A COMMENTARY ON

A Commentary on Vergil, *Aeneid* 3

S. J. HEYWORTH
&
J. H. W. MORWOOD

OXFORD
UNIVERSITY PRESS

OXFORD
UNIVERSITY PRESS

Great Clarendon Street, Oxford, OX2 6DP,
United Kingdom

Oxford University Press is a department of the University of Oxford.
It furthers the University's objective of excellence in research, scholarship,
and education by publishing worldwide. Oxford is a registered trade mark of
Oxford University Press in the UK and in certain other countries

© S. J. Heyworth and J. H. W. Morwood 2017

The moral rights of the author have been asserted

First Edition published in 2017

All rights reserved. No part of this publication may be reproduced, stored in
a retrieval system, or transmitted, in any form or by any means, without the
prior permission in writing of Oxford University Press, or as expressly permitted
by law, by licence or under terms agreed with the appropriate reprographics
rights organization. Enquiries concerning reproduction outside the scope of the
above should be sent to the Rights Department, Oxford University Press, at the
address above

You must not circulate this work in any other form
and you must impose this same condition on any acquirer

Published in the United States of America by Oxford University Press
198 Madison Avenue, New York, NY 10016, United States of America

British Library Cataloguing in Publication Data
Data available

Library of Congress Control Number: 2016943363

ISBN 978-0-19-872782-8

Links to third party websites are provided by Oxford in good faith and
for information only. Oxford disclaims any responsibility for the materials
contained in any third party website referenced in this work.

*In memory of E. L. Harrison
who loved Vergil, illuminated* Aeneid 3,
and inspired this book

Contents

Preface	ix
Introduction	1
1. Vergil's poetic career, life, and times	1
Life and times	1
The *Eclogues*	4
The *Georgics*	7
2. The *Aeneid*: a synopsis	10
3. Intertexts and influences	18
Homer	18
Tragedy	22
Hellenistic poetry	25
Latin poetry	28
4. Style	30
5. Context and themes	35
6. Metre, scansion, and versification	44
7. Text and transmission	52
8. Glossary	54
Maps	60
1. The voyage of Aeneas	60
2. The Aegean Sea	62
3. The Ionian Sea: Western Greece and South Italy	63
4. Sicily	64
Aeneid 3	65
Commentary	83
Appendix of Major Intertexts	271
Bibliography	303
Index	309
Index of passages cited, discussed, or scanned	319
Index of Latin words	324

Preface

The *Aeneid* is a story of migration, and Book 3 is the heart of this story. It takes Aeneas from Troy to Italy, and begins the process of turning Trojans into Romans. The journey sees them visit some of the most extraordinary places in the central Mediterranean, both real and imaginary: shrines and volcanoes, moving islands and monsters. This is a traveller's tale with a sublime goal, set in myth but headed towards Augustan Rome. It expresses the fear, exhaustion, and occasional moments of relief or joy that were inevitable ingredients of sea travel in the ancient world, as well as the attractions of lingering on land even when there are destinations to be reached. In writing this tale, Vergil drew on the breadth of the ancient literature, melding material from the *Odyssey* and the *Argonautica*, the classic tales of voyaging, with accounts, both in poetry and prose, of specific places and migrations.

In December 2010 we celebrated the publication of our collaborative commentary on Book 3 of Propertius. Both of us then had commitments to various other projects, and no immediate thought was given to a sequel. However, our enjoyment of the composition and pride in the apparent success of the book led to notions of renewing the partnership. The *Aeneid* was an obvious area where our interests overlap,[1] and Book 3 quickly made sense as a possible focus for our attention. When SJH came to Oxford from Leeds, he brought with him Ted Harrison's enthusiasm for the book as a way into Vergil's handling of a range of sources, and found that the book worked especially well in reading classes where there was time to look in detail at some of the models; consequently he has read it with Wadham undergraduates in roughly twenty of the last twenty-seven years. To them we owe a considerable debt, particularly those in recent years who have obligingly responded to drafts: James Oakley and Grace Hutchison are two who helped bring details into focus—but so did many others.

On the assumption that readers never penetrate beyond the first and last paragraph of a preface we hide here what we shall ignore in the

---

[1] JHWM has published *Virgil, A Poet in Augustan Rome* (Cambridge, 2008), a preface to an edition of Dryden's translation of the *Aeneid* (Ware, 1997), and articles (*JRS* 75 (1985), 51–9; *G&R* 38 (1991), 212–23); SJH a note on Book 3 (*CQ* 43 (1993), 255–7) and a review of Conte's Teubner text (*BMCR* 2010.10.03).

rest of this volume. As should be obvious from its very composition, we do not think Book 3 is the 'dullest' of the *Aeneid*,[2] nor do we think it worthwhile to speculate on whether it was written early or late in the sequence of the poem's books. There is an entertainingly confused section in Gordon Williams' book on the *Aeneid* (1983: 262–78), which tries to explain why the book is a 'general failure' (277) with many dissonant moments: he claims that the book was written early, as a third person narrative, before V. had worked out an appropriate style, but that Polydorus, the Harpies, much of Buthrotum—and of course all the first person verbs and pronouns—are later changes; in other words most of the composition, on this theory, is late! The introduction to Horsfall's 2006 edition has a section on the chronology of composition (xx–xl); this is properly sceptical on how much we know, but even he lapses in the commentary and at times talks of the book as an early one. Though it was written over many years, and not quite finished, the *Aeneid* is a unified conception, and best treated as such.

One regret is that constraints of space restricted what could be said on the rich reception of the book: its exploration of the marvellous (the Harpies[3] and Etna in particular) has appealed to many authors. In the century after Vergil's death, besides allusions in the epics of Lucan, Statius, Valerius, and Silius, it was frequently quoted by Seneca, both in the Letters and the *Naturales Quaestiones*. The memorable description of the Cyclops (*monstrum horrendum informe ingens*, 658) was redeployed to comically obscene effect in the climactic bedroom section of Ausonius' *Cento Nuptialis* (108). Dante repeatedly recalls the book for more lofty purposes: *Poscia* (Italian equivalent of *Postquam*, *Aen*. 3.1) is the first word of *Paradiso*, Canto 6, at the start of Justinian's review of Roman history, beginning from Aeneas; at *Inferno* 1.106 Virgilio uses the phrase 'umile Italia' (cf. *Aen*. 3.522–3), to describe the land for which Camilla, Euryalus, Turnus, and Nisus all die; at *Inf.* 10.60 *mio figlio ov' è* is a reverberant echo of Andromache's *Hector ubi est?* (312). On a rather different text see J. A. Jacquier, 'From Paris to Rome: Virgil's Andromache between politics and poetics in Charles Baudelaire's *Le Cygne*', in J. Farrell & D. P. Nelis (eds), *Augustan Poetry and the Roman Republic* (Oxford, 2013), 161–79.

---

[2] So the apologetic title of A. W. Allen, 'The dullest book of the *Aeneid*', *CJ* 47 (1951–2), 119–23.

[3] On the influence of Vergil's Harpies see P. R. Hardie, *The Last Trojan Hero* (London, 2014), 160ff. (including Frascatoro's *Syphilis* and *The Tempest*): Book 3 plays a large part in the New World narratives that draw on Vergil.

Preface

As in the commentary on Propertius 3, we have freely used those technical terms we find useful, trying to do so in ways that clarify the meaning, either in the commentary or in the glossary included in the Introduction: words to be found in the glossary are marked with an asterisk throughout. An appendix includes twenty passages or groups of passages (each allocated a letter in bold) that are important as background to *Aeneid* 3: these include material from the *Odyssey*, Pindar, Euripides, four of Callimachus' *Hymns*, Apollonius, Lucretius, other parts of the *Aeneid*, as well as Ovid's version of Aeneas' journey, each accompanied by a translation, as is the case with almost all Greek and Latin cited in the commentary. The text has been established anew, with the help of the information available from the editions of Mynors, Geymonat, and Conte; as is normal in Vergilian editions we use the *-is* ending for third-declension accusative plurals.

An enormous amount has been published on the *Aeneid*, and we have not seen it as part of our task to read more than a small proportion of this. Any potential urge to encyclopaedic inclusiveness has been lessened by the existence of Horsfall's polemical volume, which often reads as a commentary more on the traditions of Vergilian scholarship than on the text itself. Readers who wish to know more about the bibliography on any passage are encouraged to look at this *tour de force*, or the collections put together by Suerbaum (*ANRW* 2.31.1 (1980), 1–358) and Niklas Holzberg (available online). In the hope that he will himself publish his work, we deliberately did not consult Matthew Carter's 2004 thesis until we had completed drafting our commentary: the thesis starts from a spirited enthusiasm for the excellence of *Aeneid* 3, and goes on to offer many important insights on individual passages, e.g. (on v. 1) 'the word *postquam*, so prominently placed, trumpets book 3's status as a sequel on many levels' (15). Though we hope that our commentary will be useful to advanced scholars, we have not tried to serve their needs by giving exhaustive references, or listing multiple items of bibliography, especially for work in languages other than English. Papers or books that are referred to once usually have their bibliographical details given directly; items that recur, or that are of general importance to the appreciation and understanding of *Aeneid* 3, may be found in the Bibliography.

We have again been very fortunate in the encouraging assistance of many friends and colleagues. Bryan Morwood drew the maps. Sections of the commentary were carefully read by David Bloch, Joe Farrell, Laurel Fulkerson, Stephen Harrison, Laura Holloway, Alex Smith,

Katherine van Schaik, and various parts of the introduction by Tristan Franklinos, John Penney, Katherine van Schaik, and Jane Burkowski, who also checked references for a substantial portion of the commentary. They helped us avoid many errors and omissions; we are very grateful for that, and for the insights they have offered; if we had had more room, we would have gladly included more.

Stephen Heyworth
James Morwood

*Wadham College
Oxford, February 2016*

Thanks are due also to Malcolm Todd for his careful copy-editing, and to Tim Beck for his sharp-eyed reading of the proofs. We have added Lowe 2015 to the bibliography: this book, which we came to know only after our typescript had been submitted, includes discussions of Vergil's monsters that are rather different from ours.

S. J. H., J. H. W. M.
December 2016

INTRODUCTION

1. VERGIL'S POETIC CAREER, LIFE, AND TIMES

Tityrus et segetes Aeneiaque arma legentur,
Roma triumphati dum caput orbis erit.

Tityrus and *Crops* and the *Arms of Aeneas* shall be read while Rome is the imperial capital of the world.[1]

Ovid, at *Amores* 1.15.25–6, thus foresees (and underestimates) Vergil's poetic immortality through the sequence of his published works: the pastoral *Eclogues* (or *Bucolica*), the *Georgics*, a didactic* poem on farming, and his narrative epic, the *Aeneid*. Each is acknowledged as among the greatest and most influential poems in its genre, and as the works increase in length (one book; four shorter books; twelve), in seriousness and in stylistic level, Vergil's was quickly seen as the perfect poetic career, a model to emulate (or to reject) for poets ever since.[2] Geographically, the sequence takes the reader from the mountains of Italy and Sicily, down through the fields that the *Georgics* teaches us to cultivate, to the city that is the goal of Aeneas' journey in the *Aeneid* (a journey figured already in *Eclogue* 9); and at the same time it leads us through human history, from a nomadic lifestyle to agricultural settlement and then on to the cities that provide established communities with protection and legal order—and also with war. At the same time, in his focused use of key vocabulary (e.g. *siluae*, *umbra*; *labor*; *arma uirumque*) Vergil took important steps along the road towards codifying the genres.

Life and times

Ancient accounts of the lives of poets are notoriously unreliable,[3] and those of Vergil that have survived are no exception. The fullest is

---

[1] Ovid adopts the practice of treating key words from the first line of each poem as equivalent to a title; *Tityrus* is the name of a herdsman/singer in the *Eclogues* (see Introduction, pp. 5–6), and an *alter ego* of Vergil himself at *Ecl.* 6.4.
[2] See e.g. J. Farrell, 'Ovid's Virgilian career', *MD* 52 (2004), 41–55; P. Hardie & H. Moore (eds), *Classical Literary Careers and their Reception* (Cambridge, 2010).
[3] See esp. M. R. Lefkowitz, *The Lives of the Greek Poets* (London, 1981).

attributed to Aelius Donatus, a grammarian of the fourth century AD, which probably derives closely from the account of Suetonius, the biographer of the Caesars, who also wrote on men of letters. Though Suetonius worked closely with the emperor Hadrian and may have had access to letters to or from Vergil in the imperial archive, he was still writing well over 100 years after the poet's death; not surprisingly the ancient lives are full of charming, but implausible anecdotes, e.g. that the poet was born in a ditch (*Vita Don.* 3).

A not entirely implausible account of the poet's life runs as follows: he was born on 15 October 70 BC in a village called Andes not far from Mantua (in the Po valley in northern Italy). He spent the first years of his life in the north, and moved to Rome after assuming the *toga uirilis*. In later years he had a house on the Esquiline Hill next to the Gardens of Maecenas, to whose circle he belonged, but he preferred seclusion and spent most of his time in Campania, especially Naples (which he gives as his home, under the name Parthenope, at *Georgics* 4.564), and Sicily. In 19 BC he decided to go to Greece to revise the *Aeneid*, on which he had been working for ten years. However, in Athens he met Augustus, who was on his way back to Italy, and decided to stay with him. After a sight-seeing visit to Megara he fell ill but even so took ship for Italy. Vergil died at Brundisium on 21 September. He had asked that, if anything happened to him, the manuscript of his still unfinished poem should be burnt, but his friend Varius Rufus edited the poem for publication on the emperor's instruction (*Vita Don.* 38–41). There is a famous epitaph, written for his tomb in Naples, in the voice of the deceased (as is common):

> Mantua me genuit, Calabri rapuere, tenet nunc
> Parthenope; cecini pascua, rura, duces.[4]

This records the place of birth, of death, and of burial (which was also his home), with emphasis given to the first and third; and then with even greater brevity than Ovid it celebrates his three works, *Eclogues*, *Georgics*, and *Aeneid*.

Much of this life was lived against a backdrop of severe political and military unrest. During the first century BC the Roman republican

---

[4] 'Mantua gave me birth; Calabria snatched me away; now Naples holds me. I sang of pastures, farms, leaders.' I. Frings, '*Mantua me genuit*—Vergils Grabepigramm auf Stein und Pergament', *ZPE* 123 (1998), 89–100 explores the tradition of epigrams to which this belongs.

system broke down in the course of an unremitting succession of violent struggles between leading figures, until after 31 BC power became concentrated in the person of Julius Caesar's great-nephew and adopted son Caesar Octavianus, who came to be called Augustus from 27 BC and whose long life (from 63 BC to AD 14) instituted the line of Roman emperors. Vergil's twenties witnessed the civil war between Julius Caesar and the armies commanded by Pompey and his successors (49–45 BC). Caesar proved the victor, but was assassinated on the Ides (15th) of March 44 BC. Another civil war broke out between the Triumvirate (made up of Caesar's two closest political allies, Lepidus and Mark Antony, and Octavian, his heir) and Brutus and Cassius, the two leading assassins. The latter were defeated at Philippi in northern Greece in 42 BC. But then Italy was flung into unrest yet again when Octavian seized large areas of land on which he could settle the thousands of veterans of the victorious army; and conditions were worsened when Sextus, the youngest son of Pompey, who in the late 40s had gained control of Sicily and the seas around southern Italy, disrupted the corn supplies to Rome.

The young Caesar,[5] and his general Agrippa, eventually defeated Sextus Pompeius in 36 (and he was caught and executed by Antony in the East in 35); Lepidus' power was gradually reduced, and finally removed later in 36. This allowed the tensions between Antony and Caesar to escalate. Antony was in command of Roman territories in the eastern Mediterranean and, as well as suffering serious military setbacks, engaged in a lasting affair with the Egyptian queen Cleopatra, in favour of whom he divorced his Roman wife Octavia, his colleague's sister. What was in effect another civil war flared up. It ended with Caesar's victories over Antony and Cleopatra at the battle of Actium in 31 BC and at Alexandria the following year, after which the defeated pair each committed suicide.

One man was now the unquestioned master of Rome and its empire: in August 29 BC he celebrated an unprecedented triple triumph on three consecutive days; in 27 he ostentatiously gave up his extraordinary official powers (*Res Gestae* 34)—and the senate immediately restored them to him. He became not 'emperor',[6] but *princeps*, first

---

[5] From this point we use 'Caesar' to refer to the son, 'Julius Caesar' for the adopting father.

[6] But *Imperator* was part of his official name: *Imperator Caesar Diui Filius* [son of the god] *Augustus*. In the commentary we call him 'Augustus', or 'Caesar' when describing events prior to 27 BC.

man of the state, endowed with the powers of republican magistrates and priests; but whereas previously different men had different powers (e.g. legal and personal inviolability, the right to introduce legislation, the authority to command armies) and for limited periods, Augustus had all the powers that mattered, and they were either lifelong or constantly renewed. Through the following four decades he maintained a programme designed to stabilize and glorify the empire, as he proudly claimed in the *Res Gestae*, an enormous inscription erected on his mausoleum in Rome.[7] There were military campaigns, e.g. in Spain till 19 BC (Augustus himself was there 26 to 24); there was legislation on marriage intended to promote morality and the population; and from 27 there was a major programme of building in Rome, and elsewhere. The *Aeneid* commemorates Augustan building throughout the poem, including Book 3.[8] Soon after the battle of Actium work began at Nicopolis ('Victory City') on the site of Caesar's camp in southern Epirus, and the temple of Apollo at Actium itself was rebuilt to celebrate the victory (see 276–88 for Aeneas' visit). Again some stress is given to the fact that Thrace and Delos, the first two places visited by the migrating Trojans, are sacred in turn to Mars (13, 35) and Apollo (79–101); the two major new temples constructed by Augustus in Rome were those of Mars Ultor in the Forum Augustum and of Apollo on the Palatine. Another restoration relevant to Book 3 was that of the shrine of the Penates on the Velia (*Res Gestae* 19): the presence of these deities with Aeneas is highlighted as he sets out (12) and when they address him in a dream (147–79).

The Eclogues

The *Eclogues* is a book of ten poems, and 828 lines, written in the late 40s and early 30s; the odd-numbered poems are mimes (i.e. structured as dialogues).[9] They evoke the Greek pastoral world of the third-century

---

[7] See Cooley 2009. A further fragment of a Greek version has now been identified: P. Thonemann, 'A copy of Augustus' *Res Gestae* at Sardis', *Historia* 61 (2012), 282–8.

[8] See further Morwood, *G&R* 38 (1991), 217–21, and S. J. Harrison, 'The epic and monuments: interactions between Virgil's *Aeneid* and the Augustan building programme', in M. J. Clarke et al. (eds), *Epic Interactions* (Oxford, 2006), 159–83.

[9] Accounts often give the dates 37 for the publication of the *Eclogues* and 29 for the *Georgics*, but this may antedate the poems by some years, and goes along with a view that separates the works into discrete periods, ignoring the possibility of overlap and the signs that something was known to Vergil of his planned epic before the *Eclogues* was finished.

Syracusan poet Theocritus:[10] herdsmen living in the isolation of the mountains pass time while watching the flocks by composing tunes on their rustic pipes and singing songs. Herding was an activity of the young, and all in the *Eclogues* are male, so it is fitting that their songs are often competitive (3, 7), or erotic (2, 8, 10), or abusive (3). They reflect on the business of the shepherd's life and the beauties of the countryside. But Vergil also introduces into his pastorals topics that Theocritus had kept in separate poems: myth (6), and direct honouring of patrons as well as friends (Pollio, Varus, and the love elegist* Gallus are named); and he shows a strong concern to engage with weightier matters, a desire most directly enunciated at *Ecl.* 4.1 *Sicelides Musae, paulo maiora canamus* ('Muses of Sicily [*i.e.* Theocritean], let us sing of things a little grander'), which leads on to an extraordinarily influential and prophetic poem that announces the birth of a child, predicts the coming of a second Golden Age, and provides iconography* of fertility that will bear fruit in Augustan art. One stage of the child's life is marked by the ability to read; this will be accompanied by new fertility in the countryside (4.26–30), and, as mankind learns not to sin, the adventures of the age of heroes, with the sailing of a second Argo and the coming again of Achilles to Troy (31–6). Given the reference to reading, it is easy to see these as pointers to Vergil's own later poems, one on agriculture, the other an epic imitating Apollonius' *Argonautica* and Homer's *Iliad*. The following poem, 5, sets together the songs of two collaborative singers, of whom Mopsus laments the death of a mythical herdsman Daphnis, and Menalcas celebrates his ascent to the stars and deification: in a poem from the years after 44 this is clearly to be read allegorically, as a reflection on the death and deification of Julius Caesar. Poem 5 stands in the idyllic centre of the book; on the margins there is more disturbance, and the city is allowed to intrude into the pastoral life. In particular 1 and 9 movingly convey the chaos and misery caused by the contemporary confiscations of land.

Eclogue 1 acts as a programme* poem for the whole Vergilian corpus*, and begins thus (1.1–5):

> Tityre, tu patulae recubans sub tegmine fagi
> siluestrem tenui Musam meditaris auena;

---

[10] Two of Theocritus' pastoral *Idylls* feature a lovesick Polyphemus, who will be recalled at *Aen.* 3.641–61; 3.692–6 pay homage to Syracuse.

> nos patriae fines et dulcia linquimus arua.
> nos patriam fugimus; tu, Tityre, lentus in umbra
> formosam resonare doces Amaryllida siluas.

Tityrus, lying under the cover of the spreading beech-tree, you rehearse the woodland Muse on your fine pipe; we are leaving the territory of our homeland and the sweet fields. We are fleeing our homeland; you, Tityrus, at ease in the shade teach the woods to echo <your song about> the beautiful Amaryllis.

The beauty and ease of the opening two lines are deliberately deceptive. Meliboeus, the speaker, is already leaving this delightful scene (as are 'we': the author? the readers?). The corpus* begins with exile. Meliboeus has been forced off his land by the confiscations; there is no future for his herd of goats (symbolized in 13–15 by the loss of two new-born kids), and his future leads he knows not where: Africa, Scythia, Britain (64–6)? Yet it is he who provides the vivid description of the landscape, while Tityrus tells us about his visit to Rome, and explains that his contentment depends upon support won from a young man whom he saw in Rome and now regards as a god. His bliss comes not from primitive innocence, but depends upon his successful hunt for patronage, and an accommodation with the city. The poem encourages the reader to consider the way Rome dominates Italy (19–25), and how its empire has given a reality to geographical fantasy (61–6): as a prospective Roman legionary Meliboeus can expect to see unimaginably distant places (so too Gallus at 10.64–8). The *Aeneid* is of course a poem of exile, and Book 3 is set in Africa and narrates haphazard journeying such as Meliboeus faces; Aeneas, like Tityrus, will in Book 8 seek assistance from a leader (Evander) who lives on the site of the future Rome. But the *Aeneid* also features Italians who fear that they are being driven from their lands to provide somewhere for others to settle: thus at 12.236–7 Juturna (disguised as Camers) incites Rutulian hatred of the immigrant Trojans:

> **nos patria** amissa dominis parere superbis
> cogemur, qui nunc **lent**i consedimus **aru**is.

We, having lost **our homeland**, shall be compelled to obey haughty masters, we who now are settled **in peace on the fields**.

Like Andromache's *nos patria incensa* at 3.325, the opening tag alludes to *Ecl.* 1.3–4 (cited above), and the importance of the allusion* is underlined by the further echoes in the following line: we are invited to see the Rutulians as like the sympathetically presented Meliboeus with whom V. has begun. But in that case *Eclogue* 1 gives us a disturbing way to read the incoming settlers, Aeneas and his men (1.70–1, Meliboeus speaking):

> impius haec tam culta noualia miles habebit,
> barbarus has segetes.

An impious soldier will occupy these ploughlands so carefully cultivated, a barbarian these crops.

It seems that Vergil already knew what would be the key characteristic of his epic hero, and wished to show that *pietas* lies in the eye of the beholder.

The Georgics

As we know from the contemporary *Satires* of Horace (1.5, 6, 10), Vergil had by the early 30s become a member of the poetic circle surrounding Maecenas, friend of the young Caesar and patron of the arts. To Maecenas[11] he dedicates the *Georgics*, a poem in four books (each of between 514 and 566 lines) in the didactic* tradition founded by Hesiod, a seventh-century poet from Boeotia, who produced works in the two poetic sub-genres of didactic, the encyclopaedic *Theogony* ('The origin of the gods') and *Works and Days*, a miscellany of advice on how to be a farmer and citizen. The subject of the *Georgics* is also farming:[12] Book 1 on crops, 2 on trees, and especially viticulture, 3 on cattle, horses, sheep and goats, 4 on bee-keeping. Whereas Theocritus is the dominant (though by no means the only) model throughout the *Eclogues*, the *Georgics* displays its transitional position in the corpus* by changing models as it progresses: the first half of Book 1 is dominated by reworking of material from *Works and Days*, but the second half moves on to Aratus' *Phaenomena*, a Hellenistic* poem on the constellations, and their marking of the annual calendar, followed by a section on weather signs (V. imitates the second and third parts).

---

[11] He is addressed in programmatic* passages in each book: 1.2, 2.41, 3.41, 4.2: a neat pattern. Maecenas does not appear in either *Eclogues* or *Aeneid*; the latter absence has been found puzzling—it may simply reflect Maecenas' wish.

[12] M. S. Spurr, 'Agriculture and the *Georgics*', *G&R* 33 (1986), 164–87 discusses the work's utility as a farming manual.

8   *A Commentary on Vergil*, Aeneid 3

Towards the end of Book 2, and especially in Book 3, a more recent Latin poem, Lucretius' *de Rerum Natura* ('On Nature') takes over; while the second half of Book 4 moves into mythical narrative with the entwined stories of Aristaeus, and Orpheus and Eurydice, and for this Homer is the main model, with episodes from the *Iliad* (Achilles and Thetis in Book 1) and *Odyssey* (Menelaus' tale from Book 4) combined.[13] Along with the change in models, there are stylistic moves towards epic, with a decrease in the number of vocatives and an increase in the use of simile and of reference to myth. From the first the poem stresses hard work and persistence (themes that will continue in the *Aeneid*) and the primary need to maintain a good relationship with the gods (*in primis uenerare deos*, 1.338); despite such human efforts disaster may strike, and the poem contains vivid descriptions of a storm just before harvest (1.313–34), a fire in an olive grove (2.303–11; cf. 573 n.), and especially a horrifying plague (3.478–566; cf. 137–9 n.). Book 4 practises for epic, but in miniature, as verses 4–6 announce:

> magnanimosque duces totiusque ordine gentis
> mores et studia et populos et proelia dicam.
> in tenui labor; at tenuis non gloria, ...

I shall tell of great-hearted leaders and in orderly fashion of the behaviour of the whole race [*i.e.* of bees], their efforts, their population, their battles. The labour is over something slight; but not slight the glory to be won ...

Verses 67–85 describe a swarm in terms that could be used for a human battle.

The *Georgics* has an important political dimension. The living Caesar, who is never named in the *Eclogues* (though the *iuuenis deus* of poem 1 can be understood as a reference to him), now appears in person. He is first summoned to assist in the writing of the poem (1.24–42), an invocation longer than that to the gods of agriculture (5–23); he is saluted as Rome's hope to escape from the disorder that followed the assassination of Julius Caesar (1.466–514), and as *maxime Caesar* (2.170) at the climax of the so-called *laudes Italiae* (2.136–76).[14] After debate about the future course of his poetry at the end of 2, Book 3 provides instruction in animal husbandry, and is thus in a sense a return to pastoral, but the style is didactic*,

---

[13] On this developing intertextuality see especially J. Farrell, *Vergil's Georgics and the Traditions of Ancient Epic: The Art of Allusion in Literary History* (New York, 1991).

[14] See 539–42 n. for an important allusion˙ to this passage—as the Trojans first reach Italy.

and rarely reminiscent of the *Eclogues*. However, V. starts the book considering, and rejecting, the possibilities of mythological subjects as a route to the poetic heavens (3–9), before declaring his intention to build a temple by the river Mincius in Mantua to celebrate Caesar (10–39). The doors of the temple will depict Roman victories over the East (the Nile is mentioned at 28–9); sculptures will mark the descent from Troy (34–6).[15] After returning to the topics of *Georgics* 3 (40–5), he glosses* the metaphorical temple as something he is preparing to write (46–8):

> mox tamen ardentis accingar dicere pugnas,
> Caesaris et nomen fama tot ferre per annos,
> Tithoni prima quot abest ab origine Caesar.

Nevertheless I shall be girding myself up to tell of the fierce battles and to carry the name of Caesar in fame through as many years as Caesar is distant from the original birth of Tithonus.[16]

In the closing lines of the whole poem Augustus appears again, his imperial activity set against Vergil's idleness (*Geo.* 4.559–66):

> haec super aruorum cultu pecorumque canebam
> et super arboribus, Caesar dum magnus ad altum   560
> fulminat Euphraten bello uictorque uolentes
> per populos dat iura uiamque adfectat Olympo.
> illo Vergilium me tempore dulcis alebat
> Parthenope studiis florentem ignobilis oti,
> carmina qui lusi pastorum audaxque iuuenta,   565
> Tityre, te patulae cecini sub tegmine fagi.

This I was singing on the cultivation of fields and of flocks and on trees, while mighty Caesar was thundering in war by the deep Euphrates and as a victor was laying down the law for willing peoples and making a road to Olympus [*i.e.* to godhead]. At the time sweet Parthenope [*i.e.* Naples] nurtured me, Vergil, as I flourished in the pursuits of ignoble peace, who played at the songs of shepherds and daring with youth sang of you, Tityrus, under the cover of the spreading beech-tree.

---

[15] The *Aeneid* will invert this: Rome's Trojan ancestry provides the main narrative and the Augustan material comes in the ecphrasis* of a work of art, Aeneas' shield (8.626–728), as well as in the proleptic* speeches of Jupiter (1.257–96) and Anchises (6.756–886).

[16] As the ageing but immortal husband of Aurora, goddess of the dawn, Tithonus is a symbol of extended time; but as Priam's brother he is also a cousin of Anchises and another hint of the Trojan subject matter of the epic to be. V. only hints: Aeneas (e.g.) is not mentioned.

The passage is a *sphragis**, marking the poet's name and home on his text (both appear only here in the corpus*). The lines on Vergil sum up the *Georgics*, and with the near repetition of *Ecl.* 1.1 at the end enclose* his early career as a unified whole. But the lines on Caesar are dominated by epic motifs and point ahead, once again, to the *Aeneid*.

2. THE *AENEID*: A SYNOPSIS

Work on the *Aeneid* dominated the last decade or more of Vergil's life, and it was complete but unfinished[17] when he died in 19 BC. An epic, originally in twelve rolls, set in the era of the *Iliad* and the *Odyssey*, it tells of the voyage of a Trojan prince Aeneas, son of the goddess Venus, and a fleet of allies, fellow exiles from Troy after its sack by the Greeks. They head across the Mediterranean in search of a new home, guided by omens and prophecies of gradually increasing clarity that direct them to the west coast of Italy, and eventually to the site of the future Rome. The poem thus sets Rome's origin in an heroic past.[18]

Book 1

The poem begins thus (1.1–7; n.b. *primus* in 1):

> Arma uirumque cano Troiae qui primus ab oris
> Italiam fato profugus Lauiniaque uenit
> litora, multum ille et terris iactatus et alto
> ui superum, saeuae memorem Iunonis ob iram,
> multa quoque et bello passus, dum conderet urbem   5
> inferretque deos Latio; genus unde Latinum
> Albanique patres atque altae moenia Romae.

Arms and the man I sing who first from the shores of Troy in exile by fate came to Italy and the Lavinian shores, that man much harried on lands and on the deep through the power of the gods, because of savage Juno's ever-remembering anger, and enduring much too in war, until he could found a city and bring gods into Latium; from which origin came the Latin race, the Alban fathers, and the walls of lofty Rome.

---

[17] Cf. p. 51, on 'half-lines'.
[18] V. takes over an existing story, from sources both Greek and Roman: also derived from these is a detailed prose account by his contemporary, Dionysius of Halicarnassus, in 1.45–60 of *Roman Antiquities*, to which we regularly refer in the commentary.

Introduction 11

Vergil brings out the centrality of the evocatively unnamed Aeneas, the importance of arms and war (for the poem, and for Rome), the way that narrative falls into two halves (*multum ille et terris iactatus et alto* = Books 1–6; *multa quoque et bello passus* = 7–12), the control that fate and Juno exert over the narrative, and the fact that this is an aetiological* tale about Rome. He also misleads: Aeneas will bring gods from Troy to Latium, but he will not within the poem found a city in Latium, never mind Rome itself. V. goes on to invoke the Muse, and asks her to explain the causes of Juno's hostility to an individual outstanding in his piety.

The story begins, not at the beginning, but as the Trojans seem to be nearing the end of their journey, heading from Sicily to the west coast of Italy; unfortunately their voyage catches the attention of the goddess Juno, opponent of Troy under her Greek name Hera in the *Iliad*, and the prime deity of Carthage, the city in Africa that will be Rome's rival in the third and second centuries BC after they have first clashed in Sicily. She arranges for a storm to wreck Aeneas' fleet, and the ships are only saved by the timely intervention of the god of the sea, Neptune. The ships are scattered, and driven to land near Carthage in Africa.[19] Believing that he has lost thirteen of his twenty ships, Aeneas is deeply demoralized but puts on a show of optimism for his comrades. In heaven, Venus protests to Jupiter that he is failing to keep his promise to grant the refugees a glorious future. He reassures her by unfolding their imperial destiny, which will culminate in the deification of Aeneas' Julian descendants and the peace of the Augustan age.[20] [34–304]

The next day Aeneas, while exploring the Carthaginian countryside with his regular companion Achates, meets Venus disguised as a huntress. She tells him the story of Dido,[21] a refugee from Tyre in Phoenicia after her impious brother, the king Pygmalion, had murdered her wealthy husband Sychaeus. Dido is building the city of Carthage. As Aeneas proceeds thither, he observes the energetic construction work, and then on the walls of the temple of Juno depictions of the Trojan War. The majority of these are scenes of sorrow and destruction for the

---

[19] Of some importance as background for the journeying in Book 3 are verses 1.159–219, in which V. shows how the Trojans provide the necessities of human life after landing: shelter (159–66), fresh water (167), fire (174–6), bread (177–9), meat (187–94, 210–13), wine (195–7), conversation (197–207, 216–19).
[20] See p. 36 for text and discussion of this important speech.
[21] See **P** for a text and translation of 1.343–64.

Trojans, and he is deeply moved by the thought that their experiences are commemorated here. Queen Dido then arrives, and Aeneas, made invisible by enveloping mist, sees entering under arrest the captains of the ships that he had feared lost in the storm. When Dido greets them with generosity, Venus dispels the mist and the hero addresses the queen in deep gratitude. [305–612]

Dido welcomes Aeneas and his people, supplying sacrifices (i.e. meat) for the crews while Aeneas' son Ascanius[22] is summoned to the banquet that is prepared in the palace. Venus, however, is worried about the dangers of hospitality in a Punic city and substitutes Cupid for Ascanius. Thus, when Dido dandles Cupid on her lap thinking him to be the boy Ascanius, she is filled with passion for Aeneas, and begins to forget her love of her dead husband Sychaeus. She asks Aeneas to tell the story of the fall of Troy and his subsequent wanderings. [613–756]

Book 2

Aeneas tells how the Greeks, after ten years of unsuccessful warfare, pretended to sail home, leaving behind them on the shore a wooden horse filled with leading Greek warriors. The Trojans were tricked by the skilful deception of the Greek Sinon, who claimed falsely that he had been victimized by his fellow-Greeks, above all by Ulysses, and threw himself on the mercy of the Trojans. Misled by their compassion, the latter were persuaded that the horse was an offering to the goddess Minerva and should be brought into their city. The priest Laocoon who opposed this was killed by two giant sea-serpents together with his two sons, a breach was made in the walls and the horse hauled inside, amid general rejoicing. [1–249] That night the Greek warriors climbed down from the horse and let their fellow Greeks, who had sailed back to Troy, into the city. The ghost of Hector appeared to Aeneas in a dream, urging him to escape, and handing over to him the Penates (household gods) of Troy and Vesta's holy fire. Aeneas initially joined with other Trojans in mounting resistance but eventually they were overwhelmed by Greek numbers; Priam's palace was taken and the king was himself horrifically killed at the household altar by Achilles' son Pyrrhus. [250–558] Aeneas was only then persuaded by his mother Venus and an apocalyptic vision of falling Troy that it was

---

[22] Also called Iulus.

his duty to flee from the city with his family. He returned home and when divine portents had at last persuaded the reluctant Anchises to leave, he raised his crippled father onto his shoulders and took his young son by the hand,[23] telling his wife Creusa to follow on behind as they left the city. When they reached a shrine outside the city, he found that Creusa was no longer accompanying him and in desperation rushed back to look for her. Her ghost appeared to him, telling him cryptically that it was his lot to come to Hesperia where the Lydian Tiber flows,[24] and bidding him farewell. He rejoined the others and found that a large number of refugees had assembled. [559–804]

Book 3

[Aeneas continues.] After leaving Asia, the Trojans landed in Thrace. Aeneas' attempt to found a city was interrupted by the ghost of Polydorus, the youngest son of Priam, who had been slaughtered by the Thracian king in a shocking violation of hospitality. They sailed on to Delos, where the voice of Apollo told them to seek their ancient mother. Anchises understood this to be Crete, but when they settled there, a dreadful pestilence broke out, and a vision of the Penates told them to make instead for Italy. They were then driven by a storm to the island of the Harpies, disgusting bird-women, one of whom, Celaeno, warned them that they would not found a city before hunger forced them to gnaw their tables. [1–269] They sailed up the west coast of Greece, stopping at Actium, before reaching Buthrotum, where the Trojan seer Helenus and Andromache, Hector's widow, had built a reproduction Troy. In a prophecy Helenus instructed Aeneas that he must go to the far side of Italy, circumnavigating Sicily to avoid the monsters Scylla and Charybdis. [270–569] Landing near the erupting Mount Etna, they had a narrow escape from the Cyclopes, with the help of a Greek suppliant called Achaemenides who had been left behind by Ulysses. The voyage round Sicily ends with the death of Anchises at Drepanum. And then the storm drove them to Dido's shores. [570–718]

---

[23] This moment confirms the classic image of *pietas* and the ideal Roman family (grandfather, father, and son) as depicted on coins, in sculpture and wall-paintings.
[24] Lydia is in Asia Minor, whence the Etruscans, the inhabitants of central Italy, were thought to have come.

Book 4

In the course of the banquet and Aeneas' narration, Dido has fallen deeply in love with the Trojan hero. Despite her oath not to marry again, she is persuaded by her sister Anna that a union with Aeneas will benefit Carthage, and they seek divine aid. Juno now falls in with Venus' plan, hoping that Aeneas will stay in Carthage with the result that Rome will never be founded. The goddesses arrange that Dido and Aeneas are separated from the rest of the company on a hunt during a storm sent by Juno and seek refuge in the same cave. Dido treats the resulting relationship as a marriage. [1–172] Fama [the personification* of rumour] brings the news to the jealous African king Iarbas, who angrily prays to his father Jupiter. Thereupon the god sends Mercury to tell Aeneas (found building Carthage) to be mindful of his destiny and make for Italy. Aeneas starts to organize the departure while awaiting the right moment to tell Dido. She discovers the truth and a terrible confrontation ensues. Aeneas, despite his own love, remains determined. [173–449] Dido wants to die, has vain recourse to magic, and, when after a further intervention from Mercury the Trojans sail away, she utters a curse foretelling the grim history of warfare between Rome and Carthage, and stabs herself on a huge pyre. [450–705]

Book 5

The Trojans see Carthage in flames behind them as they sail to Sicily, where they celebrate the anniversary of Anchises' death with games: a boat-race, running, boxing, and archery. [1–544] The proceedings end with an equestrian pageant performed by the boys, led by Iulus. However, the women, who are not present at the games, are tricked by Juno into setting fire to the ships in the hope of preventing the onward journey to Italy. Aeneas, aided by a rainstorm sent by Jupiter, saves all but four of the ships. [545–699] He leaves behind the old and weak in the new city of Segesta (named from the Trojan Acestes). Before the departure, Anchises appears to Aeneas in a dream and tells him to come to the Elysian Fields with the help of the Sibyl. Venus now intercedes with Neptune to grant the fleet a safe voyage. The sea-god promises to do so at the cost of one of Aeneas' men—the helmsman Palinurus, whom the god of sleep lulls to sleep and thrusts overboard. [700–871]

Book 6

Aeneas visits the temple of Apollo at Cumae, where the Sibyl, inspired by Apollo, predicts an Iliadic war in Latium, and then instructs him on gaining safe access to the underworld. He must find a golden bough and bury one of his men who has just died: this proves to be Misenus, the trumpeter. After the discovery of the bough and the funeral, the Sibyl leads Aeneas into the world below. [1–267] They encounter horrific monsters and personifications*, then come to the River Styx, where the bank is thronged with those awaiting passage, especially the unburied, among them the helmsman Palinurus, with whom they have a poignant conversation. The initially reluctant ferryman Charon is persuaded to take Aeneas over the river. The Sibyl drugs the three-headed dog Cerberus and they see first those who died in infancy, then suicides, then those who died for love, including Dido, who does not respond to Aeneas' emotional words. In a section for brave warriors he sees fighters from the Trojan War, most poignantly his cousin Deiphobus, killed on Troy's final night, who bids him go towards the future. [268–547] As they walk past the walls of Tartarus, the Sibyl gives a vivid account of the dreadful punishments endured by sinners there. Finally they reach Elysium, the dwelling place of the happy spirits, and meet Anchises, who is reviewing the souls of his future descendants as they wait to drink the waters of Lethe, the river of forgetfulness, before they are born again. He expounds a theology of purification and reincarnation, and then identifies a number of heroes of the Roman race, including Romulus and Augustus. He ends with inspirational words on the Roman arts (empire, civilization, clemency, and conquest), but the scene closes in sadness as he tells of the early death of Marcellus (son of Augustus' sister Octavia, and his intended successor). Aeneas and the Sibyl now leave the underworld through the Gate of False Dreams. [548–901]

Book 7

Caieta, Aeneas' nurse, dies and is buried in a place that takes her name. The Trojans pass Circe's island and come to the mouth of the Tiber, and land there. (The poet addresses the Muse Erato and announces war as the subject of the poem's grander half.) The area is ruled by king Latinus, the hand of whose daughter Lavinia had been sought by the Rutulian prince Turnus. However, portents and oracles have warned that she should marry a foreigner. The Trojans eat thin cakes of meal ('tables', jokes Iulus) and Aeneas realizes that now they have fulfilled the prophecy: having consumed their tables, they can finally build their city.[25] Latinus welcomes the Trojan embassy, and judging Aeneas to be the portended foreigner he invites him to marry Lavinia. [1–285] However, Juno rouses the Fury Allecto to inflame first Latinus' wife Amata and then Turnus with frenzied anger against the Trojans. Allecto also arranges that Ascanius should kill a pet deer belonging to the family of one of Latinus' herdsmen, which leads to conflict between Trojans and Latins. [286–510] Juno dismisses Allecto and opens the Gates of War. Italian forces gather, and Vergil catalogues the contingents, including the brutal and impious Etruscan Mezentius, Turnus himself, and a Volscian warrior maiden Camilla. [511–817]

Book 8

An envoy is sent to seek help against the Trojans from the Greek hero Diomedes, now in Italy. In a dream the river god Tiber tells Aeneas to sail upstream to a city called Pallanteum, built by immigrant Arcadians on the site of future Rome: they will be allies. When he reaches this city on the next day, the king Evander, his son Pallas, and his people are feasting in honour of Hercules. Evander invites the Trojans to join them and tells how, when Hercules passed through the area on a journey from the west with Geryon's cattle, eight of them were stolen by a monster named Cācus who lived on the Aventine hill; Hercules killed him in retaliation. [1–305] As Evander leads Aeneas to his humble house, he points out various sites which will become landmarks in Rome. That night Venus persuades Vulcan to make a new set of armour for Aeneas. Next morning, Evander formalizes the alliance with the Trojans, and Aeneas goes with Pallas on a mission to gain the support of the Etruscans. [306–607] Venus presents Aeneas with his new armour. He gazes joyously but uncomprehendingly at the huge shield which is embossed with scenes from future Roman history, culminating in the battle of Actium and the triumph which Caesar celebrated after defeating Antony and Cleopatra in Egypt.[26] [608–731]

---

[25] See **Q**, and 266 n.   [26] See **R**.

Book 9

In Aeneas' absence Turnus attacks the Trojan camp, with Juno's encouragement. He attempts to provoke the Trojans into leaving their encampment by burning their ships, but through the power of Cybele, mother of the gods, from whose grove they originate, the boats are transformed into sea-nymphs. [1–122] The camp is now besieged and two Trojans, Nisus and his beloved young friend Euryalus, propose that they should go on a night-mission through the Italian lines to take a message to Aeneas. They seize the chance to butcher the sleeping enemy and take booty: they are revealed when the reflection of the moon's light gleams from a looted helmet; Nisus escapes but sacrifices himself when he sees Euryalus being killed. [123–449] Next day a fierce battle takes place around the camp. Ascanius shoots a boastful Rutulian called Remulus Numanus, but is then warned by Apollo to desist from the fighting. Ultimately Turnus gets into the camp, and is trapped inside the gates. He escapes by diving into the Tiber. [450–818]

Book 10

There is an angry debate in heaven: Venus protests at the war being fought against the Trojans, Juno at their invasion of Italy; Jupiter orders the gods to let the war take its course, to leave things to the fates. [1–117] The Trojans are holding out in their camp with difficulty, but Aeneas arrives by sea with his Etruscan and Arcadian allies. For a time the battle is dominated by the younger fighters, Pallas, Evander's son, and Lausus, the son of Mezentius, the expelled king of the Etruscans. [118–438] However, Turnus kills Pallas and takes his sword-belt. Aeneas responds to the news with furious bloodshed. Juno diverts Turnus from the battle by creating an image of Aeneas; he pursues this onto a ship, which Juno drives out to sea. Lausus helps the wounded Mezentius but Aeneas kills both son and father. [439–908]

Book 11

Aeneas sets up a trophy to celebrate the victory over Mezentius, and sadly sends back to Evander the body of Pallas, who had been entrusted to his care: the procession includes human victims for sacrifice. The Italians and Trojans make a truce and bury their dead. [1–224] At a council summoned by Latinus, news comes that Diomedes has declined to help the Italians: he has too high an opinion of his former opponent's qualities. Latinus proposes peace and is supported by Drances, who provokes Turnus into an uncompromising pro-war speech. Before a decision is made, the Trojans and their allies attack, whereupon Turnus leads the Italians into battle. [225–497] He himself sets up an ambush for Aeneas and entrusts the defence of the city to Camilla. She sweeps all before her but is eventually killed. As she dies, she sends a message begging Turnus to return, and he is thus forced to abandon his ambush. Night falls. [498–915]

Book 12

Turnus agrees to settle the matter in single combat, though Amata says she will never accept Aeneas as son-in-law. Trojans and Italians collaborate in setting up the duel; Aeneas promises the Trojans will depart if he is defeated, and that he will not claim sovereignty in victory; Latinus also swears to keep the agreed terms. [1–215] However, before the ceremony is finished, on Juno's prompting, Juturna, Turnus' nymph-sister, persuades the Italians to start fighting again. Aeneas is wounded and Turnus dominates the fighting until, after the intervention of Venus, Aeneas' wound is healed: he puts his armour back on and embraces and addresses Ascanius (for the only time in the poem). [216–440] Juturna takes over as charioteer of Turnus' chariot and keeps him away from Aeneas, who now attacks the city; Amata hangs herself. Turnus stops the conflict and faces Aeneas in single combat. As they fight,[27] Jupiter and Juno confer. She agrees that the Trojans may settle in Italy as long as the hated name of Troy is lost. Juturna leaves Turnus, who falls wounded, and submissively concedes defeat. Aeneas is about to spare him when he sees on his shoulder the sword-belt taken from Pallas. Fired with frenzy and anger, he kills him. [441–952]

3. INTERTEXTS AND INFLUENCES

Homer

The *Georgics* provided a programme* for the *Aeneid*, the proem to Book 3 announcing an intention to celebrate the young Caesar (as we

---

[27] See **S** for one incident in the fight, involving a sacred tree: 12.766–87.

have seen) and Book 4 exploring in miniature the possibilities of hexameters about kings and battles (in the first half), and in the second the artistic combination of material from both Homeric epics. Earlier Latin epics had set themselves up as responses to Homer: in the third century BC Livius Andronicus produced a version of the *Odyssey* in Latin 'saturnians'; in the second, Ennius in his *Annales* naturalized the Homeric hexameter, and described a dream in which he was visited by the ghost of Homer (fr. ii–x Skutsch), as is reported by the didactic* Lucretius, who admires both Ennius and Homer as poets, but disdains their inconsistencies and misconceptions about the world and the nature of death in particular (1.112–26). It is little surprise therefore that Propertius (in a context that sheds doubt on his enthusiasm) hailed the *Aeneid* as *nescioquid maius Iliade* ('something bigger than the Iliad', 2.34.66) even before it was published.

Awareness of the poem's close relationship with Homer persists implicitly through the epics of the first century of our era and explicitly in the writings of the fourth/fifth-century scholars Servius and Macrobius. The latter's *Saturnalia*, which is constructed as a series of discussions between Roman nobles and intellectuals over the holiday period of the Saturnalia, has the qualities of Vergil as its overriding concern: 5.2.6–5.3.17 is a disorderly account of episodes, characters, and lines that Vergil drew from Homer, and an ordered comparison, working through the text of the *Aeneid*, then begins from 5.3.17, and continues to 5.10.13 (*Aen.* 3 at 5.6.1–8), before turning into more discursive form once more.[28] Servius confirms the success of the *Georgics* in guiding reception of the *Aeneid*, when he announces that Vergil's twin intention was to imitate Homer and to praise Augustus through his ancestors (*Homerum imitari et Augustum laudare a parentibus*, 1.*pr*).

Imitation of the *Iliad* and the *Odyssey* works on every level:[29] the *Aeneid* is (save for rare moments) a third-person narrative, with speeches and

---

[28] Comparison with other poets follows, e.g. Pindar, Pythian 1 [F] at *Sat.* 5.17.9–14, and Latin authors, especially Ennius and Lucretius in 6.1–5. For further discussion of V.'s use of Pindar, see Thomas 1999: 267–87 (he does not deal with the use of fr. 33 [E] in the account of Delos at 3.73–7).

[29] The classic, systematic, account is Knauer 1964 (see 181–202 for discussion of Book 3); also important, especially on the second half, are R. R. Schlunk, *The Homeric Scholia and the Aeneid: A Study of the Influence of Ancient Homeric Literary Criticism on Vergil* (Ann Arbor, 1974); A. Barchiesi, *Homeric Effects in Vergil's Narrative* (Princeton, 2015; translation of *La traccia del modello*, Pisa, 1984).

similes used to vary pace, tone, and content (see further pp. 30–2); it is on a high stylistic level, at times archaizing* or formulaic* (though far less so than Homer).[30] Even the first letter of *Arma* (1.1) repeats that of the *Odyssey*'s Ἄνδρα ('man'), while the whole word reworks the aggressive theme of the *Iliad*[31] before the second word (*uirum*) returns us to the *Odyssey*'s *incipit**.[32] The story is set in an heroic past, and tells of leadership, voyaging and battles, of hospitality, sacrifice, and contests, of relations between men and gods, men and their families, men and their enemies; like Homer, V. gives prominent and poignant roles to women. Both poets include prophecies and narratives of past events (in particular *Od.* 9–12 is matched by *Aen.* 2–3), debates in heaven and on earth (*Il.* 1 and *Od.* 1–2 have both, e.g.; *Aen.* 10 and 11 respectively), catalogues of participants in the war (*Il.* 2; *Aen.* 7), ecphrases* of places and works of art (notably the shields of Achilles in *Iliad* 18 and of Aeneas in Book 8).

The *Aeneid* is easily seen as falling into an Odyssean and an Iliadic half. Books 1–6 are like *Odyssey* 5–12 in narrating voyages after the fall of Troy in search of (a new) home, together with the adventures that threaten the hero and his men or delay progress—storms; monsters such as the Cyclops, Scylla and Charybdis; erotic encounters (Dido plays the part of Circe, Calypso, Nausicaa); and a visit to the world of the dead (*Aeneid* 6 < *Odyssey* 11). Books 7–12 then present an account of a war that is provoked by an argument over a bride (Turnus thinks Aeneas is stealing Lavinia from him, as Paris took Helen from Menelaus). Many of the episodes are based on passages of the *Iliad*, e.g. the attempted burning of the ships (9 < *Il.* 15–16); the night episode involving Nisus and Euryalus (9 < Odysseus and Diomedes in 10); the killing of Pallas and despoiling of his body (10 < Patroclus in 16–17); and the climactic encounter between Aeneas and Turnus reworks that between Achilles and Hector in *Iliad* 22. However, the plot of the second half, in which Aeneas tries to secure his rightful wife and home, is also parallel to the *Odyssey*;[33] and the first half has many allusions* to the

---

[30] On formulae* and repetitions, see pp. 33–4.
[31] The first word (Μῆνιν, 'Wrath') is echoed by *men(e) in(cepto)*, the opening of Juno's prologic monologue (1.37): so W. Levitan, *LCM* 18.1 (1993), 14.
[32] Mostly scholars think of the exploitation of the two poems as collaborative (*Vita Don.* §21 *argumentum uarium ac multiplex et quasi amborum Homeri carminum instar*, 'a varied and complex narrative, almost equivalent to both Homeric poems') but J. Farrell in a forthcoming book will offer a reading in which they persistently struggle for mastery over their successor.
[33] For a detailed argument on the presence of *Odyssey* throughout, see Cairns 1989: 177–214.

Iliad,[34] especially the games of Book 5, based mainly on the funeral games for Patroclus in *Iliad* 23.

As part of the hero's narrative, and a description of voyages,[35] with Scylla, Charybdis, and Polyphemus prominent in the second half, Book 3 is clearly one of the most Odyssean parts of the poem; but even here major parts are played by three figures from the *Iliad*: the mourning widow Andromache, the seer Helenus, and Aeneas himself, now king of the remaining Trojans, and founder of a house that will rule a wider empire (3.97-8), as Poseidon had foretold at *Iliad* 20.307-8.[36] Odysseus' narrative of his wanderings in *Od.* 9-12 comes at a feast in a foreign court, and follows Demodocus' account of the Trojan Horse and the city's fall at 8.499-520, to which the preceding book (*Aen.* 2) thus corresponds. Both Phaeacians (*Od.* 7.30-6) and Carthaginians (1.520-78) are cautious about foreigners, and both heroes have been assisted by their usual divine helper: Odysseus by Athena (7.14-77), Aeneas by Venus; but Venus' information (1.338-68: **P**) and involvement is much more far-reaching. Though the interest of the Phaeacian princess Nausicaa in Odysseus hints at a further possible delay (6.236-46), they part in mutual admiration (8.457-68), whereas Dido has Cupid on her lap while Aeneas speaks, and his words will contribute to her desperate love for him.

Because of the familiarity of Greek literature in Rome, and Homer in particular, V. would expect readers to pick up his allusions* and imitations: they give pleasure when they are seen, and they provide meaning, not least when changes are made. The introduction of Achaemenides (588-691) is a clear instance of this: Odysseus arrives home alone, having lost all his boats and followers; but Aeneas cannot arrive alone in Italy if he is to found a city with a Trojan past. What better way to bring out the contrast between the Homeric individualist and the Roman colonist than to invent a man whom Odysseus has abandoned

---

[34] And to the now fragmentary 'Cyclic' epics on Troy's fall: E. C. Kopff, 'Virgil and the Cyclic Epics', *ANRW* II.31.2 (1981), 919-47 M. L. West, *The Epic Cycle* (Oxford, 2013), 48 (and see indices).

[35] For a passing echo that marks this similarity, see 269. Examples of more substantial imitation, not discussed below, may be seen in the first arrival on the Italian coast (521-36; n.b. *Od.* 13.93-104: **C**) and when the conversation with Achaemenides (608-15) recalls Telemachus' meeting with Theoclymenus (*Od.* 15.256-70: **D**).

[36] Cf. also *Hom. Hymn* 5.196-7. The citation is neatly embedded in a Callimachean context (pp. 25-6). For further allusions* to the *Iliad*, see e.g. the notes on the following lines: 109-10, 119, 271, 308-10, 343.

and who can be accepted onto the Trojan boats? The Trojans are more like the Ithacans when they offend divine powers by eating cattle (219–24); but they do not break an explicit injunction and they are protected by their piety (266); they will therefore not be wiped out. On the other hand, by casting Aeneas in the role of Odysseus the storyteller, V. necessarily awakens doubts about the accuracy of the narrative: most of Odysseus' tales in his poem are false;[37] and his reputation for pretence grew in later literature (e.g. Sophocles' *Philoctetes*). This matters more for Book 2, where (by putting the account into Aeneas' mouth) V. leaves open the alarming possibilities that he has not fought with heroic desperation, but got out quickly, or even betrayed the city, as other versions told the tale (Dionysius Hal., *Rom.* 1.48). In Book 3 one point may be to maintain[38] the succession of uncanny events and fearsome monsters, but at a distance from the authorial voice. Repeatedly he stresses the bypassing of places that appear in the *Odyssey* (272 n.): Aeneas heads to a real world, and does so in Book 3 via the influence of other texts.

Tragedy

The Romans of Vergil's day were keen theatre-goers. The audiences that crowded Pompey's vast theatre of 55 BC were certainly responsive (Cic. *Att.* 2.19.3), and by the time of Augustus there were about forty-three days of scenic performance a year. Augustus built his own theatre, the Theatre of Marcellus, its walls appropriately decorated with masks; and he paid a million sesterces to commission a new tragedy, the *Thyestes*, from Varius (later V's literary executor), as a feature of the celebrations of his triple triumph in 29 BC. Vergil was certainly not immune to this passion for drama, and when Aeneas arrives in Carthage theatre-building is the climax of the activity he so admires in the new city (1.427–9).[39] Many modern scholars have explored Vergil's

---

[37] He repeatedly casts himself as a Cretan when keeping his identity hidden on Ithaca (see 104 n., and de Jong on 13.253–86), and when at 11.363–76 his host Alcinous compliments him on his bard-like skill, and asks for more, he pointedly adds that he is obviously not a purveyor of fiction.

[38] Indeed to extend: he adds the Harpies, ghosts, earthquakes, volcanoes, and ever-bleeding corpses to the Odyssean material.

[39] See also the theatrical image from the promised festival at *Georgics* 3.24–5 'how the scenery departs as the sets revolve and how Britons raise the crimson curtain they are woven into'.

debt to Greek tragedy and its Roman adaptations.[40] The presence of tragedy as a genre in Latin goes back (like epic) to Livius Andronicus, and his successors Naevius, Ennius, Pacuvius, and Accius.[41] Their works survive only as titles and brief fragments, but we can see that they often followed the precedent of the three great dramatists of fifth-century Athens, Aeschylus, Sophocles, and (especially) Euripides, in selecting as their subjects myths connected with the Trojan War and its aftermath.

Evocations of the Graeco-Roman stage are woven into the fabric of the *Aeneid*. At 1.164, we encounter the word *scaena* ('theatrical scenery') used of the woods that were the backdrop to the African harbour in which the Trojans come to the shore. Then, for her expository speech to her son about Dido (**P**), Venus assumes the role of the divine speaker of a Euripidean prologue, dressing up in a costume that includes the buskin (*cothurno*, 1.337), a feature that strongly underlines the theatrical associations here.[42] Book 4 will build on this foundation, and the story of Dido is structured as a tragedy, and has repeated evocations of the genre.[43] Dido moves from felicitous greatness to suicide, brought down like Sophocles' Ajax, or Hippolytus and Phaedra in Euripides' *Hippolytus*,[44] by the machinations of deities. At 4.601–2 Dido wonders why she did not kill the boy Ascanius and feed him to his father—like Atreus or Procne and Philomela in famous tragic plots; and at 4.469–73, Vergil employs the similes of two characters from Greek tragedy to convey Dido's distraught mental state: Pentheus is described as seeing a double sun and a twofold Thebes, as he does in Euripides' *Bacchae*; and Orestes (borrowed from Aeschylus' *Libation Bearers* and/or Euripides' *Orestes*) is evoked fleeing his mother's avenging Furies.

It is worth wondering how far the performance of Graeco-Roman tragedy informs Vergil's poetic procedure. In Books 2 and 3 of the

---

[40] e.g. P. Hardie, 'Virgil and tragedy', *CCV* 312–26, explores the notion of the 'tragic'; and Panoussi 2009 focuses on ritual acts in the poem, as well as links with individual plays.

[41] For a recent survey, see G. Manuwald, *Roman Republican Theatre* (Cambridge, 2011); for linguistic debts see 28, 593, 618, 622 nn.

[42] E. L. Harrison, 'Why did Venus wear boots? Some reflections on *Aeneid* 1.341f.', *Proceedings of the Virgil Society* 12 (1972–3), 10–25.

[43] E. L. Harrison, 'The tragedy of Dido', *EMC* 8 (1989), 1–21; M. Pobjoy, 'Dido on the tragic stage: an invitation to the theatre of Carthage', in M. Burden (ed.), *A Woman Scorn'd* (London, 1998), 41–64; Harrison 2007: 208–14.

[44] And Seneca's *Phaedra* (from sixty to seventy years after V.).

Aeneid the hero is putting his story across before an audience that is listening to him with rapt attention (2.1): he is giving a recitation, like that of Curiatius Maternus which is the starting point for Tacitus' *Dialogus de Oratoribus*.[45] In the course of Book 3 Aeneas assumes two roles familiar from the dramatic repertoire, playing the ghost of Polydorus and Andromache. We should envisage Aeneas as bringing them to theatrical life. In his dialogue *de Oratore* Cicero has the character Antonius comment on how the good actors of his day brought off the feat of presenting living human beings. They empathized with the character they were portraying and adapted their delivery to the appropriate emotional states (2.193). Later in the dialogue Crassus outlines the tones of voice called for by various emotions: e.g. appropriate to the tone of dejection is 'a somewhat heavy kind of utterance, not appealing to compassion, and drawn out with a single expression and tone' (3.219); he lays considerable emphasis on the expressiveness of the eyes as the communicators of emotion (3.216–23). These are the dramatic resources that Aeneas was harnessing as he performed before Dido both on that first night and during the repetition upon which Dido insisted (4.78–9), and the reader must try to hear his delivery in the mind's ear.

Sometimes the text affords stage directions as to how the speeches in *Aeneid* 3 should be delivered (e.g. *gemitus lacrimabilis*, 39; *rumpit*, 246; 313–14, 320). This helps the reader to visualize the story, but also takes us away from the norms of tragedy, which very rarely has such pointers. Because it presents nothing directly, epic allows a less distanced encounter with episodes that ancient tragedy would present through 'messenger' speeches (as when the episodes involving the Maenads on Cithaeron are reported in the *Bacchae*, or the death of Jason's new bride in the *Medea*); but in Books 2–3 we have something equivalent to a long messenger speech, which permits the accumulation of violent and monstrous events. Above all V. saw the opportunity to explore the emotions of dislocation, loss, and misery that were key elements in the post-Trojan War plays of Euripides. Polydorus' story, drawn from the *Hecuba*, symbolizes Troy's continuing woe with his still-bleeding corpse; Aeneas' Trojans provide closure with the formalities of funeral rites and a burial mound (19–68). The figure of

---

[45] Tacitus, *Dial.* 2–3. C. Whitton (Cambridge, 2013) on Pliny, *Ep.* 2.10.6 provides up-to-date bibliography on the recitation/publication process.

Andromache combines the immediate grief of the *Iliad* with the ongoing despair of *Troades* and *Andromache*: the availability of the latter allows Vergil to be brief and bold in implying the existence of a new son, here significantly omitted (327). And Andromache's fixation on her past, with Troy's destruction, provides an important contrast to Aeneas, who may hanker after a return (351, 4.340–4), but who has an epic future towards which he must head (462).

Hellenistic poetry

Archaic and classical Greek poetry is mediated to Rome through the writings and practices of the Hellenistic* age, particularly the scholars and poets connected with the Library of Alexandria, set up by Ptolemy I as a centre to attract the best Greek minds to the new city.[46] The centre of literary culture moved to Egypt; and the places of reception typical of Athens, theatre, gymnasium, symposium, where texts were received aurally, on particular occasions, and (for drama) by very large numbers at once, were replaced in fame by an institution that was dedicated to preserving texts in written form, so that they could be read, annotated, and copied by individuals, for generations to come. The dominant aesthetic became scholarly, delighting in learning, finesse, wit, variety, small scale, and interaction with other texts: this is conveniently known to Latinists as 'Callimacheanism',[47] after the scholar who prepared the Library's catalogue, known as the *Pinakes* ('Tablets'); this must have been an extraordinary undertaking, requiring decisions on the titles, texts, genres, and authenticity of every author's work. An early librarian was Callimachus' pupil, Apollonius. Both of these men were also poets, and both wrote works that are of major importance to *Aeneid* 3.

Callimachus' most substantial poem was the elegiac* *Aetia*,[48] a lively, varied, and learned account of the origins of rites, customs, and cities all over the Greek world and beyond. Aetiology* is present in the Homeric poems, tragedy, and especially didactic*, but it becomes a

---

[46] See e.g. A. Erskine, 'Culture and power in Ptolemaic Egypt: the Museum and Library of Alexandria', *G&R* 42 (1995), 38–48.

[47] For a good introduction, see R. L. Hunter, *The Shadow of Callimachus: Studies in the Reception of Hellenistic Poetry at Rome* (Cambridge, 2006), esp. 1–6, 141–6.

[48] For the surviving fragments see A. Harder, *Callimachus: Aetia* (2 vols, Oxford, 2012); 1.24–7 briefly examine 'Aetiology in ancient literature'.

major concern in Alexandria, whence it passes to the Romans:[49] the *Aeneid* is an aetiology not only of Rome but also of its history, its great men, and its practices both religious and political. Within Book 3, we see the foundations also of cities in Thrace (16–18) and Crete (132–4, 190), and of Rome's close relationship with Epirus (500–5); we see the origins of the Roman form of sacrifice (403–9), and Aeneas behaving like a consul at 58–9. Besides these generic debts we find specific allusion* to *Aetia* fr. 43 (on the foundations of Sicilian cities), when Aeneas lists the places the Trojans passed as they sailed round the island.

Callimachus wrote much else too, of which six hymns and about sixty epigrams survive in manuscript tradition. Epigram is again a characteristic genre of Hellenistic* Greek, and influences a wide range of Latin poetry, including the *Aeneid*, which contains a number of epigrammatic moments, including a formal inscription at 3.288. The poem also contains hymnic moments, such as 8.285–305 and 3.119–20: the latter closes an episode dominated by allusion* to three of Callimachus' hymns—to Delos (73–7 n.), Apollo (90–2), Zeus (103–17).[50] From the opening of the Hymn to Apollo V. derives a sense of the uncanniness of divine revelation; from the Hymn to Zeus the debate about origins: in the *Aeneid* this leads first, mistakenly, to Crete, and eventually to Pallanteum in Book 8. Though this little city is in Italy, not Arcadia (as in the hymn), it is a place inhabited by Arcadians. The Delos Hymn provides a model for the hatred of Juno and for the everfleeing destination: Hera denies Leto solid ground on which to give birth (55–159), and she tries land after land until her son Apollo tells her to head for the wandering island Asteria (162–204), which after the birth becomes fixed, and is granted the name Delos ('conspicuous': 51–4). In Book 3 the Trojans themselves visit Delos, now fixed (73–9), and then another set of once turning islands, the Strophades (209–10 n.); but still Juno pursues them, and still they seek their destination.

Frightening and at times hopeless travel is a major theme also of Apollonius, *Argonautica* (especially Book 4). That epic is a concerted imitation of the Homeric poems; it provides a pervasive model for the

---

[49] We may think of Cato's *Origines*, e.g., and Ennius' *Annales*; and both of Ovid's most substantial works, the *Metamorphoses* and the *Fasti*, are essentially aetiological in mode.
[50] See Barchiesi, *CQ* 44 (1994), 438–43; Heyworth, *CQ* 43 (1993), 255–7. For texts and translation of some relevant passages, see **I**, **J**, **L**; **K** is a piece from Hymn 3, to Artemis, exploited by V. in his description of Etna.

Aeneid.⁵¹ The opening tells how Jason gathers together a shipload of heroes to sail from Pagasae in Thessaly to Colchis at the eastern end of the Black Sea. Book 1 takes them across the Aegean to Lemnos (where they linger for a while with the Lemnian women, who have murdered their neglectful men), then through the Hellespont. In Book 2 they have further adventures on the coasts of Propontis, including saving the blind seer Phineus from the Harpies,⁵² before passing through the Clashing Rocks, into and across the Black Sea. Book 3 begins in heaven: Hera and Athena arrange with Aphrodite that Medea, the daughter of king Aeetes, be shot by Eros (= Cupid) and fall in love with Jason; her intense passion will be a model for Dido's in *Aeneid* 4, but Medea does not distract the hero from his mission—she gives him advice and a potion that are vital in his successfully dealing with the fire-breathing oxen that Aeetes challenges him to yoke. Book 4 begins with Aeetes still angry; on Medea's urging Jason seizes the Golden Fleece, and the Argo sails away, pursued by Aeetes' ships, across the Black Sea, up the Danube, and (by geographical sleight of hand) into the Adriatic: here they at last shake off the pursuit, but encounter various figures from the *Odyssey* (Circe, Alcinous, the Sirens, Scylla and Charybdis), before tortuously returning to Thessaly via Africa and Crete. V. derives from Apollonius his mix of geographical scope, specificity, and fantasy, and much of his technique for adapting Homeric material; often indeed (as Nelis stresses) the *Argonautica* serves as a window through which V. glances at passages of the *Odyssey* or *Iliad*. Like the *Odyssey*, Apollonius provides both the material a sailing narrative requires, including the Black Storm and its aftermath,⁵³ and a sense of the monstrous other that must be left behind in the journey to Rome: he is the essential model for the horror of V.'s Harpies (209–69) and the prophecy of Helenus (< Phineus) that follows (374–462).

The handling of prophecy in Book 3 has also been influenced by a more recondite Hellenistic* text: Lycophron's *Alexandra*.⁵⁴ This poem is a messenger speech in 1,474 iambic trimeters (equivalent to the length of a full tragedy): a guard who has been instructed to watch

---

⁵¹ What had been glimpsed fleetingly is now as clear as day, thanks to Nelis' monumental work (2001). There is an illuminating sketch of where things stood in Chapter 7 of Hunter 1993 (170–89; 173–5 concern Book 3).
⁵² *Arg.* 2.178–316 [M].
⁵³ *Arg.* 4.1694–1730 [N], reworked at *Aen.* 3.192-208, 274–83. Cf. also 356, 692–715 nn.
⁵⁴ See Hornblower 2015.

over Cassandra (= Alexandra) reports to her father Priam the prophecy that he has heard her utter (31–1460). In riddling language she foresees the fall of Troy, and the travels, disasters, and triumphs subsequently experienced by many of those involved, including (to mention those most relevant to the *Aeneid*) Odysseus (648–819), Diomedes (592–632), Idomeneus (1214–25), Aeneas and his descendants (1226–80). The material on Rome is controversial, because it seems to point to a date in the second century BC,[55] whereas Lycophron of Chalcis, the tragedian to whom the work has been attributed, belongs to the early third century. But it is clear it was known, and used, by Vergil, as also by his contemporaries Propertius and Ovid.[56] Book 3 contains phrasing that recalls the guard's account of Cassandra (183–4, 381, 457), as well as the substance of her prophecies about Aeneas (e.g. 257, 392, 686).

Latin poetry

Vergil follows his Latin predecessors in imitating Homer (as has been mentioned) and Apollonius.[57] Some, including the *Bellum Punicum* by the third-century poet Naevius, used the old Latin metre 'saturnians' to tell stories of Rome's origin and history. The First Punic War was fought in Sicily and the waters around it, and if more of Naevius' poem survived we might well see greater influence on Books 1, 3, and 5.[58] But it also described Aeneas' departure from Troy, Anchises' piety and religious observation, a storm equivalent to that which sends the Trojans to Carthage in Book 1, and a resulting conversation between Venus and Jupiter, as well as details about the arrival in Italy (fr. 2–20 Warmington). As we note in the commentary some of Vergil's language seems to draw on Naevius: *arquitenens* (75), the form *Anchisā*

---

[55] The culmination at 1446–50 apparently celebrates the victory of Flamininus at Cynoscephalae in 196 and the subsequent proclamation of Greek freedom at the Isthmian Games. Hornblower argues persuasively for a unified second-century date, against the dominant view previously that a third-century text had been interpolated* with later material: see S. West, 'Lycophron italicised', *JHS* 104 (1984), 127–51.

[56] See Hornblower, esp. 96–7, for references. Useful on 'Lycophron and Vergil' is S. West, *CQ* 33 (1983), 132–5.

[57] Varro of Atax wrote a Latin *Argonautae* (see Hollis, *FRP* 122–32), and for exploration of Apollonius' fundamental importance for an extant poem, see Clare on Catullus 64, *PCPhS* 42 (1996), 60–88: V. seems to pick up on this with an allusion* at 208.

[58] See Goldschmidt 2013: 106–22.

(475). Like his successor Ennius, Naevius was also a tragedian and titles such as *Lycurgus, Andromacha, Equus Troianus* suggest that these too may have influenced the *Aeneid*; in the case of Ennius' *Hecuba* we can see this for certain from the fragments (13–68 nn.). Ennius' hexameter *Annales* was a roughly chronological account of Rome's history from its origins to the poet's own day; military material inevitably played a large part. Goldschmidt's book now provides the reader of the *Aeneid* with a systematic treatment of the debts that we can identify from the fragments; though these are far more considerable than for Naevius, they still often come with little sense of context, and so we can rarely engage in 'the large-scale analysis of structural parallels' possible in the cases of Homer and Apollonius.[59] Thus it seems appropriate that the ancient Penates should use the language of Ennius, *Annales* 1 when revealing to Aeneas his Italian future (163–6); but we do not know who the speaker was in the *Annales*.[60]

Vergil's enthusiasm for two rather different poets of the previous generation is shown already at the opening two verses of the *Eclogues*, where the phrase *siluestrem...musam* ('woodland muse') is borrowed from Lucretius' discussion of countryside echoes (4.589; cf. 442 n.), and the slightly strange *sub tegmine fagi* ('under the cover of a beech tree') echoes *subtegmina* 'threads' from Catullus' refrain (64.327 etc.: see 483 n.). Their influence on *Aeneid* 3 is intermittent and fleeting,[61] but at times profound (325, 487, 617, 658), especially in the responses to Lucretius' insistence on the non-existence of ghosts (29–33), and the wonders of Sicily (414–32, 570–87; cf. **O**). To poets younger than himself V. plays little or no discernible attention in the *Aeneid*. But those writing in the 20s are insistently aware of the *Aeneid*;[62] and in the Appendix we have illustrated Ovid's reactions to Book 3 with the narrative of the Trojans' voyage from Troy to Carthage[63]

---

[59] Goldschmidt 2013: 6. Also important for the topic is Elliott 2013.
[60] A prophet? Aeneas? Anchises? Or even the narrator (as Skutsch postulates on *Ann.* 20)? For further details that may be more significant than we can now see, cf. 1, 175, 375, 630 nn.
[61] Cf. also 113 (which combines allusion* to both), 199, 360, 390, 680.
[62] In addition to the explicit references in Propertius 2.34 and Ovid, *Amores* 1.15, already cited, we note Horace, *Odes* 1.3, 4.15, and the *Carmen Saeculare*; Tibullus 2.5; Propertius 4.1, 6, 9; Ovid, *Heroides* 7 (Dido) and *Fasti* 3.545–656.
[63] Miller 2009: 355 n. 68 has bibliography on Ovid's version of the *Aeneid*; see also S. Casali, 'Correcting Aeneas's voyage: Ovid's commentary on Aeneid 3', *TAPhA* 137 (2007), 181–210.

(13.623–14.81: T).⁶⁴ The latter characteristically lingers (13.640–74) over the magical powers and eventual transformation of the daughter of Anius, whom V. totally ignores at 73–120 (Delos has no women), and gives less than a verse (14.76) to the storm of Book 1, and an epigrammatic four lines to the whole of the Carthage episode (14.77–81).

4. STYLE

Vergil's style depends upon his intimate knowledge and creative imitation of his predecessors in Greek and Latin; yet the way he writes is unique and inimitable, marked by control—and the occasional unorthodox twist. We think for example of *dare fatis uela* (9): the phrase is grammatically simple, but the replacement of the usual *uentis* (cf. Dido's *uentis dare uela iubebo*, 4.546) turns the moment of departure from Troy into something historically momentous.⁶⁵ There are many fine observations on Vergil's style in Books 3–7 of Macrobius' *Saturnalia*, among them Eusebius' enthusiasm for the brevity in 3.11 (5.1.8): 'Would you like to hear him speaking with such brevity that brevity itself could not be confined within a narrower compass? *et campos ubi Troia fuit*: there, you see, in the smallest number of words he drained the largest city, swallowed it down, and left it not even a remnant.' In general, however, style is something best observed on the small scale, and we defer to the commentary observations on topics such as word order, sound effects, archaic* diction. Here we gather together some broader thoughts, concentrating on aspects that are distinctive in Book 3.⁶⁶

Narrative variety; time and place

In general Book 3 alternates between swift description of travel and more emotionally engaged episodes on land, usually told with greater length and detail. The structural alternation is matched by an alterna-

---

⁶⁴ The commentary on 22–68 discusses Ovid's account of Dryope's inadvertent tree-violation (*Met.* 9.336–93).
⁶⁵ See pp. 35–8 on the role of *fata*.
⁶⁶ Also relevant is the section on 'Metre', 6, below. For more extended attempts to characterize V.'s style see Lyne 1989; Conte 2007: 58–122; Horsfall 1995: 217–48; and O'Hara, *CCV* 241–58 (as well as the following chapters: Fowler on narrative, Barchiesi on ecphrasis*, Laird on characterization).

tion in mood. Sailing is exhausting, and when the fleet comes to land the crews are regularly *fessi* (78 n.), and the same epithet characterizes their distress in bereavement (145, 710); when they reach a destination or are given a prophecy that promisingly points to one, they are *laeti* (100 n.) or *ouantes* (189). However, V. varies the pattern in masterly ways: the journeys from Delos to Crete (124–31) and from Buthrotum to the south Italian coast (506–11, 519–32) take place swiftly amid brightness, hope, and excitement, whereas after the Cretan plague the 'Black Storm' creates a dark and repetitive passage to the Strophades (192–208). For some voyages V. uses the manner of geographical writers and lists the places passed (124–31, 270–5, 291–3, 548–57, 687–708), but during others he concentrates on the destination (see next paragraph). Likewise on land we may note the variety in the length: the settlement on Crete apparently lasts some seasons, perhaps years (131–42), but attention is mainly directed to one night's dream, and the immediate departure in response to that dream (147–91); almost as many lines are given to the short stops in Thrace (16–71) and Delos (78–120). The few lines spent at Actium are measured as a year's passing (284), whereas the lengthy sojourn in Buthrotum (294–505) is measured in days (356). The single night and early morning spent on the beach below Etna is developed by the meeting with Achaemenides into an episode (570–683) several times longer than the space given to the rest of the circumnavigation of Sicily and the landings this will have involved, including the final one, at Drepanum, where Anchises dies: that most emotive moment in the book is told with poignant, if mysterious, brevity (708–14).

Often as the Trojans sail towards a new destination, Aeneas' account leaps ahead and uses a geographical ecphrasis* to describe the place that they will reach. Such ecphrases regularly begin with part of the verb 'to be' followed by the kind of topography described (thus scholars use the phrase *est locus* to evoke them). We then return to narrative of action with some verb indicating arrival or an adverb of place or both. Vergil carefully varies his diction, however, so the structure never seems formulaic*:

   3.13 *terra...colitur* [Thrace]; 16 *feror huc*
   3.22 *fuit...tumulus* [Polydorus' covered body]; 24 *accessi*
   3.73 *sacra...colitur...tellus* [Delos]; 78 *huc feror*
   3.210–11 *Strophades...stant...insulae*; 219 *huc...delati* [cf. 209]
   3.533 *portus...curuatus* [Castrum Mineruae?]; 537 *hic...uidi*
   3.570 *portus...immotus* [the bay below Etna]; [cf. 569 *adlabimur oris*]
   3.692 *iacet insula* [Ortygia]; 697 *numina magna loci ueneramur, et inde...*

The contents of the ecphrases also vary: in some cases there is merely a description of the vegetation (22–3) or the topography (533–6), but after 570 this opens out into an account of Etna—and the giant who lies uneasily beneath it. Similar aetiology* is found also in the Delos and Ortygia passages, whereas for Thrace and the Strophades Aeneas tells his audience about the inhabitants.

Misdirection

Much of the pleasure of narrative comes from surprise; authors achieve that through variety, but also through misdirection. *Aeneid* 3 displays this by giving the Trojans directions in the prophecies that they cannot fully understand, and by showing Anchises mulling over Apollo's oracle (102–17)—and coming to a false conclusion—and then reconsidering and correcting his view in the light of the Penates' clarification (147–89). Helenus' speech seems to give a full account of the Trojans' future travels, but as we note on 374–462, he says nothing about major episodes that lie ahead, and much about things that will pass relatively quickly. In part this speech serves as a correction: at 279–83 the Trojans have celebrated because they are beyond Greek territory, whereas Helenus will reveal that more Greeks, and hostile ones, lie ahead (396–402). But in fact the *mali Grai* of southern Italy prove to be no active threat. The announcement at 356–7 that time is passing and conditions are good for sailing promises an early embarkation; but they do not sail away till 506. The departure from Andromache and Helenus will be treated as the final separation from Trojan family—but Acestes will appear on Sicily, and welcome Aeneas and his followers too (5.35–41; cf. also 5.711–71); even the separation from Anchises (710–11) is not final (6.679–898).

Speech

All bar the final three lines of Book 3 are part of Aeneas' long narrative to Dido and her court. There is no manifest effort to characterize the hero's voice as different from that of the poet,[67] but there are aspects

---

[67] There is e.g. no change in the way Anchises is mentioned: he appears five times as *pater Anchises* in narrative in Book 3 (out of sixteen in the poem), four times as *Anchises* (of seventeen), only once as simply *pater* (of five).

that seem to suit his role.[68] For example, the book has only one epic simile (679–81); this is analogous to the comparative paucity of similes in speeches in the *Iliad*.[69] But caution is needed: Book 2 is notably rich in similes, as Aeneas strives to evoke the horror of Troy's destruction. There are limits on the knowledge of an internal narrator, and Aeneas repeatedly ascribes information to *Fama* (see on 121); beyond this personification* gods play no direct part in the narrative, however—the Penates speak in a dream (147–76), and even the voice of Apollo is disembodied (93), heard as many in antiquity must have 'heard' divine voices mediated by priests or their assistants. Neither of these revelations is as uncanny as two other prophetic voices, the ghost of the butchered Polydorus, speaking with tragic urgency at 41–6, and Celaeno, the frightening Harpy, who is in turn abusive, authoritative, confusing (245–57). By contrast, Helenus is friendly, clear where he can be, encouraging and helpful (374–462 n.)

Aeneas reports many other utterances within his own; these tend to be characterized too. The most frequent speaker is Anchises, who responds to prophecies and omens, at times ruminatively (539–43) and using language that emphasizes memory (*recordor*, 107; *repeto*, 184), at times serving as a model in piety, with direct address to the gods (265–6, 528–9). Andromache's three speeches (310–12, 321–43, 486–91) are marked as emotional by the brokenness of the phrasing, the repetitions, and the persistent harping back to Hector; her style infects Aeneas' response at 315–19. Achaemenides is emotional too, desperate to gain the Trojans' pity: again his first speech (599–606) is abrupt, repetitive, disorderly; as he warms to his story-telling his style becomes more expansive, but he reverts to a more broken style when he wishes to convey the urgency of the situation (615, 639–40, 652–4).

Repetition and epic style

Homeric epic makes vast use of repeated formulae*: out of the total 27,853 lines which make up the *Iliad* and the *Odyssey*, about one-third are repeated or contain repeated phrases.[70] In the *Aeneid* the same line

---

[68] On the importance to a reader of awareness of the situation as Aeneas speaks see pp. 23–4. For an account of the ways in which speech is different from direct narrative in Homer, see J. Griffin, 'Homeric words and speakers', *JHS* 106 (1986), 36–57.
[69] C. Moulton, *Similes in the Homeric Poems* (Göttingen, 1977), 100.
[70] So C. M. Bowra, *Tradition and Design in the Iliad* (Oxford, 1930), 88.

occurs on more than one occasion only twice and never more than three times. Sparrow points out that far more frequently 'Vergil varied the lines in which he described such events as are usually the material for Homer's repeated lines.'[71] However, we may feel inclined to part company with Sparrow when he concludes that the straight repetitions are 'a sort of stopgap' and that, if he had completed the poem, Vergil would have revisited them (110–11): they are often supremely effective, as when the last line of the poem (12.952) describing Turnus' flight to the underworld repeats 11.831 on Camilla's equivalent journey (matching the repetitions at *Iliad* 16.856–7, 22.362–3, of the deaths of Patroclus and Hector respectively). These heroic victims of Rome's destiny are thus linked in a tragic nexus. In Book 3 material repeated elsewhere falls into two main categories: there are prophecies that get recalled in identical language at later moments in the story, namely 163–6 (the Penates' verses on Italy, repeated by Ilioneus at 1.530–3) and 390–2 (Helenus' prediction of the sow, repeated by Tiberinus at 8.43–5); and there are lines used to describe habitual action, e.g. 589 (dawn), and 192–5 (the arrival of stormy weather); when this is repeated at 5.8–11, Palinurus and Aeneas himself quickly see the danger and how to avoid it (12–34), as if they have learnt something through their experience. Repeated half-lines link important moments within the poem: *cum... penatibus et magnis dis*, of the departure from Troy (12), recurs of Augustus on his ship in the depiction of Actium on the shield (8.679); and *stans celsa in puppi*, of Anchises when he celebrates the first sight of Italy (527), returns at 8.680 (also of Augustus) and at 10.261, of Aeneas appearing with reinforcements for the embattled Trojan camp.

Such repetitions mimic the Homeric style, but what in oral poems was functional (though sometimes highly effective) here gains literary significance. V.'s version of the formulaic* style[72] is also to be seen when he repeats diction, but fundamentally varies the expression: a good example is the way that elements from the opening of Aeneas' speech at 2.1–2 are picked up at the close (see on 716–18). Compound epithets are another feature of the epic style, naturalized in Latin, and Book 3 contains a scatter of examples: *arquitenens* (75), *letifer* (139), *caprigenum* (221), *armisonae* (544), *nauifragum* (553), *horrificis* (571), *lanigeras* (642), *coniferae* (680), *magnanimum* (704).

---

[71] Sparrow 1931: 81–3 lists the repetitions.
[72] Elliott 2013: 82–117 has a valuable discussion of formulaic style in the Latin epic tradition, in the light of Macrobius, *Sat.* 6.

Etymology and learning

The speakers in Macrobius' *Saturnalia* repeatedly stress the learning shown by V., especially in his choice of diction, e.g. at 3.2.7 'We can often discover our poet's profound learning in a single word that ordinary readers suppose was used at random.'[73] Concern with etymology is of particular importance, as it is in Latin more generally: for the Romans etymology is not a precise and factual science, but rather a creative art, as a perusal of some chapters in Varro's *de Lingua Latina* quickly reveals. Both Macrobius (e.g. 3.2.12 on 6.657) and Servius (see e.g. 6, 35, 589, 698 nn.) comment on this aspect of the *Aeneid*; the modern reader may make use of Maltby 1991, and O'Hara 1996 (an updated version is promised).[74]

5. CONTEXT AND THEMES

Fatum and Fortuna

Fate plays a role of programmatic* prominence in the early lines of the *Aeneid*.[75] Aeneas is 'exiled by fate' (*fato profugus*, 1.2); and the Trojans are 'forced by the fates' to wander the seas (32).[76] The Fates are a force that has power even over the goddess Juno (*uetor fatis*, 'I am forbidden by the Fates', 39; *si qua fata sinant*, 'if the fates should allow it', 18). But it is with the fundamental speech of Jupiter that the nature of Fate is fully defined (1.254–71):

---

[73] Discussion of suggestive religious language follows. At 3.11.9 he is described as 'devoted to scholarship where matters of fact are concerned and to elegance in choosing his words'. Our note on *magnis dis* (12) should illustrate the way V. can encapsulate his knowledge in a short phrase.

[74] See the index under 'etymology' for examples in Book 3.

[75] Bailey's chapter on 'Fate and the gods' (1935: 204–40) usefully gathers the material together, and comes to a sensible conclusion on the *fata Iouis* (228–32), but seems misguided at other points (e.g. in too easily equating *fortuna* and *fatum*, and in the Christianizing 'he is feeling towards a monotheism', 233). On Jupiter and Fate, see Feeney 1991: 139–41, 154–5; for ideas on the difference between fate for V. and for Aeneas, see Williams 1983: 260–2.

[76] Singular and plural are used with little distinction of meaning; and it is hard for a modern editor to decide whether or not to use a capital F, as if to indicate divine beings. The term *Parcae* is also used by V. of the goddesses who spin the thread of life, often equated with the Fates.

Olli subridens hominum sator atque deorum
uultu, quo caelum tempestatesque serenat, 255
oscula libauit natae, dehinc talia **fatur**:
'parce metu, Cytherea: manent **immota** tuorum
fata tibi—cernes urbem et promissa Lauini
moenia, sublimemque feres ad sidera caeli
magnanimum Aenean—**neque** me sententia **uertit**. 260
hic tibi (**fabor** enim, quando haec te cura remordet,
longius et **uoluens fatorum arcana mouebo**)
bellum ingens geret Italia populosque ferocis
contundet moresque uiris et moenia ponet,
tertia dum Latio regnantem uiderit aestas 265
ternaque transierint Rutulis hiberna subactis.
at puer Ascanius, cui nunc cognomen Iulo
additur (Ilus erat dum res stetit Ilia regno),
triginta magnos **uoluendis** mensibus orbis
imperio explebit regnumque ab sede Lauini 270
transferet et Longam multa ui muniet Albam....'

Smiling at her with the expression he uses when he calms the sky and storms, the father of men and gods offered kisses to his daughter, then spoke as follows: 'Cease to fear, Cytherea: the fates of your family remain unmoved for you—you shall see the city and the promised walls of Lavinium, and you shall raise noble Aeneas aloft to the stars of heaven—nor does my opinion change me. I tell you he (for I shall speak at greater length, since this anxiety torments you, and I shall set in motion the secrets of the fates, unrolling them), he shall wage a great war in Italy and crush fierce races and establish practices and a city for the people, until the third summer sees him reigning in Latium and the third winter has passed since he subjugated the Rutulians. The boy Ascanius, to whom the name Iulus is now added (he was Ilus while the Ilian state stood with its kingdom), shall fill out thirty great cycles of rolling months in power and transfer the kingdom from the seat in Lavinium and fortify Alba Longa with much might....'[77]

An etymological link is implied at the start between *fatur* ('speaks', 256) and *fata* ('things spoken', 258); and *immota* is an important addition here: fate should be something unchangeable, and Jupiter implies his unwillingness to break that universal rule (260).[78] If the reader

---

[77] The speech continues with the 300 years of Alba Longa; Romulus' foundation of Rome; *imperium sine fine dedi*, 279; Juno's future support for the Romans; the conquest of Greece; the coming of Caesar Iulius (who could be either Julius or Augustus, or both), and the shutting of the gates of war.

[78] Cf. 4.489 *uertere sidera retro* for *uertere* used of breaking the laws of nature.

misses the association between Jupiter's speech and fate in the opening lines, another, clearer opportunity is granted by 261–2: again Jupiter's speech, expressed now by the future *fabor*, is followed by *fata*; but with the complication that *fatorum arcana mouebo* now has him setting the immovable in motion. The riddle can be understood if we see that what Jupiter expresses as a future will happen: once spoken (*fatum*) it cannot be changed, but the initial speaking begins the process of fated history. Before being spoken these truths were hidden (*arcana*); if we think of the Fates as beings with will independent of Jupiter, he is simply producing their secrets; but in the *Aeneid* they have little separate existence, and, when mentioned, function to preserve his will (e.g. 8.398, 10.113 *fata uiam inuenient*). *uoluens* ('scrolling') turns the image from speech to text; again repetition (in 269) helps bring out the point—time rolls through history like the simultaneous unrolling and rolling of an ancient book (*uolumen*).[79] Though fate, like history, is immovable and unchanging, not turned back on itself (c.f. *neque... uertit*, 260), the process continually rolls on.

The antithesis* between *fatum* and *fortuna* is basic to the divine sphere of the *Aeneid* (see e.g. 493–4). Though both terms are at times used more loosely, *fatum* has been defined (as we have seen) as the expressed will of Jupiter: his unambiguous prophecy at 1.257–96 (along with the plot of history) demands that Aeneas' Trojans reach Latium and go on to found Rome. The point is reinforced by 1.205–6, where the combination of *fatum* and *fas* establishes the necessity of that historical outcome. Others have their futures determined by the uncertainties of *fortuna*:[80] at Carthage Aeneas wonders *quae fortuna sit urbi* (1.454), Dido represents her people as harried by a fortune similar to the Trojans' (1.628–9), and seeks a time in which to learn how to cope with the unhappiness *fortuna* has inflicted on her (4.433–4); it is *fortuna* that sustained Achaemenides' early years, and *fortuna* that overwhelms him (3.615, 609). At times the same applies to the Trojans, when temporary disaster (or success) will not permanently affect their progress towards the long-term dictates of Fate: note e.g. how the

---

[79] The image goes back to Ennius' use of *euoluere* in *Ann.* 164 Skutsch *quis potis ingentis oras euoluere belli?* ('who could roll out the great extent of the war?'); cf. Anchises *uoluens monumenta* at 3.102. The diction also exploits the image of the Fates twirling their spindles, as at 1.22 *sic uoluere Parcas*, Catullus 64.314.

[80] In Book 4 (save for two instances where it refers specifically to death, of Sychaeus at 20, of Dido at 678) the word *fatum* is used not of Dido and the Carthaginians, but always of Aeneas or wider historical ends.

first attempt at Trojan resistance during the sack is blessed by *Fortuna* at 2.385, or Troy's success at withstanding the Greek attack is attributed to *fortuna* (3.16, 53). It is the *fortuna* of bad weather that sends them back to Sicily at 5.22. At 5.604 we get a strong pointer to how we should read *fortuna* on the divine level: *fortuna mutata* comes about through the interference of Juno. This is reinforced at 7.559–60, where she dismisses Allecto with the assertion that she will herself organize any further occurrence of (mis)fortune (*ego, si qua super fortuna laborum est, | ipsa regam*). Juno repeatedly acts as the instigator of vicissitudes until *Fatum*, the overarching plan of Jupiter (cf. 1.18), reasserts itself.[81] This sense of distinction is enhanced when Nautes says to Aeneas at 5.710 *superanda omnis fortuna ferendo est* (similarly 6.96): fate is not something that a character in the poem could hope to overcome by endurance—or at all.

Hospitality and flight

The narration of Books 2 and 3 takes place at a banquet in Dido's palace in Carthage while the queen, under the influence of Jupiter and Mercury (1.297–304), Venus and Cupid (1.314–409, 657–722), is falling in love with her shipwrecked guest. These circumstances encourage the reader to focus on references to love and marriage,[82] hospitality and eating, and to the ways in which Aeneas' story as a refugee in search of a new home matches the woes of Dido, as reported to him by his mother Venus (340–68: **P**). The Trojan willingness to provide succour to those in need, even if they have previously been enemies (Sinon at 2.57–198; Achaemenides at 3.588–691), provides models for the generosity the Carthaginians are also showing; Pyrrhus (330–2) and (implicitly) Polymestor are images of impiety punished. Dido's banquet is like that of Helenus (352–5), and (despite the brief signs of excess at 1.738–9) it stands in contrast to the meal thrice disrupted by the Harpies (222–58) and the monstrous anthropophagy of the Cyclops (620–7).

---

[81] This relationship between Jupiter and Juno reproduces on the historical plane the relationship between the *aether* (*Iuppiter aethere summo*, 1.223) and the *aer* (ἀήρ = Hera [by anagram] = Juno) on the meteorological; see e.g. Feeney 1991: 133, 138, 147–50. 'Juno is generally regarded as symbolizing the forces of chaos, irrationality, and femininity that threaten to derail Aeneas from his mission of founding proto-Rome' (Hejduk, *VE* 'Juno').

[82] N.b. *si tantus amor* (2.10); *conubiis* at 3.136 is a word likely to affect Dido: marriage is a necessary part of setting up a new colony.

The story of the Trojans within the *Aeneid* is one of repeated moving on—until the moment when ships are transformed into sea-nymphs in Book 9.[83] There will be departures from Carthage in 4, Sicily in 5, for Aeneas from the new settlement when he rows up the Tiber in 8; and at 6.546 Deiphobus will solemnly instruct the hero to head on towards his Roman future (*i, decus, i, nostrum; melioribus utere fatis*, 'go, glory of our race, go on; enjoy better fates'). But the theme is at its most insistent in Books 2 and 3: *fuge* says Hector's ghost at 2.289; *eripe, nate, fugam* says his mother (2.619); *fuge* says his father (2.733); *fuge...fuge* repeats the ghost of Polydorus (3.44); *fugae ne linque laborem* command the Penates (160); *effuge* (398), *fuge* (413) are Helenus' instructions to avoid southern Italy and the straits of Messina; *uade* he bids Anchises at the moment of departure (480); *fugite, o miseri, fugite* Achaemenides urges. And flee they do: Troy lies in ruins; Andromache and Helenus are stalled in a recreated past; coast after coast is found wanting. At the same time the land they seek seems to flee them: 496, 536.

Greatness

The *Penates* are *magni di*, and so are those Aeneas carries with him (12); it is his duty to establish a city to match, as the Penates tell him at 159 *moenia magnis | magna para*. Other great gods named in the book are Jupiter (104, 107), and Juno (437); and at 263-4 Anchises responds to the grim prophecy of Celaeno (*Furiarum maxima*, 252) with an address to *numina magna*. The adjective *magnus* is used twenty-six times in total in the book: greatness reinforces the point about the appropriate scale for Trojan ambition, in particular when the seer Helenus is able to apprehend *maioribus auspiciis* (374-5); and it is not an incidental detail when the epithet is applied at 525 to the *crater* used by Anchises to mark the first sight of Italy. Thus there is thematic point to the number of episodes in the book that have elemental scope: the dark storm (192-200);[84] Scylla and Charybdis, both in advance (414-23), and in reality (564-7);[85] Etna (570-87),[86] and

---

[83] Turnus celebrates because there is not for the Trojans *spes ulla fugae* (9.131). The theme of flight persists, but is transferred to the victims of war, including Turnus himself (cf. *fugere* at 12.753, 758, 952).

[84] *magnus* appears twice of the seas crossed (196, 211), and again at 226 in the following encounter with the chthonic* Harpies; the more emphatic (and desolate) *uastus* at 191, 197.

[85] Again *uastus* contributes to the scale: 414, 421, 431.

[86] Etna is accompanied by *ingens*, another synonym, at 555, 570, 579, the Cyclops at 619, 636, 658 (as by *uastus* at 617, 647, 656).

Etna's avatar Polyphemus (616–81): repeatedly the terrestrial reaches the stars (567 n.).

Such size may be seen as compounding the element of monstrosity within the book (most obvious in Polydorus' blood, the Harpies, the Cyclopes, and Scylla); but we are also given visions of the greatness of cities—another function, it seems, of the circumnavigation of Sicily and the visit to Crete: hence *centum urbes habitant magnas* of Crete at 106; *numina magna loci* at 697, of Syracuse; and *maxima...moenia* of Agrigentum at 703–4. These are set against the little cities Aeneas encounters: the *parua urbs* near Actium at 276, Petelia at 402, and especially the emphatically minuscule Buthrotum, at 349–50 *paruam Troiam simulataque magnis | Pergama*. Troy itself is a great city flattened by its fall (2–3, 11). When Aeneas reaches Pallanteum in Book 8, it is only a little city he finds there, as is brought out by the limited scale of Evander's palace (*angusti subter fastigia tecti | ingentem Aenean duxit*, 'he led the huge Aeneas beneath the roof of his ungrand house', 8.366–7); though Hercules ('the great son of Amphitryon', 8.103) and his *ara maxima* (8.271–2) point the way to the future greatness of the *Aeneadae* (8.340–1), here the Penates are still small (8.543). Pallanteum is a precursor to Rome (and Romans prided themselves on the small beginnings of their city), but it is not yet the *ingens Troia* which Helenus bids Aeneas raise (462).

Prophecy, piety, political leadership

Consultation of oracles and fulfilment of omens are staples of foundation narratives,[87] and V. uses Book 3 to set up the eating of tables and the discovery of the huge white sow that will be fulfilled in Books 7 and 8. But the prophetic mode, which occupies much of the book, also provides a satisfying sense of direction—and misdirection[88]—to the narrative. Hector and Venus have told Aeneas to depart from Troy in Book 2. Creusa's ghost has been more explicit, though barely more helpful (2.780–2):

> longa tibi exsilia et uastum maris aequor arandum,
> et terram Hesperiam uenies, ubi Lydius arua
> inter opima uirum leni fluit agmine Thybris.

---

[87] See e.g. C. Dougherty, *The Poetics of Colonization* (Oxford, 1993); Horsfall, *Vergilius* 35 (1989), 8–27; Harrison, *PLLS* 5 (1985), 131–64.

[88] See p. 32.

You must plough long exile and the vast expanse of the sea, and you will come to the land of the Evening Star, where the Lydian river flows with gentle stream through the rich ploughland of men, the Thybris.

It is important that *Hesperia* ('Westerland') is an ambiguous term (the Penates will gloss* it with nine further lines at 3.163–71, including the first explicit naming of Italy), and that *Lydius* in 781 confuses in advance the message of *Thybris*: Lydia is a place a Trojan thinks he knows, but the river's name is as obscure for Aeneas when it is spoken as it is familiar to Roman readers.[89] The sense of partial and gradual revelation, as Aeneas hears and understands more, is basic to the narrative of Book 3 and the poem more broadly;[90] but so is the feeling of unpredictability—portents will be fulfilled, but the characters do not know how. There is no attempt by the Trojans to eat their tables and so immediately satisfy Celaeno's prophecy: they, like the reader, have to wait for Iulus' jest (7.116–17), and Aeneas' reading of it (266 n.). There Aeneas will act as a priest, confirming that a portent has been satisfied, ordering silence, and arranging sacrifice; this is a role he regularly performs in Book 3, but he also serves as a prophet, most obviously when he describes the future alliance between Rome and Epirus (500–5), but also in his description of Sicily, where he foresees cities that will be founded in the sixth century (703–4 nn.).

Aeneas has paraded his *pietas* when he describes how he carried his father out of Troy but carefully refrained from touching the Penates, polluted as he was with the blood of slaughter (2.707–23). By the start of Book 3 he has been cleansed, and he repeatedly remembers acts of worship: as part of the community at Aeneadae (62–8), Delos (79), Actium (278–83, cleansing again after the pollution of the Harpies), Castrum Mineruae (543–7), and Syracuse (697); and in person when founding Aeneadae (19–21) and appealing to the local deities as things turn strange (34–6), at Apollo's temple (84), in response to the manifestation of the Penates (176–8), and by making a dedication at Actium (286–8). He is the recipient of requested prophecies from Apollo (93–9) and Helenus (358–463). In all of this he functions like a priest

---

[89] The point is totally missed by Williams 1983: 272. Aeneas may surmise more by the time he repeats the words.
[90] And to fiction in general, one might add.

in Rome, a role that comfortably combines with that of political leader, for example when he founds cities (17–18, 132–7), acts as a consul (58–9), and orders the commencement of war (234–7) or a journey (289). Anchises displays a similar combination. He takes the lead in sacrifice after his mistaken interpretation of Apollo's oracle (118–20), and on arrival at the Italian coast (525–43); and he prays to the gods to avert Celaeno's threats (263–6). But he is not simply a religious leader or consultant on ancient lore (58, 102–17, 180–8)—he is regularly the one who gives significant orders, not least to sail or change course (9, 144–6, 472–3, 558–60) and he offers his hand to the suppliant Achaemenides (610–11).[91] Palinurus, the helmsman, having been introduced at a moment of mystification (201–2), is given control of the route (269), which he repays with due care and authority in later episodes (513–20, 561–3). The society, as Aeneas presents it, is able to accept shared leadership, and mature debate too, as is shown by the unanimity of the 'senatorial' meeting at 58–61.

Looking ahead: history and Rome

The previous paragraph has illustrated ways in which the Trojans act as proto-Romans in Book 3; the proem in Book 1 foregrounds such a reading throughout. And because the poem instils a sense of aetiology*, readers will look for aspects that evoke the long history between the narrative time and the present. Thus Aeneas founds two cities in Book 3: Aeneadae in Thrace, apparently the prototype of Aenus (13–68 n.), and Pergamea in Crete, which will become Pergamum (133). We also get a sense of *magna Graecia* (396–402) and (through the etymologies: 692–715 n.) the extent of Greek settlement in Sicily. The Trojans celebrate Actian Games (280–2), as people did in the Augustan age, and visit places made famous by the campaigns and subsequent monuments in the area (276–88). In Buthrotum they revisit a degraded 'Troy' as tourists, much as Julius Caesar had done with the real site of Troy.[92] At 403–9 and 435–9 Helenus enjoins the Roman mode of sacrifice, with covered head, and the worship of Juno, who will become part of the Capitoline

---

[91] See also Sanderlin, *CJ* 71 (1975–6), 53–6.
[92] Lucan suggests the similarity when he recalls *Aen.* 3.350 *arentem Xanthi cognomine riuum* at 9.974–5 *inscius in sicco serpentem puluere riuum | transierat qui Xanthus erat* ('unaware he [*i.e.* Caesar] had crossed the stream that was Xanthus, meandering in the dry dust').

triad: both instructions are first obeyed at 545–7. Above all, we are invited to consider Roman links with Epirus and Sicily. Though it is the future alliance that Aeneas looks forward to at 500–5, the name of Pyrrhus as a king in Epirus brings to mind one of Rome's great enemies. Pyrrhus, born c.319 BC, and in power in Epirus from 297, having tried to expand his kingdom in northern Greece with only temporary success, responded to an appeal for assistance from the Greek city of Tarentum, on the coast of southern Italy: they wanted help in resisting Roman expansion. He crossed to Italy in 280, and was victorious in major, but destructive, battles, and eventually withdrew after the battle of Beneventum in 275: see notes on 383, 398, 503 for possible resonances. Sicily will be the focus of Rome's conflict with Carthage, especially in the First Punic War (264–241 BC); but for Book 3 recent history plays a more loaded part: it was the base of Sextus Pompey in the 30s, an enemy who was a real danger to Julius Caesar's heir.[93]

Family

The book begins with Anchises ordering departure from the Troad (9), and Aeneas leaving for exile accompanied by comrades and his son (*cum sociis natoque*, 12). Anchises, as we have seen, plays an important role in the book, which ends with his death (707–13). But Ascanius, the son, hardly appears thereafter: indeed he is mentioned only in the words spoken by Andromache (339, 484). We might compare the absence of the travelling Trojan women from this book, present only when there is a death to mourn (65).[94] However, it seems as though the absence is more than just an example of the non-appearance of women and children in adventure narratives: this is a poem where Aeneas addresses his son just once, without much intimacy, when freshly arrayed in arms for the final battle (12.432–40), though he twice summons him through others (1.643–6, 5.545–51), and Ascanius performs memorable actions when his father is not present (hunting in 4 and 7; killing Remulus Numanus with an arrow in 9). Brutus, who will drive the Tarquins out from Rome, is saluted by Anchises for executing his sons when they threaten the liberty of the nascent republic (6.817–23); Aeneas is a less

---

[93] See Powell 2008; and our notes on 413, 424–5, 553.
[94] So Fantham 2015: 116. The observation remains a good one even though Fantham excludes a female presence in instances of *socii* such as 71, 259, 524. Andromache too laments in her appearances, explicitly at 301–5, effectively at 482–91.

brutal model of the *pater* who has more care for his *patria* than his children. Andromache's concern for Ascanius is hardly a comforting alternative, however: she sees him as a substitute for her own dead son (489-91), and alarmingly elides her living son, the future king and eponym* of the Molossi, remembering only the pain of childbirth (327).

One point that Aeneas makes forcefully, if implicitly, in Book 2, is that leadership of the Trojans has passed to him: Hector is dead, and his ghost conveys religious and political authority to his cousin (2.288-95); Priam is dead (2.554-8), and so is another of his sons, Polites (2.526-32). Priam's descendants continue to be discarded in Book 3: the youngest son Polydorus has been killed by his host in Thrace (3.55-6), and Helenus, a surviving son, has become ruler of Greek cities, and acknowledges that his Troy is a miniature version, not a rival for the *ingens Troia* that Aeneas is fated to found (462).

6. METRE, SCANSION, AND VERSIFICATION

Quantity

The scansion of Latin verse of the classical period is quantitative, not based on speech stress as in English. Syllables are either light or heavy, regardless of where the speech stress falls in each word.

(a) All syllables which contain a long vowel or a diphthong are heavy, e.g. both syllables in each of *aēstās, fātīs, nātō*. For the purposes of scansion heavy syllables are marked with a macron ⁻, light syllables with the symbol ˘. This convention sometimes results in a syllable containing a short vowel being marked with a macron; see below.

(b) If a short vowel is followed by two consonants whether in the same or in different words, the syllable is heavy, e.g.:

īmmĕrītām uīsūm sŭpĕrīs, cĕcĭdītquĕ sŭpērbŭm [2]

In this line the syllables underlined are heavy although in each case the vowel is—and should be pronounced—short.

(c) *h* has no metrical value; it does not count as a consonant.
qu functions as a single consonant.
x and *z* both count as double consonants (= *cs, ds/sd*).

(d) Exceptions to rule (b)
(i) if a short vowel is followed by a combination of mute (*p, t, c, b, d, g*) and liquid (*r* and less commonly *l*), the syllable may be scanned either light or heavy, depending on whether the syllable is treated as

Introduction 45

dividing between or before the pair of consonants, e.g. *pă-trĕm* (35) but *sāc-ră* (19); *uŏlūc-rīs* (241) but *uŏlŭ-crūm* (216, 361); *Cȳ-clōpăs* (647) but *Cȳc-lōpum* at 569 (similarly at 617, 644, 675, and everywhere else in V.); *āttōllītquĕ glŏbōs* (574), but *spīcŭlăquĕ c-lĭpĕīquĕ* (7.186).[95]

(ii) As in Homer, metrical necessity can cause a short consonant to remain light even when it comes before two consonants which are not mute and liquid, or before a double consonant, as at 270 *nĕmŏrōsă Zăcȳnthŏs*.

(iii) Homer is also imitated when V. places a syllable with a short vowel before only one consonant when a heavy syllable is required, e.g. in *nemus* at 112: *Īdaēūmquĕ nĕmūs, hīnc*.

(e) The second *i* in *mihi* and *tibi* can be short (29 *mihĭ*, 453 *tibĭ*, and commonly) or long (*mihī* 183, *tibī* 388, 412). Also variable is the *i* in the pronominal genitive ending -*ius*: it is short in *āltĕrĭūs* at 31 and 33, but long in *īpsīŭs* at 5.55.

Elision (and prodelision)

A vowel at the end of a word followed by a vowel at the start of the next word is elided (as in French *c'est*, but in normal Latin texts the elision is not marked), e.g.

dīuērs(a) ēxsĭlĭ(a) ēt dēsērtās quaērĕrĕ tērrās [3]

The final *as* of *diuersa* and *exsilia* elide before the *es* of *exsilia* and *et. h*, having no metrical value, does not stop elision:

māiōr(e) hāstīlĭă nīsū [37]

The *e* of *maiore* elides before *(h)astilia*.

For the purposes of reading Latin, the best advice is not to pronounce the elided vowel unless it makes a vital contribution to the meaning.

More surprisingly, a final syllable ending -*m* elides before a following vowel, e.g.:

mōnstr(um) hōrrēnd(um), īnfōrm(e), īngēns, cuī lūmĕn ădēmptŭm [658][96]

---

[95] Though V. occasionally treats *que* as heavy when the following word begins with two consonants (or even one: 91), it is anomalous when we find *Gelā fluuii* at 702 (a line we follow Wagner in deleting).

[96] A remarkable line, with its heavy spondaic start emphasized by the three elisions.

When reading, do not pronounce the elided syllable ending -*m* fully but nasalize the vowel (Allen 1989: 31).

A vowel before *est* is liable to prodelision, i.e. the *e* of *est* disappears, not the vowel at the end of the word before, e.g.: *Apollo (e)st* (154), *locuta (e)st* (320), *amico (e)st* (463), *necesse (e)st* (478), *fama (e)st* (694).[97]

Types of elision may be classified in order of ascending gravity: (a) short vowels (of which that in *que* is especially easily lost); (b) vowels + final *m*; (c) long vowels; (d) diphthongs. For examples of (c), cf. *erg(o) agite* (114), *erg(o) auidus* (132), *erg(o) animis* (250: V. regularly elides *ergo*, 13 times before a short *a*); *inconsult(i) abeunt* (452); and (d) cf. *aduers(ae) obluctor* (38), *com(ae) et* (48), *subit(ae) horrifico* (225), *Harpyi(ae) et* (226), *dir(ae) obscenae* (262), *optat(ae) aurae* (530).

Elisions of monosyllabic words are relatively rare: in *Aeneid* 3 V. elides *iam* (192, 260), *se* (205), *te* (410), *me* (605).[98]

The hexameter

All three of Vergil's main Greek models used the hexameter: Homer, writing epic; Hesiod, writing didactic*; Theocritus, writing pastoral. Ennius developed a Latin equivalent. By the time V. employed it the line has attained great regularity. It scans as follows:

$$\underset{1}{-\smile\smile} \mid \underset{2}{-\smile\smile} \mid \underset{3}{-} \mid\mid \underset{4}{\smile\smile} \mid \underset{5}{-\smile\smile} \mid \underset{6}{-\smile\smile} \mid -\smile$$

The hexameter consists of six feet, the first five of them basically dactylic* in pattern (—⏑⏑). However, a spondee (— —) may be substituted for a dactyl in any of the first four feet; the fifth foot is nearly always a dactyl and the sixth foot is always a spondee or trochee (—⏑), i.e. the final syllable can be either long or short ('anceps'). Verses 5–6 scan thus:

ău̅gŭrī̆|īs ăgī̆|mūr || dī̆|uū̆m clās|sēmquĕ sŭ|b īpsā

Āntān|dr(o) ēt| Phrў̄gī̆|ae̅ || mō|līmūr| mōntĭbŭs| Īdae̅

Book 3 contains four hexameters with a fifth-foot spondee (often called a 'spondeiazon'[99]), 12, 74, 517, 549:

cūm sŏcĭīs nātōquĕ pĕnātĭbŭs e̅t mā̅gnīs dīs [12]

---

[97] Of these examples all bar the last occur in the sixth foot (where elision, unlike prodelision, would not be permitted); likewise *ille (e)s* at 6.845.

[98] *ne qu(a)* (406) and *si qu(a)* (433) might rather be treated as disyllabic units, and so hardly fall into this category.

[99] Cf. Cicero, *Att.* 7.2.1.

Caesurae

There is usually a strong caesura (literally 'a cutting'), a break between words, after the first long syllable of the foot, in the middle of the third foot, e.g.:

> Pōstquām rēs Ăsīae ‖ Prĭămīqu(e) ēuērtĕrĕ gēntĕm [1]

This third-foot caesura is designated '3s' ('s' = 'strong', as opposed to 'w' = 'weak', where the word break follows a light syllable).[100] Where this is missing, V. usually has a caesura after the first syllable of the fourth (4s) or the second foot (2s), and often both, e.g. verse 7:

> īncērtī ‖ quō fātă fĕrānt ‖ ŭbī sīstĕrĕ dētŭr

In Book 3 in verses 12, 269,[101] 531, 674, 707 the only strong caesura is in the second foot. There is a caesura after *et* (the normal break comes before it) in 4, 61, 222, 244, 520, 567; and the extraordinary 549 has its only possible caesura at an elision.

Hiatus

Hiatus* occurs when a vowel at the end of a word is not elided before another vowel. It is found in 74 (twice), 464, 606:

> sī pĕrĕō, hŏmĭnūm mănĭbūs pĕrīssĕ iŭuābĭt [606]

Verse 211 has correption*, the form of hiatus that affects quantity:

> īnsŭlae Ĭŏnĭ(ō) īn māgnō, quās dīră Cĕlaenō

The diphthong at the end of the cretic* *īnsŭlae* is shortened (as regularly happens in Homer) so that it can fit in the dactylic* line—a Greek usage appropriate to the Greek place-names, as in 74 (see n.).

Alternative forms, number, and case

Metrical flexibility is provided by the alternative endings (a) in passive and deponent forms of the second person singular of the present indicative (*rērĕ* rather than *reris*, 381), present subjunctive (*praeterlabārĕ*, 478), future indicative (*mittērĕ*, 440); and (b) of the third person plural of the perfect indicative active: there are fourteen instances of -*ērĕ* in the book,[102] which is thus more

---

[100] '3d' indicates word break ('diaeresis') at the end of the third foot.
[101] An imitation of an Homeric line (*Od.* 11.10) and Homeric rhythm.
[102] This is not a purely metrical choice: see on *dedērĕ*, 238.

common than both the standard *-ērunt* (only *suasērunt*, 363, *posuērunt*, 399) and *-ĕrunt* (as required in *stetĕrunt*, 48, *constitĕrunt*, 681).

Another word where the quantity changes according to the needs of the metre is *cōnūbĭă* (319); contrast *cōnŭbīīs* (136); similarly *Ītălĭam* (166 etc.), *Ītălă* (185), but *Ītălī* (396), *Ītălōs* (440). In both *rēlĭquĭae* (87) and *rēlĭgĭo* (363, 409) the *e* was properly short, but for the words to appear in dactylic* verse it had to be lengthened.

It is also partly for metrical convenience that V. makes use of vocatives (119), the collective singular* (400), poetic plurals* (84, 307, 602 nn.), and (very frequently) historic presents (e.g. *ăgĭmur*, 5: note the short syllables). He more often has the genitive plurals *deum* and *diuum* (59 n.) than *deorum* and *diuorum*; similarly for compounds such as *caelicolum* (21; cf. 221, 550, 704).

Start of the verse

Though spondees are freely used as the alternative to dactyls* in the first four feet of the hexameter, at the start of the line poets often prefer a dactyl (and they try to avoid opening with a word that forms a spondee in itself). This can be illustrated by the use of *neque* rather than *nec* after an opening monosyllable, e.g. at 242:

> sēd nĕquĕ uim plumis ullam nec uulnera tergo

and by the introduction of *ego* after first person verbs, as in 623:

> uīd(i) ĕgŏmet

This tendency adds weight to those spondaic words that do coincide with the first foot: 1, 57, 61, 81, 108, 119, 158, 205, 268, 353, 420, 429, 450, 454, 466, 495, 518, 563, 636, 684, 697.[103]

One striking effect is the use of polysyllabic Greek names that fill the opening two and a half feet of the line: *Lāŏmĕdōntĭădāē* (248).

End of the verse

The final word of the hexameter is almost always trisyllabic or disyllabic. The major group of exceptions involve four- or five-syllable Greek words or other manifestations of Greek rhythm; the examples in Book 3 are all four-syllable words:

> Lēdāē(am) Hērmĭŏnēn Lăcĕdāēmŏnĭōsqu(e) hўmĕnāēōs [328]
> dōnă dĕhīnc āūrō grăuĭ(a) āc sēctō ĕlĕphāntō [464][104]

---

[103] Even rarer is the spondaic word in the fourth foot, which has a marked, and sometimes expressive, slowing effect: see Williams on 9.

[104] Note also the Homeric hiatus˙.

Caulōnīsqu(e) ārcēs ēt naufrāgūm Scўlăcēŭm [553]
āĕrĭāē quērcūs aut cōnĭfĕrāē cўpărīssī [680]

While there are inevitably some clashes in the first four feet of a hexameter between the way the words are pronounced (accent*)[105] and the way they are emphasized by the rhythm of the line (ictus*), these restrictions on the final feet ensure that the hexameter usually ends with the two in harmony.[106] Occasionally there are monosyllables in the sixth foot.[107] When there are two it does not in itself much disrupt the harmony. Contrast for example the harmony of the second half of 151 (the accent is marked by acute accents, ictus by underlining, as occasionally in the commentary):

in sómnis múlto manifésti lúmine, quí sé

and the disharmony in 695, cause by the presence of a dibrach* (a word consisting of two short syllables) in the fifth foot:[108]

occúltas egísse uías súbter máre, quí núnc[109]

A single monosyllable in the sixth foot violently prevents the coincidence of ictus and accent:

litóreis íngens inuénta sub ilícibus sús [390][110]

Book 3 has one instance of a hypermetric line, i.e. with an elided extra syllable at the end (684):

cōntrā iūssă mŏnēnt Hĕlĕnī, Scўllāmquĕ Chărўbdīnqu(e) | inter

Rhythm

Vergil is a master at varying his pace, and using the rhythm to enhance the meaning of his words. Thus there are quick-moving lines with five dactyls*,[111] such as 90 (which marks the start of the earthquake on Delos) and 489, which seems expressive of Andromache's emotion; and slower-moving spondaic verses, of which 208 depicts the effort of rowing, and 579 evokes the weight of Etna on top of the giant Enceladus.[112]

---

[105] For a quick summary of the rules see below, on 'reading'.
[106] See 207, 560, 579, 581 for particular effects.
[107] See also p. 46, on prodelision.
[108] So too 42, 207.
[109] See *ad loc.* for the contrast with the following two lines.
[110] There are final monosyllables also at 12, 375.
[111] See also 418, 666.   [112] See also 430, 465–8, 655–8.

Enjambment* and sentence length

Continuity between lines and the placing of pauses is important in articulating the flow of the verse and in creating memorable effects. Thus we move from the sequence of 514–21, where there are pauses in sense, of varying intensity, at the end of every line (even if editors do not always include punctuation) to the wonderful enjambment *humilemque uidemus* | *Italiam* (followed by sentence end) in 522–3. The climax of Achaemenides' account of the blinding of Polyphemus comes in the long sentence 630–8, which is immediately followed by the three urgent vocatives of 639–40, ending with the enjambed *rumpite* isolated in 640. Counter-enjambment* (where the flow of thought begins near line end) is also used effectively: see 219, 480.

Word order

A common feature of Augustan poetry is the separation of adjective and noun, often with the adjective in pre- or post-caesural position and the noun at the end (or vice versa), as in these three consecutive lines (481–3):

> prouehor et fando || surgentis demoror Austros
> nec minus Andromache || digressu maesta supremo
> fert picturatas || auri subtemine uestis

V. also likes chiasmus* (e.g. *prolem ambiguam geminosque parentis*, 180), and the similar effect produced when a line is enclosed* by two parallel words, such as the verbs in these verses:

> linquimus Ortygiae portus pelagoque uolamus [124]
> cedamus Phoebo et moniti meliora sequamur [188]

Postponement* of conjunctions (and pronouns usually placed at the start of clauses) is also a standard part of poetic style in V.'s day.[113] It can be used to help make the verse scan, or feel rhythmically effective (e.g. by enabling the poet to have a dactyl in the first foot). Here is a list (we hope tolerably complete) of the instances in Book 3 (asterisks indicate postponement to later than second position):

cum 10, 137 (n.), 623*, 626, 655
et 67, 668
ne 453*, 473*
neque 496
postquam 212 (n.), 463

---

[113] The following prepositions are postponed: *circum* (75), *iuxta* (506), *inter* (685: a striking enjambment*).

qua 114*
quae 397, 486*, 546 (n.)
qui 337 (n.)
a quo 168
quotiens 581
sed 37, 586
si 434
ubi 105*, 219
unde 107
ut 25 (n.)
utinam 615

Word order is used to create balanced lines, especially to end paragraphs or speeches, or to mark a moment of resolution in the narrative, for example the balanced chiasmus* in these lines:

> placemus uentos et Cnosia regna petamus [115]
> ancora de prora iacitur, stant litore puppes [277]

Cf. also 119–20, 718. For the different kind of balance in golden* and silver* lines see 280, 175.

Half-lines

Donatus (23–4) describes Vergil's compositional method as he wrote the *Aeneid* as follows:

He sketched it out first in prose, divided it up into twelve books and set about turning it into a poem bit by bit just as he felt inclined and not in any particular order. And so that he wouldn't hold up the flow of his inspiration, he left some passages unfinished, and in others he inserted the most trivial verses to preserve continuity; these he jokingly used to say were set in place as 'props' to hold up the fabric of his work until the solid columns should come to replace them.

This may not be based on independent evidence, but makes good sense of the poem as we have it: complete, but with signs of lack of finish in every book. Among these the most striking are the fifty-eight 'half-lines' (in fact part lines of varying lengths) scattered through our text, of which seven are in Book 3. Half-lines often remain where passages appear unfinished (470) or joins have not been resolved (218, 661), including instances before direct speech (527). The other three in Book 3 are strikingly effective (316, 640; even 340 with its incomplete sense), and in each case one can perceive why V. may not immediately have seen how to complete the verse without damaging the effect.[114]

---

[114] See e.g. Sparrow 1931: 30–45; *VE* 'half lines'.

Reading

Learning how to scan helps in accurate reading of Latin verse (and prose too, in time); reading aloud often makes the text easier to understand—one begins to see and hear how the words fit together. The verse should be read using the natural pronunciation of the Latin words, with the stress normally on the penultimate syllable when that is heavy (*diuérsa, Anchíses*) and in disyllabic words (*páter*), and on the previous one when the penultimate syllable is light (*hospítium, nómine*); when enclitics such as *-que* and *-ne* are added, the word accent falls immediately before the enclitic, e.g. *gradit́urque* (664). The rhythm of the verse may be left to look after itself: it will still come across.[115]

7. TEXT AND TRANSMISSION

The text of the *Aeneid* was published (i.e. formally made available for copying) shortly after Vergil's death in 19 BC. For the next millennium and a half all substantial copies were made by scribes writing out, line by line, what they saw in the manuscript in front of them. Such copying inevitably leads to errors: anyone who writes a text that is above a few lines in length makes mistakes, whether he is the author or a scribe reproducing the material of another; the cause is fundamentally psychological, a function of the human incapacity for sustained attention and coordination of mind and hand. A glance at the apparatus criticus of a scholarly edition such as Mynors' Oxford Classical Text or Conte's Teubner edition will reveal the kinds of errors made: adjacent forms are repeatedly confused, e.g. moods and tenses of verbs, cases of nouns. Scribes replace words with synonyms (and antonyms too), and with words of the same metrical pattern. The beginnings and ends of lines are vulnerable though failures of memory and physical damage. Mistakes are made in writing letters pronounced the same, and in reading letter forms that look alike. The context often has an effect, with one word assimilated to another nearby in meaning or in form. Words change places. Lines are omitted, especially where some similarity in phrasing makes it easy for the scribe's eye to skip (e.g. 3.210 in F); if the missing material is restored in the margin, it may not find its way to its proper home in any subsequent copy. But material is often interpolated* from the margin, even though it may have been written there not as a correction, but for some other purpose, e.g. as a parallel, a gloss*, or a reader's embellishment.[116]

---

[115] Williams' commentary on Book 3 is rich in comments on metrical features and effects. For an introduction that explores some topics we do not have room for see Tarrant 2012: 37–42.

[116] e.g. Servius reports that some MSS had three additional verses after 3.204.

Introduction 53

In Vergil's case, however, the manuscript tradition is both early and strong, and the text is better preserved than any other classical Latin author. Thus every verse of *Aeneid* 3 is extant in two, three, or four copies from the fifth or sixth century. In addition, the text is indirectly transmitted through citations in other authors,[117] including the various commentaries. The material gathered under the name of Servius is especially important, because it is so full and detailed, and explains much that might otherwise be mystifying.[118] Nevertheless, there are places where the MSS and the indirect tradition do not give a reading that is likely to be Vergil's, and conjectures are adopted by editors. Thus Mynors in Book 3:[119]

230 deleted by Ribbeck
464 *grauia ac secto* Schaper: *grauia sectoque* MSS, Servius, etc.
684 *Scyllamque Charybdinque* Heinsius: *Scyllam atque Charybdin* MSS
685 *utrimque* Nisbet: *utramque* MSS

It is not clear whether this is the result of descent from a single common ancestor (an 'archetype'),[120] or whether comparison of other manuscripts and the interest of readers in Vergilian oddities led to 'horizontal' transmission of corruption. There are other places of doubt where conjectures seem to remove difficulties, and we thus print these readings not found in ancient MSS:

127 *consita* a few later MSS: *concita* MSS, Servius, etc.
360 *laurusque Clari* Ottaviano: *clari laurus* MSS (*clarii* or *clarii et* later MSS)
419 *limite* Baehrens: *litore* MSS: *aequore* in Seneca's citation at *Nat. Quaest.* 6.30.1[121]
460 *sacerdos* a few later MSS, Bentley: *secundos* MSS
558 *haec* later MSS: *hic* MP and some later MSS
561 *tridentem* Heinsius: *rudentem* MSS
702 deleted by Wagner[122]

Besides trying to preserve what is rightly transmitted and to restore what has been corrupted, the editor of a classical text has to use the most helpful paragraphing, punctuation, and orthography.[123] V. will have expected his text

---

[117] Such transmission may not always be independent: see Heyworth, in Günther 2015: 218–19, nn. 36, 38.

[118] For the purposes of our commentary it has not seemed important to distinguish between Servius and Servius *auctus*, or *Danielis*: the work is fundamentally a compilation. For a stimulating introduction to Servius, see D. P. Fowler, *CCV* 73–8.

[119] We discuss each case, briefly, *ad loc.*

[120] So E. Courtney, 'The formation of the text of Vergil', *BICS* 28 (1981), 13–29, and 'The formation of the text of Vergil—again', *BICS* 46 (2002–3), 189–94.

[121] Seneca cites 3.414–19; as transmitted the quotation has other oddities too.

[122] There are other places where the text seems dubious but no plausible conjecture has yet been suggested: see on 134, 152, 428, 510, 606, 607.

[123] Thus at 324 we follow Horsfall in preferring *eri* to the *heri* printed by Mynors.

to be read in capitals, without any differentiation of proper nouns; but modern readers expect a mix of lower and upper case, and it confuses if we abandon the convention. This enforces an inauthentic distinction between *Fama* and *fama* (121), *Fata* and *fata* (see p. 35, n. 76), *Furiae* and *furiae* (331). Modern punctuation is very different from that of Vergil's day (of which we in any case know little); again current usage is our guide. We have punctuated and paragraphed the text anew for this edition, and (in comparison with Mynors' OCT) there are significant differences of sentence structure at 9–11, 253–4, 318–19, 416–17, 620–1.[124]

8. GLOSSARY

References are normally to notes in the commentary.

accent: the accent falls on the naturally stressed syllable in a word: see p. 52.

adynaton: things that can never happen, cited in order to emphasize the unlikelihood of something else: 255–7.

aetiology (aetiological): the study or description of the origins of peoples, places, creatures, customs: 82, 113, and pp. 25–6.

Alexandrian: connected with the Hellenistic* city of Alexandria in Egypt, famous for its literary culture, centred round the Museum and Library. Notable authors who worked there in the third century BC are Callimachus, Apollonius, Theocritus. See pp. 25–7.

Alexandrian footnote: a marker of an allusion* to an earlier text, often explicit through *ut fertur*, *dicunt* etc., but also less directly with reference to echo, theft, memory, repetition or the like: 90, 416, 578, 694.

allusion: an indirect but significant reference to another text: 90, 110.

anacoluthon: a passage where the sense does not follow on to make a grammatically logical sentence: 502–5.

anaphora: the repetition of a word or phrase in two or more successive clauses: 119, 490, 566–7.

anastrophe: inversion of normal grammatical word order: 75, 506, 685.

antithesis: semantic or syntactical opposition: 448, 478.

ἀπὸ κοινοῦ ('apo coenu'): literally 'in common' with each noun, phrase, or clause: 76, 250, 337, 408.

aposiopesis: 'breaking off into silence', used to describe a sentence where the sense is left incomplete: 340.

---

[124] For a fuller account, see e.g. Tarrant 2012: 45–51, and in *VE* ('Text and transmission'). More generally see L. D. Reynolds and N. G. Wilson, *Scribes and Scholars: A Guide to the Transmission of Greek and Latin Literature* (4th edn, Oxford 2013), especially 223–35 on 'Corruptions'.

apostrophe: address of a character within a narrative (from which the writer 'turns away'): 119, 371.
apposition (appositional): the placing of a noun or phrase alongside another in the same case, without grammatical connexion: 7, 60–1, 516. A similar meaning is sometimes conveyed by an appositional genitive: 477. Sometimes one noun is 'enclosed' within a phrase with which it agrees: 537.
archaic (archaizing): old-fashioned, particularly of language, whether in form or diction: 354, 671.
captatio beneuolentiae: an attempt to gain favour in prayers or pleas: 85, 359.
catasterism: metamorphosis into a star or constellation: 517.
chiasmus (chiastic): phrasing where the order of the second half reverses that of the first: 192.
chthonic: literally 'of the earth' but used of what dwells below the earth, especially the powers of the underworld: 252.
corpus: 'body' of text, the works collected under an author's name.
correption: in metre, the shortening of a long vowel or diphthong at the end of a word when the next word starts with a vowel: 211 (*īnsŭlāĕ Ionio*).
cosmology: the study of the physical world and its origin: 516.
counter-enjambment: the anticipation of the start of a new clause in the final word(s) of a line: 219.
cretic: the metrical pattern —⏑— (impossible in dactylic* verse): 211.
dactyl: the metrical pattern —⏑⏑: 90, p. 46. **Dactylic verse** is poetry written using this pattern, i.e. (dactylic) hexameters (the usual metre of epic, didactic*, pastoral, and satire) and elegiac* couplets.
deictic: literally 'pointing', used of pronouns and adverbs that direct attention to something present: 396, 490.
deliberative questions: questions which show the questioner in the act of deliberating, e.g. 'What am I to do?': 88, 367.
dental: a consonant articulated with the tongue against the upper teeth (i.e. *t*, *d*, *n*): 572–3, 620.
dibrach: the metrical pattern consisting of 'two short' syllables (⏑⏑): 695.
didactic: the genre of dactylic* poetry (originally in hexameters) that sets out to teach either information, in an encyclopaedic way (Hesiod's *Theogony*, Callimachus' *Aetia*, Aratus' *Phaenomena*, Ovid's *Fasti*), or a craft (Hesiod's *Works and Days*, Vergil's *Georgics*, Ovid's *Ars Amatoria*), or both (Lucretius, *de Rerum Natura*).
Du-Stil: German term meaning 'you-style', used for the mannered repetition of second person pronouns frequent in hymns: 119.
ecphrasis: a formal description of a place or work of art: 78, and pp. 20, 31–2.
elegy (elegiac): a metrical form that alternates dactylic* hexameter and a shorter, less flexible verse (called a pentameter). Traditionally the form was used especially for lament and epigram, in Vergil's time (in the hands of

Gallus, Propertius, Tibullus, and then Ovid) for the expression of sentiments about love: 23, 305.
enclitic: a short word attached to the end of another word, e.g. *-que*: 91. (In an English translation enclitics are usually rendered before the word to which they are attached.).
enclosure: the existence of links between the start and finish of a poem or passage: 461–2, and p. 50.
encomium (encomiastic): formal praise: 119.
enjambment (enjambed): the continuation of closely connected sense from one line of poetry into the next, sometimes giving emphasis to the word that is carried over: 2, 100, 497, 630–6.
epexegetic: explanatory: 148, 336, 442, 466.
epiphany: the appearance of a god to human beings: 90.
eponym: the source of a name or title: 556. **Eponymous** means 'taking its name from a person or character'.
ethic dative: a dative that expresses an individual's general interest in the substance of the sentence, usually *mihi* ('I reckon') or *tibi* ('I tell you'): 183, 475.
formulae (formulaic): repeated phrases or lines, especially as used in oral poetry: pp. 33–4; 516.
frequentative: a verb that communicates repeated action: 425, 555.
gloss: an explanatory phrase or word, whether added by the poet, a commentator, or a scribe in a manuscript: 226–7, 374–5. Also a verb (= 'to provide a gloss for'): 209–30, 264.
gnomic: 'generalizing', applied to the use of the perfect tense in Latin in generalizations and similes (like the aorist in Greek): 681. See Wackernagel 2009: 229–31.
golden line: consisting of two adjectives and two nouns with a verb in the middle: the first adjective agrees with the first noun, the second with the second: 280. See e.g. Wilkinson 1963: 215–16 (he goes on to define a 'silver' and a 'bronze' pattern).
Hellenistic: belonging to the period of Greek culture after the death of Alexander in 323 BC and ending either with the sack of Corinth in 146 or with the death of Cleopatra in 30 BC: 22–68. (Cf. Alexandrian*.).
hendiadys: 'one' object or idea expressed 'by two' nouns: 47, 414, 575.
hiatus: the gap (literally 'gaping') that occurs between two adjacent vowels when there is no elision: 211, 329, 464. For 'prosodic hiatus', see correption*.
historic: referring to the past (applied to present tense verbs and infinitives): 100, 141, 666.
hypallage: transference of epithet from one noun to another (usually from a genitive to the noun on which it depends): 131.
hyperbole (hyperbolic): the use of exaggerated terms, not to be taken literally: 565, 663.

hysteron proteron: inversion of the natural order of expression: 289, 597–8.
iambic (iambus): a metrical unit having one light syllable followed by one heavy syllable (⌣—): 464.
iconography: visual representation of any kind: 113.
ictus: the ictus falls on a syllable which is stressed by the metre: see p. 49.
inchoative: (of a verb) describing a process of becoming or beginning: 530.
incipit: the opening word or words of a piece of text: 32.
interpolation (interpolated): phrasing deliberately altered or added by a reader: 230, 428.
intertext: a text with which the text in question has a link, not necessarily of a kind intended by the author: 13–68, 419. **Intertextuality** is the nature or the exploration of such links.
jussive: literally 'ordering', applied to subjunctives or imperatives: 88, 234.
litotes: emphatic understatement, especially where a negative is used to assert a positive: 621.
makarismos: e.g. 'happy the one who…': 321, 493.
metapoetic: discussing the nature of poetry: 692–6.
metonym (metonymy): a word associated with someone or something used in place of that person or thing (e.g. 'the Crown' for 'the Queen'): 296. This is fundamental to Latin poetic style; Vergil uses *astra* ('the stars'), for example, to evoke the gods, and in particular the deification of Julius Casear (158). A significant group of metonyms in Latin comes in the use of the names of divinities, e.g. *Doris* for the sea: 74 n. Cf. also synecdoche*.
middle: a usage of the passive form of the verb where the subject is responsible for (or at 428 fundamentally involved in) the action (in Greek, this 'voice' exists as a different, third form for many verbs): 405, 635.
mise en abyme: literally 'put into the abyss', used to describe a passage (or an image) that contains a smaller copy of itself, in a sequence that might recur infinitely, as when Aeneas at 10.261 stands at the stern of his ship and holds up a shield that depicts shields—and Augustus standing at the stern of his ship (8.680): 354.
nasal: a consonant produced when breath goes through the nose rather than the mouth (i.e. *m*, *n*): 572–3, 655–8.
neoteric: a modern term (derived from Cicero, *Att.* 7.2.1) referring to the 'modern' poets of the middle of the first century BC such as Catullus, Calvus, and Cinna: 588.
onomatopoeia (onomatopoeic): the phenomenon through which the sound of a word or a phrase suggests its sense: 92, 571ff., 655.
oxymoron: the juxtaposition of two words of contradictory meaning to emphasize the contradiction, e.g. 'bitter sweet': 383.
paradoxography (paradoxographical): the collection of marvels from geography, biology, and anthropology: 26.

parataxis (paratactic): the juxtaposition of logically related clauses or sentences without the use of subordinating conjunctions: 207, 356–8, 456–7, 478, 512–13.

pejorative: carrying a negative connotation, often expressive of contempt: 228, 613.

periplus (a transliterated Greek word meaning 'sailing around'): a document that lists ports and coastal landmarks in order: 551, 690.

personification (personify): the representation of an idea or thing as having human characteristics: 574–7.

pleonasm (pleonastic): the use of words that reinforce but do not change the sense: 533, 548.

plural, poetic: an irrational use of plural for singular, such as is common in poetry, sometimes for metrical benefit, sometimes with other effects: 84, 307, 602.

polyptoton: the repetition of a word in different forms or cases: 98, 329, 500.

postponement, postponed: the placing of conjunctions (and interrogatives) that normally begin clauses at a second or subsequent position; see pp. 50–1 for a list of examples.

praeteritio: 'passing over' of a topic, usually explicit: 272.

predicative: completing the sense of the verb (used of adjectives attached to subjects and objects): 69–70, 196; cf. prolepsis*.

preterite: past, i.e. the so-called 'perfect' tense of Latin in historic sequence, where *feci* means 'I did', not 'I have done': 565.

programme (programmatic): announcing or implying the style and/or content of the literary work that follows: 374–462; pp. 18–19.

prolepsis (proleptic): anticipation of a future event (667, 706); or the use of an adjective before it actually becomes applicable: 141, 237, 508.

scholia (scholiast): an ancient commentary (commentator): 694.

sententia: a memorably phrased generalization: 56–7.

sibilance: a hissing or whistling sound, as produced by the **sibilant** letter *s*: 215, 273.

silver line: consisting of two adjectives and two nouns with a verb in the middle: the first adjective agrees with the second noun, the second with the first (Wilkinson 1963: 216–17): 175.

singular, collective: referring to the use of a singular noun to denote a whole group: 400.

sphragis: a passage in which a poet identifies himself, especially at the beginning and end of a poem or a collection: p. 10.

spondee (spondaic): a metrical unit having two heavy syllables (— —): 12, 48, 655.

styleme: a distinctive feature of an author's style: 684–5.

substantive (substantival): a noun, or another word (e.g. pronoun, adjective, or clause) acting as a noun: 240.

syllepsis: an expression in which the same verb is used in two different senses, usually literal and metaphorical (contrast zeugma*): 125–7, 385.
syncope (syncopated): the compression of a word into a shorter form: 3, 99, 143, 364, 501.
synecdoche: the part for the whole (a subset of metonymy*): 57, 61, 465, 513, 586, 616, 686.
synizesis: a process whereby two vowels within a word coalesce into a single long syllable: 327, 464.
tautology: repetition of the same notion in different words: 123, 455, 548.
tmesis: separation (literally 'cutting') of the prefix from its verb: 634–5.
topos: a commonplace or frequently handled topic: 570–87. (*Topos* is the Greek for place, and Latin authors use *locus* with equivalent force.)
trochee (trochaic): a metrical unit having one heavy syllable followed by a light one (—⌣): 327, 480, 618.
tutelary: 'protecting', used of the deities who look after cities, households, or individuals: 16.
zeugma: a figure of speech in which a verb or adjective is applied to two nouns, though it is properly applicable to only one of them: 260–1, 304–5.

Also worth noting are the following conventions:

Annales fr. 1 Skutsch: for authors (like Ennius) whose fragments are collected together under different numerations, the numbering used is indicated with the name of the editor (sometimes in abbreviated form, e.g. 'Sk.').

[Seneca]: such brackets indicate that a work edited under the name of an author is not actually by him, as is the case with the plays *Octavia* and *Hercules Oetaeus*, transmitted with the tragedies of Seneca.

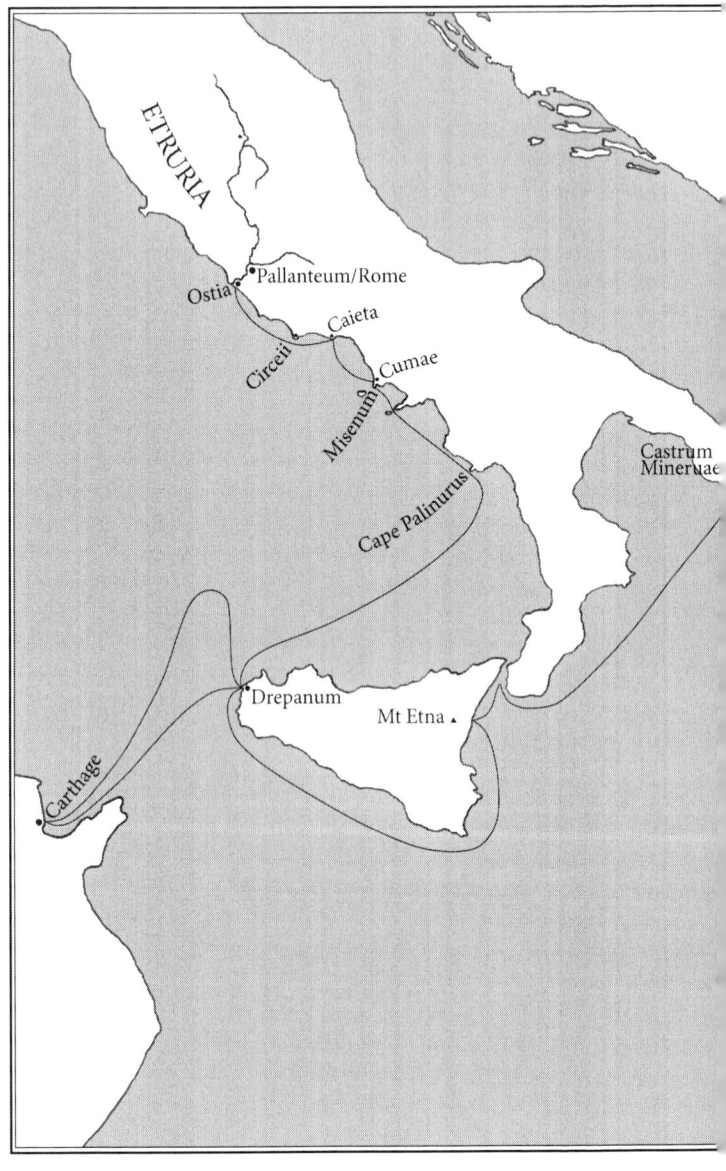

Map 1. The voyage of Aeneas

Maps 61

The Voyage of Aeneas

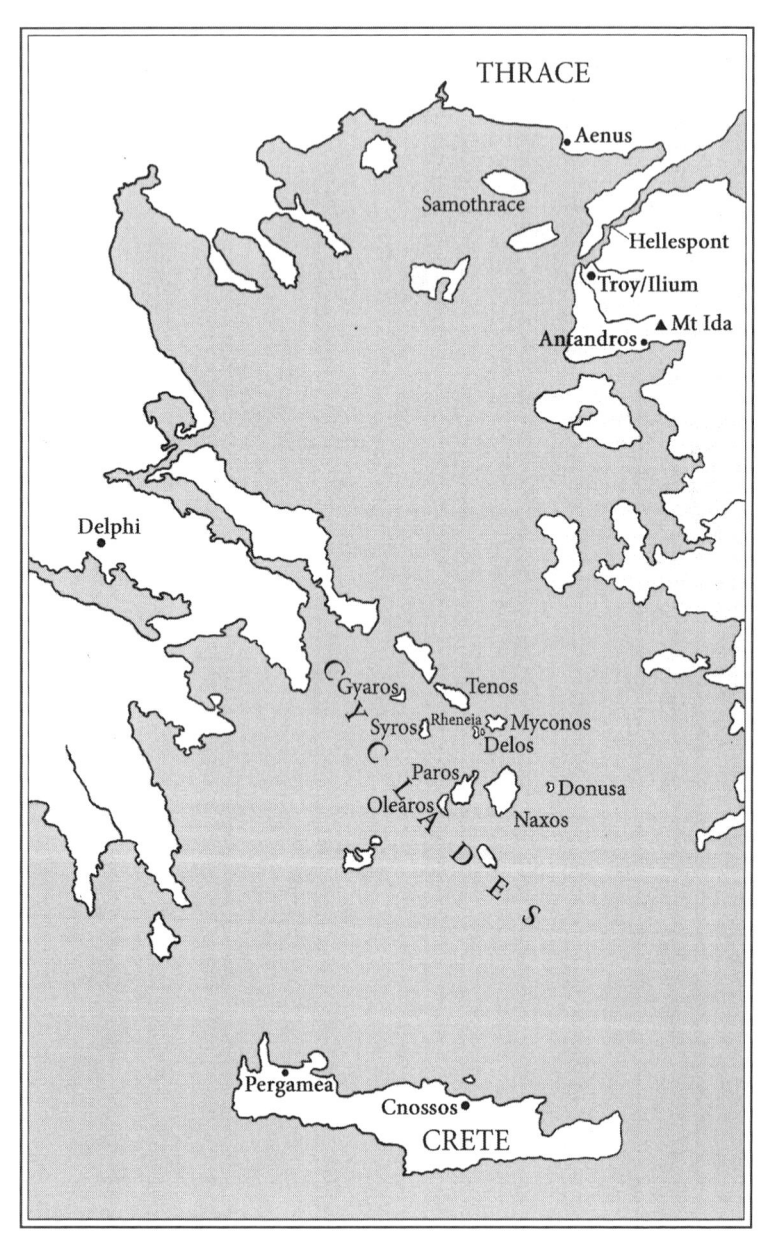

Map 2. The Aegean Sea

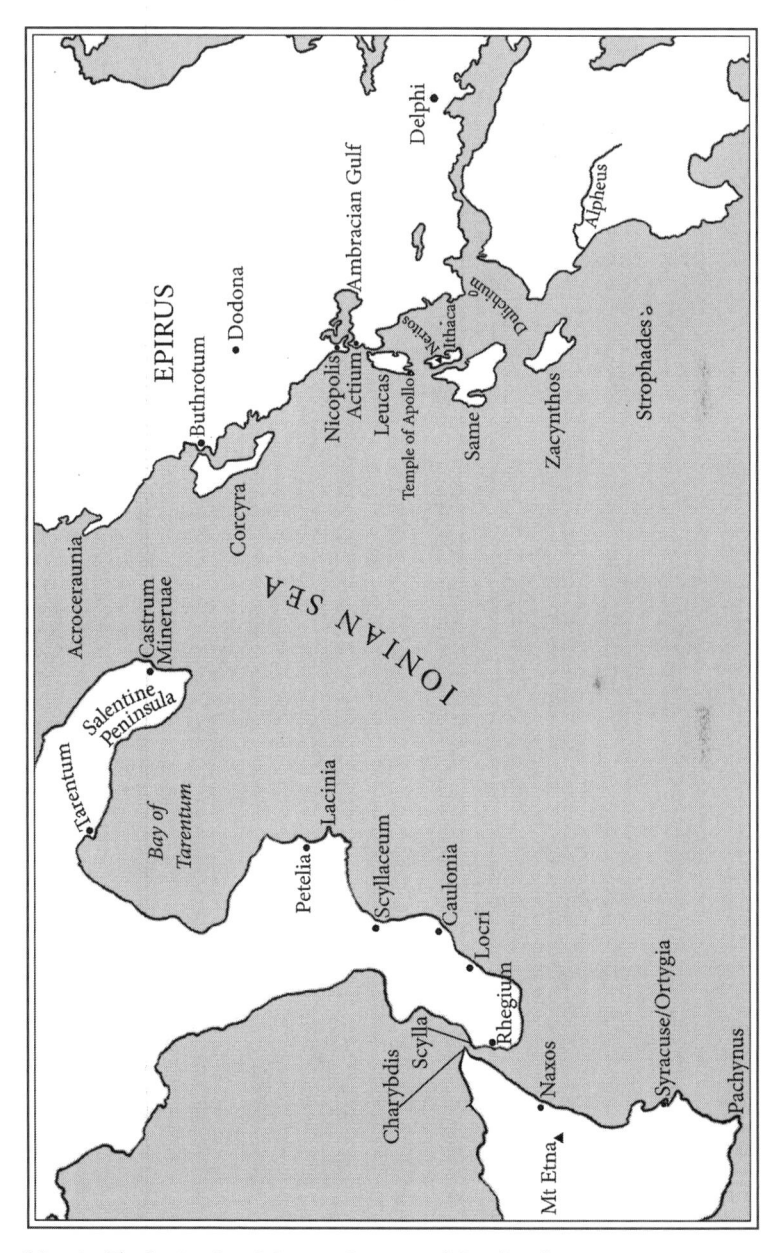

Map 3. The Ionian Sea: Western Greece and South Italy

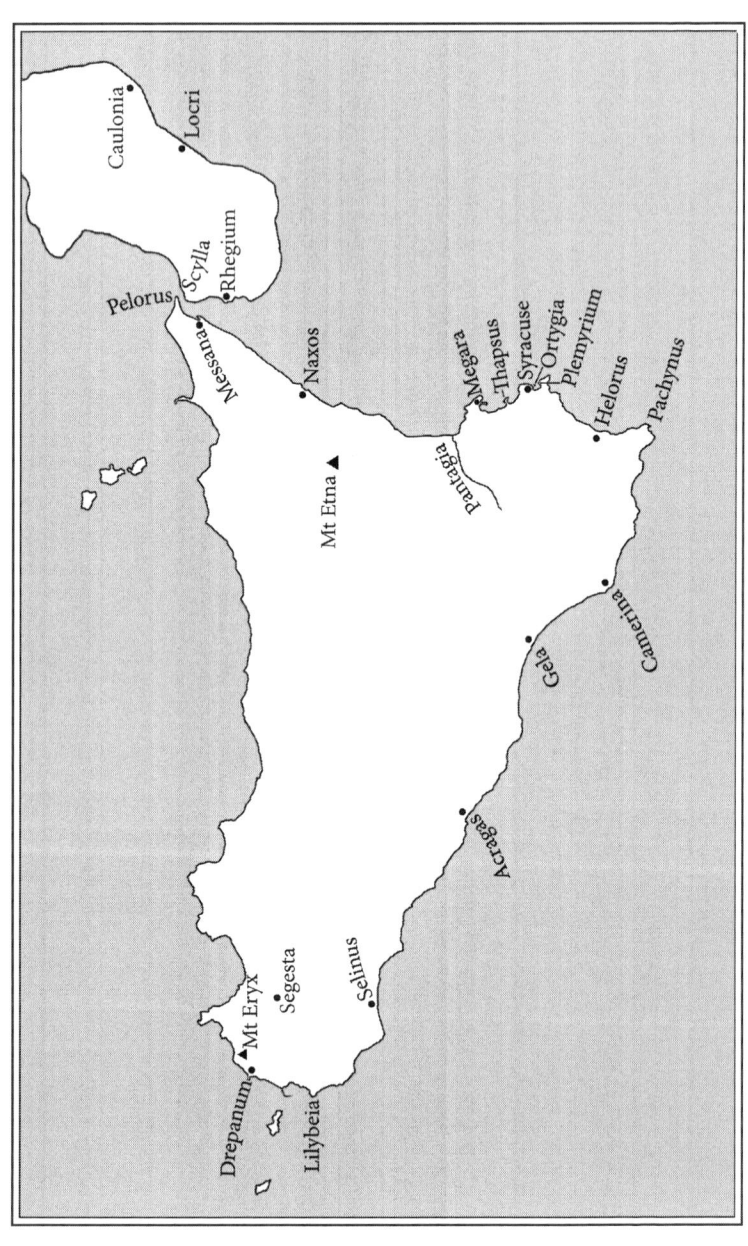

Map 4. Sicily

VERGIL, *AENEID* 3

   Postquam res Asiae Priamique euertere gentem
immeritam uisum superis, ceciditque superbum
Ilium et omnis humo fumat Neptunia Troia,
diuersa exilia et desertas quaerere terras
auguriis agimur diuum, classemque sub ipsa   5
Antandro et Phrygiae molimur montibus Idae,
incerti quo fata ferant, ubi sistere detur,
contrahimusque uiros. uix prima inceperat aestas
et pater Anchises dare fatis uela iubebat.
litora cum patriae lacrimans portusque relinquo   10
et campos ubi Troia fuit, feror exul in altum
cum sociis natoque penatibus et magnis dis.
   Terra procul uastis colitur Mauortia campis
(Thraces arant) acri quondam regnata Lycurgo,
hospitium antiquum Troiae sociique penates   15
dum fortuna fuit. feror huc et litore curuo
moenia prima loco fatis ingressus iniquis
Aeneadasque meo nomen de nomine fingo.
sacra Dionaeae matri diuisque ferebam
auspicibus coeptorum operum, superoque nitentem   20
caelicolum regi mactabam in litore taurum.
forte fuit iuxta tumulus, quo cornea summo
uirgulta et densis hastilibus horrida myrtus.
accessi uiridemque ab humo conuellere siluam
conatus, ramis tegerem ut frondentibus aras,   25
horrendum et dictu uideo mirabile monstrum.
nam quae prima solo ruptis radicibus arbos
uellitur, huic atro liquuntur sanguine guttae
et terram tabo maculant. mihi frigidus horror
membra quatit gelidusque coit formidine sanguis.   30
rursus et alterius lentum conuellere uimen
insequor et causas penitus temptare latentis;
ater et alterius sequitur de cortice sanguis.
multa mouens animo Nymphas uenerabar agrestis
Gradiuumque patrem, Geticis qui praesidet aruis,   35
rite secundarent uisus omenque leuarent.
tertia sed postquam maiore hastilia nisu

adgredior genibusque aduersae obluctor harenae,
(eloquar an sileam?) gemitus lacrimabilis imo
auditur tumulo et uox reddita fertur ad auris: 40
'quid miserum, Aenea, laceras? iam parce sepulto,
parce pias scelerare manus. non me tibi Troia
externum tulit aut cruor hic de stipite manat.
heu fuge crudelis terras, fuge litus auarum:
nam Polydorus ego. hic confixum ferrea texit 45
telorum seges et iaculis increuit acutis.'
tum uero ancipiti mentem formidine pressus
obstipui steteruntque comae et uox faucibus haesit.
    Hunc Polydorum auri quondam cum pondere magno
infelix Priamus furtim mandarat alendum 50
Threicio regi, cum iam diffideret armis
Dardaniae cingique urbem obsidione uideret.
ille, ut opes fractae Teucrum et Fortuna recessit,
res Agamemnonias uictriciaque arma secutus
fas omne abrumpit: Polydorum obtruncat, et auro 55
ui potitur. quid non mortalia pectora cogis,
auri sacra fames! postquam pauor ossa reliquit,
delectos populi ad proceres primumque parentem
monstra deum refero, et quae sit sententia posco.
omnibus idem animus, scelerata excedere terra, 60
linqui pollutum hospitium et dare classibus Austros.
ergo instauramus Polydoro funus, et ingens
aggeritur tumulo tellus; stant Manibus arae
caeruleis maestae uittis atraque cupresso,
et circum Iliades crinem de more solutae; 65
inferimus tepido spumantia cymbia lacte
sanguinis et sacri pateras, animamque sepulcro
condimus et magna supremum uoce ciemus.
    Inde ubi prima fides pelago placataque uenti
dant maria et lenis crepitans uocat Auster in altum, 70
deducunt socii naues et litora complent;
prouehimur portu, terraeque urbesque recedunt.
sacra mari colitur medio gratissima tellus
Nereidum matri et Neptuno Aegaeo,
quam pius arquitenens oras et litora circum 75
errantem Mycono e celsa Gyaroque reuinxit
immotamque coli dedit et contemnere uentos.

huc feror, haec fessos tuto placidissima portu
accipit; egressi ueneramur Apollinis urbem.
rex Anius, rex idem hominum Phoebique sacerdos, 80
uittis et sacra redimitus tempora lauro
occurrit: ueterem Anchisen agnouit amicum.
iungimus hospitio dextras et tecta subimus.
   Templa dei saxo uenerabar structa uetusto:
'da propriam, Thymbraee, domum; da moenia fessis 85
et genus et mansuram urbem; serua altera Troiae
Pergama, reliquias Danaum atque immitis Achilli.
quem sequimur? quoue ire iubes? ubi ponere sedes?
da, pater, augurium atque animis inlabere nostris.'
uix ea fatus eram: tremere omnia uisa repente, 90
liminaque laurusque dei, totusque moueri
mons circum et mugire adytis cortina reclusis.
summissi petimus terram et uox fertur ad auris:
'Dardanidae duri, quae uos a stirpe parentum
prima tulit tellus, eadem uos ubere laeto 95
accipiet reduces. antiquam exquirite matrem.
hic domus Aeneae cunctis dominabitur oris
et nati natorum et qui nascentur ab illis.'
haec Phoebus; mixtoque ingens exorta tumultu
laetitia, et cuncti quae sint ea moenia quaerunt, 100
quo Phoebus uocet errantes iubeatque reuerti.
tum genitor ueterum uoluens monumenta uirorum
'audite, o proceres,' ait 'et spes discite uestras.
Creta Iouis magni medio iacet insula ponto,
mons Idaeus ubi et gentis cunabula nostrae. 105
centum urbes habitant magnas, uberrima regna,
maximus unde pater, si rite audita recordor,
Teucrus Rhoeteas primum est aduectus in oras,
optauitque locum regno. nondum Ilium et arces
Pergameae steterant; habitabant uallibus imis. 110
hinc mater cultrix Cybeli Corybantiaque aera
Idaeumque nemus, hinc fida silentia sacris
et iuncti currum dominae subiere leones.
ergo agite et diuum ducunt qua iussa sequamur;
placemus uentos et Cnosia regna petamus. 115
nec longo distant cursu: modo Iuppiter adsit,
tertia lux classem Cretaeis sistet in oris.'

sic fatus meritos aris mactauit honores,
taurum Neptuno, taurum tibi, pulcher Apollo,
nigram Hiemi pecudem, Zephyris felicibus albam.   120
   Fama uolat pulsum regnis cessisse paternis
Idomenea ducem, desertaque litora Cretae:
hoste uacare domum sedesque astare relictas.
linquimus Ortygiae portus pelagoque uolamus
bacchatamque iugis Naxon uiridemque Donusam,   125
Olearon niueamque Paron sparsasque per aequor
Cycladas, et crebris legimus freta consita terris.
nauticus exoritur uario certamine clamor:
hortantur socii Cretam proauosque petamus.
prosequitur surgens a puppi uentus euntis,   130
et tandem antiquis Curetum adlabimur oris.
ergo auidus muros optatae molior urbis
Pergameamque uoco et laetam cognomine gentem
hortor amare focos arcemque attollere tectis.
   Iamque fere sicco subductae litore puppes,   135
conubiis aruisque nouis operata iuuentus,
iura domosque dabam, subito cum tabida membris
corrupto caeli tractu miserandaque uenit
arboribusque satisque lues et letifer annus.
linquebant dulcis animas aut aegra trahebant   140
corpora; tum sterilis exurere Sirius agros;
arebant herbae et uictum seges aegra negabat.
rursus ad oraclum Ortygiae Phoebumque remenso
hortatur pater ire mari ueniamque precari:
quam fessis finem rebus ferat, unde laborum   145
temptare auxilium iubeat, quo uertere cursus.
   Nox erat et terris animalia somnus habebat:
effigies sacrae diuum Phrygiique penates,
quos mecum a Troia mediisque ex ignibus urbis
extuleram, uisi ante oculos astare iacentis,   150
in somnis multo manifesti lumine qua se
plena per insertas fundebat luna fenestras;
tum sic adfari et curas his demere dictis:
'quod tibi delato Ortygiam dicturus Apollo est,
hic canit et tua nos en ultro ad limina mittit.   155
nos te Dardania incensa tuaque arma secuti;
nos tumidum sub te permensi classibus aequor;

idem uenturos tollemus in astra nepotes
imperiumque urbi dabimus. tu moenia magnis
magna para longumque fugae ne linque laborem. 160
mutandae sedes: non haec tibi litora suasit
Delius aut Cretae iussit considere Apollo.
est locus—Hesperiam Grai cognomine dicunt—
terra antiqua, potens armis atque ubere glaebae.
Oenotri coluere uiri; nunc fama minores 165
Italiam dixisse ducis de nomine gentem.
hae nobis propriae sedes; hinc Dardanus ortus
Iasiusque pater, genus a quo principe nostrum.
surge age et haec laetus longaeuo dicta parenti
haud dubitanda refer: Corythum terrasque requirat 170
Ausonias: Dictaea negat tibi Iuppiter arua.'
talibus attonitus uisis et uoce deorum
(nec sopor illud erat, sed coram agnoscere uultus
uelatasque comas praesentiaque ora uidebar;
tum gelidus toto manabat corpore sudor) 175
corripio e stratis corpus tendoque supinas
ad caelum cum uoce manus et munera libo
intemerata focis. perfecto laetus honore
Anchisen facio certum remque ordine pando.
agnouit prolem ambiguam geminosque parentis, 180
seque nouo ueterum deceptum errore locorum.
tum memorat: 'nate Iliacis exercite fatis,
sola mihi talis casus Cassandra canebat.
nunc repeto haec generi portendere debita nostro,
et saepe Hesperiam, saepe Itala regna uocare. 185
sed quis ad Hesperiae uenturos litora Teucros
crederet? aut quem tum uates Cassandra moueret?
cedamus Phoebo et moniti meliora sequamur.'
sic ait, et cuncti dicto paremus ouantes.
hanc quoque deserimus sedem paucisque relictis 190
uela damus uastumque caua trabe currimus aequor.

    Postquam altum tenuere rates nec iam amplius ullae
apparent terrae, caelum undique et undique pontus,
tum mihi caeruleus supra caput astitit imber
noctem hiememque ferens, et inhorruit unda tenebris. 195
continuo uenti uoluunt mare magnaque surgunt
aequora: dispersi iactamur gurgite uasto.

inuoluere diem nimbi et nox umida caelum
abstulit; ingeminant abruptis nubibus ignes:
excutimur cursu et caecis erramus in undis.   200
ipse diem noctemque negat discernere caelo
nec meminisse uiae media Palinurus in unda.
tris adeo incertos caeca caligine soles
erramus pelago, totidem sine sidere noctes.
quarto terra die primum se attollere tandem   205
uisa, aperire procul montis ac uoluere fumum.
uela cadunt; remis insurgimus: haud mora, nautae
adnixi torquent spumas et caerula uerrunt.
  Seruatum ex undis Strophadum me litora primum
excipiunt. Strophades Graio stant nomine dictae   210
insulae Ionio in magno, quas dira Celaeno
Harpyiaeque colunt aliae, Phineia postquam
clausa domus mensasque metu liquere priores.
tristius haud illis monstrum, nec saeuior ulla
pestis et ira deum Stygiis sese extulit undis.   215
uirginei uolucrum uultus, foedissima uentris
proluuies uncaeque manus et pallida semper
ora fame.
huc ubi delati portus intrauimus, ecce
laeta boum passim campis armenta uidemus   220
caprigenumque pecus nullo custode per herbas.
inruimus ferro et diuos ipsumque uocamus
in partem praedamque Iouem; tum litore curuo
exstruimusque toros dapibusque epulamur opimis.
at subitae horrifico lapsu de montibus adsunt   225
Harpyiae et magnis quatiunt clangoribus alas,
diripiuntque dapes contactuque omnia foedant
immundo; tum uox taetrum dira inter odorem.
rursum in secessu longo sub rupe cauata   229
instruimus mensas arisque reponimus ignem;   231
rursum ex diuerso caeli caecisque latebris
turba sonans praedam pedibus circumuolat uncis,
polluit ore dapes. sociis tunc arma capessant
edico, et dira bellum cum gente gerendum.   235
haud secus ac iussi faciunt tectosque per herbam
disponunt ensis et scuta latentia condunt.
ergo ubi delapsae sonitum per curua dedere

litora, dat signum specula Misenus ab alta
aere cauo. inuadunt socii et noua proelia temptant, 240
obscenas pelagi ferro foedare uolucris.
sed neque uim plumis ullam nec uulnera tergo
accipiunt, celerique fuga sub sidera lapsae
semesam praedam et uestigia foeda relinquunt.
una in praecelsa consedit rupe Celaeno, 245
infelix uates, rumpitque hanc pectore uocem;
'bellum etiam pro caede boum stratisque iuuencis,
Laomedontiadae? bellumne inferre paratis
et patrio Harpyias insontis pellere regno?
accipite ergo animis atque haec mea figite dicta, 250
quae Phoebo pater omnipotens, mihi Phoebus Apollo
praedixit; uobis Furiarum ego maxima pando.
Italiam cursu petitis, uentisque uocatis
ibitis Italiam, portusque intrare licebit.
sed non ante datam cingetis moenibus urbem 255
quam uos dira fames nostraeque iniuria caedis
ambesas subigat malis absumere mensas.'
dixit, et in siluam pennis ablata refugit.
at sociis subita gelidus formidine sanguis
deriguit; cecidere animi, nec iam amplius armis, 260
sed uotis precibusque iubent exposcere pacem,
siue deae seu sint dirae obscenaeque uolucres.
et pater Anchises passis de litore palmis
numina magna uocat meritosque indicit honores:
'di, prohibete minas; di, talem auertite casum 265
et placidi seruate pios.' tum litore funem
deripere excussosque iubet laxare rudentis.
tendunt uela Noti: fugimus spumantibus undis
qua cursum uentusque gubernatorque uocabat.

    Iam medio apparet fluctu nemorosa Zacynthos 270
Dulichiumque Sameque et Neritos ardua saxis.
effugimus scopulos Ithacae, Laertia regna,
et terram altricem saeui exsecramur Vlixi.
mox et Leucatae nimbosa cacumina montis
et formidatus nautis aperitur Apollo. 275
hunc petimus fessi et paruae succedimus urbi:
ancora de prora iacitur; stant litore puppes.
ergo insperata tandem tellure potiti

lustramurque Ioui uotisque incendimus aras,
Actiaque Iliacis celebramus litora ludis. 280
exercent patrias oleo labente palaestras
nudati socii: iuuat euasisse tot urbes
Argolicas mediosque fugam tenuisse per hostis.
interea magnum sol circumuoluitur annum
et glacialis hiems Aquilonibus asperat undas. 285
aere cauo clipeum, magni gestamen Abantis,
postibus aduersis figo et rem carmine signo:
AENEAS HAEC DE DANAIS VICTORIBVS ARMA.
linquere tum portus iubeo et considere transtris:
certatim socii feriunt mare et aequora uerrunt. 290
protinus aërias Phaeacum abscondimus arces,
litoraque Epiri legimus, portuque subimus
Chaonio et celsam Buthroti accedimus urbem.
   Hic incredibilis rerum fama occupat auris,
Priamiden Helenum Graias regnare per urbis 295
coniugio Aeacidae Pyrrhi sceptrisque potitum,
et patrio Andromachen iterum cessisse marito.
obstipui miroque incensum pectus amore
compellare uirum et casus cognoscere tantos.
progredior portu classis et litora linquens, 300
sollemnis cum forte dapes et tristia dona
ante urbem in luco falsi Simoëntis ad undam
libabat cineri Andromache manisque uocabat
Hectoreum ad tumulum, uiridi quem caespite inanem
et geminas, causam lacrimis, sacrauerat aras. 305
ut me conspexit uenientem et Troia circum
arma amens uidit, magnis exterrita monstris
deriguit uisu in medio, calor ossa reliquit,
labitur; et longo uix tandem tempore fatur:
'uerane te facies, uerus mihi nuntius adfers, 310
nate dea? uiuisne? aut, si lux alma recessit,
Hector ubi est?' dixit, lacrimasque effudit et omnem
impleuit clamore locum. uix pauca furenti
subicio et raris turbatus uocibus hisco:
'uiuo equidem uitamque extrema per omnia duco; 315
ne dubita, nam uera uides.
heu! quis te casus deiectam coniuge tanto
excipit, aut quae digna satis fortuna reuisit?

Hectoris Andromache, Pyrrhin conubia seruas?'
deiecit uultum et demissa uoce locuta est: 320
'o felix una ante alias Priameia uirgo
hostilem ad tumulum Troiae sub moenibus altis
iussa mori, quae sortitus non pertulit ullos
nec uictoris eri tetigit captiua cubile.
nos patria incensa diuersa per aequora uectae 325
stirpis Achilleae fastus iuuenemque superbum
seruitio enixae tulimus; qui deinde secutus
Ledaeam Hermionen Lacedaemoniosque hymenaeos
me famulo famulamque Heleno transmisit habendam.
ast illum ereptae magno flammatus amore 330
coniugis et scelerum Furiis agitatus Orestes
excipit incautum patriasque obtruncat ad aras.
morte Neoptolemi regnorum reddita cessit
pars Heleno, qui Chaonios cognomine campos
Chaoniamque omnem Troiano a Chaone dixit, 335
Pergamaque Iliacamque iugis hanc addidit arcem.
sed tibi qui cursum uenti, quae fata dedere?
aut quisnam ignarum nostris deus appulit oris?
quid puer Ascanius? superatne et uescitur aura?
quem tibi iam Troia— 340
ecqua tamen puero est amissae cura parentis?
ecquid in antiquam uirtutem animosque uirilis
et pater Aeneas et auunculus excitat Hector?'
talia fundebat lacrimans longosque ciebat
incassum fletus, cum sese a moenibus heros 345
Priamides multis Helenus comitantibus adfert,
agnoscitque suos laetusque ad limina ducit,
et multum lacrimas uerba inter singula fundit.
procedo et paruam Troiam simulataque magnis
Pergama et arentem Xanthi cognomine riuum 350
agnosco, Scaeaeque amplector limina portae;
nec non et Teucri socia simul urbe fruuntur.
illos porticibus rex accipiebat in amplis:
aulai medio libabant pocula Bacchi
impositis auro dapibus, paterasque tenebant. 355

   Iamque dies alterque dies processit, et aurae
uela uocant tumidoque inflatur carbasus Austro:
his uatem adgredior dictis ac talia quaeso:

'Troiugena, interpres diuum, qui numina Phoebi,
qui tripodas laurusque Clari, qui sidera sentis 360
et uolucrum linguas et praepetis omina pennae,
fare age—namque omnis cursum mihi prospera dixit
religio, et cuncti suaserunt numine diui
Italiam petere et terras temptare repostas;
sola nouum dictuque nefas Harpyia Celaeno 365
prodigium canit et tristis denuntiat iras
obscenamque famem—quae prima pericula uito?
quidue sequens tantos possim superare labores?'
hic Helenus caesis primum de more iuuencis
exorat pacem diuum, uittasque resoluit 370
sacrati capitis meque ad tua limina, Phoebe,
ipse manu multo suspensum numine ducit,
atque haec deinde canit diuino ex ore sacerdos:
  'Nate dea (nam te maioribus ire per altum
auspiciis manifesta fides; sic fata deum rex 375
sortitur uoluitque uices, is uertitur ordo),
pauca tibi e multis, quo tutior hospita lustres
aequora et Ausonio possis considere portu,
expediam dictis; prohibent nam cetera Parcae
scire Helenum farique uetat Saturnia Iuno. 380
  Principio Italiam, quam tu iam rere propinquam
uicinosque, ignare, paras inuadere portus,
longa procul longis uia diuidit inuia terris.
ante et Trinacria lentandus remus in unda
et salis Ausonii lustrandum nauibus aequor 385
infernique lacus Aeaeaeque insula Circae,
quam tuta possis urbem componere terra.
signa tibi dicam, tu condita mente teneto:
cum tibi sollicito secreti ad fluminis undam
litoreis ingens inuenta sub ilicibus sus 390
triginta capitum fetus enixa iacebit,
alba solo recubans, albi circum ubera nati,
is locus urbis erit, requies ea certa laborum.
nec tu mensarum morsus horresce futuros:
fata uiam inuenient aderitque uocatus Apollo. 395
  Has autem terras Italique hanc litoris oram,
proxima quae nostri perfunditur aequoris aestu,
effuge: cuncta malis habitantur moenia Grais.

hic et Narycii posuerunt moenia Locri,
et Sallentinos obsedit milite campos 400
Lyctius Idomeneus; hic illa ducis Meliboei
parua Philoctetae subnixa Petelia muro.
quin ubi transmissae steterint trans aequora classes
et positis aris iam uota in litore solues,
purpureo uelare comas adopertus amictu, 405
ne qua inter sanctos ignis in honore deorum
hostilis facies occurrat et omina turbet.
hunc socii morem sacrorum, hunc ipse teneto;
hac casti maneant in religione nepotes.
ast ubi digressum Siculae te admouerit orae 410
uentus et angusti rarescent claustra Pelori,
laeua tibi tellus et longo laeua petantur
aequora circuitu; dextrum fuge litus et undas.
haec loca ui quondam et uasta conuulsa ruina
(tantum aeui longinqua ualet mutare uetustas) 415
dissiluisse ferunt; cum protinus utraque tellus
una foret, uenit medio ui pontus et undis
Hesperium Siculo latus abscidit, aruaque et urbes
limite diductas angusto interluit aestu.
dextrum Scylla latus, laeuum implacata Charybdis 420
obsidet atque imo barathri ter gurgite uastos
sorbet in abruptum fluctus rursusque sub auras
erigit alternos, et sidera uerberat unda.
at Scyllam caecis cohibet spelunca latebris
ora exsertantem et nauis in saxa trahentem. 425
prima hominis facies et pulchro pectore uirgo
pube tenus, postrema immani corpore pistrix
delphinum caudas utero commissa luporum.
praestat Trinacrii metas lustrare Pachyni
cessantem, longos et circumflectere cursus, 430
quam semel informem uasto uidisse sub antro
Scyllam et caeruleis canibus resonantia saxa.
    Praeterea, si qua est Heleno prudentia uati,
si qua fides, animum si ueris implet Apollo,
unum illud tibi, nate dea, proque omnibus unum 435
praedicam et repetens iterumque iterumque monebo:
Iunonis magnae primum prece numen adora,
Iunoni cane uota libens dominamque potentem

supplicibus supera donis; sic denique uictor
Trinacria finis Italos mittere relicta.   440
huc ubi delatus Cumaeam acceseris urbem
diuinosque lacus et Auerna sonantia siluis,
insanam uatem aspicies quae rupe sub ima
fata canit foliisque notas et nomina mandat.
quaecumque in foliis descripsit carmina uirgo   445
digerit in numerum atque antro seclusa relinquit:
illa manent immota locis neque ab ordine cedunt.
uerum eadem, uerso tenuis cum cardine uentus
impulit et teneras turbauit ianua frondes,
numquam deinde cauo uolitantia prendere saxo   450
nec reuocare situs aut iungere carmina curat:
inconsulti abeunt sedemque odere Sibyllae.
hic tibi ne qua morae fuerint dispendia tanti,
quamuis increpitent socii et ui cursus in altum
uela uocet possisque sinus implere secundos,   455
quin adeas uatem precibusque oracula poscas
ipsa canat uocemque uolens atque ora resoluat.
illa tibi Italiae populos uenturaque bella
et quo quemque modo fugiasque ferasque laborem
expediet, cursusque dabit uenerata sacerdos.   460
haec sunt quae nostra liceat te uoce moneri.
uade age et ingentem factis fer ad aethera Troiam.'
    Quae postquam uates sic ore effatus amico est,
dona dehinc auro grauia ac secto elephanto
imperat ad nauis ferri, stipatque carinis   465
ingens argentum Dodonaeosque lebetas,
loricam consertam hamis auroque trilicem,
et conum insignis galeae cristasque comantis,
arma Neoptolemi. sunt et sua dona parenti.
addit equos, additque duces,   470
remigium supplet, socios simul instruit armis.
interea classem uelis aptare iubebat
Anchises, fieret uento mora ne qua ferenti.
quem Phoebi interpres multo compellat honore:
'coniugio, Anchisa, Veneris dignate superbo,   475
cura deum, bis Pergameis erepte ruinis,
ecce tibi Ausoniae tellus: hanc arripe uelis.
et tamen hanc pelago praeterlabare necesse est:

Ausoniae pars illa procul quam pandit Apollo.
uade,' ait 'o felix nati pietate. quid ultra   480
prouehor et fando surgentis demoror Austros?'
nec minus Andromache digressu maesta supremo
fert picturatas auri subtemine uestis
et Phrygiam Ascanio chlamydem (nec cedit honore),
textilibusque onerat donis, ac talia fatur: 485
'accipe et haec, manuum tibi quae monumenta mearum
sint, puer, et longum Andromachae testentur amorem,
coniugis Hectoreae. cape dona extrema tuorum,
o mihi sola mei super Astyanactis imago.
sic oculos, sic ille manus, sic ora ferebat;   490
et nunc aequali tecum pubesceret aeuo.'
hos ego digrediens lacrimis adfabar obortis:
'uiuite felices, quibus est fortuna peracta
iam sua; nos alia ex aliis in fata uocamur.
uobis parta quies: nullum maris aequor arandum,   495
arua neque Ausoniae semper cedentia retro
quaerenda. effigiem Xanthi Troiamque uidetis
quam uestrae fecere manus, melioribus, opto,
auspiciis, et quae fuerit minus obuia Grais.
si quando Thybrim uicinaque Thybridis arua   500
intraro gentique meae data moenia cernam,
cognatas urbes olim populosque propinquos,
Epiro Hesperiam (quibus idem Dardanus auctor
atque idem casus), unam faciemus utramque
Troiam animis: maneat nostros ea cura nepotes.'   505
   Prouehimur pelago uicina Ceraunia iuxta,
unde iter Italiam cursusque breuissimus undis.
sol ruit interea et montes umbrantur opaci:
sternimur optatae gremio telluris ad undam
sortiti remos passimque in litore sicco   510
corpora curamus; fessos sopor inrigat artus.
necdum orbem medium Nox Horis acta subibat:
haud segnis strato surgit Palinurus et omnis
explorat uentos atque auribus aëra captat;
sidera cuncta notat tacito labentia caelo,   515
Arcturum pluuiasque Hyadas geminosque Triones,
armatumque auro circumspicit Oriona.
postquam cuncta uidet caelo constare sereno,

dat clarum e puppi signum; nos castra mouemus
temptamusque uiam et uelorum pandimus alas.   520
   Iamque rubescebat stellis Aurora fugatis
cum procul obscuros collis humilemque uidemus
Italiam. Italiam primus conclamat Achates,
Italiam laeto socii clamore salutant.
tum pater Anchises magnum cratera corona   525
induit impleuitque mero, diuosque uocauit
stans celsa in puppi:
'di maris et terrae tempestatumque potentes,
ferte uiam uento facilem et spirate secundi.'
crebrescunt optatae aurae portusque patescit   530
iam propior, templumque apparet in arce Mineruae;
uela legunt socii et proras ad litora torquent.
portus ab Euroo fluctu curuatus in arcum,
obiectae salsa spumant aspargine cautes,
ipse latet: gemino demittunt bracchia muro   535
turriti scopuli refugitque ab litore templum.
quattuor hic, primum omen, equos in gramine uidi
tondentis campum late, candore niuali.
et pater Anchises 'bellum, o terra hospita, portas:
bello armantur equi; bellum haec armenta minantur.   540
sed tamen idem olim curru succedere sueti
quadrupedes et frena iugo concordia ferre:
spes et pacis' ait. tum numina sancta precamur
Palladis armisonae, quae prima accepit ouantes,
et capita ante aras Phrygio uelamur amictu,   545
praeceptisque Heleni dederat quae maxima rite
Iunoni Argiuae iussos adolemus honores.
   Haud mora, continuo perfectis ordine uotis
cornua uelatarum obuertimus antemnarum,
Graiugenumque domos suspectaque linquimus arua.   550
hinc sinus Herculei (si uera est fama) Tarenti
cernitur; attollit se diua Lacinia contra
Caulonisque arces et naufragum Scylaceum.
tum procul e fluctu Trinacria cernitur Aetna,
et gemitum ingentem pelagi pulsataque saxa   555
audimus longe fractasque ad litora uoces,
exsultantque uada atque aestu miscentur harenae.
et pater Anchises 'nimirum haec illa Charybdis:

hos Helenus scopulos, haec saxa horrenda canebat.
eripite, o socii, pariterque insurgite remis.'   560
haud minus ac iussi faciunt, primusque tridentem
contorsit laeuas proram Palinurus ad undas;
laeuam cuncta cohors remis uentisque petiuit.
tollimur in caelum curuato gurgite et idem
subducta ad Manis imos desedimus unda.   565
ter scopuli clamorem inter caua saxa dedere;
ter spumam elisam et rorantia uidimus astra.
interea fessos uentus cum sole reliquit
ignarique uiae Cyclopum adlabimur oris.
   Portus ab accessu uentorum immotus et ingens   570
ipse; sed horrificis iuxta tonat Aetna ruinis,
interdumque atram prorumpit ad aethera nubem
turbine fumantem piceo et candente fauilla,
attollitque globos flammarum et sidera lambit;
interdum scopulos auulsaque uiscera montis   575
erigit eructans, liquefactaque saxa sub auras
cum gemitu glomerat fundoque exaestuat imo.
fama est Enceladi semustum fulmine corpus
urgeri mole hac, ingentemque insuper Aetnam
impositam ruptis flammam exspirare caminis,   580
et fessum quotiens mutet latus, intremere omnem
murmure Trinacriam et caelum subtexere fumo.
noctem illam tecti siluis immania monstra
perferimus, nec quae sonitum det causa uidemus.
nam neque erant astrorum ignes nec lucidus aethra   585
siderea polus, obscuro sed nubila caelo,
et lunam in nimbo nox intempesta tenebat.
   Postera iamque dies primo surgebat Eoo
umentemque Aurora polo dimouerat umbram,
cum subito e siluis macie confecta suprema   590
ignoti noua forma uiri miserandaque cultu
procedit supplexque manus ad litora tendit.
respicimus: dira inluuies immissaque barba,
consertum tegimen spinis; at cetera Graius,
et quondam patriis ad Troiam missus in armis.   595
isque ubi Dardanios habitus et Troia uidit
arma procul, paulum aspectu conterritus haesit
continuitque gradum; mox sese ad litora praeceps

cum fletu precibusque tulit: 'per sidera testor,
per superos atque hoc caeli spirabile lumen, 600
tollite me, Teucri. quascumque abducite terras:
hoc sat erit. scio me Danais e classibus unum
et bello Iliacos fateor petiisse penatis.
pro quo, si sceleris tanta est iniuria nostri,
spargite me in fluctus uastoque immergite ponto: 605
si pereo, hominum manibus periisse iuuabit.'
dixerat et genua amplexus genibusque uolutans
haerebat. qui sit fari, quo sanguine cretus,
hortamur, quae deinde agitet fortuna fateri.
ipse pater dextram Anchises haud multa moratus 610
dat iuueni atque animum praesenti pignore firmat.
ille haec deposita tandem formidine fatur:
'sum patria ex Ithaca, comes infelicis Vlixi,
nomine Achaemenides, Troiam genitore Adamasto
paupere (mansissetque utinam fortuna!) profectus. 615
hic me, dum trepidi crudelia limina linquunt,
immemores socii uasto Cyclopis in antro
deseruere. domus sanie dapibusque cruentis,
intus opaca, ingens. ipse arduus, altaque pulsat
sidera: di talem terris auertite pestem! 620
nec uisu facilis nec dictu adfabilis ulli,
uisceribus miserorum et sanguine uescitur atro.
uidi egomet duo de numero cum corpora nostro
prensa manu magna medio resupinus in antro
frangeret ad saxum, sanieque aspersa natarent 625
limina; uidi atro cum membra fluentia tabo
manderet et tepidi tremerent sub dentibus artus,
haud impune quidem, nec talia passus Vlixes
oblitusue sui est Ithacus discrimine tanto.
nam simul expletus dapibus uinoque sepultus 630
ceruicem inflexam posuit iacuitque per antrum
immensus saniem eructans et frusta cruento
per somnum commixta mero, nos magna precati
numina sortitique uices una undique circum
fundimur, et telo lumen terebramus acuto 635
ingens quod torua solum sub fronte latebat,
Argolici clipei aut Phoebeae lampadis instar,
et tandem laeti sociorum ulciscimur umbras.

sed fugite, o miseri, fugite atque ab litore funem
rumpite. 640
nam qualis quantusque cauo Polyphemus in antro
lanigeras claudit pecudes atque ubera pressat,
centum alii curua haec habitant ad litora uulgo
infandi Cyclopes et altis montibus errant.
tertia iam lunae se cornua lumine complent 645
cum uitam in siluis inter deserta ferarum
lustra domosque traho uastosque ab rupe Cyclopas
prospicio sonitumque pedum uocemque tremesco.
uictum infelicem, bacas lapidosaque corna,
dant rami, et uulsis pascunt radicibus herbae. 650
omnia conlustrans hanc primum ad litora classem
conspexi uenientem. huic me, quaecumque fuisset,
addixi: satis est gentem effugisse nefandam.
uos animam hanc potius quocumque absumite leto.'
   Vix ea fatus erat summo cum monte uidemus 655
ipsum inter pecudes uasta se mole mouentem
pastorem Polyphemum et litora nota petentem:
monstrum horrendum, informe, ingens, cui lumen ademptum.
trunca manum pinus regit et uestigia firmat;
lanigerae comitantur oues: ea sola uoluptas 660
solamenque mali.
postquam altos tetigit fluctus et ad aequora uenit,
luminis effossi fluidum lauit inde cruorem
dentibus infrendens gemitu, graditurque per aequor
iam medium, necdum fluctus latera ardua tinxit. 665
nos procul inde fugam trepidi celerare recepto
supplice sic merito tacitique incidere funem,
uertimus et proni certantibus aequora remis.
sensit, et ad sonitum uocis uestigia torsit.
uerum ubi nulla datur dextra adfectare potestas 670
nec potis Ionios fluctus aequare sequendo,
clamorem immensum tollit, quo pontus et omnes
intremuere undae, penitusque exterrita tellus
Italiae curuisque immugiit Aetna cauernis.
at genus e siluis Cyclopum et montibus altis 675
excitum ruit ad portus et litora complent.
cernimus astantis nequiquam lumine toruo,
Aetnaeos fratres caelo capita alta ferentis,

concilium horrendum, quales cum uertice celso
aëriae quercus aut coniferae cyparissi   680
constiterunt, silua alta Iouis lucusue Dianae.
praecipitis metus acer agit quocumque rudentis
excutere et uentis intendere uela secundis.
contra iussa monent Heleni, Scyllamque Charybdinque
inter, utrimque uiam leti discrimine paruo,   685
ni teneam cursus: certum est dare lintea retro.
ecce autem Boreas angusta ab sede Pelori
missus adest; uiuo praeteruehor ostia saxo
Pantagiae Megarosque sinus Thapsumque iacentem.
talia monstrabat relegens errata retrorsus   690
litora Achaemenides, comes infelicis Vlixi.
   Sicanio praetenta sinu iacet insula contra
Plemyrium undosum; nomen dixere priores
Ortygiam. Alpheum fama est huc Elidis amnem
occultas egisse uias subter mare, qui nunc   695
ore, Arethusa, tuo Siculis confunditur undis.
iussi numina magna loci ueneramur, et inde
exsupero praepingue solum stagnantis Helori.
hinc altas cautes proiectaque saxa Pachyni
radimus, et fatis numquam concessa moueri   700
apparet Camerina procul campique Geloi.
[immanisque Gela fluuii cognomine dicta]
arduus inde Acragas ostentat maxima longe
moenia, magnanimum quondam generator equorum;
teque datis linquo uentis, palmosa Selinus,   705
et uada dura lego saxis Lilybeia caecis.
hinc Drepani me portus et inlaetabilis ora
accipit. hic pelagi tot tempestatibus actus
heu, genitorem, omnis curae casusque leuamen,
amitto Anchisen. hic me, pater optime, fessum   710
deseris, heu, tantis nequiquam erepte periclis.
nec uates Helenus, cum multa horrenda moneret,
hos mihi praedixit luctus, non dira Celaeno.
hic labor extremus, longarum haec meta uiarum,
hinc me digressum uestris deus appulit oris.   715
   Sic pater Aeneas intentis omnibus unus
fata renarrabat diuum cursusque docebat.
conticuit tandem factoque hic fine quieuit.

Commentary

1–12 *Departure from the Troad*
All bar the opening two lines of Book 2 are narrated by Aeneas to Dido and the mix of Phoenicians and Trojans present at the feast in her palace. Book 3 continues his narrative, uninterrupted until his closing silence is signalled in the final three verses (716–18). On the narrative of Book 2, see Introduction, pp. 12–13; it ends with the coming of dawn after the terrible night in which Troy has fallen. Aeneas, having encountered only the ghost of his wife Creusa on his return to the city, leaves once more, and finds that a significant number of refugees have gathered, ready to follow him into exile. At last, he says, he yields, and, raising his father on his shoulder, he heads for the hills (*cessi et sublato montis genitore petiui*, 804).

Dido's request at 1.753–5 was that her guest tell 'from the very beginning the trickery of the Greeks, the misfortunes of your people and your own wanderings' (*a prima...origine...insidias...Danaum casusque tuorum erroresque tuos*). Book 3 turns to the final part of the request, but verses 1–5 begin with a summary of the events of Book 2; the opening paragraph then briefly describes what happens before they leave the Troad (5–8), before culminating in yet another departure from Troy (10–12). Odysseus also narrates twice his leaving of Troy, but briefly in adjacent lines (*Od.* 9.38–9), and both times in unemotional participial phrases: '... the careworn return Zeus imposed on me departing from Troy (ἀπὸ Τροίηθεν ἰόντι). The wind bearing me from Ilion (Ἰλιόθεν με φέρων ἄνεμος) took me to the Cicones.'

1–5 Postquam: a traditional opening to an epic book. *Odyssey* 2, 8, 17 begin with Ἧμος ('when', introducing the arrival of dawn in each case), and two books within Odysseus' narrative (11 and 12) with Αὐτὰρ ἐπεί ('but when'; so too *Iliad* 3, 15; similar is 20.1). More significant may be that *Postquam* itself starts what seems to have been the first line of the third book of Ennius' *Annales* (fr. 137 Skutsch) *Postquam lumina sis oculis bonus Ancus reliquit* ('after noble Ancus left the light with his eyes'). Silius too begins his third book with *Postquam*. The word occurs eight times in Book 3, more than any other book of the poem: narrative sequence is an important element here (cf. 192 n.).   **euertere...uisum**

<est> **superis, ceciditque...et...fumat**: A sequence of three verbs describes the fall. *euertere* has been used to mark the responsibility of the gods in Venus' words at 2.602–3 *inclementia diuum | has euertit opes sternitque a culmine Troiam* ('the harshness of the gods overturns this empire and throws Troy down from its height'); as V. uses the verb of felling trees at 11.136, *Geo.* 1.256, 2.208, it also recalls the simile of the uprooted mountain ash with which Aeneas ends his vision of the gods destroying the city (2.626–31). *(oc)casus* is used of the city's fall at 2.432, 507. After the divine decision and the climactic event, *fumat* expresses the ongoing result (as when smoke is still visible at verse 823 of Euripides' *Hecuba*, a play that is the major source for 13–68). **res Asiae Priamique...gentem**: Troy is presented first as the capital of an Asian empire (*OLD res* 16) and then through its royal family, who have played a large part in Aeneas' account in Book 2 (in addition to 453–558, the scenes in the palace, he has told of Hector's ghost at 268–97 and of Cassandra at 403–15). He is just about to leave Asia. **immeritam** is given extra weight by the enjambment*. Aeneas brings out the way that not everything determined by the gods is deserved by mortals; but the epithet may also evoke the ongoing debate about the culpability of the Trojans in the *Iliad* (see, e.g., 13.622–7). **superbum**: 'lofty' (*OLD* 1c): the sense of height contrasts with *humo* (3). The epithet is commonly negative ('arrogant'), but also used more positively ('magnificent'), e.g. in the description of Aeneas' shield, for the doorposts of the temple of Palatine Apollo (8.721). Fowler (2000: 49–50) suggests that both connotations are present here, with the poet, or rather the gods, seeing the pride that comes before the fall: the Greek equivalent ὑπερφίαλος is used of the Trojans by Athena and Poseidon at *Iliad* 21.414 and 459. **Ilium...Troia**: the grandeur of the city is symbolized by the co-existence of two equally famous names, a fact with which poets liked to play through such juxtapositions (2.624–5 *omne...uisum considere in ignis | Ilium et ex imo uerti Neptunia Troia* 'All Ilium seemed to sink into fire and Neptune's Troy to be overturned from its foundation', pointedly echoed here; Hor. *Odes* 1.10.14–15; Prop. 3.1.31–2). **omnis humo fumat**: 'was entirely smoking from the ground'. Each word contributes to the picture of utter destruction: the whole city has been levelled to the ground and reduced to smoke. For the present tense we may compare Venus' vivid appeal at 10.45–6 *per euersae...fumantia Troiae | excidia* ('by the smoking ruins of overturned Troy'), and for the combination of present and past after *postquam*, cf. 192, and *Ecl.* 1.30 *postquam nos Amaryllis habet, Galatea*

reliquit ('once Amaryllis was caring for me and Galatea had left'). The ancient commentator Probus thought that *fumat* was syncopated* from *fumauit*, but this seems far-fetched when the form is easily understood as a present. Aeneas will threaten to burn Latinus' city to the ground at 12.569 *aequa solo fumantia culmina ponam*.   **Neptunia**: Neptune (and Apollo) built Troy's walls, only to be defrauded of payment by the then king Laomedon: hence his comment towards the end of the voyage, 5.810-11 *cuperem cum uertere ab imo | structa meis manibus periurae moenia Troiae*, 'though I wanted to overturn the walls of perjured Troy that had been constructed by my hands'; Venus describes this scene of destruction at 2.610-12.   **diuersa**: they do not 'seek' exile 'in various places' so best taken as 'distant' (12.621; *OLD* 4), though V. may have chosen the epithet to hint at the different outcomes for different groups.   **exilia**: cf. 11. Anchises has refused to countenance exile at 2.638; but at 2.780-2 Creusa's ghost foretells *longa exsilia* and a distant destination described in riddling terms, and by 2.798 it is the purpose of the gathering band (*collectam exilio*).   **desertas...terras**: the theme reappears several times in Book 3, notably at 121-3 where excitement at a Trojan return to Crete is raised by the rumour that Idomeneus has abandoned his kingdom (*deserta...litora, sedes...relictas*). The fact that Latium is far from deserted will prove problematic in the second half of the poem, notably at 7.475-510 where Iulus shoots a stag, which turns out to be a domesticated animal and thus causes the initial conflict. However, the participle has a general validity, in the manner of an oracle: Latium was 'left' by the Trojans' ancestor Dardanus (so Servius; cf. 167). **quaerere...agimur**: 'we are driven to seek'. The same infinitive appears after *agere* also at 7.393, *rudentis excutere* at 682-3: see J. Penney in Adams & Mayer 1999: 254.   **auguriis...diuum**: 'by omens from the gods'. This refers to the instructions and portents Aeneas has received in Book 2 (see Introduction, pp. 12-13): in particular Aeneas recalls his father's words *uestrum hoc augurium* (703), addressed to the *di patrii*. But the present tense also allows for further portents in the period before they actually set sail: 4.345-6 imply contact with oracles in Asia.

5-8 classem: the building of the fleet is treated at greater length in Book 9 (77-122): Cybele (111 n.) is there revealed to have allowed Aeneas to cut down her sacred grove on Ida (she retains his wife Creusa in Asia, 2.788, perhaps as recompense); Turnus' attack on the boats becomes the moment when (as Jupiter had promised) they turn to sea-nymphs.

sub ipsa | Antandro 'under the very walls of Antandros': within the single place-name V. combines realism and mythography. Antandros was a ship-building town, on the coast but close to Ida and its supplies of timber and pitch (Thuc. 4.52.3; Xen. *Hell.* 1.1.25, 2.1.10; *Geo.* 3.450, 4.41); as it stood some 40 miles south-east of Troy it was unlikely to be visited by Greeks returning home. The geographer Pomponius Mela (1.92) reports, as an alternative to derivation from the island of Andros, a story that Ascanius ruled in the area and gave up the town as a ransom when he was captured by the Greeks; the town gained its name from ἀντ' ἀνδρὸς 'in place of the man'. The same derivation is given by Servius, but linked to a ransom for Polydorus, who will be prominent in V.'s next episode. Neither of these fits the narrative of the *Aeneid*, but passing evocation of rejected stories is part of the learned poet's style. **montibus Idae**: the first of seven mountains in the book, culminating in the biggest, Etna, which will dominate the final major episode. **incerti** stands in apposition* to the unexpressed subject of *molimur* and on it depend the two indirect questions ('uncertain where the fates are bearing us, where it is granted that we settle'). It begins the book on a note of suspense, and is nicely at odds with the fixity implied by *fata* (Introduction, pp. 35–8). At 5.2 in his departure from Carthage, a city then lit by flames, he is by contrast *certus iter* ('certain in his route'). **contrahimusque uiros**: the phrase again reprises the end of Book 2: at 796–800, Aeneas is amazed by the number of people who have collected at the temple of Ceres along with the members of his household.

8–9 uix prima inceperat aestas, | et: V. frequently co-ordinates *uix* + pluperfect with *et* (5.857, 6.498) or *que* (2.692; similarly 11.296) or no conjunction at all (3.90, 10.659, 12.650), instead of inverted *cum*. The start of summer is of course the expected time to begin sailing (Hesiod, *Works & Days* 678–82; Ov. *Fast.* 4.131–2; Apul. *Met.* 11.5.5, 11.16.5–17). The book begins with a precise marker of time; such details will recur (notably at 284), but without the precision to match Dido's reference to *septima aestas* at 1.755–6. *prima* initiates the Trojans' travels (523 n.).   **pater Anchises**: the combination is repeated eleven times in the poem: he is *paterfamilias*, head of the household, and thus takes command; but at other times Aeneas leads (Introduction, pp. 41–2).   **iubebat** may be taken as inceptive imperfect ('began to order'): as in the parallel usage at 472 reluctance to leave may be implied.   **dare fatis uela**: the expected dative after *uela dare* is *uentis*

Commentary: lines 1–12

(as at 4.546, 8.707–8). As in the words *quo fata ferant* (7), Aeneas marks his departure as something portentous, dependent on the will of Jupiter and not the whim of the winds.

10–12 cum ... relinquo: editors have this as a continuation of the previous sentence; but the reader does not look for a further temporal clause after *uix ... et* (cf. Williams 1983: 271). On the other hand, this clause, looking back, makes a good setting for the movement of the exile at the start of his long voyage, out onto the open sea, accompanied by his people and the gods: 'When in tears I leave the shores of my homeland and the harbours, and the plains where Troy once was, I am carried onto the deep, an exile, along with my comrades and my son, the gods of the household and the Olympian gods.' **patriae lacrimans**: both words bring out the emotion of the departure, especially for Dido and the Carthaginians, also forced to leave their *patria* (1.357: **P**). Jason weeps as he leaves his homeland at Apollonius, *Arg.* 1.535, and according to Servius (*ad loc.*) Naevius had the wives (*sic*) of Aeneas and Anchises weeping as they left Troy. **campos ubi Troia fuit, feror ... in altum**: as in verse 3 (*humo*) Troy is figured as flat (see Introduction, p. 40), and in choosing *altum* ('the deep' or 'the high <sea>') rather than e.g. *aequor* V. reprises the contrast between what Aeneas leaves and where he heads (n.b. *montis* at 2.804, hinting at Rome as well as the immediate destination of Ida). *fuit* recalls the words of Panthus to Aeneas, announcing the end of Troy (2.325: *fuimus Troes, fuit Ilium*): the perfect tense of *esse* regularly implies 'is no more'. **feror** once more reworks *fata ferant* (7). **cum sociis natoque penatibus et magnis dis**: a line that looks magnificently back and forward, back to Pyrrhus' words when he releases Roman captives in Book 6 of Ennius' *Annales* (fr. 190 Sk.: *dono—ducite—doque uolentibus cum magnis dis*; 'I grant—do take them—and give them with the good grace of the great gods'), and ahead to 8.679 [**R**], where it is Augustus at the battle of Actium who is accompanied by 'the senators and people, the Penates and the great gods': the religious aspect remains the same, but the more intimate 'comrades and son' have grown to the full identity of Rome, *senatus populusque Romanorum* (or *SPQR*, as drain covers in the city still attest). In the Ennian line *cum* means 'with the support of', as it must also at 8.679; but Aeneas has with him his comrades and son, the *penates* too (1.68, 378; 2.293, 717, 747; 3.148), and presumably also the *magni di*: but what does that phrase signify? The balanced phrasing of the line implies that they are to be taken as separate from the Penates, hence perhaps the Olympian deities (Servius lists Jupiter, Juno, Minerva, Mercury), accompanying Aeneas most famously in the form of the fire of Vesta and the Palladium, the image of Pallas Athena. There are complications, however. Varro (cited by Probus on *Ecl.* 6.31) reports three altar bases in the middle of the Circus dedicated to *di magni, di potentes, di <uicuentes>*; these evoke the Θεοὶ Μεγάλοι, who had a famous shrine on Samothrace, an Aegean island north-west of Troy (S. G. Cole, *Theoi Megaloi: The Cult of the Great Gods at Samothrace*, Leiden, 1984). Macrobius (*Sat.* 3.4.9) and Servius (1.378) give Greek equivalents for all three phrases (θεοὺς μεγάλους, θεοὺς δυνατούς, θεοὺς χρηστούς), and report that Cassius Hemina identified these Samothracian gods as the Penates. Moreover, the Penates are themselves described as *magni* at *Aen.* 9.258 (and perhaps 3.160). Varro (*Ling. Lat.* 5.58-9) links the *di magni* with Samothrace, but identifies them as *Caelum et Terra* ('Sky and Earth'). He also notes the common belief (attributed to him by Servius on 3.12) that they are Castor and Pollux, to whom offerings were made there by shipwrecked sailors: this pair would certainly be apt deities for Aeneas to carry with him on his voyage, and the ancient statues in the temple of the Penates on the Velia suggest them in their youth and military garb (Dionysius Hal., *Rom.* 1.68.1-2; Augustus had the temple restored, *R.G.* 19.2; a surviving panel from the Ara Pacis apparently depicts them). Dionysius gives the fullest account, and one that is compatible with Vergil's (1.67-9, 2.66): the holy objects transported to Italy by Aeneas were the images of the Great Gods and the Palladium, previously brought to the Troad by Dardanus, when he migrated from Samothrace (as Latinus will recall at *Aen.* 7.207-8), after founding the temple. V.'s brevity thus opens up a host of meanings; and (as Horsfall points out) the phrase neatly marks the journey from the Troad (11) to Thrace (13-14), past Samothrace itself. For the spondaic* fifth foot and closing monosyllable, see Introduction, pp. 46, 49.

13-68 *Thrace*
Immediately on landing in Thrace, Aeneas sets to work on a new city for the Trojan refugees, the first of five occasions in the *Aeneid* on which he works on new settlements (3.132-4: Pergamea; 4.260: Carthage; 5.755-7: Segesta; 7.157-9: the camp at the mouth of the Tiber); after the action of the poem is finished, he will build another city in Italy, Lavinium. His city-building in Thrace is aborted after a blood-curdling encounter with the speaking body of his buried cousin Polydorus.

Commentary: lines 13-68

In one of a number of evocations of Greek tragedy in the *Aeneid* (see Introduction), Vergil here makes striking use of the prologue of Euripides' revenge play *Hecuba*, in which Polydorus' ghost appears and tells the same story of his murder by the local king Polymestor as Aeneas does here (49-57): **G(a)**. There was a Latin version by Ennius, which survives only in fragments (171-84 Jocelyn); for an English translation see Warmington's Loeb (1.290-9). Similarity and difference characterize the intertextual* play. The Euripidean story of Polydorus and Polymestor, implanted in the Aeneas legend by V., allows Aeneas to appeal to Dido's ready sympathy by exploiting the similar saga of gold-induced impiety, told him by his disguised mother Venus at 1.343-64 (**P**), which Dido has suffered when her husband Sychaeus was murdered at an altar by her brother Pygmalion. (The link here suggests that the underground concealment of the treasure (1.358-9) is borrowed from Eur. *Hec.* 1002.) Through Pygmalion's *furor* for gold and the Thracian king's violation of hospitality, both tales powerfully embody the fundamental theme of impiety.

A key point of difference is that in the play Polydorus is in two places: his body is being washed along the shore (28-9: cf. Ennius, *Hec.* fr. 179 Jocelyn *undantem salum*) while his spirit is hovering above his captive mother's tent (30-2: the actor probably appeared above the stage building). In the *Aeneid* Polydorus is neither on the sea nor in the air: he lies covered in an overgrown mound. (As in the plays V.'s Polydorus has not been duly buried: the word *sepulto* in 41 has bitterly ironical overtones.) Missing from the *Aeneid* episode is the figure of Hecuba, who will be confronted with the corpse (*Hec.* 679-720) and react with utter horror and vengeful violence towards Polymestor (1035-55). In Aeneas' version pious ritual ends the story. He presents Dido with a tale of inhuman abuse of hospitality; she will not abuse hospitality (n.b. 4.600-6), but she will end up seeking vengeance (4.615-29).

Another difference is geographical. Euripides' Polydorus was killed on the Thracian Chersonese north of the Hellespont, the narrow channel (bridged by Xerxes and swum by Leander and Lord Byron) that parts Europe from Asia (see Map 2). It is a liminal location eminently suitable for an exploration of Greek and barbarian behaviour. But since the smoke of Troy is visible from there (*Hec.* 823), it would be too close for a sensible creation of a new Trojan city. Vergil is unspecific about where Aeneas starts building. In line with the legend (Lycophron 1236, Dionysius Hal., *Rom.* 1.49.4, Livy 1.1.4), he comes to Thrace, and calls the city he founds *Aeneadae* (18). There was a city Aenus at the mouth of the river Hebrus: in addition to the similarity of the name (though Servius writes on 17 that it was derived from a companion of Odysseus), Pliny (*Nat.* 4.43) tells us that Polydorus' tumulus was here. Though Aenus is referred to by Homer (*Il.* 4.520) and so would have existed before the arrival of Aeneas, another city called Aeneia is too far to the west to be a likely candidate (but see Erskine 2001: 93–8 and Hornblower on Lycophron 1236).

The ceremony in which the Trojans accord Polydorus proper burial combines Greek and Roman elements (Bailey 1935: 59–60, 290–1). The offerings of milk and blood sacrifices (66–7) look forward to the honours paid to Anchises on the anniversary of his death (5.77–8) and are suggestive of Greek hero cult (Panoussi 2009: 160–4). Though the shortest of the poem's funeral scenes (cf. 5.72–103 (commemoration of Anchises' death), 6.212–35 (Misenus), 11.139–81 (Pallas)), it is substantial enough to serve as a pious correction of the perfunctory reference at Eur. *Hec.* 894–7.

13–14 procul: 'at a distance'; Servius points out that the word can mean either *satis longe* ('rather far') or 'not very far'. Aenus is some 130 miles from Antandros, but subsequently the Trojans have travelled much farther.   **uastis…campis**: ablative of quality (G&L §400) or description ('a country of vast plains'), or ablative of place where ('is inhabited/tilled on its vast plains').   **colitur** means both 'is inhabited' and, in view of the ploughing mentioned in the following line, 'is tilled'; for the fertility of Thrace, cf. *Iliad* 9.71–2, 11.222, 20.485, and esp. Eur. *Hec.* 8–9 (**G(a)**).   **Mauortia**: *Mauors* is a poetic form of Mars, the god of war; Ares, his Greek equivalent, was traditionally of Thracian origin (see Janko on *Iliad* 13.301–3; cf. *Od.* 8.361). In the *Iliad* he is on the side of the Trojans in the Trojan War, even fighting for them in Book 5; but if this fact offers any consolation to Aeneas, he is soon to be disabused: the god rather prefigures the role of spears in the episode.   **Thracēs**: a Greek nominative plural.   **regnata** 'ruled over': V. uses the previously intransitive verb *regno* in the passive (6.770, 793).   **acri…Lycurgo**: dative of the agent. The name evokes impiety and tragedy. Homer (*Il.* 6.130–40) says that for attacking the nurses of Dionysus Lycurgus was first blinded by Zeus and then died. We also know of two lost plays of Aeschylus about Lycurgus (*Edonians*, i.e. maenads, and the satyr-play *Lycurgus*) and a Latin *Lycurgus* by Naevius. These apparently told how he resisted the introduction of the worship of Dionysus into Thrace, and was led by a mad vision of the hated vine to attack his own son: violence against plants/people is a feature of V.'s episode too (S. Casali, 'La vite dietro il mirto: Lycurgus, Polydorus e la violazione delle piante in *Eneide* 3', *SIFC* 4.3 (2005), 233–50).

15-16 hospitium antiquum Troiae sociique penates: 'of old a place friendly to Troy with allied tutelary* gods': *hospitium* (83 n.) has a local meaning here. The Thracians are allies of the Trojans in Homer (*Il.* 2.844–5). Here the Thracian king links himself with Agamemnon when he realizes that the Trojans are finished (53–4). The Penates of Troy are of course travelling with Aeneas (12, 148).   **dum fortuna fuit**: a précis of Eur. *Hec.* 16–18 (**G(a)**). *dum* (= while) with a past tense means 'exactly as long as (and no longer)': the Thracian king is a fair-weather friend; cf. Ennius, fr. 351 (Jocelyn) *amicus certus in re incerta cernitur*, which has been taken by some scholars as a line of the *Hecuba* referring to Polymestor.

16-18 feror huc: after description of the destination, Aeneas moves on to narrate the Trojans' arrival, a pattern that recurs across the book: p. 31.   **moenia prima loco**: *prima* marks the start of the building, but also that these are Aeneas' 'first walls'. Here we have a statement of the city-building theme established at 1.7 *altae moenia Romae*.   **fatis ingressus iniquis**: 'entering <on a venture> to which the fates were ill-disposed'. *Fatis iniquis*, a pointer to what ensues, may be regarded grammatically as an ablative of attendant circumstances.   **Aeneadasque meo nomen de nomine fingo**: *fingo* is regularly used of coining a name: *OLD* 6b. For a discussion of whether the city was Aeneia in Chalcidice or Aenus at the mouth of the Hebrus, see 13–68 n. The interlaced word order helps to convey the identity of Aeneas' name with the one he gives his city. The phrasing recalls Jupiter's prophecy of the foundation of Rome at 1.276–7 *Romulus...condet | moenia Romanosque suo de nomine dicet* ('Romulus shall found a city and call them Romans from his own name'): on the one hand this must not be the place, but on the other Aeneas provides a model for his descendant.

19-21 sacra: the first of many instances within the book where Aeneas brings out his religious commitment.   **Dionaeae matri**: Aeneas' mother, Venus, daughter (by Jupiter) of Dione, child of Oceanus and Tethys: cf. *Iliad* 5.370–1. Elsewhere in Latin Dione is used for Venus herself (Cat. 56.6, Cicero, *de Natura Deorum* 3.59).   **diuis...**

auspicibus coeptorum operum: 'to the gods who are the supporters (*auspex*, *OLD* 3) of work <newly> begun'. According to Servius 'the gods who preside over new undertakings' are Jupiter (cf. 9.625), the god of the citadel, Apollo, the god of prophecy, and Liber (= Bacchus), the god of liberty. **supero...caelicolum regi**: lit. 'to the king above of the heaven-dwellers': an elevated periphrasis for Jupiter, well adapted to the sacrificial context. *caelicolum* uses the shorter ending of the first declension genitive plural; from Ennius on it is the normal poetic form. **nitentem...taurum**: 'a sleek bull', i.e. one gleaming with health. There is an odd notion, deriving from Servius and Macrobius (*Sat.* 3.10.3–4), that the subsequent prodigy occurs because Aeneas had sacrificed an inappropriate victim to Jupiter: see Dyson 2001: 29–35. But bulls are regularly sacrificed to Jupiter elsewhere, e.g. *Geo.* 2.146–7, Ovid, *Met.* 4.756, *Fasti* 1.579, and the pious hero is proceeding with due religious propriety.

22–68 The violation of trees and subsequent punishment is a repeated motif in Hellenistic* poetry: Callimachus, *Hymn* 6.24–115: Erysichthon; Apollonius, *Arg.* 2.469–89: the son of Paraebius; Nicander, fr. 41: Dryope. The first and last of these myths recur in Ovid's *Metamorphoses* (8.739–878: Erysicthon; 9.336–93: Dryope). Erysichthon and the father of Paraebius ignore warnings given to protect the nymph who lives in the tree; Dryope innocently picks lotus flowers to give to her son, not realizing that she is attacking Lotis herself, who has been transformed into the tree in escaping from Priapus. Ovid bases his Dryope narrative on this passage: as well as motifs and diction (e.g. *guttae* of blood 28/9.344; *horror*, 29/9.345; *conuellere*, 31/9.351; *lentus* 31/9.353) he imitates Vergil's structure (personal witness followed by history of the hidden individual), as does Dante in *Inferno*, Canto 13, which has clear allusions* to both episodes (Durling & Martinez 1996, *ad loc.*). Blood and sound also come from a plant at *Argonautica* 3.846–66, when Medea gathers sap from the root of the 'Prometheion', which looks like fresh-cut flesh: as Hunter puts it (1993: 173), 'what brings safety in the *Argonautica* (Medea's potion) is rejected in the *Aeneid*.... from such a vision Aeneas and his men must flee'. But we should also note that the Trojans flee unharmed, protected perhaps by their piety and their sense of due process (58–9) as well as their innocence. R. Thomas, 'Tree violation and ambivalence in Vergil', *TAPhA* 118 (1988), 261–73, points out links with 12.766–87 (**S**), where the Trojans are not punished for cutting down a wild olive sacred to Faunus that might have obstructed their movements in battle. In response to Turnus' prayer to Faunus the stump holds fast Aeneas' spear; but Venus plucks it out. Both passages begin with *forte* (22/12.766); note also e.g. *accessi(t)* 24/12.787; *uellitur* 28/ *reuellit* 12.787; *lentus*, 31/12.773, 781; *conuellere*, 31/12.774; *obluctor* 38/*luctans* 12.781. Unlike Thomas, we would stress the contrasts: though the greater god still protects them, the Trojans are neither pious nor innocent in Book 12.

22–3 forte: Aeneas says that the mound just happened (*forte*) to be close by; but the wood-gathering necessary for the decking of the altars leads into the portent in a way that seems more than mere chance (cf. 6.179–211, where Aeneas is led to the Golden Bough while collecting wood for Misenus' funeral pyre). **tumulus**, as Servius points out, can mean both a natural and a burial mound (*OLD* 1, 2). **quo...summo**: 'on the top of which'. The absence of a verb in this relative clause may add to the impression of a dense and impenetrable bristle of shoots. **cornea...| uirgulta <sunt> et densis hastibilus horrida myrtus**: 'cornel bushes and a myrtle bristling with close-packed shafts'. Both plants were used for making spears: *Geo.* 2.447–8: *myrtus ualidis hastilibus et bona bello | cornus* ('myrtle is good for strong spear-shafts and cornel for war'), *Aen.* 7.817 *pastoralem praefixa cuspide myrtum* ('pastoral myrtle with a spear point fixed on'). The spear metaphor evokes the spiky growth of the myrtle, but the shafts will before long prove to contain their literal meaning. Myrtle is also relevant here as the plant sacred to Venus: cf. 5.72 *uelat materna tempora myrto* (Aeneas 'covers his brow with his mother's myrtle'); Pliny, *Nat.* 12.3, 15.120; and various passages in Ovid where it symbolizes love elegy* (*Amores* 1.1.29, 3.1.34) or is carried by the goddess (*Ars* 3.53, *Fasti* 4.15). For the breathy alliteration here cf. *Aen.* 10.178 (*horrentibus hastis*) and 11.601–2 (*hastis | horret*). Coo (*MD* 59 (2007), 196) notes the proleptic* force of *horrida*: emotional horror quickly follows (26, 29).

24–6 uiridem...siluam: 'verdant undergrowth' (*Geo.* 1.76, 152); but *siluam* is used of the forest of spears in Aeneas' shield at 10.887, a much-imitated image (cf. Lucan 6.205, Stat. *Theb.* 5.533, Silius 4.619). *uiridem* coupled with *frondentibus* in 25 suggests healthy growth, an impression soon to be horrifically subverted. **ab humo**: prepositions of motion are normally (as at 3) not used with *humus*, but V. writes *ab* *humo* also at 5.452, and later writers sometimes follow his lead. **tegerem ut**: the postponement* of subordinating conjunctions such as *ut* from the head of their clause is fairly common (see Introduction, pp. 50–1); it is especially striking when the verb precedes, and V. is not averse to this effect: *Aen.* 11.161, 796, 856, 12.555. **horrendum et dictu uideo mirabile monstrum**: the interlacing of the word order here—*horrendum* agrees with *monstrum* and the ablative supine *dictu* must be taken with *mirabile* ('wondrous to relate': see G&L §436)—is expressive, and adds emphasis to the mind-numbing impression that the portent made on the narrator. There is a leap from the sequence of historic* verbs to the vivid present of *uideo*, and the resonantly nasal* *m*s and *n*s add to the effect. A *monstrum* is an inexplicable phenomenon; it can be favourable (as at *Aen.* 2.680, the flame on Ascanius' head), or neutral (3.307), or horrific, as often in this paradoxographical* book, e.g. when the words *monstrum horrendum* are used again of the Cyclops (658). *dictu* may remind us that Aeneas is recounting these events at Dido's banquet.

27–9 quae prima...huic: as frequently in Latin, both in prose and poetry, when the relative clause launches a sentence, its antecedent (*prima arbos*) is taken into the clause, if necessary adapting its case to its new position. *huic* refers to the tree and might be classed as 'dative of the thing concerned' or 'dative of disadvantage': 'in the case of' or 'from the first tree'. **ruptis radicibus**: 'an admirable rending, ripping alliteration' (Horsfall). **atro liquuntur sanguine guttae**: 'there trickle drops of black blood' (ablative of material). For blood flowing from plants, see 22–68 n., and Ovid, *Met.* 2.360, where Clymene pulls off branches as she tries to stop her daughters, the sisters of Phaethon, turning into poplars. *atro sanguine* (repeated in 33 and 622) nods to Homer's μέλαν αἷμα (*Il.* 4.149); cf. Ennius *fr.* 297 Jocelyn *tabo sanie et sanguine atro* ('pus, gore and black blood'), *Geo.* 3.221, Livy 38.21.9: in all these instances it is used of the dead. **terram tabo maculant**: a grisly echo of the self-castration of Attis in Catullus 63.7 *recente terrae sola sanguine maculans* ('spotting [*or* defiling] the surface of the earth with fresh blood'). More gore will appear in the caves of Polyphemus (618–27) and Cacus (8.197).

29–30 mihi: possessive dative ('my limbs...my blood'). **frigidus... gelidus**: horror and fear are associated with cold in ancient as in modern thought from Homer on (e.g. 'chilling fear' at *Il.* 9.2). Aristotle states that 'coldness accompanies fear' (*Part. An.* 2.650b28); and at 3.290–1 Lucretius follows two lines on the heat of anger in the mind with *est et frigida multa, comes formidinis, aura,* | *quae ciet horrorem membris et concitat artus* ('there is also a great chill wind, companion of fear, which rouses horror in the body and shakes the limbs'). **coit formidine sanguis**: For the congealing of the blood, cf. 259, 10.452, 12.905. The phrase is cited by Isidore of Seville, at *Etymologiae* 10.102, as evidence to back up his claim *timor sanguinem gelat, qui coactus gignit formidinem* ('fear freezes the blood, and when that congeals it produces dread'). Quintilian, the teacher of rhetoric (*c.* AD 35–100), at 8.3.70 cites 69–70 to show how descriptive detail creates vividness: *contingit... claritas etiam ex accidentibus* ('vividness can be obtained also by describing the incidental features of a situation').

31–3 rursus et alterius lentum conuellere uimen: 'again to pull up the tough shoot of a second <tree> too'. The first three words stress the repetition of the action. *et alterius* is replicated at the same position in 33, *et* comes second in all three lines, and *sequitur* (33) follows on from *insequor* (32): the idea of identical consequences is driven home. *lentum* here combines the meanings of 'pliant', 'tough', and 'clinging' (*OLD* 1, 2, 3): the shoot will not break; it has to be pulled out of the mound. **conuellere... insequor et... temptare**: 'I press on to tear up and to investigate' (*OLD tempto*, 2); for the bold use of infinitives cf. 4–5 *quaerere... agimur*. Aeneas understandably needs to find out the causes of the portent. Adler 2003: 282–4 represents him as a sceptical inquirer, eager to find out 'the deeply hidden causes' but disabled by his fearful reaction and retreating into conventional piety. **causas penitus temptare latentis**: a reworking of Lucretius, who at 1.145 promises to enable the reader to 'perceive things deeply hidden' (*res... occultas penitus conuisere*). At *Geo.* 2.490 *felix qui potuit rerum cognoscere causas* ('blessed is the man who can recognize the causes of things') V. has saluted the natural philosopher; but *causae* can be not only scientific explanations, but also the stories that explain origins (e.g. in the *incipit** at Ovid, *Fasti* 1.1, *Tempora cum causis,* 'The times of the year and the stories behind them'); the tale of Polydorus is far from scientific, and at odds with Lucretius' Epicureanism, which stresses the non-existence of ghosts.

34–6 multa mouens animo: modelled, in alliteration as well as sense, on *Odyssey* 1.427 πολλὰ φρεσὶ μερμηρίζων, 'turning over much in his thoughts' (Harrison on *Aen.* 10.890, where the formula* is repeated).

96   *A Commentary on Vergil*, Aeneid 3

Nymphas uenerabar agrestis: there is no doubt some inceptive force in this imperfect ('I began to worship') but the tense also implies that he continues to pray as he acts. The Elder Cato (*Agr.* 139) and Ovid (*Fasti* 4.753–5) suggest prayers designed to escape the offence of cutting sacred trees. The wood-nymphs (Dryads or Hamadryads) could clearly be helpful with this particular situation.   **Gradiuum...patrem**: Mars is appealed to, as the local god (13 n.). The origin of the name *Grādiuus* is uncertain. Despite the *a* (long save at Ovid, *Met.* 6.427), Latin writers regularly connect it with *grădior* ('the marching god'): so Servius here, and Festus 97 *a gradiendo in bella*.   **Geticis**: the Getae lived in northern Thrace.   **qui...praesidet** is a conventional Roman usage to identify tutelary* deities: cf. Cicero, *Verr.* 5.188, Livy 38.51.8 *deos qui Capitolio atque arci praesident*; Hickson 1993: 38–9.   **rite**: 'with due response to prayer' (*OLD* 1b).   **secundarent...leuarent**: 'grant a favourable outcome to what I had seen and lighten the omen'. For *secundare* cf. *secundus* of winds (529 n). The subjunctives are used after the idea of praying present in *uenerabar* (*OLD* 1b). The technical name for the internal rhyme of *secundarent* and *leuarent* is 'leonine': other instances involving verbs come at 344, 5.853, 10.756. The effect here adds a sense of ritual to Aeneas' prayer.

37–8 tertia marks the third, climactic assault upon the shrubs. Effortfulness is conveyed by the words *maiore...nisu*, *adgredior*, *aduersae* and *obluctor*, as well as by the hero's posture, on his knees straining against the sand. The elisions at the caesura in the third and fourth feet of 38 (*genibusqu(e) aduers(ae) obluctor*) add to the effect.   **hastilia** may be poetic plural*, or Aeneas may be pulling at a collection of stalks.

39–40 eloquar an sileam: Servius comments with a fine appreciation: *parenthesis ad miraculum posita, qua magnitudinem monstri ostendit. et bene auditorem attentum uult facere* ('a miraculously well-placed parenthesis through which he conveys the greatness of the portent. And he wants to make his auditor thoroughly attentive.'). As at 26, we are reminded that Aeneas is narrating these events (Williams 1983: 274). Under such circumstances silence is not an option. Again the phrasing evokes Greek tragedy: for the antithesis* speech vs silence Horsfall directs us to Eur. *Ion* 758, *Andr.* 679, *I.T.* 938, *Orest.* 1539–40.   **lacrimabilis**: 'tearful' (*OLD* 2) or 'worthy of tears' (*OLD* 1)? asks Servius. No doubt both. Adjectives ending in

-bilis are usually passive (i.e. 'to be cried over') but for the active sense cf. e.g. *Aen.* 10.481 *penetrabile telum* ('a weapon that can pierce'); and Horace uses *illacrimabilis* as an epithet for Pluto, god of the underworld, 'who cannot cry' (*Odes* 2.14.6), as well as in a passive sense ('unwept') at 4.9.26. The word is a concealed stage direction, letting us know the emotional register in which Aeneas will deliver Polydorus' speech.   **uox reddita**: a voice in answer to Aeneas' attack on the mound.   **fertur ad auris**: a frequent phrase, but here the sound 'is carried to' Aeneas' ears not in normal conversation but from the depths of the mound.

41–3 miserum: supply *me* (and likewise *mihi* with *sepulto*, *me* with *confixum*, 45 n.). Though the epithet is regularly applied to the dead, here it is no cliché: Polydorus, his shade, and his corpse have undergone the utmost misery.   **Aenea**: the normal form of the Greek vocative. The horror of the unknowing assault on the corpse is increased by the expression of familiarity.   **iam parce sepulto, | parce pias scelerare manus**: *parce* is constructed first with a dative ('spare a buried man'), then with an infinitive ('refrain from desecrating'), a mainly poetic usage: cf. Cat. 64.146 *nihil promittere parcunt* ('there is nothing they refrain from promising'), Lucr. 2.680, Hor. *Odes* 3.8.26. Ovid removes the linguistic complexity when he echoes the phrasing *laceras...parce...parce* at *Met.* 2.361–2, as the sisters of Phaethon react to their mother's desperate assault (28 n.): *'parce, precor, mater,' quaecumque est saucia clamat, | 'parce, precor: nostrum laceratur in arbore corpus'* (' "Spare me, mother, I pray," whichever is wounded cries out, "spare me: my body is torn in the form of the tree" ').   **iam** = *tandem*: Aeneas has been making his third assault on the mound; *now at last* he should stop.   **sepulto**: there is a bitter irony here (13–68 n.): Polydorus has not been granted burial; on the contrary he has suffered a hideous perversion of it. The Trojans will rectify this at 62–8: note the echoing *sepulcro* at the end of 67.   **pias...manus**: Aeneas' Polydorus knows his Aeneas, reinforces the image being given to Dido, and exculpates his relative.   **non me tibi Troia**: Polydorus' first use of the first person is negated, but he then shows his closeness to Aeneas with the juxtaposed pronouns. For the unusual rhythm, see Introduction, p. 49.   **non...tibi...externum**: 'not a stranger to you'. Both Polydorus and Aeneas were members of the Trojan royal family and the reference here is to their shared ancestry, as well as their shared nationality.   **tulit**: 'produced me': a pointed reference to birth in the voice of a dead man.   **aut cruor hic de stipite manat**: the *non* that began the sentence is picked up again and taken with *de stipite*: 'nor is it from the trunk of a tree that this blood is welling'. This oddly phrased sentence suggests the confused anguish of the ghost.

44–6 fuge...fuge: the placing of these urgent repeated imperatives leads to a dramatic clash between ictus* and accent*: cf. 639. Polydorus repeats the earlier ghostly instruction to Aeneas, Hector's *fuge* at 2.289, and re-establishes from 1.2 (*fato profugus*) a programme* for a book in which Aeneas will repeatedly hurry away (Introduction, p. 39).   **crudelis...auarum**: Aeneas' narration will soon explain what these mean (49, 55–7). The Trojans are to avoid places marked by cruelty and greed, as well as *monstra*.   **nam Polydorus ego**: supply *sum*, often omitted when subject and complement are present (again at 60, e.g.). At last he speaks directly of himself without a negative, but the fine simplicity of the self-identification is complicated by the elision of *ego* before *hic*, all the more marked over a strong pause in sense. Polydorus then elides himself completely in his final sentence, by leaving *me* to be understood again, with *confixum* (45).   **iaculis... acutis** is an ablative of description or material (cf. *Ecl.* 5.39 *spinis surgit paliurus acutis* 'the thorn with its sharp spikes rises up', *Geo.* 2.362 *nouis adolescit frondibus aetas* 'their youthful life matures with fresh leaves'). The metaphor of the iron crop of weapons is a favourite one of V.'s (Williams cites 7.526, 11.601–2, 12.663–4, *Geo.* 2.142), but here we have no metaphor. Polydorus was pierced and killed by a volley of iron-tipped spears; the myrtle and cornel shafts have taken root in his body and started growing. Around them wind and waves have created a mound.

47–8 ancipiti...formidine: perhaps best translated as a hendiadys* 'uncertainty and fear'   **mentem...pressus**: 'oppressed in my mind': *mentem* is accusative of the part of the body affected (G&L §338; Woodcock §19): it was the mind that was put under pressure, so it remains in the accusative even when the verb is in the passive. *premere* is regularly used of emotional pressure (*OLD* 8a).   **obstipui steteruntque comae et uox faucibus haesit**: this line also occurs at 2.774 when Aeneas sees the ghost of his wife Creusa. A variant beginning *arrectaeque horrore comae* appears at 4.280, when Mercury forcefully reminds him to pursue his mission (and also at 12.868). There is a fine pathos in the fact that the very line that Aeneas twice uses of his own extreme emotion in his speech to Dido will be echoed when the poet tells us that he experienced the same feeling at the moment when he resolved to leave her.   **com(ae) et**: the elision may express the voice sticking in the throat (cf. Austin on 2.774); and the effect may be enhanced by the fact that *et uox* is a spondee* consisting of two monosyllables, an unusual pattern for this foot.   **stetĕrunt**: see Introduction, p. 48.

49–52 Having used Polydorus' voice to address himself, Aeneas narrates in his own words the story told by the Euripidean Polydorus [**G(a)**]; it is as if, like V.'s reader, he had access to the tragedy.   **hunc Polydorum**: the narration starts in a naturalistic way, picking up on the just-mentioned name.   **quondam** 'once upon a time' reinforces the story-telling mode.   **auri...cum pondere magno** = *Hec.* 10: Priam's aim was that if Troy fell, his surviving children should have plenty to live on (11–12).   **infelix Priamus**: the epithet is applied seven times in the poem to the listening Dido. Priam has died as his city burns; Dido's death will be marked by a simile imagining the burning of Carthage (4.670–1).   **mandarat** = *mandauerat* (syncope*); with *furtim* a precise equivalent to Euripides' ὑπεξέπεμψεν (14).   **alendum** 'to be brought up': the gerundive expresses purpose after the verb of sending (G&L 430). Cf. *Hecuba* 20 and Polymestor's account at 1133–4 [**G(c)**].   **Threicio regi**: *Thrēĭcĭus* provides a metrically tractable alternative to *Thrācĭus*. Aeneas manages the narrative without naming Polymestor. He thus implies his unwillingness to distinguish the villain, and avoids the potential confusion of Polydorus and Polymestor. Servius suggests that to use the expression 'Thracian king' emphasizes the cruelty of the area: from here came the kings Diomedes, the owner of horses which fed on human flesh, Lycurgus, the opponent of Bacchus (14 n.), and Tereus, who raped his sister-in-law and cut out her tongue (Ovid, *Met.* 6.424–562).   **Dardaniae**: Troy, named after Dardanus, an ancestor of Priam and Aeneas (94 n.).

53–6 ille marks the change of subject from Priam to Polymestor.   **ut opes fractae**: 'When the might of the Trojans was shattered': supply *sunt* (cf. e.g. 2, 65, 90, 495).   **Teucrum**: genitive plural, alternative to *Teucrorum* (which V. also uses freely). *Teucri* is by far the commonest of V.'s synonyms for the Trojans.   **res Agamemnonias**: 'the interests of Agamemnon' (*OLD res* 13). At *Hec.* 1175–7 Polymestor claims to Agamnenon that his killing of Polydorus was promoting the Greek king's interests (σπεύδων χάριν...τὴν σήν). **uictricia... arma**: the earliest extant instance of the originally feminine *uictrix* applied to a neuter noun (Wackernagel 468). **fas omne abrumpit**: 'he violates all that is right': strong language. Both kinship and hospitality have been violated (Servius). When she sees Polydorus' corpse in Euripides' play (714–20: **G(b)**), Hecuba laments the loss of basic trust between guest and host (cf. 25–6, 790–2, 803–5). **obtruncat** 'hacks to pieces, butchers' also recalls *Hec.* 716–20. The verb literally means 'lops off limbs to leave a body like a trunk' (Oakley on Livy 7.26.5); it appears already in a fragment about Medea cited by Cicero at *D.N.D.* 3.67 (= *TrRF* adesp. 74.3) *puerum interea obtruncat membraque articulatim diuidit* ('in the meantime she butchers the child [Apsyrtus] and divides the limbs joint by joint'). The verb recalls the death of Priam (2.663, 557), and Coo (*MD* 59 (2007), 196–8) suggests that it suits the arboreal theme of the episode. **auro ui**: The first ablative completes the sense of *potitur* ('takes possession of the gold'; cf. *Hec.* 25), the second is an ablative of manner ('by force'). **potĭtur**: V. has the form also at 4.217; both are scanned with a short *i*, as already in Ennius (*Ann.* 71 Skutsch) and in dactylic* poetry after Lucilius; likewise V.'s three instances of another nominally fourth-conjugation form, *orĭtur*. Williams draws attention to 'the staccato effect of the phrases which conclude the narrative about Polymestor, with three main verbs in nine words, and marked mid-line sense pauses'.

56–7 quid non mortalia pectora cogis, | auri sacra fames: Aeneas' wording here is echoed elsewhere in Vergil, most famously in the next book: *improbe Amor, quid non mortalia pectora cogis?* (4.412; 10.501–2 has a similar authorial *sententia**); but here on Aeneas' lips it has a special significance. It will appeal with great immediacy to Dido, whose husband Sychaeus was singled out for murder by her impious brother because of his wealth (1.343, 349 *auri caecus amore*). After the personal narrative of 16–48, Polydorus' story in 49–56 does not involve Aeneas and is told with matter-of-fact abruptness. Now he shows his emotional reaction, before describing his dutiful actions in response. At *Hecuba* 775 Agamemnon expresses similar emotion when he grasps Polymestor's motivation ('O hard-hearted man! Did he lust to take the gold?'). *cogere*, like other verbs that take infinitives (cf. *OLD soleo* 2b), is used with an 'internal accusative', functioning as

Commentary: lines 13–68   101

if it were the object of an unexpressed *facere* (*OLD cogo* 12): 'what do you not drive the hearts of men <to do>?'. **sacra**, 'accursed' (*OLD* 2c) develops from a meaning found already in Rome's archaic law code, the Twelve Tables, cited by Servius on 6.609: *patronus si clienti fraudem fecerit, sacer esto* ('if a patron defrauds a client, let him be accursed [i.e. outlawed]'; Warmington 3.490–1). Statius will use it of the highly polluting Oedipus (*Thebaid* 2.442).

57–9 pauor returns us to the emotions of 47–8 before the narrative resumes. **ossa**: synecdoche* for 'body'; it brings out Aeneas' awareness of his physical state as he recovers from his shock (cf. *OLD* 1e). **delectos populi ad proceres ... refero**: already Aeneas acts like a Roman consul referring a matter to the senate ('the leading men chosen from the people'): see pp. 41–3 for such aetiology*. In defining this proto-senate he uses *populus*, the other official part of the Roman state (*senatus populusque Romanorum*). For *refero* so (*OLD* 7), see e.g. Cicero addressing the senate as consul in his fourth Catilinarian: *sed ego institui referre ad vos, patres conscripti, ... et de facto quid iudicetis et de poena quid censeatis* (*Cat.* 4.6: 'I have decided to refer to you, senators, ... the questions of what you think about the deed and what you judge about the punishment'). **monstra deum** 'portents sent by [*lit.* of] the gods': reports of supernatural phenomena were a regular part of senatorial business, and the histories of Livy and Tacitus are full of lists of prodigies (D. S. Levene, *Religion in Livy* (Leiden, 1993), 38–77; Feeney in Rüpke 2011: 140–1). The alternative genitive plural (which we can trace back to Naevius) is also found at 215, 375, 476 in Book 3; likewise *diuum* at 5, 114, 148, 359, 370, 717. **primum ... parentem** 'my father first of all': as the senior figure in the party Anchises is consulted first, just like the *princeps senatus* (*OLD princeps* 4a; normally the senior consular) in the senate. The heavy alliteration of *ps* in 57–8 may suggest the purposeful energy in the now *pauor*-free Aeneas. **quae sit sententia**: again the standard language of senatorial business: cf. e.g. Cic. *Cat.* 1.9 *sententiam rogo*, and *OLD rogo* 4.

60–1 omnibus idem animus (supply *est*, 45 n.): lit. 'all had the same mind' (but compare the English idiom 'all were of the same mind') leading on to the infinitives *excedere, linqui, dare* in apposition*. **scelerata ... terra**: 'from the land of crime'. **linqui** 'to be left': in such lists of infinitives V. sometimes varies between active and passive, e.g. at 7.468–9 *iubet arma parari, | tutari Italiam, detrudere finibus* *hostem* ('he orders arms to be prepared, to protect Italy, to drive the enemy from its bounds'); 11.83–4; and perhaps *Ecl.* 6.85–6 *cogere...ouis stabulis numerumque referri | iussit... Vesper* ('Evening gave orders to collect sheep in folds and the number to be counted'; but part of the manuscript tradition reads *referre*). Here he could easily have written *linquere* (found in some late MSS) and thus avoided, as he generally prefers, a spondaic* word at the start of the line; but the emphatic and impersonal usage gives an appropriate stress to the concept of leaving.   **pollutum hospitium**: '(the site of) polluted guest-friendship' (see 15, and *OLD* 3 for *hospitium* used of a place). *pollutum* stresses the religious dimension of the violation of hospitality. See also 83.   **dare classibus Austros**: as Williams well remarks (following the ancient commentator Donatus), 'this inversion of the more obvious phrasing, as in *uentis uela dare* [cf. 9 n.], personifies the fleet as impatient to leave, waiting to be given its winds.' He compares 4.417 *uocat iam carbasus auras* ('the canvas sail now summons the breezes'). *Austros*, literally 'South Winds', stands by synecdoche* for the winds generally: South Winds would in fact not be helpful to them as they sail south from the north coast of the Aegean.   **classibus**: like other collective nouns, such as *populus* (e.g. at Ovid, *Her.* 12.45, *Met.* 6.179) and *examen* (*Ecl.* 7.13), *classis* is sometimes used in the plural without true plural sense: so again at 157, 7.436.

62–5 instauramus: 'we begin again': *OLD* 1 gives the meaning 'start afresh (a ceremony which has been wrongly performed or interrupted)'. Though the burial process that Polydorus has undergone as Polymestor's victim is an horrific perversion, and the accumulation of the mound has happened by chance, he lies beneath the ground (*sepulto* 41) and it is on the original site that the Trojans heap up the new one.   **Polydoro**: 'for Polydorus', dative of advantage.   **ingens**: a favourite word of Vergil: Henry (n. at 118) calls it 'our author's maid of all work'. Here, as elsewhere (see O'Hara 1996 on *Geo.* 2.131), it may play on the etymological senses 'native' or 'natural'.   **tumulo**: local ablative, 'over the mound', or perhaps a purposive dative 'for [i.e. to produce] a mound'.   **stant**: the present matches the rest of the verbs in 62–8, but may also hint at the continuing presence of the altars, like the mound and the cypress trees.   **Manibus**: 'the departed spirit' of Polydorus: for the setting up of altars for the dead cf. 304–5 (Hector) and 5.99–101 (Anchises).   **caeruleis...uittis**: either an associative ablative 'with dark bands' or instrumental with *maestae*

'<made to appear mournful> by dark bands'. *caeruleus* covers a range of colour from the blue of the sky and the sea to the glossy greenish-blue of snakes. In this funereal context it means 'dark-coloured' (*OLD* 1, 2, 4, 9); thus Servius writes that the ancients understood *caeruleum* as *nigrum*.   **atraque cupresso**: with its dark foliage, the cypress is the tree of death: cf. 6.216–17 (Misenus' funeral) and Watson on Horace, *Epodes* 5.18.   **et circum Iliades crinem de more solutae** 'around them are the women of Troy, their hair flowing free after the custom': an expanded version appears at 11.34–5 (the funeral of Pallas), where *sunt* is to be supplied, as here. The combination of *Iliades* ('women of Troy') and lamentation shows that we are still in the world of Greek tragedy, specifically Euripides' two great plays of lament, *Hecuba* and *The Trojan Women*; cf. also *Iliad* 24.699–776. *crinem* is an accusative of the part of the body affected (47 n.).

66–8 inferimus: 'we offer': the word is a technical term: cf. *inferiae* ('offerings to the dead'), which could include wine, honey, perfume, and flowers, as well as the milk and sacrificial blood offered here: cf. e.g. 5.77–9, Prop. 4.7.32–4, Aesch. *Pers.* 611, Soph. *El.* 894–6. **sanguinis et sacri pateras** 'and dishes of the blood of sacrificial victims': for the use of *sacer* in this sense, cf. 5.78, 333, *Geo.* 4.542. **sepulcro | condimus**: cf. 6.152 *conde sepulcro*.   **magna supremum uoce ciemus**: this was a regular procedure at Roman funerals: cf. 6.506 *magna Manis ter uoce uocaui* (Aeneas to Deiphobus: 'with a loud cry I called three times on your Manes'), Propertius 1.17.23 *illa meum extremo clamasset puluere nomen* ('she would have called my name over the final dust and ashes').

69–120 *Delos*
When the weather is calm, the Trojans set sail again, southward across the Aegean Sea (Map 2), to Delos, birthplace of Apollo, where they do not try to settle, but receive a prophecy (94–8), which Anchises interprets as an instruction to sail on to Crete, the island that marks the southern edge of the Aegean. Though a small island, Delos was from the eighth century a major sanctuary and from the third to the first a key trading port (and slave market). Vergil exploits the presence of Apollo, and the rich literary tradition about the island. After the Polydorus episode, based on a Euripidean tragedy, V. turns to the third-century Alexandrian* poet Callimachus as his model, exploiting in turn the Hymns to Delos (4: **L**), Apollo (2: **J**) and Zeus (1: **I**): see

on 73–7, 90–2, and 103–17, and Introduction, pp. 25–6 for some background.

69–72 ubi prima: 'as soon as', a frequent combination in a variety of genres, especially narrative and didactic*. It here marks a new beginning.   **fides pelago**: a surprising phrase: confidence in the sea is not normally expressed by sailors: contrast Palinurus' words at 5.850–1 *fallacibus auris | et caeli totiens deceptus fraude sereni* ('so often deceived by deceptive winds and the delusion of a clear sky'), and *si qua fides uentis, Zephyro date carbasa nautae* ('if you have any confidence in the winds, set your canvas for the West Wind, sailors') at Ovid, *Fasti* 6.715. By choosing *fides* rather than the expected *quies* (cf. *inde ubi prima quies*, of night, at 8.407), V. evokes the thoughts of the crew, as more explicitly of Palinurus at 513–19.   **pelago... uenti... maria... Auster... altum**: the alternation of sea and wind represents effectively the combination that dominates the sailor's life.   **placata... uenti dant maria**: 'the winds provide calmed seas', a predicative* use of the participle.   **lenis crepitans... Auster**: the wind is smooth, but blowing enough to make rigging creak or waves sound, and thus to carry ships along at a good pace. *Auster* is again generic here (61 n.): Ovid corrects with the phrase *utilibus uentis* at *Met.* 13.630 (**T(a)**). It is not habitually a gentle wind (as *Zephyrus* is: 120); having crossed the Mediterranean, it regularly brings rain (e.g. *Geo.* 1.462 *umidus* ('dank'), 3.278 *unde nigerrimus Auster | nascitur et pluuio contristat frigore caelum* ('whence the very black South Wind originates and makes the sky gloomy with rain and cold'); Ovid, *Met.* 13.725 *imbrifer* [**T(c)**]) and can be alarming or destructive (*Aen.* 2.111 *terruit*, 6.336 *obruit*). The epithets thus matter, as in the Elder Cato's *inde omnem classem uentus auster lenis fert* (*Orat.* fr. 29: 'from there the wind, a gentle southerly, carries the whole fleet'), and in the very similar passage at 5.763–4 *placidi strauerunt aequora uenti | creber et aspirans rursus uocat Auster in altum* ('the calm winds settled the sea and a frequent blowing South Wind summons them to the deep'). That passage also has adjective and participle baldly placed with a single substantive*; for this rare combination, see e.g. *Geo.* 3.28–9 *magnum... fluentem | Nilum* ('big-flowing Nile'); 1.163 *tarda... uoluentia plaustra* ('slow rolling wagons').   **uocat**: 'summons', i.e. attracts (*OLD* 2b): cf. 8.711–13 *Nilum |... uocantem | caeruleum in gremium latebrosaque flumina uictos*; 2.338.   **deducunt socii naues**: ancient boats were typically brought up on to a beach when

Commentary: lines 69–120

not sailing; here they are hauled down again, and the Trojans throng the shore, preparing to depart. **terraeque urbesque recedunt**: Latin poets love to evoke the phenomenon by which to the individual on a smooth-sailing boat it is the land that seems to move: so Lucretius at 4.387–9 describes the way the mind is deceived by perception, *qua uehimur naui, fertur, cum stare uidetur...et fugere ad puppim colles campique uidentur* ('the ship on which we are travelling moves when it seems to stand,...and hills and plains seem to fly astern'). This leads on pointedly to Delos, the island that once (according to myth) literally floated across the Aegean.

73–7 sacra: Delos is not indicated by name (until *Ortygiae*, 124, at the moment of departure), but it is the most prominent sacred island of the Aegean (described as 'holy' in the first words of Callimachus' *Hymn to Delos*, 4.1 τὴν ἱερήν), and the reference to Apollo in 75–6 confirms the identity. *mari medio* may call to mind the way that the island is in the middle of the Cyclades ('the encircling islands': 127 n.). **colitur**: 'is inhabited', as in 13, but here (like *coli*, 77) also 'is venerated' (*OLD* 6; cf. *ueneramur*, 79): in his insightful essay, from which we draw much, Barchiesi observes (1994: 439 n. 4) that this points to the Callimachean hymn, as well as the predictions of the Homeric Hymn to Apollo (e.g. 88). **gratissima...Nereïdum matri et Neptuno Aegaeo**: a tease before the confirmation that this is Apollo's island, but echoing Pindar's phrasing at fr. 33c.2 [E]. The Nereids are sea nymphs, daughters of Nereus and Doris, whose name is used as a metonym* for the sea at *Ecl.* 10.5: any island may be of delight to marine deities. According to Strabo (8.6.14), Poseidon (the Greek equivalent of Neptune, and Olympian god of the sea) exchanged Delos for another island, while the mythographer Hyginus (*Fab.* 140) has him taking Latona to Delos when she is about to give birth to Apollo and Diana; more significant for V. may be that Poseidon's prophetic words from the *Iliad* will be heard reworked by Apollo in 97–8. Moreover he combines allusion* to two parts of Callimachus' *Hymn* 4: 17 on the senior pair of sea gods, Oceanus and Tethys, as visited by islands, and 268–70, the prophecy that Delos will be more beloved than any other land to any god, including the Isthmus of Corinth to Poseidon [**L(d)**]. The line (repeated in full at verse 474 by the Vergilian imitator who wrote the short epic *Ciris*) is one of those V. uses to create a striking recall of Greek diction and metre, with two Greek names (*Nereidum*, *Aegaeo*), and two instances of hiatus* (*mātrī ēt, Nēptūnō*

Āegāeō: cf. *Ecl.* 7.53); it is not only a *spondeiazon*, but every foot bar the first is spondaic* (every foot bar the second at 7.634). For similar combinations of Greek names and metrical anomalies, cf. *Ecl.* 2.24 *Amphion Dircaeus in Actaeō Ărăcȳnthō*; *Geo.* 1.221 *ante tib(i) Eoāe Ātlāntĭdĕs ābscōndāntŭr*; 1.437 *Glāūcō* [*Glaucoque* Wagner] *ēt Pănŏpeāe ĕt Īnōō Mĕlĭcērtāe*; *Aen.* 1.617 *tune ille Aeneas quem Dārdănĭō Ānchīsāe*.   **pius**: here means 'showing due respect to his birthplace and his mother', and implies that Aeneas too should respect the oracular instruction to seek out his motherland (96): the nineteen other instances of the form *pius* refer to Aeneas (including two where he applies it to himself: 1.378, 10.826). The equation between Aeneas and Apollo will be strengthened in the simile describing the hero's youthfully divine beauty at 4.141–50: there Apollo is imagined visiting 'maternal Delos' for a festival; on this visit sacrifice is delayed until the very end (118–20).   **arquitenens**: the compound ('bowholder', equivalent of the Greek τοξοφόρος, used of Apollo at *Hom. Hymn* 3.13) is first used of Apollo (and his sister Diana) by Naevius in his epic *Bellum Punicum*, cited by Macrobius (*Sat.* 6.5.8). Apollo will repeatedly appear in the narrative as far as 479, mainly as the oracular god; but his bow may remind us not only of his filial piety in using it to protect his mother (Miller 2009: 104) but also of *Iliad* 1, where he supports his priest Chryses, dishonoured by Agamemnon, and attacks the Greek army with plague arrows. Chryses significantly addresses Apollo as 'god of the silver bow' (*Il.* 1.37); the similar title here anticipates the plague that strikes the Trojans on Crete.   **oras et litora circum**: 'round coasts and shores', anastrophe*: poets often find it convenient to place disyllabic prepositions after their nouns; V. has fourteen other instances with *circum*, and uses the licence also with *contra, inter* (685), *iuxta* (506), *penes, propter, supra*, and *subter*, e.g. in the similar 12.532 *lora et iuga subter*.   **errantem**: Delos, first wandering, then settled, evokes the Trojans themselves (*errantes*, 101: see Miller 2009: 105 for further such points). In the Homeric Hymn to Apollo the island is not floating, but fears being sunk through Apollo's disdain (3.70–8); V.'s account here is based on Pindar, *Hymns* fr. 33 [**E**], and Callimachus, *Hymn* 4.35–54, 191–5 [**L**].   **Mycono e celsa Gyaroque**: the adjective may be taken ἀπὸ κοινοῦ* (i.e. 'in common' with each noun), but neither Myconos, a slightly larger island immediately east of Delos, nor Gyarus is especially 'high' (Myconos rises to 341 metres, Gyaros to 489), a point on which Ovid corrects Vergil by applying the epithet *humilis* to Myconos at *Met.* 7.463. Gyaros lies west-north-west, much further away, beyond both

Rheneia and Syros (west) and Tenos (north); it is barren and essentially uninhabited, but was treated as a grim place of exile under the emperors. Though Cicero (*Att.* 5.12) talks of landing there on his way to Delos in 51 BC, Vergil may have chosen the names for their obscurity, to contrast with Delos, in Greek literally 'visible', even when not named. *celsa* perhaps figures the two neighbouring islands as pillars to which Delos is attached (cf. Pindar, fr. 33d.5–9: E).   **immotam**: 'stationary', in contrast to *errantem*, but also 'unaffected by earthquakes', a tradition mentioned by several authors (Pindar, fr. 33c.4: E; Call. *H.* 4.306 ἀσφαλὲς οὖδας, 'firm ground'), usually when they are describing just such an event (Herodotus 6.98.3, Thucydides 2.8.3; cf. 90–2). Statius evokes this (and with *times* inverts *contemnere uentos*) in the closing lines of a simile describing a storm created by Neptune in the Aegean (*Theb.* 3.437–9: 'the Cyclades resist uncertainly, their roots quaking; even you, Delos, fear to be torn from your Myconos and Gyaros, and you call on the promise of your great nursling [Apollo]'):

> dubiae motis radicibus obstant
> Cyclades; ipsa tua Mycono Gyaroque reuelli,
> Dele, times magnique fidem testaris alumni.

78–9 huc: marks the return to narrative at the end of the short digression. As often, the preceding ecphrasis* covers the time of the journey: cf. 13–16, 210–19, 1.159–70. The varied anaphora* *huc... haec* creates a hymnic effect appropriate to Delos, backed up by the continued praise of the island (*tuto placidissima portu*: the phrase implies the relief of a safe landing).   **fessos**: the first of eight instances of the adjective in this book (85, 145, 276, 511, 568, 581, 710). All bar that at 581 (of the giant Enceladus) are applied to the Trojans, their circumstances, or Aeneas himself, wearied by sea travel, or their tribulations in general (145, 710).   **accipit**: 'receives as a visitor', *OLD* 12b; so, of places, also at 96, 708 (plus *excipiunt* at 210); and, of a deity, at 544.

80–3 Anius: son of Apollo, and revered as the founder of Delos. He, or rather his daughters, who had the power to turn what they touched into wheat, wine, and olive oil, play a part in the Trojan cycle, either helping the hungry Greek army (*Cypria* fr. 26 West; Lycophron 570–83) or refusing to do so (Ovid, *Met.* 13.652–74, where they escape by turning into doves). Aeneas passes over this fantastic story.   **rex idem hominum Phoebique sacerdos**: the phrasing calls to mind both Jupiter (*diuum pater atque hominum rex*, 2.648) and Augustus, who ruled the empire (though the poets do not apply the term *rex* and its cognates directly to him before the later works of Ovid), dedicated the temple on the Palatine, and as *quindecimuir* functioned as a priest of Apollo (Miller 2009: 242). Anius is not only described as *sacerdos*; he is dressed as a priest of Apollo too, as the *uittae* ('headband') and laurel of 81 show. The sanctity of Delos continues to be revealed.   **sacra redimitus tempora lauro**: like other verbs that describe what a person does to their own body, *redimire* can be used in the passive (especially in the participle) with a 'retained' accusative, equivalent to that accompanying the active voice ('I encircle *x* with': *OLD* 1). Laurel is the plant sacred to Apollo, and thus worn by his worshippers: for an aetiology*, see Ovid, *Met.* 1.452–567, who ends his account of Apollo's thwarted rape of the nymph Daphne with the god's prophecy of how the transformed maiden will stand outside the door of Augustus.   **ueterem Anchisen agnouit amicum**: the friendship is not explained, but at 117 Anchises shows knowledge of the southern Aegean, and his earlier travels have made him a friend of the Arcadian Evander too (8.155–68). *Anchisen* is the Greek accusative, the form always used in Latin dactylic* verse (Housman, *CP* 2.823–5).   **iungimus...dextras**: a simple but significant gesture of affection in the *Aeneid* (Wills 1996: 204–5). **hospitio**: 'in guest-friendship': both Anius as host and the Trojans as guests are *hospites*. Contrast *hospitium* of Thrace at 15: there proper behaviour is overturned (55); on Delos it is maintained. Hospitality is a major theme of the enclosing Dido episode and there is considerable irony in the fact that in the queen's view Aeneas will violate it. Ovid remarks that 'he has the reputation of piety, yet as a guest he provided both a sword and the cause of your death, Dido' (*Ars* 3.39–40). For a finely calibrated response to Aeneas' possible abuse of hospitality, see R. K. Gibson, 'Aeneas as *hospes* in Vergil, *Aeneid* 1 and 4', *CQ* 49 (1999), 184–202.

84–120 Those intending to found new cities regularly consulted the oracle at Delphi (so e.g. the people of Thera are advised by Delphi to send a colony out under Battus to Cyrene in Libya at Herodotus 4.151–7; Cadmus before founding Thebes at Ovid, *Met.* 3.8–13; Parke & Wormell 1956: 1.49–81, Fontenrose 1978: 120–3, 137–44), and Latin narratives report many other consultations (94–6 n.). Delos is not normally an oracular shrine (though the island hopes for this status in bargaining with Leto at *Hom. Hymn* 3.81: see Richardson (Cambridge, 2010) *ad loc.*, Miller 2009: 107–8), but V. uses the presence of Apollo

Commentary: lines 69–120 109

on one of the islands traditionally visited by Aeneas (Dionysius Hal., *Rom.* 1.50.1) to introduce the oracular theme (which will be continued in the episodes on Crete and the Strophades, with Helenus, at Cumae in Book 6, and through Latinus' incubation at 7.81–106).

84 Aeneas, having entered the palace of Anius in 83, is suddenly addressing the god in his temple. There is apparently a gap between the paragraphs, which Ovid's narrative (*Met.* 13.638–77: cf. **T**) pointedly fills with dinner, conversation, and a night's sleep. Macrobius (*Sat.* 3.6.1–4) thinks V. evokes an altar of Apollo Genetor (mentioned by the scholar Cloatius Verus), where the god was worshipped with prayer, but no sacrifice. **templa dei saxo...structa uetusto**: The poem celebrates temples both old (2.713) and new (1.446-51, implicitly 8.720); but Macrobius (*Sat.* 3.6.6–8) argues that the description rather brings out the 'long-lasting stability of the rock, i.e. the island' (cf. 77). *templa* is poetic plural*, as is shown by the singular *dei* and the following event: see Williams on 307, and 5.98.

85–9 da: like the Greek equivalent δός, a common opening of prayers (Harrison on 10.421), but in this address to the prophetic god, asking for information (88), best taken as 'reveal' (*OLD* 28), rather than as 'grant' (*OLD* 3), the sense that it clearly has in *da augurium* (89), the culminating request for a sign. **propriam...domum**: 'a home of our own', as the similar phrasing at 167 confirms: *hae nobis propriae sedes*. But *proprius* also carries the connotation 'in perpetuity' (*OLD* 1), and this leads on well to *mansuram urbem*. **Thymbraee**: Aeneas characterizes Apollo as a fellow Trojan, the god with a temple at Thymbra, close to Troy. On such *captationes beneuolentiae** (attempts to gain favour) in the *Aeneid*, see S. J. Harrison, *CQ* 34 (1984), 488. **moenia...et genus et mansuram urbem**: *moenia* often stands for a city by synecdoche* (17, 100, 1.7, e.g.), but here Aeneas seems to think of the walls, then the inhabitants, before combining them in *urbem*. *mansuram* ('destined to last', 'enduring') may be read with all three nouns (ἀπὸ κοινοῦ*). **serua altera Troiae | Pergama, rēliquias Danaum atque immitis Achilli**: in providing guidance on their goal, Apollo will preserve the remnants of the Trojan people left after the destruction wrought by Achilles and the other Greeks (for the genitive after *reliquiae*, see *OLD* 1c): the whole phrase *reliquias...Achilli* is in apposition* to *Troas* at 1.30, and *reliquias Danaum* to *nos* when Aeneas thanks Dido for her compassion at 1.598. It is thus clear that *altera Troiae Pergama* does not refer to the new city ('a second Troy'), but metaphorically to the city's other 'citadel'—its surviving people (as *Pergama* again at 8.37): the sentiment that men, not walls, make a city can be traced back to Alcaeus fr. 112.10, Sophocles, *O.T.* 56–7, and the words of Nicias at Thucydides 7.77.7. If we can trust the capital manuscripts, V. prefers the second-declension genitive *Achilli* on four occasions; once (12.352) they have the third-declension form *Achillis*; and at 2.476 and 1.30 (where R produces the easy assimilation *immitis Achillis*) they are divided. V. always uses *Vlixi* (273 n.).   **quem sequimur?** 'who is it that we are following?', but perhaps with the implication 'whom are we to follow?'; for indicative in deliberative* questions, cf. 367, Fordyce on 7.359, Tarrant on 12.637 *quid ago?* Deliberative questions are classically answered by jussives*, and Apollo's response does include the command *exquirite matrem* (as if answering 'whom are we to follow'); but he also provides information: it is Aeneas' house that will dominate (97), not another's. Here then is a divine resolution of the question 'who is in charge?' that is provoked by the events of Book 2 and the underlying contradiction between *Anchises...iubebat* (9: see n.) and *Aeneadas* (18). It is with some irony then that Anchises takes the lead in responding to the oracle (102–20)—and reads it mistakenly.   **pater**: an honorific title for any god, not common for Apollo in comparison with Jupiter, Bacchus, and Mars, but used for him also at 11.789. The phrasing echoes Anchises' appeal to Jupiter at 2.691, *da deinde auxilium, pater*, and perhaps evokes Apollo Γενέτωρ ('the father'): 84 n.

90–2 uix ea fatus eram: as ancient texts had no equivalent to inverted commas, the end of speech is often marked (90, 118, 344), and in a way that can seem excessive in a modern, punctuated text (189, 258, 312, 463, 607); but in this instance the addition of *uix* makes the sentence look ahead: see 8–9 n., 655. Though freer than some other poets in using parts of *is*, in the plural V. has only *ea* (27 times, including 3.100, 655) and *eos* (twice).   **tremere omnia uisa** <*sunt*> **repente**: the shaking immediately succeeds the speech in the text as in the narrative. The address to Phoebus provokes an epiphany*, expressed through a reworking of the opening lines of Callimachus' Hymn to Apollo (J; see Heyworth 1993 for more details): there too the whole shrine shakes (2), and the laurel (1), as a sign of the god's imminent arrival. *repente* reproduces ἐξαπίνης ('suddenly', 5). *uisa* allows the earthquake to be read as an illusion, if we wish. It also marks the allusion* (an 'Alexandrian footnote'*): readers have already 'seen' this scene. The dactylic* rhythm helps convey the pace of the action. **liminaquē laurusquĕ dei**: an imitation of the frequent Homeric treatment of the equivalent Greek enclitic* τε...τε. In all bar two cases V. has the lengthening before words beginning with two consonants (e.g. 4.146 *Cretesquē Dryopesquĕ*); the two exceptions (here and at 12.363 *Chloreaquē Sybarimquĕ*) recall another aspect of Homeric practice, which occasionally lengthens short syllables before λ (= *l*) and σ (= *s*): see West 1982: 15–16, 38 (and for stylistic discussion of V.'s imitations, Wills 1996: 376–7, 380). Lucan inverts the phrasing to signal a false prophecy at 5.154–5 *nulloque horrore comarum | excussae laurus immotaque limina templi* ('the laurels were shaken by no trembling of the foliage and the doorway of the temple was unmoved'). **laurus...mons circum...cortina**: the laurel is more often associated with Delphi (Hom. *Hymn* 3.396; Callimachus, *Iambi* fr. 194.26–36) than Delos, where it was the palm and the olive-tree that were famous, as the trunks grasped by Leto in labour (Hom. *Hymn* 3.117, Theognis 5–6, Callimachus, *Hymn* 4.210, 262; but Euripides includes a laurel: *I.T.* 1100, *Hecuba* 459, *Ion* 919). The sense that we have suddenly been transported to another Apolline site is then strengthened by *mons*; this must be the 112 metres high Mount Cynthus on Delos; but that merely slopes up from the sacred area, whereas Delphi is surrounded by the spurs of Parnassus. And the *cortina*, a cauldron attached to a tripod, is a conventional part of the equipment of the Pythia, the priestess at Delphi (Parke & Wormell 1956: 1.24–6; Bonnechere in Ogden 2010: 155; Euripides, *I.T.* 976, *Orestes* 329; Lucretius 1.739 [cited on 360]; Ovid, *Met.* 15.635; *OLD* s.v. *cortina* 1b). She or Apollo is represented sitting on it (Berlin Antikenmuseen F 2538 = Beazley 217214, reproduced by Fontenrose 1978: 205; Euripides, *I.T.* 1253, *Orestes* 956); here it amplifies the noise the Trojans hear (the onomatopoeic* *mūgire*); but one may suspect that at some periods it was used to produce hallucinatory fumes as part of the ritual of consultation. **adytis...reclūsis**: the sanctuary within the temple opens up to reveal the god. Callimachus, *Hymn* 2.6–7 instructs the doors to open automatically (the attendants would take care not to be seen on such an occasion); Vergil shows the result.

93 summissi petimus terram: the participle shows that the Trojans are forced down to the ground in terrified supplication (Lucr. 1.92 *muta metu terram genibus summissa petebat*, 'dumb with fear Iphianassa sank to her knees, seeking the ground'). But *petimus terram* also reprises Aeneas' request; and Apollo will offer not only a land (*tellus*, 95), but the earth itself (97–8).   **uox fertur ad auris**: *haec Phoebus* in 99 confirms that it is Apollo who speaks, but the mechanics of the revelation are left obscure: cf. 9.112–17, Ovid, *Met.* 3.96–7; contrast the vivid account of the Sibyl's possession at 6.77–101.

94–6 Dardanidae duri: the pronouncement begins with a significant word, and an example of alliteration, which will recur. In addressing the Trojans as descendants of Dardanus, Apollo gives them a clue about the origin they are to seek (167; so Macrobius, *Som.* 1.7.7–8); Anchises will think of them rather as *Teucri* (108). *duri* points to the need for endurance and the hardiness of the male band who will finally reach Latium: see McGushin, *AJPh* 85 (1964), 225–53.   **quae uos a stirpe parentum | prima tulit tellus, eadem uos ubere laeto | accipiet… matrem**: after the masculine *duri* and the paternal 'from the stock of your forefathers' the promised land is repeatedly figured as a mother, giving birth (*tulit*) and welcoming with a breast (*ubere*: *OLD* 1, 2): Keith 2000: 46–8. When Aeneas travels up the Tiber in Book 8, he finds a huge white sow, as the river-god promises in a dream, with thirty young around her udders (*albi circum ubera nati*, 8.45); but the prophecy will also be fulfilled by the sustaining 'fertility' of Latium (1.531, 2.781–2)—the poet exploits the sense of *uber* he has developed in the *Georgics* (see Mynors on 2.275). Such ambiguous indirectness is typical of the language of oracles, especially in literature: at Pindar, *Pyth.* 4.6–8 Apollo is cited as telling Battus to found Cyrene 'on a bright shining breast'; *Anth. Pal.* 14.66 plays on 'mother', and so do Livy 1.56.4–13 (*mater = Terra*), Ovid. *Met.* 1.367–402 (*ossa parentis* = clods of earth), and *Fasti* 4.259 *mater abest; matrem iubeo, Romane, requiras*, 'mother is missing; I bid you look for mother, Roman' (Apollo solves this riddle from the Sibylline books at 263–4, pointing them towards Cybele, the mother of the gods): 'motherland' turns out to be the correct interpretation, but Anchises will first try a solution that involves Cybele.

97–8 At *Iliad* 20.290 Achilles is about to kill Aeneas, until Poseidon intervenes and saves him, drawing attention to his piety towards the gods (298–9). He says that Apollo will not save Aeneas, despite his encouragement to fight (79–111), and that Zeus, who previously favoured the race of Dardanus (304), now hates the race of Priam, before concluding (307–8: there is a Romanizing variant γένος πάντεσσιν ἀνάξει in 307, found in the geographer Strabo, 13.1.53):

Commentary: lines 69–120

νῦν δὲ δὴ Αἰνείαο βίη Τρώεσσιν ἀνάξει
καὶ παίδων παῖδες, τοί κεν μετόπισθε γένωνται.

But now the might/race of Aeneas is going to rule the Trojans/everyone, and his sons' sons, who will come hereafter.

V. keeps the shape of the lines in rendering the Romanizing version into Latin. In *nati natorum* he inverts the word order of the Homeric polyptoton* παίδων παῖδες, but produces an equally spondaic* equivalent and amplifies it with *nascentur*; and he introduces his own similar word-play in 97 with the pair *domus... dominabitur*. He changes the initial temporal adverb to a local one (*hic*) to suit the new context, and significantly adds *et* before the relative clause so that the prophesied supremacy continues into the ongoing future. At the same time we hear echoes of 1.284–5 *domus Assaraci... uictis dominabitur Argis* (Jupiter's announcement of Roman conquest and domination of Greece) and even 2.327 *incensa Danai dominantur in urbe*, the words of Apollo's priest Panthus (on this and other ramifications see Miller 2009: 108–15); the verb will recur in later prophecies (6.766, 7.70). As in Book 1, it is the god who imposes an empire; Aeneas has simply asked for a home, generalized into a city for his band of migrants: the move from *domus* to *dominabitur* should shock.

99–101 haec Phoebus: verbs of speech are (save for *esse*) the most commonly omitted. **mixto... tumultu**: literally 'with confusion mixed in', equivalent to *mixta tumultu*, as at 2.609 *mixto... undantem puluere fumum* ('smoke swirling mixed with dust'). **laetitia**: the enjambment* and the word order are expressive, with joy only now emerging from the hubbub (which is then evoked by the repetitions of cuncti quae... quaerunt as everyone talks at once). Throughout the book pleasure regularly alternates with exhaustion (cf. 78, *fessos*): see 133, 169, 178, 347, 524 for *laetus* applied to Trojans. **sint**: after the historic* present (*quaerunt*) Latin allows either primary or historic subjunctive: the former is normal in Caesar, e.g., and Vergil (e.g. 608–9). **quo Phoebus uocet errantes iubeatque reuerti**: like many oracles this raises questions as much as answering them. The Trojans essentially repeat Aeneas' *quo ire iubes?* (88). The one new detail is saved till last: from *reduces* and *matrem* (96) they understand that their journey is in some sense a 'return'; but *errantes*, while meaning 'us who wander', also hints at the error they are about to make (*errore*, 181).

102–3 genitor: Anchises, as the senior member of the group, is the obvious intrepreter of Apollo's words, but in reviewing what he knows of his people's ancestry, described in a sonorous and weighty verse, he follows the wrong line.   **uoluens monumenta**: 'pondering the traditions', but *monumenta* are frequently written texts (*OLD* 4, 5) and *uoluere* (*OLD* 10) and its compound are used for unrolling scrolls, so there is also a passing image of Anchises engaged in archival research.   **proceres**: the leaders among the migrants: cf. 58.   **spes discite uestras**: 'learn what you may hope for': Servius' comments bring out the way that *uestras* (rather than *nostras*) hints at Anchises' impending death.

104–6 Creta: announcement of the next stage on the Trojans' route, described in advance, including the further detail at 121–3 (contrast 13–16, 73–7, where the ecphrases* come while they are at sea). V. apparently innovates in including the island on the itinerary. He saves till later books dark tales associated with Minos (Armstrong 2002): the Labyrinth in a simile at 5.588–91, Daedalus and Icarus, Pasiphae and the Minotaur at 6.14–33; the abandoned Ariadne of Catullus 64 is a prototype for Dido in Book 4. More significant here is the association of Crete with trickery and deceit (*deceptum*, 181). This goes back to the lying tales of Odysseus, who repeatedly claims to be a Cretan traveller (*Od*. 13.256, 14.199, 19.172–81), and is encapsulated in the paradox of the Cretan Epimenides, 'Cretans are always liars', cited by Callimachus, in his *Hymn to Zeus* (1.8: **I(a)**), a text to which we are directed by V.'s next word.   **Iouis magni**: the phrase is a significant addition to Vergil's Homeric model here: Κρήτη τις γαῖ᾽ ἔστι, μεσῶι ἐνὶ οἴνοπι πόντωι (*Od*. 19.172, 'Crete is a land in the middle of the wine-dark sea'). At 2.647–9, when Anchises at first refuses to leave Troy, he focuses on his crippling by Jupiter (the punishment for sex with Venus); he then appeals to *Iuppiter omnipotens* to confirm the omen of the unburning flame on Iulus' head (2.689–91): the lover of Venus is used to thinking in grand terms. But *magni* (reprised in *magnas*, 106) does not pick up anything in Apollo's words. Moreover, though Jupiter was strongly associated with Crete, his birthplace was disputed: the opening of Callimachus' Hymn provides a pattern for the debate about the origin of the Trojans.   **mons Idaeus**: recalls 'in the Idaean mountains' at Call. *H*. 1.6, 51 [**I**]. The presence of a Mount Ida on Crete and in the hinterland of Troy (6, 112) underpins the narrative of Trojan migration.   **cunabula**: the key word of Anchises' misinterpretation: a cradle is not a mother, and in the Callimachean hymn Zeus is an infant on Crete (with direct reference to

Commentary: lines 69–120 115

his cradle at 48), but was born in Arcadia (see on 170–1). **centum urbes...magnas, uberrima regna**: Anchises now begins to respond to precise details of the prophecy, first *ubere*. 'Hundred-citied Crete' is a Homeric phrase (*Il.* 2.649), and it is described as 'fertile' (πίειρα) at *Od.* 19.173; the hundred cities imply fertility, and the point is enhanced by *magnas* (they are thriving), and then by the implied link between *urbes* and *uber*. **habitant**: the subject is implied: 'people', 'the Cretans' (similarly *habitabant*, referring to the proto-Trojans, at 110).

107–10 maximus...pater: *prima tellus* invites the Trojans to look for the origin of their earliest ancestor; Anchises thinks of Teucer, but according to Servius (perhaps simply deducing from V.'s narrative) Dardanus was older. Traditions about the two are confused; each is said to have married the other's daughter, e.g. (Servius; Dionysius Hal., *Rom.* 1.62.1), and thus to have combined the two blood-lines; so the error is understandable. (Hardy 1996 argues that Anchises focuses on Batea, daughter of Teucer, wife of Dardanus, and thus the mother the Trojans seek; but though she appears in person at Dion. Hal. 1.62.1, no Latin writer mentions her, and there is no clear pointer to her here.) **si rite audita recordor**: there is irony here: Anchises' memory is not obviously at fault, but his interpretation is. *audita* (like *audite*, 103) may remind us that Aeneas is narrating to an audience. **Teucrus Rhoeteas primum est aductus in oras**: Anchises' account is the same as one of two versions given by Servius; the other has Teucer as the son of a Scamander who migrated from Crete, whereas Dion. Hal. 1.61.5 reports that he came from Attica. Rhoeteum is at the eastern end of the long shallow bay on the Hellespont, north of Troy. Teucer is not known to have had a particular connexion, so the epithet *Rhoeteas* functions as a synecdoche* for the Troad. As Apollonius uses the Greek equivalent, when the Argo passes Troy (*Arg.* 1.929), it also conjures up the tradition of the epic voyage: Teucer was a proto-Aeneas, travelling in the opposite direction (cf. 1.1–3; Nelis 31). *Teucrus* is an alternative nominative, the Latin equivalent to Greek Τεῦκρος, found only here. **nondum Ilium et arces | Pergameae steterant; habitabant uallibus imis**: this imitates the shape, but inverts the topography, of Aeneas' words in vaunting his distinguished ancestry to Achilles at *Iliad* 20.216–18:

κτίσσε δὲ Δαρδανίην, ἐπεὶ <u>οὔπω</u> Ἴλιος ἱρή
ἐν πεδίῳ <u>πεπόλιστο</u> πόλις μερόπων ἀνθρώπων,
ἀλλ' ἔθ' ὑπωρείας <u>ᾤκεον</u> πολυπίδακος Ἴδης.

('Dardanus founded Dardania, when holy Ilium had not yet been founded in the plain as a city of mortal men, but they still inhabited the slopes of Ida with its many springs.') The allusion* helps clarify that *steterant* = 'had been made to stand/established' (*OLD* 13–15). Such concern with the pre-history of a city will recur in Book 8 (especially 337–68).

111–13 hinc seems to have two common, but normally separate functions, causal ('it is for this reason that') and geographical ('from here, i.e. Crete'). **mater cultrix Cybeli**: the paternal Anchises, having begun with the *pater* (107), moves on to the *mater*, Cybĕle (or Cybēbe), identified with Rhea, mother of Jupiter, Neptune, Dis, Juno, and Ceres; but she is less present in Crete than in the Troad, and though her trees have formed the boats on which the Trojans sail (5 n.), she will follow them to Rome much later (Ovid, *Fasti* 4.255–70). Cybelus is a mountain in Phrygia where she had a shrine (Servius). **Corybantiaque aera | Idaeumque nemūs**: a first allusion* to Catullus 63 (*Idae...nemora*, 52; cf. 113), and further allusions to Callimachus' Hymn to Zeus [**I(b)**]: the Idaean woods belong on Mount Ida, where Zeus was brought up (*H.* 1.51), protected from his father Cronus (1.53–4) by the clanging of the armour of the Curetes (1.52; cf. 131) and the Corybantes (1.46). Lucretius reports the myth, with typical scepticism, at 2.633–9 (n.b. *pulsarent aeribus aera* at 2.637), though without naming the Corybantes; both groups appear when the chorus describe the noisy dance around the infant god at Euripides, *Bacchae* 120–5; and the Argonauts set up a similar rite for the 'Idaean Mother' (Apollonius 1.1117–39), but in Phrygia, where the Trojans have come from. For *nemūs*, see Introduction, p. 45. **fida silentia sacris**: 'conscientious silence for the sacred rites': commentators associate this with Horace, *Odes* 3.2.25–6 *est et fideli tuta silentio | merces*, itself an embellishment of Simonides fr. 582 ἔστι καὶ σιγᾶς ἀκίνδυνον γέρας ('there is an unassailable reward for silence too'), reported by Plutarch as a saying of Augustus. Horace's point is different, whatever it is (see Nisbet & Rudd 2004 for discussion), but both poets are surely complimenting their patron in asserting formal silence as essential to the Roman/Trojan way of life. **iuncti currum dominae subiere leones**: V. reworks a scene from Catullus' Hymn to Cybĕle/Cybēbe, in which 'the mistress of Dindymus' looses one of the lions from her chariot to chase Attis back under her control: 63.76 *iuncta iuga resoluens Cybele leonibus*, 91 *dea Cybebe, dea domina Dindymi*; cf. also Lucretius 2.601 *in curru bii-*

ugos agitare leones ('on her chariot drives a yoked pair of lions'). Anchises' aetiology* has moved on from cult to story-telling or iconography*: Teucer's coming from Crete made Cybele's lions part of Trojan (and hence Roman) myth.

114–17 ergo agite: a vigorous call to action, leading from explanatory observations (here, 5.58, *Geo.* 1.63) or change of circumstances (2.707).   **diuum ducunt qua iussa sequamur**: even now that the Trojans have a plan to pursue they are still the object of the gods' direction. *sequamur* suggests an answer to *quem sequimur?* (88), but the Trojans are about to follow the misguided instructions of the wrong leader. Aeneas and his listeners (and Vergil and his readers) also head on the route determined by Anchises' reading of the gods' orders.   **Cnosia regna**: after the calming good sense of *placemus uentos* (an instruction fulfilled in 118–20), this introduces a disquieting note: Crete has been the seat of kingdoms before, notably that of Minos, and his unfortunate and bestial family, instantly evoked by reference to Cnossos (104, 121–2 nn.). The Trojans are not far from such a world (**nec longo distant cursu**): this is a route best not taken.   **modo Iuppiter adsit**: 'provided Jupiter is with us', i.e., on the most basic level, 'if the weather is kind to us': Jupiter replaces Poseidon from Achilles' analogous lines when he is thinking of returning home at *Iliad* 9.362–3. For the final time Anchises' words remind us of the Callimachean hymn: though Jupiter may be present in Crete, it is still not his or the Trojans' motherland.   **tertia lux classem Cretaeis sistet in oris**: just as Crete has been described in advance (104), here the expected time of arrival is given.

118–20 meritos aris mactauit honores: 'he made the deserved sacrifices (*OLD honor* 2b) on the altars': Apollo, who has given the requested prophecy, and Neptune, whose words from *Iliad* 20.307–8 he retransmits, already deserve their offerings; Storm and the West Winds are rewarded in hopeful anticipation. In addition, Neptune is a god that seafarers should keep in good humour, as is shown by 1.124–56 and 5.779–826; and the Argonauts sacrifice to Apollo, asking for a fair voyage at Apollonius 1.402–24. *aris* is presumably a real plural: sacrifices are made outside the shrine of each deity.   **taurum Neptuno, taurum tibi, pulcher Apollo**: a reworking of *Iliad* 11.728 ταῦρον δ' Ἀλφειῶι, ταῦρον δὲ Ποσειδάωνι ('a bull to Alpheus, and a bull to Poseidon'). The episode on Delos ends, as it began, with Neptune (74) and Apollo (75), with *sacra*, and with another nod to hymnic style in the encomiastic* epithet, the anaphora*, and the echo of Du-Stil* in the mannered initial alliteration of *taurum…, taurum tibi* and in the apostrophe* to Apollo (cf. 6.251 *tibi, Proserpina, uaccam* [a cow for you, Proserpina], and 8.84 *tibi enim, tibi, maxima Iuno*, as Aeneas sacrifices the white sow).   **nigram Hiemi pecudem, Zephyris felicibus albam**: the Olympian gods are granted bulls, grand offerings; lesser ones for the weather deities, a black ewe for the deity to be kept at a distance (cf. 6.249), a white one for the fair winds that are sought for the voyage (Homer has a similar pair for Earth and Sun at *Il.* 3.103–4).

121–46 *The voyage to Crete and the settlement there*
There is warm encouragement to find a new home in Crete (Map 2): first news of the expulsion of king Idomeneus and then a fair voyage through the famously dangerous Cyclades (Horace, *Odes* 1.14.20, Livy 36.43.1) look to be positive omens. But shortly after their new city Pergamea has been established, a plague strikes.

121–3 Fama uolat: the image of Rumour as flying is repeated in the same words at 7.392, 8.554 (similarly *uolans*, 11.139; *uolitans*, 7.104; *uolitans pennata*, 9.474). All of them are enriched by the full realization of Fama as a personification* at 4.173–97: the swiftest of monsters, growing as she travels, covered in eyes, tongues, ears, as well as feathers, sleeplessly flying through the darkness of night, surveying and terrifying cities from high towers in daylight, tenacious of lies as well as a source of truth: see Hardie 2012: 78–112. V. has *fama* introducing acc. + inf. clauses on four further occasions in Book 3 (165 [= 1.532], 294, 578, 694 (and on just seven other occasions): the construction, which continues to the end of the sentence here, is well suited to first-person narrative, where it loosely explains how the internal narrator knows something that might simply be revealed by the poet himself. In this case the rumour is accurate, and supports the decision to sail to Crete: Idomeneus, a prominent figure in the *Iliad* as the king who has led Cretan forces against Troy, has abandoned the kingdom of his grandfather Minos, and there is an invitingly vacant home for the Trojans to take over.   **Idomenēa**: equivalent to the Homeric accusative Ἰδομενῆα (e.g. *Iliad* 2.405; Servius compares *Ilionēa*, 1.611). Helenus will supply more information at 400–1—Idomeneus has gone to the *campi Sallentini* of south-eastern Italy; at 11.265 Diomedes is reported as mentioning his *uersos penates* ('overthrown', or simply 'changed', 'home'). But V./Aeneas leaves it unclear why he has been expelled (**pulsum**) from Crete: was it thanks to a usurper? to the gods, when he either did (Servius *ad loc.*) or did not sacrifice his son, the first creature he saw on return home, as he had vowed to Neptune? or to the Cretans, who thought him responsible for incurring a plague (cf. 137–42; Herodotus 7.171)?   **hoste uacare domum sedesque astare relictas**: a tautological* doublet, as if the news is so suprising that it needs repetition. *hoste* (emphasized by position) is a collective singular* (though also reflecting the reference to Idomeneus in particular), and ablative after *uacare*, 'to be without'. After *deserta litora*, *uacare* recalls the aftermath of the Noric plague at *Geo.* 3.476–7 <u>deserta</u>*que regna | pastorum et longe saltus lateque* <u>uacantis</u> ('the realms of the shepherds are deserted and the pasture-land empty far and wide': cf. 137–42), and *relictas* the previous occasion on which Greeks have left a shore empty, at 2.28 *desertosque...locos litusque relictum*—a snare, as this inviting space will prove a delusion. *relictas* also brings out the similarity between conqueror and conquered: cf. *relinquo* (10) for the departure from Troy, and *linquimus*, starting the very next line.

124–7 Ortygiae: an alternative name for Delos (literally 'Quail Island'); the Trojans will visit another Ortygia at 692–7.   **uolamus**: the ease and speed of Rumour (121) is matched by the Trojans' voyage. **bacchatamque iugis Naxon**: Naxos, a mountainous island, the largest of the Cyclades, south of Delos (and thus in the direction of Crete), was famous as the place where Bacchus found Ariadne after her abandonment by Theseus: this reflects the importance there of Dionysiac cult. V. recalls his use of the participle *bacchatus* at *Geo.* 2.487 *uirginibus bacchata Lacaenis | Taygeta* ('Mount Taygetus, danced over by Spartan maidens'); cf. also *bacchantes* in Catullus' account of the ecstatic troupe that accompanies the god when he meets Ariadne (64.255). *iugis* is 'ablative of place where'. *Naxon* (like *Olearon* and *Paron*) is a Greek accusative, equivalent to the Latin *-um* ending (though feminine in gender). The route from Delos to Crete would most naturally go south between Naxos and the island of Paros to the west; the other two islands mentioned form an east–west chain (see Map 2), and would hardly be passed on the same southerly voyage: V. is more interested in the names than the geography.   **uiridemque Donusam**: Donusa is a small island east of Naxos, and not notably fertile, as the epithet might suggest: V. is presumably looking for the contrast with 'snow-white

Paros' (Servius implausibly offers, as an alternative, reference to green marble).   **Olearon niueamque Paron**: Olearos (spelled *Oliaros* at Ovid, *Met.* 7.469; now Antiparos) lies off the west coast of its larger neighbour Paros, which was famous in antiquity for its pure white marble, used for sculpture (1.593): hence *niueam* (and *marmoreamque Paron* at Ovid, *Met.* 7.465), and comparisons such as Horace, *Odes* 1.19.6 *splendentis Pario marmore purius* ('shining more spotlessly than Parian marble').   **sparsas...Cycladăs** (third-declension Greek accusative plural): the phrase generalizes the islands named to the whole archipelago of the south-east Aegean. Etymologically *Cyclades* means 'forming a circle' (Pliny, *Nat. Hist.* 4.65 *circa Delum in orbem sitae, unde et nomen traxere Cyclades*, 'organized into a circle round Delos, as a result of which they also gained the name Cyclades'; O'Hara 1996 also cites a Greek equivalent, Callimachus, *Hymn* 4.198 περιηγέας); *sparsas* plays on an alternative name *Sporades* ('scattered'), more often used for outlying islands or other groups: cf. Pomponius Mela 2.111, Pliny, *Nat. Hist.* 4.68. Mention of the Cyclades (and in 291 of Phaeacia = Corcyra) makes for a link with an epigram of Vergil's contemporary Crinagoras of Mitylene (*Anth. Pal.* 9.559 = 32 G.-P.), in which he prepares to sail to Italy, via the Cyclades and Corcyra, and asks the assistance of Menippus, author of a *periplus**; Gow & Page, *Garland of Philip* 2.243 date this to 27 or 26 BC, just before his participation in an embassy to Augustus. The similarity of the voyages is perhaps due to chance—but Crinagoras, who writes for Marcellus, Augustus' son-in-law, was well connected with the regime.   **et...legimus freta**: after the catalogue of islands we come to *legimus*, the verb of which they are objects; given that *freta* ('seas') is an object too, we should see this as a mild syllepsis*, first 'skirt' (*litoraque Epiri legimus*, 292; *OLD* 7b), then 'traverse' (*OLD* 7a), i.e. 'sail through'.   **crebris...freta consita terris**: 'seas sown [*or* scattered] with frequent lands': for the phrasing cf. e.g. Livy 33.6.7, *ager consitus crebris arboribus* ('land planted with many trees'), Curtius 10.1.14 *insulam palmetis frequentibus consitam* ('an island scattered with many palm-groves'); and for metaphorical usage *OLD* 1b, as well as Pliny, *Nat. Hist.* 4.65 cited above (Horsfall 2000 and Conte 2009 see *consitae* as hinting at *Sporades* again). For *crebri* marking the crowding of a number of discrete items in an area cf. also 11.209 *crebris conluent ignibus agri* ('the fields shine with numerous fires'). However, *consita* is a reading found only in a few late MSS; the tradition has *concita* ('stirred into action'), which is (despite Servius) a very odd way to express the effect of land on water.

128–31 nauticus…uario certamine clamor: | hortantur socii: in earlier voyages the Trojans have been passively carried by wind and water (*feror*, 11, 16, 78; *prouehimur*, 72); here they have a keen urgency in heading to their mistaken destination. *uario certamine* (ablative of description, or perhaps of cause, with *exoritur*) suggests a variety of contests as the voyage progresses: between different vessels; now with oar, now under sail (when the following wind rises in 130). **proauos** perhaps hints at the error they are making: they have been told to seek not 'forefathers' but the *antiquam matrem* (96). **petamus**: either indirect command after *hortantur*, without expressed *ut* (as at Cicero, *Att.* 4.15.10; Caesar, *Bell. Gall.* 6.33.5, Livy 6.15.10 e.g.), or direct speech, which is rare after *hortari*; in either case the crews are encouraging each other: 'Let's head for Crete.' **euntis**: supply *nos*, 'as we proceed'. **tandem** marks the end of the voyage, which is thus made to seem long; so too at 205, 278: Hübner, *GB* 21 (1995), 102–4 sees the word as a leitmotif of the book. **antiquis Curetum…oris**: 'the ancient shores of the Curetes' standing by hypallage* for 'the shores of the ancient Curetes': these were primitive inhabitants of Crete, who protected the infant Jupiter by conducting a noisy war-dance around his cradle (Callimachus, *Hymn* 1.52: **I(b)**); they are regularly associated with the Corybantes (cf. 111; Ovid, *Fasti* 4.209–10). An etymological link between *Creta* and *Curetes* is implied by the placement of the two nouns after the caesura in 129 and 131 (cf. Apollonius, *Arg.* 2.1233–4).

132–4 ergo marks the eager building of the city walls as the culmination of the recent narrative: we may see this as going back to the failure in Thrace, and the oracular response on Delos, but the main focus must be on the voyage safely finished: cf. 278 for a similar usage. **Pergameam**: a backward-looking name, taken from Pergama, the citadel of Troy (cf. 87, 110, 336): note *arcem*, 134. However, like *Aeneadae* in Thrace (13–68 n.), the name will leave a trace in the historical record, as *paucis relictis* (190) implies; it will become Pergamum (Velleius Paterculus 1.1.2; Pliny, *Nat. Hist.* 4.59), towards the western end of the north coast of Crete (Map 2). **laetam cognomine**: apparently expressing this as a fact rather than part of Aeneas' instruction: they take joy in a name that evokes Troy. *laetam* maintains the general spirit of rejoicing from 100; the intervening journey has been so smooth for once that they have not become *fessi*. The upbeat tone prepares for the contrasting disaster to follow (n.b. 145); later in the book Aeneas will realize that it is not their destiny to look to the past, as Andromache and Helenus have done (493–9).   **amare focos**: on the thematic importance of loving their new homes (*focos* 'hearths' is a common synecdoche*), see Jenkyns (1998: 432), Fletcher (2014, esp. 1, 105–6), and cf. Aeneas' emotional words to Dido at 4.347 *hic amor, haec patria est*, describing Italy.   **arcemque attollere tectis**: 'and to raise the citadel high with roofs': striking language, not easy to clarify. An *arx* is an easily defensible highpoint, and *attollere* is used elsewhere of land masses that raise themselves naturally (the Strophades at 205, the promontory Lacinia at 552, *pater Appenninus* at 12.703). The Trojans add to the effect. However, *tectis* does not suggest fortifications, though it might refer to temples, such as that of Juno Moneta, which stood on top of the Arx in Rome (*templis* would convey this straightforwardly). In a context of city foundation the easiest sense would be 'houses', as at 1.425 *pars optare locum tecto* ('some choose a place for their house'); but an *arx* would not be a place for many homes. There is similarly evocative imprecision when Aeneas is building another city at 4.260 *fundantem arces ac tecta nouantem*: Carthage.

135–9 iamque fere: 'now...just', a combination that goes back to Ennius (*Annales* 264 Skutsch), also used by V. at 5.327, 835. The phrase helps the reader to link the sequence of unconjoined main clauses thanks to the implied imminence of the inverted *cum*-clause (137). **subductae** <*erant*>: 'had been hauled up' (*OLD* 1b), the standard term for beaching ships (normal procedure in the ancient world); the verb can be followed either by *in* + acc. or by a locative expression. Taking the boats out of the water marks the intended move from travel to settlement.   **conubiis aruisque nouis operata iuuentus, | iura domosque dabam**: symbolic activities for the new city (and what the poem will not present happening in Aeneas' foundation in Latium). As well as establishing the legal framework, Aeneas allots space for the building of homes, as happened whenever Rome founded new colonies: cf. 5.755–8 (Segesta). The correct scansion here (contrast 319) is probably *cōnŭbīis* rather than *cōnūbjīs*: see Austin on 1.73, Munro (Cambridge, 1893) on Lucretius 3.776. *nouis* (to be taken with both *conubiis* and *aruis*) and *iuuentus* bring out the hopes for the future: a new city needs families and fields. *operata* <*erant*>: 'were busy with', regularly used of religious activity (which is perhaps to be inferred here, alongside other aspects of marriage and agriculture).   **subito**

Commentary: lines 121–46

cum: *dabam* has at last expressly established the sense of continuing activity into which the plague now suddenly breaks: the postponement* of *cum* puts pointed stress on *subito*.   **tabida membris | corrupto caeli tractu miserandaque uēnit | … lues**: 'from a diseased region of the sky there came a plague, corrupting bodies and deplorable' (though in the Latin the word order begins from the symptoms and only then moves to cause). The introduction of the plague echoes the diction from the start of the long description of the disastrous Noric plague at *Georgics* 3.478–81:

> hic quondam morbo caeli miseranda coorta est
> tempestas totque autumni incanduit aestu
> et genus omne neci pecudum dedit, omne ferarum,   480
> corrupitque lacus, infecit pabula tabo.

Here once owing to a sickness in the heavens there arose a deplorable time: it burnt white with all the heat of harvest-time, and sent to death every kind of animal, domestic and wild, and spoilt the drinking pools, and infected the fodder with pestilence.

The existence of that passage (3.474–566) enables V. to cut the account here short: it is only at the end that the disease there infects human beings (*membra*, 565).   **arboribusque satīsque**: the effects of this plague spread to the worlds of *Georgics* 1 (sown crops) and 2 (trees).   **letifer annus**: the heat brings and exacerbates the plague: *annus* ('season') neatly evokes the fuller details of *Geo.* 3.479. For *letifer* see Harrison on 10.170 *letifer arcus*.

140–2 Aeneas reprises the sequence of 137–9: the effect on the settlers (implied subject of *linquebant*); then the baleful weather, and its disastrous effect on agriculture.   **dulcis animas**: another echo of *Geo.* 3, where the dying cattle 'give up their sweet lives' (*dulcis animas…reddunt*, 495). *linquere* is used with a noun qualified by *dulcis* to mark an undesired departure also for Meliboeus forced from his farm at *Ecl.* 1.3 *dulcia linquimus arua* and Aeneas driven by the gods to leave Carthage at *Aen.* 4.281 *dulcisque relinquere terras*. For the individual leaving life rather than vice versa, Servius compares Terence, *Adelphoe* 498 *animam relinquam*.   **sterilīs exurere…agros**: 'utterly parched the fields <and made them> infertile'; the adjective is proleptic*, and the infinitive historic*, equivalent here to the imperfects in 140 and 142: it stresses the effect (as does the prefix *ex-*, and the phrase *arebant herbae* in 142), and serves V.'s metrical convenience.   **Sirius**: the baneful effects of the Dog Star in late July/August is a commonplace, used e.g. to describe Priam's vision of Achilles on the battlefield (*Iliad* 22.25–31), and the Rutulians' of Aeneas' shield at 10.273–4 *Sirius ardor | ille sitim morbosque ferens mortalibus aegris* ('the familiar burning of Sirius, bringing thirst and disease for sick mortals'). The context here recalls especially *Argonautica* 2.516–27 where the farmer-hero Aristaeus is instructed by his father Apollo to move home from Phthia (in northern mainland Greece) to Ceos, one of the Cyclades, in order to help the locals ward off a plague, caused by Sirius' burning of the 'Minoan islands' (2.516–17). **uictum seges aegra negabat**: the failing crops are momentarily personified*: 'sick', like the men (140), and 'saying no' to expectations of sustenance, *uictum* (literally 'support for life'). The combination *uictum negare* alludes to *Geo*. 1.149 *uictum Dodona negaret* (where Dodona is Jupiter's oracle, as well as symbolizing oak trees at the time when mankind can no longer subsist on acorns); Armstrong (*CQ* 52 (2002), 324) suggests that this might point to Jupiter as the origin of the plague.

143–6 rursus ad oraclum Ortygiae Phoebumque: the repetition of the names *Ortygia* (124) and *Phoebus* (80, 99, 101) compounds the sense of return explicit in *rursus* and *remenso*. Ill fortune forces colonists to return to seek clarification from an oracle already in Herodotus' account of the foundation of Cyrene (4.157). V. has the syncopated* form of *oraculum* only here, elsewhere the plural (e.g. 456). **hortatur pater**: Anchises takes the plague to be a punishment and a warning; if he has made an error, Apollo's forgiveness (*ueniam*) and further guidance must be sought. We may contrast the start of the *Iliad*, where Agamemnon's folly in not returning the daughter of Chryses leads to the plague inflicted by Apollo; but it is Achilles who calls an assembly and suggests the consultation of seers (1.59–67). *me* is to be supplied as the object of *hortatur* and the subject of the infinitives. **remenso |...ire mari**: literally 'to go on the sea measured out once again'; there is a synonymous ablative at 2.181 *pelagoque remenso*, with the same passive use of the past participle of *remetior*. **quam...unde...quo**: the three indirect questions by a kind of zeugma* extend the sense of *precari* from 'pray for' to 'ask'. **quam...finem...ferat**: cf. Aeneas' optimistic claim to his shipwrecked followers at 1.199 *dabit deus his quoque finem* ('a god will put an end to these woes too'), echoed by Venus in her question to Jupiter at 1.241 (*quem das finem, rex magne, laborum?*), and the moment when Iulus' joke about eating tables marks an end to their toils at 7.118

ea uox audita laborum | prima tulit finem. In the singular *finis* can be either feminine (as here) or masculine (3.440, 718; and 1.241, just cited). **fessis**: cf. 78, 133 n. **unde laborum | temptare auxilium iubeat**: 'from where he bids us try to get succour for our difficulties': for genitives defining *auxilium*, see 1.358 *uiae*, 8.472 *belli*; Ovid, *Rem*. 48 *uulneris*; for *tempto* so, see *OLD* 8; for the omission of the object after *iubere*, cf. 9, 289, 472. **quo uertere cursus**: a brief evocation of the labyrinthine confusion in which the Trojans aptly find themselves on Crete, uncertain which way to turn. Fortunately the Penates will save them from re-treading ground just covered. *cursūs* is an apt poetic plural*, multiplying the journey to match the *labores*.

147-91 *The dream prophecy of the Penates*
Anchises' advice that Aeneas return to Delos establishes the urgency of the Trojans' plight and his own wisdom in accepting that he may have made an error. V. will play with return to the same place in the case of western Sicily, revisited in Book 5; but here he avoids narrative repetition by the familiar epic device of a warning dream, in this case the appearance of the Penates whose images have accompanied their travels. As is usual in Homer, there is 'a tacit assumption that the sleeper's senses are awake and active' (West on *Odyssey* 4.795ff., in Heubeck et al.). Aeneas is aware of the illuminating moonlight coming through the windows (151-2) and of the fact that he is asleep in bed (150); and the visitation is seen as happening there: cf. *Iliad* 2.16-36 (Oneiros in the shape of Nestor appears to Agamemnon), 23.62-102 (the ghost of Patroclus to Achilles), *Odyssey* 4.795-841 (Athena as Ipthime to Penelope), 6.16-40 (Athena as the daughter of Dymas to Nausicaa). The situation as Aeneas sleeps is similar to the despair of the Argonauts when stranded on the desolate north African coast (Apollonius 4.1232-304); the local nymphs appear to Jason (in a vision rather than a dream: 1308-31) and encourage him to seek for escape from the Syrtes: see Hunter 1993: 174. Closest in the *Aeneid* is Hector's ghost at 2.268-97 (see 150, 157-60 nn. for citations); others to appear in Aeneas' dreams are Mercury at 4.554-70, Anchises at 5.719-39, the river god Tiber at 8.26-67; Dido sees Sychaeus' ghost at 1.353-9 [P], Turnus the Fury Allecto, in the form of the priestess Calybe, at 7.413-59. Mercury and Sychaeus also advise departure.

147-53 Nox erat et terris animalia somnus habebat: the phrasing recurs in an expanded form at 8.26-7 (before Tiber visits the initially restless Aeneas) *nox erat et terras animalia fessa per omnis | alituum pecudumque genus sopor altus habebat* (epithets are given to 'lands', 'sleep', and 'animals', which is further defined by 'the race of birds and of flocks'), and 4.522-7 (where it sets up a contrast: Dido cannot sleep). **effigies sacrae diuum Phrygiique penates**: as *effigies* immediately implies, these are the images that Aeneas has brought with him, following Hector's instruction: see 12 n. As at 2.293 (cited on 157-60) and 2.717 *sacra… patriosque penatis*, the *que* is epexegetic*: it adds a phrase that makes the previous one more precise. **a Troia**: for the use of a preposition with the name of a city, see 595. **mediisque ex ignibus urbis | extuleram**: once more Aeneas recalls the horrors of Book 2, though strictly there (and in the sculptures of the event) it is Anchises who carries the Penates, as Aeneas is still polluted by the blood he has shed (2.717-20). **uisi <sunt> ante oculos astare iacentis**: *uisi* (which agrees in gender with *penates*, the nearer of the two subjects) is easily taken as 'seemed' before an infinitive, but there is no infinitive in the similar phrasing when Creusa's ghost appears to Aeneas at 2.773-4 *umbra Creusae | uisa mihi ante oculos*, so we might render it 'were/was seen' here and in another important parallel, 2.270-1 *in somnis, ecce, ante oculos maestissimus Hector | uisus adesse mihi*. It is hard to decide whether *iacentis* is genitive ('lying in sleep', *OLD* 2b) with an implied *mei*, or accusative plural ('resting', *OLD* 9a). **in somnis**: 'in sleep', a common plural in this phrase. However, Servius reports that *multi* take it as a single word *insomnis* ('unsleeping'); and some modern scholars have followed this reading; but 173-5 imply that Aeneas was asleep, and the point is confirmed by the frequency of the phrase in dream sequences from the time of Plautus (*Curc.* 260, *Mil.* 383) and Ennius (*Ann.* 212 Skutsch, *trag.* 51 Jocelyn), as well as in the *Aeneid* itself (1.353; 2.270; 4.353, 466, 557; 12.908). **multo manifesti lumine** expresses how they appeared in the dream, but also what Aeneas will see when he wakes up: he establishes credibility for the dream and authority for the words he hears by providing this circumstantial and numinous detail. **qua se | plena per insertas fundebat luna fenestras**: the light is given a realistic explanation—but the brightness of the full moon can seem supernatural, and is thus appropriate for the vision. Windows were normally shuttered, and not glazed, in antiquity; *insertas* thus apparently refers to the construction of the gap within the wall of the house, and the point of the epithet is hard to see. Alternatively we might wonder whether *fenestras* means 'shutters' (as at Horace, *Odes* 1.25.1 *iunctas* *fenestras*, *OLD* 1b), but in that case *insertas* would have to convey the sense 'parted' (cf. Prop. 1.3.31 *diuersas praecurrens luna fenestras*, 'the moon running past the parted shutters'), but this seems most implausible, as does a suggestion of Servius (followed by Horsfall), that we have a kind of hypallage* = *luna inserta per fenestras* (cf. Lucretius 2.114–15 *solis lumina ... inserti fundunt radii per opaca domorum*, 'the let-in rays pour the light of the sun through the dark parts of houses'). Is the participle perhaps corrupt? For the unusual sixth foot, consisting of the two monosyllables *qua se*, cf. 695; unlike that line, this is in other ways metrically straightforward. The unemphatic *se* carries little stress and so hardly disrupts the normal rhythm at line end.   **adfari...demere**: historic* infinitives. For the use of a pair of verbs to introduce speech, cf. e.g. 314, 358 *his...adgredior dictis ac talia quaeso*.

154–5 quod: understand *id* as antecedent, and object of *canit*.   **tibi delato Ortygiam**: 'to you once delivered to Delos'. *deferre* is 'to carry to a destination' (*OLD* 1); the past participle is used here with a conditional force, equivalent to a future perfect. *Ortygiam* is accusative of motion towards, without a preposition, as is normal with names of islands.   **dicturus Apollo est**: in promising to give the words that Apollo was going to speak had the dream not anticipated the journey, the Penates comment on the narrative route not taken. In fact, they will not reproduce Apollo's intended words, but speak for themselves, reprising and clarifying the instructions of Hector's ghost and Apollo's oracle.   **canit**: 'prophesies' (*OLD* 8), as at 183, 366, 373, 444, 457, 559 (the frequency is a measure of the prophetic nature of this book).   **tua nos** is a significant juxtaposition, bringing out the close relationship between the Penates and Aeneas; the following lines maintain the point (*nos te ..., nos...sub te*; then *idem* and *tu* starting consecutive sentences).   **en** draws attention to the vivid reality of their appearance; cf. e.g. 5.672, 8.612, 9.7, 11.365.   **ultro** stresses the willingness of the god to help: no need for prayers or travel to his special shrine; he speaks through the divinities with easy access to Aeneas. Gods are always potentially present in their sanctuaries or statues, as when Artemis overhears the accidental oath of Cydippe (to marry Acontius) at Callimachus, *Aet.* fr. 75.22–7; cf. Theocritus, *Id.* 1.66–9, reworked at *Ecl.* 10.9–12.

156–60 The Penates echo the end of the speech of Hector's ghost (2.293–5):

                    sacra suosque tibi commendat Troia penatis;
                    hos cape fatorum comites, his moenia quaere
                    magna pererrato statues quae denique ponto.

The hendiadys* of *sacra suosque...penatis* is reworked in the introduction to the speech (148); the polyptoton* *hos...his* is echoed by the anaphora* *nos...nos* (both referring to the Penates); *secuti* matches *comites*; *moenia...magna* is repeated; *pererrato...ponto* is turned into *permensi classibus aequor*. However, in 158–9 the Penates add the prophecies of apotheosis for Aeneas' descendants and *imperium* for the city.   **nos...nos...idem**: as at (e.g.) 541, 564, *idem* emphatically reprises the subject ('and we too'), here marking the move from past (*secuti*, *permensi* <*sunt*>) to future (*tollemus*, *dabimus*). The repeated *nos* echoes the homeless Meliboeus of *Ecl.* 1.3–4 (cited in the Introduction, pp. 5–6).   **te Dardania incensa tuaque arma secuti** (cf. 54 n.): like Aeneas in 149, they evoke the events of Book 2 with reference to the burning of the city and Aeneas' attempt to fight. However, *tua arma* is paired with *te* grammatically, reworking the poem's opening tag *Arma uirumque*; the phrase points to the future too, when Aeneas' arms will be used again in the second half of the poem, as well as to the military prowess of Rome to be.   **tumidum**: 'swollen', 'rising high' (*OLD* 3), a common epithet for the sea. Though the voyages so far in the book have been smooth, storms will follow, first on the next leg of the long journey (194–204).   **permensi classibus** (61 n.) **aequor**: summary of the events of Book 2 is followed by summary of Book 3 itself; the pair of verses recalls *et terris iactatus et alto* (1.3).   **idem**: 'and we too' (541, 564), serving as the pivot round which the speech moves from defeat and exile to glory and empire.   **uenturos**: 'future', but as Servius says it gives them current existence; cf. *uenientum* of the souls of future Romans at 6.755. The word recurs in a similar context, though with a different sense, at 6.789–90 *hic Caesar et omnis Iuli* | *progenies magnum caeli uentura sub axem* ('Here are Caesar and all the offspring of Iulus, fated to reach the mighty zenith of heaven').   **tollemus in astra nepotes**: Romulus, Julius Caesar, subsequently Augustus and other emperors. Here the prophecy moves to material that will (in chronological, if not textual, terms) be made more precise in Jupiter's speech in Book 1 (286–90): *nascetur...Caesar,* | *imperium Oceano, famam qui terminet astris* | *Iulius, a magno demissum nomen Iulo....uocabitur hic quoque uotis* ('Caesar will be born, who will bound the empire with the Ocean, his

Commentary: lines 147–91 129

glory with the stars, Julius, a name descended from great Iulus.... He too will be summoned in prayers'). The stars are a common metonymy* for the home of the gods, but evoke Divus Julius in particular, whose ascent to heaven was symbolized by the appearance of a comet during the funeral games held in 44 BC, a point that Vergil uses to underpin the equivalence of the pastoral hero Daphnis with Caesar (*Ecl.* 5.51 *Daphninque tuum tollemus ad astra*, 52, 57; 9.47). **imperiumque urbi dabimus**: as well as 1.287 (just cited) this prefigures/recalls Jupiter's *imperium sine fine dedi* (1.279). The word will recur prominently in another prophetic passage, Anchises' survey of future Romans in Book 6, especially 781–2 *Roma | imperium terris, animos aequabit Olympo* (under the auspices of Romulus 'Rome shall make its empire match the lands of the earth, its heart Olympus'), 794–5 *super et Garamantas et Indos | proferet imperium* (Augustus 'will extend the empire beyond the Garamantes and the Indians'). Deification and the stars appear in this speech too: 6.790 (cited above, on *uenturos*) and 795–805. The *urbs* to which the Penates will bring empire will turn out to be Rome in the long run, not Lavinium founded by Aeneas. **tu**: after the emphatic *nos*, this stresses Aeneas' role, to provide the city, and 'not abandon the long toil of migration'—as he will again, for a while, when he settles in Carthage. **moenia magnis | magna para**: for the notion that one might build walls generous enough to contain a great city, compare Ovid, *Fasti* 3.181–2 *moenia iam stabant, populis angusta futuris, | credita sed turbae tum nimis ampla suae* ('walls already stood, narrow for the future inhabitants, but then believed too generous for the city's population'). But *moenia* is also a synecdoche* for the city as a whole (85 n., 1.277, 2.252). *magnis* may refer to the great descendants of the Trojans, but also to the Penates themselves (as in the parallel passage at 2.294–5, cited at the start of this note): see 12 n. on their identity as *magni di*. Polyptoton* of words meaning 'big' is found in Homer to mark the heroic death (*Il.* 16.776 κεῖτο μέγας μεγαλωστί, 'He lay majestic in his majesty'; 18.26, of Achilles mourning Patroclus; *Od.* 24.40); V. applies the usage to a grand future. **ne linque laborem**: leaving Crete does not mean abandoning labour; 'toil cannot be dissevered from glory' (Jenkyns 1998: 436, in a lively reading of the speech).

161–2 mutandae sedes: the central point of the speech is expressed simply in five heavy syllables: 'your home [*and* our seats] must be changed': *mutandae* is gerundive of necessity or obligation, as at 235,

384–5, 495–7. The common metaphorical sense of *sedes* is picked up in *considere* ('settle', 162); the more literal application to the Penates' position by *hae nobis propriae sedes* in 167. **non haec...litora... aut Cretae**: 'not these shores...or in Crete [*locative*]': the emphatically negated words are placed in each clause; for *non...aut* beginning adjacent clauses, cf. 42–3.

163–6 These lines are also found at 1.530–3, where Ilioneus repeats the information provided by the Penates here, in explaining to Dido the presence of Trojan ships on the n. African coast.   **est locus**: a standard introduction of a geographical ecphrasis*, found also at 7.563, and seven times in Ovid. But Vergil recalls a particular passage in Book 1 of Ennius' *Annales* (fr. 20–2 Skutsch, possibly from three consecutive lines): *est locus Hesperiam quam mortales perhibebant...Saturnia terra... quam Prisci, casci populi, tenuere Latini* ('there is place which men used to call Hesperia...the land of Saturn, which the Aboriginal Latins held, an ancient people'); cf. the phrase *terra antiqua* in apposition* in 164. Saturn's part in the earlier history of Latium will be brought out by Vergil especially in Evander's account at 8.319–29.   **Hesperiam**: 'the land of the Evening Star [*or* West]', as suits the point of view of the Greeks. Aeneas has already heard the name from the ghost of Creusa in her prophecy at 2.781 *terram Hesperiam uenies*, echoing Apollonius, *Arg.* 3.311 on Circe's journey to 'the land of evening'. (Horace uses the same name for Spain, likewise west of Italy, at *Odes* 1.36.4.)   **potens armis atque ubere glaebae**: 'powerful in arms and the fertility of the soil'. The second half of the phrase looks back to *ubere laeto* (95), as the Penates begin to explain the correct solution to Apollo's riddling oracle. But the expression as a whole brings out the duality on which the Romans saw their city's greatness as founded: success in war and productivity in agriculture; so e.g. *Georgics* 2.143–76 (539–42 n.).   **Oenotri**: a name for the inhabitants of the south-eastern parts of Italy, literally 'men of the wine country', from the Greek οἶνος ('wine').   **fama** <*est*>: 121 n. It is perhaps expressive of the limited power of the Penates that they too rely on *fama*.   **minores | Italiam dixisse ducis de nomine gentem**: 'that their descendants have called the race "Italian" from the name of their leader', i.e. *Italus* (7.178; so too Dionysius Hal. 1.35.1)—just as the Romans will be called after Romulus.

167–8 propriae sedes: 85 n., 161 n.   **hinc Dardanus ortus** confirms a second detail from the oracle, the opening address to the Trojans as *Dardanidae* (94).   **Iasiusque pater**: a comparatively obscure member of the family tree, said to have been the half-brother of Dardanus; both were sons of an Electra, Dardanus fathered by Jupiter, Iasius by Corythus, according to Servius, and both emigrated from Etruria, with Dardanus finally settling in Troy, Iasius in Samothrace (12 n.; cf. 7.206–9). Both the helmsman Palinurus (5.843) and the doctor Iapyx (12.392) are called *Iasides* ('son of Iasius'), which seems to imply descent from Iasius, even if we imagine that to be the name of the actual father of each. But he is introduced here because of the link with Corythus (170).   **genus a quo principe nostrum**: 'from which beginning our race <came>'; the brothers as a pair are treated as the antecedent of *a quo principe*. The use of *nostrum* shows the Penates identifying themselves with the people; they recall 94–5 *quae uos a stirpe parentum | prima tulit tellus*.

169–71 surge age: 'come, rise', an urgent instruction to rise from bed, but also encouragement to grow into his role as founder of a great people: cf. *Ecl.* 10.75 *surgamus*, where V. urges himself to get up from his position as a shepherd sat watching his flocks and to essay something more ambitious in his future work.   **laetus**: happy once more, now things are clarified, and a glorious future reasserted: cf. 133, 145, 178. The emotion will be explicitly shared by the people as a group at 189 (*ouantes*).   **longaeuo dicta parenti | ... refer**: the new information should be passed immediately to Anchises, as the source of the error (102–17) and of the suggestion that one has been made (143–6). The expression 'long-lived father' helps present him also as a symbol of a senate (a body of *senes* or *patres*), to whom Aeneas, as if a magistrate, reports news (cf. 58–9).   **haud dubitanda**: 'certain', unlike the typically ambiguous oracle (and the question of Zeus's birthplace: Call. *H.* 1.5: **I(a)**).   **Corythum terrasque requirat | Ausonias**: 'let him seek out Corythus in the land of Ausonia'. In this hendiadys* the second element is less specific than the first; *Ausonias* adds yet another name for Italy to the three in 163–6 (compare the discussion in Dionysius Hal., *Rom.* 1.35), one that reproduces a phrase from Apollonius 4.552–3, γαῖαν | Αὐσονίην. Corythus (cf. 168 n.) is perhaps to be identified with Cortona, a town on the border of Etruria and Umbria. There is some irony in having Anchises as the subject of *requirat*: he will never reach the west coast of Italy.   **Dictaea negat tibi Iuppiter arua**: 'he denies that the Dictaean [i.e. Cretan] fields are yours', perhaps with the implication that, as 'king of Crete' (*Geo.* 2.536 *Dictaei regis*; cf. *Geo.* 4.152), Jupiter refuses to give up his land to

Aeneas. The adjective *Dictaea* and the conversational aspect to *negat* once again recall the debate about Zeus's origin in Callimachus, *Hymn* 1.4–9 [**I(a)**]; and that passage in fact gives a more accurate pointer than the Penates do to the proper destination of the Trojans: their great city will be built not at Corythus, but on the Palatine, where Aeneas in Book 8 finds Evander and his people, born like Zeus in Arcadia.

172–8 Aeneas wakes from sleep in realistic excitement at what he has seen and heard; he rises from bed, and with his customary pious diligence prays and makes an offering.   **nec sopor illud erat**: based on *Odyssey* 19.547 οὐκ ὄναρ, ἀλλ' ὕπαρ ἐσθλόν ('not a dream but a reliable waking vision'; 20.90 is similar), and deliberately paradoxical, i.e. 'that was too vivid for a dream', but the following two and a half verses provide the evidence for crediting the experience: as Aeneas wakes up, he sees what he has been dreaming (*coram agnoscere... uidebar*).   **uelatasque comas**: like Roman priests for a solemn rite (405).   **praesentiaque ora**: 'their features face to face' (*OLD praesens* 1, reinforcing *coram*), but also 'present to help' (*OLD* 3), which allows us to refer *ora* to their mouths.   **gelidus toto manabat corpore sudor**: for the sweat that accompanies the awakening from a vivid dream, cf. Turnus after his sleeping encounter with Allecto at 7.458–9: *ossaque et artus | perfundit toto proruptus corpore sudor* ('sweat bursting out from his whole body drenches his bones and limbs'). Here it seems to provide evidence to Aeneas that his vision was real. Macrobius (*Sat.* 6.1.50) notes that V. is imitating Ennius here: *Ann.* 417 Skutsch *tunc timido manat ex omni corpore sudor*, 'then sweat seeps from all his fearful body' (unfortunately we know nothing of the context); the changes produce a silver* line, neatly ordered amid the confusion of waking.   **tendoque supinas | ad caelum...manus**: the standard gesture of prayer (as when we first see Aeneas at 1.93 *duplicis tendens ad sidera palmas*), addressed *ad caelum*, Servius suggests, to include Apollo (162) and Jupiter (171) as well as the Penates themselves.   **munera libo | intemerata focis**: 'I offer pure sacrifices at the hearth', but perhaps (given that *libare* is especially used of liquid dedications) 'I pour offerings of unmixed wine'. Servius (on 11.211) notes that the hearth is the 'altar of the Penates'. After the direct manifestation of the divine, 'unadulterated offerings' seem especially important, a point reinforced by the next phrase,   **perfecto laetus honore**, in which *perfecto* stresses the proper completion of the sacrifice (118 n.).

179-81 Anchisen: 82 n. **facio certum**: a verse equivalent of *certiorem facio* (which cannot fit into a dactylic* line). **ordine**: 'in order', implying 'in full detail'. **agnouit prolem ambiguam geminosque parentis**: his son has recognized the appearance of the Penates (173); Anchises in turn recognizes how he came to be misled: 'the uncertain line of descent and the double forefathers' (i.e. Teucer and Dardanus) is appropriately expressed through a hendiadys* that looks at the family tree from the bottom first and then the top. There is a model for this realization of the truth of a past prophecy at *Odyssey* 9.507-16, when Polyphemus recalls the words of the soothsayer Telemus about his blinding. **nouo ueterum deceptum errore locorum**: in trying to ascertain the 'ancient mother' of the Trojans, Anchises mistakenly lighted on the place where Teucer came from long ago rather than the similarly ancient origin of Dardanus. *nouo* ('recent') amplifies the extent of time past through the contrast with *ueterum*, and thus excuses his error.

182-8 Iliacis exercite fatis: Anchises' phrase (repeated at 5.725) condenses the opening lines of the poem, where Aeneas is described as coming from Troy, exiled through fate, and harried on land and sea (1.1-3: *Troiae... ab oris, fato profugus, et terris iactatus et alto*). Bowra (Harrison (ed.) 1990: 370) noted that *exercite* also has an implication of 'tested'; the phrase thus contributes to the sense of Aeneas as progressing Stoic hero. **sola mihi talis casus Cassandra canebat**: usually taken as 'Cassandra alone used to prophesy such events to me', but the order might encourage us to take *sola* with *mihi*: either 'alone to me' (which would explain the absence of such predictions elsewhere in the tradition) or 'only, I think, Cassandra', taking *mihi* as an ethic* dative (*Geo.* 1.45, 3.19; Cic. *Cat.* 2.10, *Mur.* 21, 74; Livy 2.29.12; Woodcock §66). Apollo gave Cassandra the gift of prophecy to seduce her, but when she refused him he added the proviso that she never be believed (2.247; Aeschylus, *Ag.* 1202-13); consequently the Trojans ignored her prognostications of doom for the city (187)—and, Anchises now realizes (**nunc repeto**), her talk of migration to Italy. *nunc repeto* also perhaps points to Cassandra's prophecies in Lycophron (West, *CQ* 33 (1983), 134-5). **haec generi <illam> portendere debita nostro**: 'that she foretells this was owed to us'. *debita* implies 'fated': cf. Aeneas' words at 6.66-7 *non indebita posco | regna meis fatis* ('I do not seek a kingdom not owed me by my fates'), 7.120 *salue, fatis mihi debita tellus* ('hail, land owed to me by the fates'). *haec* refers to the future in Italy revealed by the Penates, as the next clause quickly makes clear.   **saepe Hesperiam, saepe Itala regna uocare**: *uocare* ('to call on') and the anaphora* evoke the ecstatic mode of Cassandra's utterance. The names directly recall 163, 166.   **ad Hesperiae... litora... uates Cassandra**: he reflects in a chiastic* pattern on how easy it was to disbelieve Cassandra's words: it was not plausible that Trojans would emigrate to the west, and no one was impressed by Cassandra's prophecies then (unlike now: *nunc*, 184). For the imperfect subjunctives **crederet** and **moueret**, see G&L §258-9 ('past potential').   **cedamus Phoebo**: i.e. let us do as he wishes; cf. *Ecl.* 10.69 *omnia uincit Amor: et nos cedamus Amori* ('Love conquers all; let us too submit to the power of Love').   **moniti meliora sequamur**: *meliora* is the object of both the participle and the main verb: 'having been advised of a better course [*lit.* better things], let us pursuit it'. See *OLD* 1b for *moneo* + double accusative, including examples where a passive form with a personal subject retains a neuter accusative.

189-91 dicto paremus: cf. Aeneas' words in response to Mercury's second warning, at 4.577 *imperioque iterum paremus ouantes*.   **ouantes**: cf. *laetus*, 169.   **hanc quoque deserimus sedem**: *hanc quoque* brings out the repetitive theme of departure in the book. The point is reinforced by *uela damus* in 191: cf. 9 *dare... uela iubebat*. The Cretan episode ends as it began with participants in the Trojan War abandoning homes in Crete (121-3, esp. 122 *deserta litora*).   **paucisque relictis** implies the continued existence of the settlement that will become the city of Pergamum (133 n.). The Trojans will leave rather more of the party behind at Segesta in Sicily: 5.746-71.   **caua trabe**: 'on a hollow ship', singular for plural; *trabs*, literally 'beam', is used, as often (*OLD* 4), by synecdoche* for 'boat', as a thing made from timber.   **uastum... currimus aequor**: 'we run across the vast sea', accusative of extent, cf. 5.235 *aequora curro*.

192-208 *The Dark Storm*
The joy of escaping from the plague in Crete does not last long: the fleet is soon overwhelmed by the darkness of a thunderstorm. Though the surface of the sea turns into swollen rollers and lightning flashes repeatedly, it is the darkness that troubles them the most: having just learned their destination, for three days they can no longer be sure of their route, or even whether it is night or day. The weather thus rehearses the darkness that afflicts Odysseus' ships as they sail south of

Commentary: lines 192–208

the Peloponnese (*Od.* 9.67–81), and the Argonauts as they leave Crete, at Apollonius 4.1694–714 [N]. But whereas Apollo quickly answers Jason's prayers in the *Argonautica*, the Trojans will arrive at an island that turns out to be as hellish as the storm, and it will not be till 275 that Apollo appears.

192–5 postquam recalls the opening word of the book, and takes us on to a new episode (cf. 463, and the famous articulation of Book 4 by the tag *At regina* in verses 1, 296, 504). These lines are a close imitation of *Odyssey* 14.301–4 (cited by Macrobius, *Sat.* 5.3.3; 5.6.1 points to the imitation of the almost identical 12.403–6, with τὴν νῆσον, 'the island', for Κρήτην μέν):

> ἀλλ' ὅτε δὴ Κρήτην μὲν ἐλείπομεν, οὐδέ τις ἄλλη
> φαίνετο γαιάων, ἀλλ' οὐρανὸς ἠδὲ θάλασσα,
> δὴ τότε κυανέην νεφέλην ἔστησε Κρονίων
> νηὸς ὕπερ γλαφυρῆς, ἤχλυσε δὲ πόντος ὑπ' αὐτῆς.

When we left Crete, and no other lands were visible, but only sky and sea, then the son of Cronos [i.e. Zeus] set a dark blue cloud above the hollow ship, and the sea grew dark beneath it.

They recur in a slightly revised form at 5.8–11 (the changes are underlined):

> <u>ut pelagus</u> tenuere rates nec iam amplius <u>ulla</u>
> <u>occurrit tellus, maria</u> undique et undique <u>caelum,</u>
> <u>olli</u> caeruleus supra caput astitit imber
> noctem hiememque ferens, et inhorruit unda tenebris.

In that case, however, the shared wisdom and experience of Palinurus and Aeneas lead to a simple change of course: they head for Sicily, and helpful West Winds begin to blow. The repetition of the lines in almost the same form is itself an imitation of the Odyssean repetition. **nec iam...| apparent terrae**: the disappearance of land presages the disappearance of sky (198) and even sea (200). **caelum undique et undique pontus**: continuation of the *postquam* clause (as *tum* in 194 helps the reader to see); *apparet* e.g. is to be supplied. The chiastic* order throws emphasis on the first and last words (cf. Wills 1996: 392–3; Tibullus 1.1.78 *dites despiciam despiciamque famem*, 'riches I shall despise and I shall despise hunger') and symbolizes the way the fleet is surrounded by sky and sea. **mihi** (unemphatic, as usual, in second position) provides a possessive sense, which in this case obviously applies to *caput* ('over my head'). **caeruleus...imber**: 'a dark rain-storm'. *caeruleus* is found of clouds already at Cicero, *Aratea* fr. 33.204. The adjective was regularly applied to the sea (432 n.), evoking the dark blue reflection of the *caelum*, with which it is also frequently associated (e.g. Ennius, *Ann.* 54 Sk. *in caerula caeli*, Lucretius 1.1090), and from which the word derives (*OLD*). At *Geo.* 1.453 *caeruleus pluuiam denuntiat* V. links the colour with rain—when it is seen on the rising sun. In the darkness and the rain the distinctions between air and water disappear. **noctem...tenebris**: again the first and last words are emphasized, in this case reinforcing one another. *nox* recurs at 198, 201, 204, and the sense of elemental darkness is compounded by *caecis* (200), *caeca caligine* (203).

196–200 con**tinu**o **ue**n**ti uoluu**n**t mare**: though the winds make the sea roll, they play no other part in this storm, in contrast to their dominant role in Book 1 (81–6, 102–3, e.g.). The repetition of sounds in the first three words perhaps evokes the rolling pattern of the water. **magnaque surgunt | aequora**: 'and the surface of the sea rises big': *magna* is used predicatively*. *aequora*, though easily taken as a poetic plural*, may suggest the succession of billowing waves. **dispersi**: separation is a real danger for the group that hopes to set up a new city. Unlike in Book 1, however, they will all reach land together. **gurgite uasto**: an echo of 1.118, where shipwrecked sailors are swimming in 'the vast ocean'. Though *gurges* is not limited to its original sense of whirlpool (see Henry on 1.118 [his 122]), the phrase effectively combines desolation, elemental scale, and the threatening pull of the sea. **inuoluere diem nimbi et nox umida caelum | abstulit**: 'clouds enveloped the light of day and damp night took away the sky [i.e. removed the stars from sight]': read so, the two clauses convey different points, but we will shortly find (201–4) that day and night cannot be distinguished, while the clouds may be identified as the night they have brought (195) along with rain. The equation suggested by the chiastic* expression (verb–object–subject/subject–object–verb) adds to the apt sense of uncertainty. **ingeminant abruptis nubibus ignes**: 'there is repeated lightning as the clouds break apart': the repetition of sounds mimics the repetition of the lightning. Ancient meteorology explained lightning as caused by the bursting of clouds: Lucretius 2.214 *abrupti nubibus ignes* (reworked here), 6.173–203, Ovid, *Met.* 6.696 *exsiliantque cauis elisi nubibus ignes* ('and fires leap out squeezed from hollow clouds'), Pliny, *Nat.* 2.192. **excutimur cursu et caecis**

Commentary: lines 192–208 137

erramus in undis: an obvious source of despair when the fated destination has just been comprehended: cf. the Argonauts at Apollonius 4.1700–1 (**N**: their despair is increased by their closeness to home). However, the claim 'we are shaken off course' is not borne out by what follows, despite the repetition of *erramus* in 204; for though the Trojans are not able to see where they are headed, wind and water drive them in the wanted direction, south of the Peloponnese and towards Italy (Map 1); they thus avoid contact with potentially hostile Greek lands (e.g. Menelaus in Sparta, Nestor at Pylos). *erramus* is strikingly inert as the only active verb of which the Trojans are subject in the passage: so Hutchinson in Günther 2015: 271.

201–4 ipse...Palinurus: Aeneas' helmsman, here mentioned for the first time, and one of the most important minor figures in Book 3 (513, 562), and the poem as a whole: he is forced overboard by the god Somnus (Sleep) at the end of Book 5, and Aeneas meets his unburied ghost in a poignant scene in the underworld (6.337–83). *ipse* implies his prowess and experience (also hinted at in *meminisse*: see Fletcher 2014: 118–19) even for those who have not heard of him previously (i.e. both the Carthaginians in the audience, and the first-time reader).   **negat <se> discernere...nec meminisse uiae**: 'he says...that he does not distinguish...nor recall the route'. *nec* repeats (and does not invert) the negative implication in *negat*. There is some irony when our first knowledge of the helmsman has him unable to find his way—and the man who will fall overboard is seen *media...in unda*. Farrell (in Perkell 1999: 98) links Palinurus' incapacity with that of Anchises in leading them to Crete (99–117). V. is likely to be drawing on one of the Argonautic passages from Callimachus' *Aetia* (fr. 17, esp. 8–9 Harder), where a character (not identified in the fragment) cannot discern the Great Bear for Tiphys, the helmsman, to steer by.   **tris adeo**: *adeo* is used here (as at 7.629 *quinque adeo*) to strengthen the number it follows ('quite three days'): *OLD* 8c.   **incertos caeca caligine soles**: 'days made uncertain by the blinding darkness', accusative of time throughout which (matched by *totidem sine sidere noctes*). Word order shows that *caeca caligine* qualifies *incertos*. For *soles = dies*, see *OLD* 2c, *Ecl.* 9.51–2 *longos...condere soles* ('to make long days set'): a striking, but easily comprehensible, synecdoche*.

205–8 quarto...die: cf. the sequence at 27–37 *prima...rursus...tertia sed...*; *Odyssey* 5.388–92 'then for two nights and two days, Odysseus wandered on the water …; but when dawn brought the third day …'; and Palinurus' account of his vain effort to swim to safety, at 6.355–7 <u>tris</u> *Notus hibernas immensa per aequora noctes* | *uexit me uiolentus aqua; uix lumine* <u>quarto</u> | *prospexi Italiam* ('three winter's nights the violent South Wind carried me on the water across the boundless sea; on the fourth day I just managed to spy Italy'): *uix* emphasizes the feeling of delay there, as **tandem** does here.   **se attollere**: the reflexive form is used of the promontory Lacinia at 552, and of the Appennine mountain range at 12.703 (*se attollens pater Appenninus ad auras*).   **uisa**: just as one of the Sporades 'appeared' (ἐφαάνθη, 4.1711: **N**) to the Argonauts after their journey through the black storm (cf. 210).   **aperire procul montis ac uoluere fumum**: 'to reveal mountains far off and to billow out smoke'. To an optimist the smoke might suggest the domestic fires of human habitation (cf. *Od.* 9.167, 10.149–52), and the possibility of hospitality; rather it implies volcanic activity, a precursor of Etna *(caelum subtexere fumo*, 582; see 209 n.), and an exhalation from the underworld, as suits the hellish inhabitants (215, 252). *aperire* echoes Apollonius' use of ἀνέφηνεν ('revealed') in giving the etymology for the island name Anaphe when Apollo shines light on a mountain top to end the Argonauts' voyage through darkness (4.1717–18: **N**); but for the Trojans the revelation is a delusion (contrast 275).   **uela cadunt**: 'our sails droop' (*OLD cado* 7d): the wind stops blowing, so they quickly turn to their oars.   **remis insurgimus**: 560 n.: here too there is coincidence of íctus* and a̲ccent* in *insúrgimus* and the following feet.   **haúd móra, naútae | adnixi torquent**: an easy parataxis* (as at 548), which neatly expresses the absence of delay. For the unusual rhythm in the fifth foot, see Introduction, p. 49. The five spondees* of 208 may be expressive of the effort of rowing. **caerula uerrunt**: 'they sweep the dark blue waters'. *uerrere* is a common metaphor for rowing (290, 5.778, 6.320; as well as when this whole verse is repeated at 4.583; already at Ennius, *Ann.* 377 Sk.). The language particularly echoes early lines of Catullus 64 (7 <u>caerula</u> <u>uerrentes</u>…*aequora*; 13 <u>tortaque</u> <u>remigio</u> <u>spumis</u> *incanuit unda*, 'and the water, churned up by the oars, grew white with foam'): pointedly, for Catullus too begins to imitate Apollonius' *Argonautica* here (see e.g. Clare, *PCPhS* 42 (1996), 60–88). Even as we seem to have entered calmer waters, *caerula* maintains the language of the dark storm (cf. 194, 211 n.).

209–69 *The Harpies*
The Trojans have been saved from the storm, and they land on an island where there is the welcome sight of unshepherded cattle and

goats. But (as Aeneas' introduction of the episode warns us) when they kill some and try to eat, they are repeatedly attacked by the Harpies, a flock of bird-like monsters, one of whom eventually utters a dire prophecy. Anchises prays that the gods alleviate the foreseen disaster, and they hurriedly depart. Though one significant model here is *Odyssey* 12.260–419, the episode in which his hungry crew eat the Cattle of the Sun, nowhere in the poem is imitation of *Argonautica* more apparent (2.178–316 [**M**]: Phineus and the Harpies [212 n.]); see Nelis 32–8, and Harrison, *PLLS* 5 (1985), 147–62 for fuller discussion of Vergil's integration of these (and other) models.

209–13 seruatum: though Aeneas (here standing for the whole group) thinks he has been saved after the uncanny darkness of the storm, the land they have reached will prove no less frightening.   **excipiunt**: in comparison to the other ancient variant *accipiunt* ('welcome'), this is appropriately neutral in connotation ('receive'); contrast the instance at 5.40–1, where Acestes' warm welcome of the returning Trojans is shown by the accompanying phrases in *gaza laetus agresti | excipit* ('he receives us joyfully with rustic riches'). The enjambment* helps express the relief of delayed arrival.   **Strophadum ... Strophades**: the formality of the repetition marks the etymological point of the lines, which is brought out explicitly in *Graio ... nomine dictae*. *Strophadum* echoes the analogous genitive plural Σποράδων ('the Scattered Islands'), used of the group that includes Anaphe, where Apollo appears providing light to the Argonauts at Apollonius 4.1711 [**N**]. *Strophades* means 'the Turning Islands'; in Apollonius this is glossed* at 2.295–7 [**M(c)**]: what had previously been the 'Floating Islands' (Πλωταί) changed their name, because this is where the sons of Boreas 'turned' from their pursuit of the Harpies. Despite Apollonius' different explanation, the two names are obvious synonyms: the islands move and shift shape, presumably because they are volcanic (206 n.; and cf. Ovid's *portubus infidis*, *Met.* 13.710: **T(c)**). Against this background, **stant** is a significant choice of diction: like Delos (of which they are a hellish equivalent) the islands are now fixed, and so is their name.   **īnsŭlāe Ionio in magno**: the cretic* sequence of syllables in *īnsŭlāe* etc. exclude the noun from use in dactylic* poetry, except in the nominative singular (e.g. 3.104, 386, 692), or with some licence, here 'prosodic hiatus' or correption*, a frequent phenomenon in Homeric versification, but rare in Latin. Vergil regularly uses hiatus* in lines with a marked Greek element (Trappes-Lomax, *PCPhS* 50 (2004), 145–9) such as the names

Ionio here and in *sub Iliŏ alto* at 5.261. The 'Ionian Sea' lies between the Peloponnese and Sicily (see Map 3); *mari* is understood, hence the neuter form.   **dira Celaeno**: the chief Harpy, who will utter a grim prophecy at 247–57. *Celaeno* derives from κελαινός 'black', suited to the Harpies' original role as personifications* of storm-winds (*Odyssey* 1.241, 20.77–8, *Iliad* 16.150; cf. the names *Aello*, 'Whirlwind' and *Ocypete*, 'Swiftwing' at Hesiod, *Theog.* 267), but also used often of the underworld and its inhabitants: the Trojans have not yet fully escaped from the uncanny dark storm of 194–204. There are thirty-five instances of *dirus* in the whole poem, but Vergil harps on it in this short episode (228, 235, 256, 262; *dira Celaeno* again in Aeneas' brief recapitulation at 713); the word thus characterizes the ominous horror of the events on the Strophades, and of Celaeno in particular. Moreover, at 252 she describes herself as the 'greatest of the Furies', who are sometimes identified with the *Dirae* (262 n.).   **Phīnēĭă postquam | clausa domus**: an unusually obvious cross-reference to the tale told in Apollonius, *Argonautica* 2 [**M**]. Phineus is there a seer, punished by Zeus for revealing too much of his intention: he has lost his sight, and, every time he tries to eat, the Harpies descend on his home and destroy his meal. Two of the Argonauts, Zetes and Calaïs, sons of Boreas, the North Wind, chase off the Harpies, and only refrain from killing them when they receive an oath from Iris, messenger of Zeus, that they will not trouble Phineus again. He then makes a carefully limited prophecy about the Argo's journey to Colchis, including an encounter with the aggressive Birds of Ares (242 n.), and the unsleeping dragon the Argonauts will find guarding the Golden Fleece. Phineus is thus an important precursor of the theme of partial prophecy that is essential to this book, with its series of revelations, sometimes incomprehensible or misleading, not least the speech of Celaeno at 247–57; cf. also Helenus' speech at 374–462 (and esp. 377–80). As a blind man, Phineus implicitly continues the theme of darkness from the storm (197–204). At *Arg.* 2.284–99 [**M(c)**] the Strophades mark the end of the pursuit, as we have seen, but in that text the Harpies then take up residence on Crete (2.299, 434), which V. has used as an implicit link in the progress of the Trojans' voyage. As well as reprising the theme of belatedness from line 1, *postquam*, emphasized by its postponement* to line end, is the first of several markers of the imitation (cf. *priores*, 213): Aeneas' voyage comes after the Argo, and V.'s story after Apollonius.

214–18 tristius haud \<est\> illis monstrum: *tristis* ('gloomy', 'grim') is often used of the underworld and its inhabitants (e.g. 4.243 *Tartara*

Commentary: lines 209–69

tristia; 6.315 *nauita tristis*, of Charon; 6.438 *tristique palus inamabilis unda*, 'and the unlovely marsh with its dismal waters'), but it is also applied to 'harsh' smells and 'bitter' tastes (*OLD* 8), which may be relevant given the connexion of the Harpies with food and the smell they leave behind them. On *monstrum*, see 26 n.   **nec saeuior ulla | pestis et ira deum Stygiis sese extulit undis**: 'nor has any plague or manifestation of divine anger raised itself more savage from the waters of the Styx'. *ira* is rarely used for those who exact punishment as a result of anger (*ThLL ira* 365.76–81), but Valerius Flaccus imitates V. by applying it to the Harpies (4.428). V. again evokes both Allecto (*pestis* at 7.505, and 'to whom grim wars and exhibitions of anger…are a delight', 7.325–6 *cui tristia bella | iraeque…cordi*), and the *Dirae* (*pestes* at 12.845), whose name is derived from *deorum irae* according to Servius on 2.519 (Harrison, *PLLS* 5 (1985), 152).   **sese**: V. likes the reduplicated form of the reflexive, especially before vowels (also 345, 598). The elision contributes to the apt ugliness of the line with its five sibilants* in five syllables (<u>S</u>tygii<u>s s</u>e<u>s</u>(e) e<u>xt</u>-), two of them strengthened by the hard *t* following (as already in *pe<u>sti</u>s*).   **uirginei <sunt> <u>u</u>olucrum <u>u</u>ultus**: the verb 'to be' has to be supplied in each clause of the sentence, as often happens in the brief encapsulation when figures are introduced, e.g. 593–5 (Achaemenides), and 426–8 *<u>p</u>rima hominis facies et <u>p</u>ulchro <u>p</u>ectore uirgo | <u>p</u>ube tenus, <u>p</u>ostrema…<u>p</u>istrix*, of the similarly monstrous Scylla, also described with emphatic alliteration. Another group of monsters depicted with the faces of maidens and the bodies of birds are the Sirens ('they were partly like birds, and partly like maidens to look at', Ap. *Arg.* 4.898–9); unlike Odysseus and the Argonauts, Aeneas will only hear a broken echo of their voices (556). **foedissima uentris | proluuies**: though epic does not use words like *cacare* (cf. Cat. 36.1 *cacata charta*, 'shitty sheets' on the *Annales* of Volusius, presumably a hexameter poem), or *merda* (Horace, *Satires* 1.8.37), and even *stercus*, favoured word of the agricultural writers, appears in verse only at Lucretius 2.872, Horace, *Epod.* 12.11, and occasionally later, V. exploits the ingrained human distaste for excrement. The picture here and in the encounter itself (225–46) is a frightening mixture of realism and mythological fantasy. The Harpies are both malevolent spirits from the underworld, with human faces and voices, and a frighteningly persistent flock of hungry and aggressive seabirds, whose attacks spoil the food they do not take themselves (227, 244).   **uncae…manus**: the phrase, reminiscent of χερσὶν ἁρπάγοις ('snatching hands', cited from Sophocles, *Phineus*, fr. 706

Radt), evokes the predatory nature of the Harpies: V. has it twice of human hands 'hooked' to grasp or pick something (6.360; *Geo.* 2.365–6), but the adjective is more commonly applied to the clawed feet of birds, notably at 233 *pedibus circumuolat uncis* (at 5.255, 9.564, 11.723, 12.250 of eagles or hawks seizing prey).   **pallida semper | ora fame**: 'faces ever pale with hunger'. *pallidus* is another epithet regularly used of the inhabitants of the underworld (cf. 1.354 [**P**]; 8.244–5 *regna…pallida*; *Geo.* 1.277 *pallidus Orcus*; 3.551–2 *Stygiis emissa tenebris | pallida Tisiphone*). *semper* evokes the Harpies' eternal nature; and *fame* resumes their link with food (252 n.). On the 'half-line', see Introduction, p. 51.

219–24 huc marks the return from the ecphrasis* of 210–18 to the narrated action.   **ecce**: though V. occasionally varies his usual placement (the start of the line), this is the only time he puts *ecce* at the end. The effect of this counter-enjambment* is a striking redirection of attention away from the calm entry into port—but not to the Harpies, rather to the delightful sight of unguarded herds of cattle and goats. However, there is an ominous note even to this, for the scene recalls Thrinacia, the island on which the cattle and sheep of the Sun, Helios, are pastured in the *Odyssey* (11.108, 12.128–9, 265–6). Despite the warnings of Tiresias and Circe, Odysseus' companions force him to land, and, when contrary winds maroon them for a month, in their hunger and desperation, while he sleeps, they sacrifice and eat some of the cattle. Zeus responds to Helios' anger by sending a storm that destroys all of the crew bar Odysseus. Vergil imitates the *Odyssey* by placing this evocation of Helios' cattle between a storm and a prophecy related to the killing of the cattle (Horsfall on 192–208); but the Trojans do not break a direct injunction and their storm comes first, and is simply unpleasant, not fatal.   **laeta**: 'thriving'. The echo of *ubere laeto* (95) might briefly suggest that the Trojans have found a potential home.   **caprigenumque pecus nullo custode per herbas**: a playful variation on a line from Cicero's version of the Hellenistic* poet Aratus (*Prognostica* fr. 6.1 = Arat. 1098), *caprigeni pecoris custos de gurgite uasto*: whereas Cicero speaks of the 'guardian of his goat-born flocks', V.'s flock has no herdsman (the potentially pastoral moment is averted); *per herbas* may also correct 'from the vast sea' (though we know from the Aratean context that that phrase applied to sea-birds).   **inruimus ferro**: after the famine on Crete (138–42) and the privations of the storm the Trojans are keen to eat, and religious observance for once comes second, almost as an afterthought. But the phrasing suggests the violence of marauders, and for a moment we get an alternative glimpse of the Trojans as an aggressive invading force: cf. 2.757 *inruerant Danai* (of the Greeks entering Aeneas' house), Ilioneus' denial of such purposes to Dido at 1.527-8 *non nos aut ferro Libycos populare penatis | uenimus, aut raptas ad litora uertere praedas* ('we have not come either to pillage Libyan homes or to snatch booty and take it back to the shore'), or the accusations of Juno at 10.77-8 *quid… Troianos uim ferre Latinis… atque auertere praedas?* ('what of the fact that the Trojans inflict violence on the Latins… and take away booty?'); and Putnam 1995: 53-5.   **diuos ipsumque uocamus… Iouem**: 'we call on the gods, and especially Jupiter himself': Jupiter is likewise picked out, amid a larger group of deities, at 19-21.   **in partem praedamque**: 'to take a share in the prey': hendiadys*. *praeda* means 'prey' as well as 'booty' (*OLD* 2, 1); the choice of word, reinforced by repetition at 233, 244, helps maintain the aggressive tone visible in 222. When the equivalent Greek word ἑλώριον occurs at *Arg.* 2.264, it is used of the food that is 'booty' for the Harpies.   **toros**: as usual V. conceives of dining as something done lying down; cf. 1.214 *fusique per herbam*, when the Trojans eat the deer killed by Aeneas after the storm. Tables are part of the equipment of the feast there (1.216), as again here (231, where it slyly looks ahead to the climactic word of Celaeno's speech, 257).

225-8 at subit(ae) horrifico lapsu: the positive delights of the feast are suddenly interrupted with another swift and horrific descent of mood, emphasized by the brutal elision.   **Hārpȳīae**: the enjambment* gives an element of suspense as the creatures arrive. The meaning of the name is implied by the etymological gloss* *diripiunt*, placed immediately below: the verb is the Latin equivalent of ἥρπαζον ('they snatched') at Ap. *Arg.* 2.189 [**M(a)**]; Ἅρπυιαι ('Harpies'/ 'Snatchers') starts the previous line. *diripiunt* may add a play on the Harpies' alternative name *Dirae* (211 n., and cf. 228).   **contactuque omnia foedant | immundo; tum <*est*> uox taetrum dira inter odorem**: along with the interruption of the feasting and the destruction of the food, there is a simultaneous assault on all the other senses (carrying on from the mainly visual description in 216-18, and *clangoribus* in 226). The emphatic enjambment* of *immundo* and the heaping up of pejorative* adjectives stress the inevitable disgust the Trojans feel; for the smell, cf. Apollonius

2.191–2, 229, 272 [**M**]. *tum* is best understood as 'in addition' here (*OLD* 9).

229–33 rursum in secessu longo sub rupe cauata: the Trojans at first treat this like the attack of a flock of seagulls, unpleasant but not ominous: they have presumably not noticed the maidenly faces or understood the *uox* as making intelligible utterances. They thus try again, sensibly retreating under an overhang for protection. *rursum*, repeated at 232, marks the revisiting of both Apollonius' Harpy episode, and the narrative pattern of 24–46 (n.b. 31 *rursus*), where Aeneas fails twice to understand the significant horror of what is happening, and it takes a third attempt to produce an explanatory voice. At 1.310–12, Aeneas makes sure the fleet is hidden away before he sets off to explore the north African coast:

> classem in conuexo nemorum sub rupe cauata
> arboribus clausam circum atque horrentibus umbris
> occulit.

He conceals the fleet in a bowl amid the woods, under a hollowed out crag, encircled by woods and shivering shadows.

The recurrence of the phrase *sub rupe cauata* in 229 provoked a reader or scribe to add 1.311 to this context too (cf. 8.46, based on 3.393; 10.278 = 9.127; the medieval MSS provide other examples), and the canonical numeration includes it as 230, even though it must be interpolated* (as the great Vergilian editor Ribbeck saw):

> rursum in secessu longo sub rupe cauata
> arboribus clausam circum atque horrentibus umbris   230
> instruimus mensas arisque reponimus ignem.

This is shown by the presence of *clausam* in MP, the two antique manuscripts available here, as well as some of the ninth-century copies; for *clausam* has no grammatical reference, and must be drawn from 1.311, where it belongs with *classem*. The tradition offers the variants *clausa* (supposedly with *rupe*—but that already has the epithet *cauata*) and *clausi* (in agreement with the first-person plural subject—but for a personal object the verb would not be idiomatic with the sense 'surrounded', rather than 'shut in'): these too are interpolations*, vain attempts by readers to integrate the intrusive verse. **caecisque latebris**: still the Trojans cannot see what is happening to them (212 n.). We might wonder whether the Harpies are coming from the sky (*ex diuerso caeli*), the woods (258), or from the underworld

(215).   **turba sonans** recalls the noise of 226 (*clangoribus*) and 228 (*uox*), and introduces the explicit notion of disorder.   **praedam**: cf. 223.   **uncis**: cf. 217.

234-7 arma capessant: V. quite often omits *ut* when expressing indirect commands, here (as at 10.258) after the magisterial *edico* (*OLD* 1b), which then introduces an indirect statement in the following line that is given jussive* force by the presence of the gerundive. *arma* reprises the first word of the poem, in an order from Aeneas, the man from 1.1; but here arms will prove useless.   **<u>bellum cum gente gerendum</u>**: the formality of the language, enhanced by the incantatory repetitions, associates this skirmish with war more generally, and especially that which the Trojans will fight in Italy: *bella gerenda* is used in the warnings of Anchises to Aeneas (6.890) and by Turnus at 7.444.   **haud secus ac iussi faciunt**: in this moment of crisis the obedient Trojans are model citizens (as again at 561).   **scuta latentia condunt**: 'they stow their shields so they are concealed', a proleptic* use of the participle.

238-41 dedere: even though in seventeen occurrences out of eighteen he places *dedere* at line end (where the choice is metrically indifferent), V. never uses the form *dederunt*.   **dat signum** responds to *sonitum...dedere* like the trumpet blast of one army answering that of another; cf. *signum* of Allecto's trumpet blast at 7.513, 519, which marks the beginning of the skirmish between Latins and Trojans, repeated at 8.1 when the conflict has extended to Turnus' Rutulians and other local tribes, as well as in the resumption of battle at 11.474 *dat signum*.   **Misenus**: V. has Aeneas introduce a figure who will be important in Book 6, where his pride in his playing of the trumpet leads him to challenge the sea-god Triton, whose power makes him fall fatally on the rocks (6.164-74); it is while purifying himself by organizing Misenus' funeral that Aeneas comes upon the Golden Bough that enables him to visit the underworld unscathed (6.183-235). (Cf. the introduction of the helmsman Palinurus at 202.)   **inuadunt**: again Aeneas uses aggressive language of his men's actions: this is an attack, not merely self-defence; cf. the use of the verb of the Greeks in Troy, at 2.265 *inuadunt urbem*, 414; and of the Rutulians attacking the Trojan camp at 9.147, 567.   **noua proelia temptant**: though this is a 'strange' form of conflict (*OLD nouus* 2), and new for the Trojans, the epithet invites the contrary reader to notice that the deployment of swords against Harpies was a feature of the Boreads' pursuit at *Arg.* 2.273–85. Like *edico* at 235, *temptant* is used with two different constructions, first the substantival* object, and then an infinitive in apposition, explaining how the battles—with birds, not Greeks—are new.   **foedare**: 'to mutilate' (*OLD* 3), but equating the Trojans to the 'polluting' Harpies (216, 227, 244): so Panoussi 2009: 86–7.   **obscenas pelagi … uolucris**: 'repulsive birds of the sea': the adjective implies ill omen, but also what should not appear on stage (*ob-scaenus*: cf. Varro, *Ling. Lat.* 7.96)—or in epic; it thus encourages us to think of the birds' excrement. *pelagi* fits the accounts according to which the Harpies were descended from Pontos or Neptune (Hesiod, *Theogony* 265–9; Servius); but the realistic element seems as important here—for a final time Aeneas presents them as a flock of seabirds such as one might in reality encounter on an uninhabited island.

242–4 sed neque uim plumis ullam nec uulnera tergo | accipiunt: the delusion is quickly exposed—there is nothing natural here: parallels for such invulnerability can be found in the Earth-born Antaeus, whom Hercules has to hold away from the earth to crush (Ovid, *Ibis* 393–5; Lucan 4.589–655), and Talos, the bronze giant of Crete killed by Medea's witchcraft (*Arg.* 4.1638–89); the Stymphalian Birds, dealt with in one of Hercules' Labours, are sometimes represented as having metal feathers; so too those encountered by the Argonauts in the Black Sea (Apollonius 2.1047–88). But the Trojans do not have to defeat these monsters—departure and prayer will achieve their purpose—so a closer analogy may lie in the personifications* Aeneas encounters at the entrance to the underworld (6.290–4): they are mere shapes without body; though he draws his sword, the Sibyl warns him it is useless, and his *pietas* allows him to pass them by. Latin poets are happy to match *neque* with *nec* (e.g. 2.197, 8.316, 11.70, 12.903); and they prefer to use *neque* after an opening monosyllable in order to secure a dactyl* in the first foot of the line: of the thirty-four times V. uses *neque* before a consonant in Mynors' OCT, fourteen are at 1s; whereas he has the far commoner *nec* only twice in this position.   **celerique fuga sub sidera lapsae**: 'and flying away with a swift escape up to the stars'. *sidera* (cf. *Arg.* 2.300 [**M(c)**]) gives an elemental note, before the next verse returns us to the mundane horrors they leave behind—half-eaten food and excrement.

245–6 una … Celaeno: 'one <of them>, Celaeno' or 'Celaeno alone': *una* focuses attention on the speaker as *unus* does at 716. Her perch on a rock is natural for a bird, and suited to her address of the people. Williams brings out the appropriateness of the slowing spondees* in this and the next line to introduce Celaeno's 'grim prophecy'.   **infelix uates** recalls Agamemnon's μάντι κακῶν at *Iliad* 1.106 (of Calchas), but whereas that means 'seer of miseries', the application of *infelix* to Celaeno evokes the greater range of misfortune involved in encountering the Harpies.   **rumpit...hanc pectore uocem**: 'she belches this speech from her chest'; see *OLD rumpo* 5b for the transitive use to describe speech, developed by V. (see Austin on 2.129). The violence of the utterance is likewise stressed at 11.376–7 *exarsit...uiolentia Turni;* | *dat gemitum rumpitque has imo pectore uoces* ('the violence of Turnus blazed up; he gives a groan and brings up these words from the depths of his chest').

247–9 bellum etiam pro caede boum stratisque iuuencis: 'Is there war too to promote' (*OLD* 4; or perhaps, with an ironical twist, 'in return for': *OLD* 10) 'the slaughter of cattle and the killing of steers.' We have punctuated this as a separate sentence, rather than a mere anticipation of *bellumne inferre paratis* in 248, partly because *est* is easily supplied and the sense feels complete in an unpunctuated text; but also because it brings out the reputation of the Trojans as aggressors. Paris stole Helen (and property: *Iliad* 3.70) from Menelaus, and the people fought to protect what he had taken; now they are fighting over the cattle they have killed though they did not own them: cf. the wounding of Silvia's stag by Ascanius, which is the immediate cause of conflict between Trojans and Latins (7.475–510). The next question also looks ahead.   **Laomedontiadae**: 'people of Laomedon', the father of Priam. Because of Laomedon's breaking of his promises to reward Apollo and Poseidon for building the walls of Troy (*Iliad* 21.441–52; Horace, *Odes* 3.3.21–2) and Hercules for killing a sea-monster (Hyginus, *Fab.* 89.3–5), he is used by V. as a symbol of Troy in contexts where lying or punishment is in mind, e.g. at 4.542 *Laomedonteae...periuria gentis*, and *Geo.* 1.501–2 *satis iam pridem sanguine nostro* | *Laomedonteae luimus periuria Troiae* ('we [i.e. the Romans] have long now paid enough with our blood for the perjuries of Laomedon's Troy').   **bellumne inferre paratis**: similar phrasing recurs in the second half of the poem to describe Trojan (11.250: the envoys reveal to Diomedes *qui bellum intulerint*), and Roman aggression (7.604 *Getis inferre manu lacrimabile bellum* |...*parant*: the Gates of War are opened when 'they prepare to carry tear-bringing war with force against the Getae'). Wills (1996: 64) notes too the echo of *bellum…bellum* in the Sibyl's prophetic speech at 6.86 *bella, horrida bella*, which reflects the way that Celaeno figures the current attack as a precursor to the invasion of Italy (cf. 222–3). **patrio Harpyias insontis pellere regno**: *patrio* ('ancestral') is a tendentious claim, given that in Apollonius (2.284–300: **M(c)**) the Harpies' association with the Strophades is the accidental end of their chase by the sons of Boreas (Hyginus, *Fab*. 14.18 follows V.). Again V. seems to look ahead: Celaeno's words foreshadow the Rutulian reaction to the coming of the Trojans to Latium, as expressed at 12.236–7 *nos patria amissa dominis parere superbis | cogemur, qui nunc lenti consedimus aruis* ('when our homeland is lost we shall be forced to obey haughty masters, we who are now settled peacefully in our fields'): cf. p. 6.

250–4 accipite ergo animis atque haec mea figite dicta: *ergo* is normally first word in its clause—forty-seven out of fifty-five times in V.—but occasionally he places it second, third, or even fourth (6.456). Both *animis* and *haec mea dicta* are to be taken ἀπὸ κοινοῦ*, i.e. in both clauses. The importance of the announcement is conveyed by the formal insistence on attention, as when the same line is repeated by Jupiter requiring divine non-interference in the battle (10.104: see Harrison *ad loc*. for further parallels). **Phoebo pater omnipotens, mihi Phoebus Apollo**: cf. Ap. *Arg*. 2.180–2 [**M(a)**], where it is Apollo who has granted the power of prophecy to Phineus and Zeus who is concerned to limit what may be foretold. Macrobius, *Sat*. 5.22.11–14 finds a source in two passages of Aeschylus (*Eum*. 19, fr. 86 *TrGF*) for the notion 'that Apollo prophesies what Jupiter has said to him'. V. may hint at versions in which the oracle of Zeus at Dodona (Varro, cited by Servius on 256) or Cassandra, taught by Apollo, is the source of the prophecy Celaeno utters. **Furiarum ego maxima**: confirmation that Celaeno is a chthonic* power, this is recalled at 6.605–6, in the Sibyl's account of the punishments in Tartarus: *Furiarum maxima iuxta | accubat et manibus prohibet contingere mensas* ('the greatest of the Furies lies nearby and prevents them touching the tables with their hands'), an activity that corresponds both to the Harpies' repeated disruption of the Trojans' meal and to the punishing hunger she prophesies. See Panoussi 2009: 83–90 for further discussion of the equation. **Italiam cursu petitis, uentisque uocatis | ibitis Italiam**: 'Italy you seek on your voyage, and with the winds you have summoned you will reach Italy.' After *ibitis*, *Italiam* is accusative of motion towards, imitating archaic* usage with the names of countries (see Penney in Adams & Mayer 1999: 261). Modern editors generally put a strong stop after *uentisque uocatis*, but the phrase extends the previous clause awkwardly, as it does not form a proper pair with *cursu*. With punctuation after *petitis* the two clauses are balanced; and *uocatis* is echoed at 395 *aderitque uocatus Apollo* in a matching announcement of Trojan success. In displaying knowledge of the winds, Celaeno perhaps evokes the Harpies' old Greek identity as wind deities (211 n.). Mention of Italy confirms the prophecy of the Penates (166), and establishes the speaker's reliability before the grim revelation that follows.

255–8 'But you shall not be granted a city and surround it with walls until terrible hunger and the harm done in slaughtering us forces you to gnaw your tables and eat them up.' As people do not eat tables, this might be taken as an *adynaton**: the city will never be founded (cf. the witches' apparition at *Macbeth* IV.i.91–3 'Macbeth shall never vanquished be, until | Great Birnam Wood to high Dunsinane Hill | Shall come against him', and Macbeth's response 'That will never be.'). Read so, these lines and the phrasing of 254 may help explain how Dido (and perhaps even Aeneas) come to believe that the Trojans are not fated to wall a city in Italy: they reach Italy and enter a port, at 521–47; but if they are never to be given their own city, why not stay in Carthage? Alternatively the lines might function as a prophecy of hunger so grim that the foundation will be a goal reached only with regret. However, the omen turns out to be a riddle with a paradoxical solution (266 n.), such as is common in stories of city foundations (Horsfall, *Vergilius* 35 (1989), 11–13). The omen is a traditional part of the Aeneas legend, mentioned by Cassandra at Lycophron 1250–2 'There he will find a food-laden table, which will be eaten later by his companions; this will remind him of old oracles' (Hornblower's translation), Varro (cited by Servius), Dionysius Hal. *Rom.* 1.55, Strabo 13.1.53. Attributing the prophecy to Celaeno is apparently a Vergilian innovation, and one that adds to the dread as well as exploiting the Harpies' association with hunger. **non ante...quam**: the standard Latin way of expressing 'not until'. *āntĕquām* has to be separated into its constituent parts in dactylic* verse, as it sometimes is in prose. **nostraeque iniuria caedis**: genitive of definition, explaining what the injury consists in (Woodcock §72.5); cf. 1.27 *spretaeque iniuria formae* ('the wrong done by the spurning of <Juno's> beauty'). Celaeno seems to collapse into one offence the killing of the cattle (*caede boum*, 247) and the assault on the Harpies themselves (241; but note 242-3).   **subigat**: the subjunctive is prospective (cf. 384-7, and Cat. 64.188-91), but perhaps also helps distance the hypothetical possibility, as in other *adynata**, e.g. *Ecl.* 1.59-63 (for other examples see H. V. Canter, 'The figure ἀδύνατον in Greek and Latin poetry', *AJPh* 51 (1930), 32-41, esp. 33-4).   **malis absumere mensas**: 'with your jaws to consume tables': the horrifying surprise is kept to the climactic final word. The addition of *malis* stresses the physical consumption of the tables (as at *Geo.* 3.268, where the mares of Glaucus 'consumed his limbs with their jaws', *malis membra absumpsere*). The word recurs at 7.114 when the omen is fulfilled (see on 265).   **in siluam pennis ablata refugit**: monstrous as her prophecy is, as Celaeno departs, she becomes a bird once more, flying off into the trees; the flying departure is like that of Iris at *Argonautica* 2.300, after her oath to the Boreads.

259-62 at sociis subita gelidus formidine sanguis | deriguit: in the Polydorus episode, it was Aeneas himself whose blood was frozen by the horror (*gelidusque coit formidine sanguis*, 30); here the whole group is affected.   **nec iam amplius armis, | sed uotis precibusque iubent exposcere pacem**: 'and now no more with arms, but with vows and prayers they bid us entreat peace': the Trojans see that not fighting, but religion is appropriate for dealing with such a *monstrum*, and the phrasing they use is almost a religious formula*: cf. 370, 4.56-7 *pacemque per aras | exquirunt*, Livy 1.16.3 *pacem precibus exposcunt* (and Ogilvie *ad loc.*). The sentence provides an instance of zeugma*: the sense shifts after *armis*, which are not normally used when requesting peace. Servius suggests that we supply *usi sunt* in the first clause, Williams *petere salutem*; but the sense is clear and a decision is not needed.   **siue deae seu sint dirae**: a complex play on the identity of the Harpies. *dirae* will turn out to be an epithet joined to *uolucres* and matching *obscenae*; but first, in its opening syllable, it hints at the prayer formula* *si deus, si dea es* (Cato, *Agr.* 139, and the discussion by Hickson 1993: 41-3). However, *Dirae* ('the Dread Ones' or 'Curses') is also an alternative name for the Furies (4.473, 610; 7.324, and Horsfall *ad loc.*), or for related powers who assist Jupiter and presage disaster (Tarrant on 12.845-52; n.b. *obscenae uolucres* at 12.876); and it is used as a name for the Harpies in Valerius Flaccus' account of the Phineus episode (*Arg.* 4.423-636) at 586 *saeuae... Dirae*. There is a similar effect at 1.293, where the *Dirae* seem to be the negative images of disorder, opposed to *Fides et Vesta*, and 'shut in by tight-fitting iron constructions' (*ferro et compagibus artis | claudentur*)—and then the words *Belli portae* are added, and *dirae* becomes an adjective ('grim gates of War'); see also 211, 215 nn. The sentence thus suggests as alternatives to 'goddesses' that they may be gods, or infernal deities—or unpleasant sea-birds. But as Servius notes, birds were habitually seen as conveyers of omens in the ancient world, to such an extent that in both Greek (Aristophanes, *Birds* 719-21, and N. Dunbar (Oxford, 1995), *ad loc.*) and Latin (*OLD auis* 3b) 'bird' can be used to mean 'portent'. *sint* marks the conditional clause as part of the indirect speech, after *iubent*.

263-6 pater Anchises: Aeneas has taken the lead at 234-7 in mistakenly ordering the use of arms, so it is appropriate that Anchises takes the lead in praying now, though leadership and religious activity are each split between the two of them over the book as a whole (see Introduction, pp. 41-2): one might compare the Cretan episode, where it is Aeneas who has the dream of the Penates that corrects Anchises' misinterpretation of Apollo's oracle. **passis...palmis**: the usual gesture in prayer, as when Aeneas supplicates the gods in the storm at 1.93 *duplicis tendens ad sidera palmas* ('stretching both hands towards the stars') or at 2.688 *caelo palmas cum uoce tetendit*, when Anchises thanks Jupiter for the omen that signified approval for departure from Troy. Though V. nowhere else has *palmas pandere*, he uses the verb of spreading wings (*Geo.* 1.398) and sails (520). **numina magna uocat**: the appeal is not to the Harpies themselves, but to the Olympians in general (*di...di*, 265), especially Jupiter and Apollo, whose words have been conveyed (251-2), and who both appear in the next paragraph (275, 279); in offering encouragement in the face of Celaeno's threat at 394-5 Helenus mentions the invocation of Apollo in particular. **meritosque indicit honores**: in this moment of crisis there is no lingering to make sacrifice (delayed till 279-88, and then 7.120-47), and Aeneas conveys the hurry in his narrative by not repeating his father's formal vows, but simply indicating that they were made: contrast the sacrifices actually performed on departure from Crete at 118 *meritos aris mactauit honores*. Here Servius glosses* *meritos* with *congruos* 'suitable', but it is hard to exclude the sense 'deserved', whether that is read as a conditional use ('if deserved') or an anticipation that the prayers will be successful—as indeed they will. **placidi** is effectively part of the imperative: 'be mild'. The close association of *placidus* and *pax* (e.g. 1.249, 7.46, 8.325; Cicero, *Tusc. Disp.* 5.48; Lucretius 1.40, 5.1154–5, 6.73) links this to *exposcere pacem* in 261, so that it becomes a ritual request for the *pax deorum*, the peaceful and supportive relationship that the Romans sought with their divinities (see 370, and e.g. Oakley on Livy 6.1.12 *neque inuenta pace deum*, 'not having found the gods' blessing'); contrast the *ira deum* of 215.   **seruate pios**: 'save those who honour you', i.e. by letting them build a city and not undergo the threatened famine. *pios* economically reminds the god of what those praying have done in the past to earn favour; cf. Turnus' prayer to Faunus and Earth at 12.777–8, *colui uestros si semper honores* ('if I have consistently honoured your rites'), 6.529–30; and Chryses' prayer to Apollo at *Iliad* 1.39–41 'if ever I have roofed over a fine temple for you, or burnt the fat thighs of bulls or goats, fulfil this prayer of mine'. Servius compares 7.21, where Neptune ensures that the *pii Troes* sail safely past Circe's island. See Akbar Khan, *Prometheus* 22 (1996), 131–44 for further discussion of Trojan piety here. Anchises' prayer will prove efficacious (cf. Helenus at 394–5): though Celaeno's threats come true, Jupiter (7.110) ensures it is achieved through a temporary shortage of wheat, and a joke by Ascanius (7.116 *heus, etiam mensas consumimus?* 'hey, are we eating our tables too?') when the Trojan leaders eat the flatbreads on which they have spread their food soon after arrival in Latium. Aeneas immediately spots the fulfilment of the omen and recognizes that they have found their *patria* (122). He attributes the prophecy to Anchises himself, with no mention of the Harpies. This silence seems odd, and might be regarded as a symptom of the poem's lack of finish or a deliberate inconsistency, but some interpretations give it thematic or narrative coherence: Harrison (*PLLS* 5 (1985), 158–62) sees a pointed removal of sinister associations (365, *dictu nefas*); and West (*CQ* 33 (1983), 133–4) points out that Anchises could have received such oracles from Cassandra (182–7). Horsfall on 7.107–47 has further discussion and references.

266–9 litore funem | deripere excussosque iubet laxare rudentis: both *deripere* ('tear away') and *excussos* ('shaken out') have a hint of violence to them that helps convey the urgency of Anchises' instructions for departure and the voyage. *funem* refers to the cable that secures the ships to the shore, *rudentis* to the brails that bind the sail to the yard (so Horsfall) or the sheets that control the setting of the sail: in either case they will be running before the wind.   **qua cursum uentusque gubernatorque uocabat**: no immediate destination having been announced, they sail at

Commentary: lines 270–93 153

the whim of the weather and the guidance of the helmsman; fortunately South Winds are blowing (268) and they head north. Macrobius, *Sat.* 5.6.3 notes the imitation of *Odyssey* 11.10 (= 12.152) τὴν δ'ἄνεμός τε κυβερνήτης τ'ἴθυνε ('wind and helmsman guided the ship'), which is marked not only by the sense, and by the use of a singular verb with two singular subjects, but also by the rhythm, with the lack of strong caesura in the third or fourth foot (unusual in Latin, common in Greek). From 202 the helmsman of Aeneas' boat is known to be Palinurus; his guiding hand and the use of *gubernator* looks ahead to his thematically significant role in Book 5 (n.b. 12, 859; revisited at 6.337, 349); though he will be lost overboard, Aeneas takes over competently (5.867–8), unlike Gyas when he angrily throws his cautious helmsman Menoetes overboard during the ship-race (5.159–82, 223–4).

270–93 *Actium and the west coast of Greece*
The fleet heads north up the coast of Greece, past the Ionian Islands (Map 3), including Ithaca, home of Odysseus, the Greek leader who had travelled furthest to reach Troy. Beyond that the Trojans feel that they have escaped their enemies. They cleanse themselves from the pollution of the encounter with the Harpies and offer sacrifices to Jupiter: after tension and chaos comes the relaxed activity of civilized peoples, first with games at Actium—Aeneas anticipates the commemoration of Augustus' naval victory of 31 BC, a victory that will be depicted on the shield made for Aeneas by Vulcan (8.675–708: **R**). (The equivalent chapter in Dionysius of Halicarnassus (*Rom.* 1.50) tells of stops on Zacynthus, at Leucas, Actium, and Ambracia; in each case they establish a temple for Aphrodite, with games too on Zacynthus. V. shifts material to give a new aetiological* focus.) Then, at the end of a winter spent in this geographically perplexing safe haven, Aeneas dedicates a shield he had taken from a Greek warrior, and they continue north, eventually arriving at Buthrotum, now Butrint in Albania. While marking progress on the voyage and the passage of time, the section continues the weaving together of Odyssean (270–3) and Argonautic (275–83) material, and takes us from the horrific mythical world of the Harpies to the Actium of Vergil's own day. There are some remarkable moments of Trojan self-assertion: they hold their own games (reminiscent of the Panhellenic Games, such as the Olympics, or those held by Achilles in *Iliad* 23), and Aeneas dedicates a shield with an inscription that both acknowledges and questions the totality of Greek victory (286–8).

270–3 In his account of the Ionian Islands, V. begins with Zacynthos and ends with Ithaca, and its kings Laertes and Odysseus, thus inverting the order of material in the lines with which Odysseus finally reveals himself to the Phaeacian court (*Od.* 9.19–24):

> εἴμ᾽ Ὀδυσεὺς Λαερτιάδης, ὅς πᾶσι δόλοισιν
> ἀνθρώποισι μέλω, καί μευ κλέος οὐρανὸν ἵκει.   20
> ναιετάω δ᾽ Ἰθάκην εὐδείελον· ἐν δ᾽ ὄρος αὐτῇ
> Νήριτον εἰνοσίφυλλον, ἀριπρεπές· ἀμφὶ δὲ νῆσοι
> πολλαὶ ναιετάουσι μάλα σχεδὸν ἀλλήλῃσι,
> Δουλίχιόν τε Σάμη τε καὶ ὑλήεσσα Ζάκυνθος.

I am Odysseus, son of Laertes, who am well known to men for all kinds of tricks, and my fame has reached heaven. I dwell in far-visible Ithaca; on it there is a conspicuous mountain, Neritum where the leaves quiver, and round it are many islands very close to one another, Dulichium and Same and wooded Zacynthos.

For Aeneas the culmination (273) is a curse, far from the Homeric hero's proud self-identification. Ovid has a similar list for the journey of his Aeneas (*Met.* 13.711–12: **T(c)**).   **apparet** perhaps echoes Odysseus' insistence on visibility in his account of his home.   **nemorosa Zacynthos** exactly matches the sense of the line-ending in *Od.* 9.24, and though it begins at 4s rather than 3d it reproduces the Homeric anomaly of a short *a* left light before the double consonant (*sd*) that makes up the Greek zeta and its Latin equivalent. The ancient name is still used for the southernmost of the major Ionian islands, nearly thirty miles north of the Strophades, and thus naturally the first to be seen by the Trojans.   **Dulichiumque Sămēqu(e) et Nērĭtŏs ardua saxis**: again the names and some of the phrasing are drawn precisely from the model; but the geography is quite unclear, and was already in antiquity. At *Iliad* 2.626–30 Dulichium is large enough to provide forty ships for the expedition against Troy, whereas Odysseus commands only twelve (2.631–7); he is described there as leader of 'the great-hearted Cephallenians who occupied Ithaca and Neritos of the shimmering leaves, and farmed Crocyleia and rugged Aegilips, and held Zacynthus, and lived around Samos'. V. has adopted the Odyssean form *Same* and the Iliadic *Neritos*; by making it feminine (the normal gender for islands in Greek) he seems to treat *Neritos* as an island (as *Iliad* 2.632 could imply), but the adjectival phrase *ardua saxis* is equivalent to τρηχεῖα, the epithet given to Aegilips at *Iliad* 2.633 and Ithaca itself at *Od.* 9.27. *Same* (a name now borne by a port) is usually

Commentary: lines 270-93

identified as the large island Cephallonia or a town on it. Some have thought that Dulichium also refers to Cephallonia, or part of it; while others (especially W. Dörpfeld) take Same to be the modern Ithaca, and Homer's Ithaca to be Leucas. V. was probably more interested in the allusive* power of the names than the precise geography. **effugimus scopulos Ithacae**: avoidance of Odyssean places becomes a theme in the book: 291, 639, and repeatedly in the case of Scylla and Charybdis; cf. also Neptune's carrying the fleet past Circe's island at 7.21-4. But there is realism here as well as literary *praeteritio**: sailors want to avoid reefs or cliffs!   **Laërtia regna**: slightly ironic in apposition* to *scopulos*, but 'the Ithacans gloried in the mountainous poverty of their island' (Horsfall).   **terr(am) altricem** recalls Odysseus' description of Ithaca at *Od*. 9.27 'rugged, but a good nurse of young men (κουροτρόφος)'. The elision is followed by another in *saeu(i)*, and contributes to the spondaic* vehemence of the line, culminating in the sibilance* of the final three words.   **s̲aeu(i) e̲xsecramur Vlix̲i**: for the ways in which Aeneas describes Ulysses, see 613 n. The genitive of the name is found in three forms: the third-declension *Vlixis*, the quadrisyllabic *Vlixei* (e.g. Horace, *Odes* 1.6.7), and this form, which V. always uses, as apparently did Cicero, *Tusc. Disp.* 1.98, 5.46 (though on such orthographical distinctions manuscript traditions are not reliable); cf. *Achilli*, 87.

274-7 mox et...| et...aperitur: 'next appear both...and'. Leucas is the northernmost of the group; the central mountains rise to over 1,000 metres.   **formidatus nautis aperitur Apollo**: V. has in mind the temple of Apollo on the cliff-top of the southern cape of Leucas: cf. Ovid, *Ep*. 15.165-6 *Phoebus ab excelso quantum patet aspicit aequor: Actiacum populi Leucadiumque uocant* ('Apollo looks from high up as far as the sea stretches: men call him Actia(ca)n and Leucadian'; Sappho there proposes to throw herself from this famous 'Lovers' Leap'). *formidatus nautis* ('feared by sailors') reflects on this position: the temple marks a route sailors would avoid. Moreover, there is evidence to suggest that the cult statue carried a warning beacon (Butrica 2001: 297; *LIMC* 470). When Jason prays to Apollo as the Argonauts pass through their dark storm, the god responds quickly (Apollonius 4.1706-18: **N**), and provides the shining light of his bow from the island that comes to be called Anaphe (205-6 n.; the god also appears to the Argonauts at 2.674-719: Nelis 61-2). At the equivalent point in the *Aeneid* the Strophades provide not light, but mountains, smoke, and the chthonic* horror of the Harpies; and it is only now that Apollo appears, *aperitur* reprising the delusive *aperire* of 206. **hunc petimus**: *hunc* must refer to Apollo, but the Apollo of 275 was explicitly not a destination sought by sailors. However, there was another temple of Apollo, at Actium (287 n.; Thucydides 1.29.3, Strabo 7.7.6), on the mainland south of the inlet to the Ambracian Gulf, close to the north of Leucas; and the Trojans will be on the *Actia litora* at 280. It has been shown that the two names *Apollo Leucadius* and *Apollo Actius* are used interchangeably, as if the cult were regarded as one (Butrica 2001; besides *Ep. Sapph.* 166, just cited, cf. Aelian, *de Natura Animalium* 11.8 'On Leucas there is an elevated cape where a temple to Apollo is sited, and the worshippers name him "Actian"'. See also Miller 2009: 73; and S. Casali, 'Terre mobili. La topografia di Azio', in C. Santini & F. Stok (eds), *Hinc Italae gentes* (Pisa, 2004), 45–74). It looks as though V. has played with this sense of identity to transport the fleet quickly north. We may compare what Callimachus does at *Hymn* 1.42–3: having given birth to Zeus, Rhea leaves Thenae in Arcadia and is instantly at Crete, where another Thenae is near to Cnossos. **fessi**: cf. 78. **paruae succedimus urbi**: as a piece of narrative to Dido this works straight-forwardly—the Trojans enter a city near the temple; but to a reader with a sense of the geography, this creates another puzzle: there was no more than a small village at Actium. Does V. aggrandize the settlement, or are we to think of another city in the area? Stahl argues that the Trojans are to be imagined as coming up the inland side of Leucas and putting in at the city Leucas (where the island was joined to the mainland by sandbanks over which boats were hauled); Cicero, e.g., halted there (and at Actium) travelling to Italy in 50 BC (*Fam.* 16.1–9), and this might seem an appropriate place to spend the winter (284). Or are we rather to think of a city on the site of Augustus' foundation at Nicopolis, north of the inlet to the Ambracian Gulf? For this is where the Actian Games (280–2) were held after Augustus re-established them (the earlier version featured in a work of Callimachus on Games: fr. 403); and when Aeneas puts up a commemorative memorial (286–8) a Roman reader might well think of the monuments of Nicopolis. We may admire the poet's ambiguity without feeling it necessary to make a decision. **ancora de prora iacitur; stant litore puppes**: the first clause marks the moment of arrival at the shore ('anchors are tossed from the prow'); the second the ongoing position of the ships ('sterns stand on the shore'). The stress on naval activity fits the proximity of Actium; but the beaching of the ships means there is

Commentary: lines 270–93   157

no hint of a naval battle, nor will there be a ship-race as part of the games—that waits till Book 5 (Goldschmidt 2013: 122–3).

278–83 ergo introduces what follows the arrival, here after a difficult and threatening journey summed up in the participial phrase in the rest of the verse: cf. 132, where the arrival (*tandem... adlabimur*) comes in the previous line; and 238, where the *ubi* clause is equivalent to the participle.   **insperata tandem tellure potiti** stresses the eventual arrival at a safe destination after the false hopes of 209–10, 219–21; Odysseus sees γαῖαν ἀελπέα ('unhoped for land') at *Od.* 5.408, but it takes prayer and enormous effort to reach the shore of Phaeacia. *tellure potiti* means 'having reached land' (cf. 1.172), but *potior* regularly implies gaining control of territory, and Stahl (1998: 56–7) sees the phrasing as evoking a moment in the Actium campaign, when Augustus' forces under Agrippa capture the city of Leucas.   **lustramurque Ioui**: after the religious and physical pollution of an encounter with the Harpies, the Trojans cleanse themselves ritually. Though V. often uses *lustrare* metaphorically, to describe the movement of people or light, occasionally as here it has religious force, describing the lustration of fields at *Ecl.* 5.75, and cleansing from the pollution of death at 6.231. Jupiter has been involved in the pollution on the Strophades (223), and the Trojans know his overarching importance for what they are engaged in (251, 171; 2.689–704). In narrative terms, then, offerings to Jupiter (cf. e.g. 19 for the dative) make good sense; but Jupiter is not a deity present in the area, nor were lustrations in Rome normally associated with his divinity. Lloyd (*AJPh* 75 (1954), 298) suggested that V. thinks of the censorial lustration of 28 BC, alongside his other evocations of religious events in the years after Actium; however, this does not explain Jupiter's presence here. Zeus is heavily involved in Circe's purification of Medea and Jason for the murder of Medea's brother Apsyrtus (*Arg.* 4.700–17), but the Trojans have not obviously committed a similar offence. Butrica (2001: 307; cf. Miller 2009: 57–66) suggests there is a link to a papyrus epigram (*Supplementum Hellenisticum* 982 = D. L. Page, *Select Literary Papyri* 113 [Loeb]) that salutes Apollo of Actium (1) and Leucas (13), and twice (8, 13) also mentions Zeus, each time equated to Augustus.   **uotisque incendimus aras**: 'and we kindle the altars with our promised offerings': cf. 8.285 *incensa altaria*, Aeschylus, *Agamemnon* 91 βωμοὶ δώροισι φλέγονται ('the altars are aflame with offerings'). The sacrifice and games is equivalent to what the Argonauts do for Apollo on Anaphe

(Apollonius 4.1719–30: **N**), though there the competition is of insults exchanged between the men and Medea's maidservants.   **Actiaque Iliacis celebramus litora ludis**: a 'golden line'*, with a celebrated etymological play: Ἄκτιος, from which *Actia* comes, means 'of the shore'; Apollonius has the equivalent gloss* at 1.403–4, when the Argonauts establish on the shore (ἐπάκτιον) an altar for Apollo Actios; Propertius repeats the play in his allusive* account of the still unpublished *Aeneid* at 2.34.61 (see Heyworth, *Cynthia* 275). *celebramus* combines both the thronging of the shore (*OLD* 1) and the religious honouring with games (5.58 *laetum cuncti celebremus honorem*, 'let us all celebrate a joyful festival'; 5.603 *celebrata...sancto certamina patri* 'contests held for the holy father' i.e. Anchises); *Actia* implies that Apollo is the recipient of the games (276 n.).   **exercent patrias... palaestras**: *patrias* reinforces *Iliacas*: as in the games for the anniversary of Anchises' death (on a larger scale), there is emphasis on ancestral tradition at the same time as the text looks ahead to the Augustan age (cf. e.g. 5.563–76). The line then brings out the complexity of cultural transmission when it ends with the quintessentially Greek notion of the *palaestra*, here 'styles of wrestling', but regularly referring to the central area of the gymnasium, the symbolic gathering place of Greek manhood, but one that V. has already associated with early Italian society at *Geo.* 2.531 *corporaque agresti nudant praedura palaestra* ('and they bare their hardened bodies in rustic wrestling'; this was the life lived by 'the ancient Sabines', by 'Remus and his brother', *Geo.* 2.532–3).   **nudati**: prepared for by the athletes' olive oil in 281. The realistic note is revisited at times in the athletics of Book 5 (e.g. 134–5). The nakedness was presumably a major reason for the exclusion of women from athletic games, despite the encouragement Augustus generally gave to such activities (Suetonius, *Aug.* 43–5), not least by his foundation of the Actian games at Nicopolis and in Rome.   **mediosque fugam tenuisse per hostis**: the Trojans have successfully travelled beyond the lands of all the Greeks who came to Troy. The picture will be complicated in the next episode, however: Buthrotum turns out now to be controlled by Priam's son Helenus, but it had till recently been the home of Neoptolemus, the most savage enemy in Book 2; and Helenus will warn that further 'bad' Greeks lie ahead, in Italy (396–402). Another complexity emerges for the reader whose attention has been caught by the reference to Actium, for the battle featured a famous flight to (temporary) safety through the midst of opposing forces—but by the ships of Cleopatra

(Plutarch, *Antony* 66.5 διὰ μέσου φεύγουσαι τῶν μαχομένων, 'fleeing through the middle of the combatants'), a surprising analogy for the Trojans (but one that will be revisited by the behaviour of Aeneas and Dido in Book 4).

284–8 interea could mean 'in the meantime, while the rituals were being prepared and carried out', but is easier to take in the sense 'subsequently', as often in narrative (*OLD* c), e.g. at 4.129, 10.1 (and Harrison, *ad loc.*). The Actian Games of Augustus were apparently held on the anniversary of the battle, 2 September; and Aeneas' sequence invites us to see his games as coinciding with this.   **magnum sol circumuoluitur annum**: 'the sun is rolling round the long year', i.e. completing its circuit by passing through winter, as the next verse explains. The stately progress of the year is expressed in spondees* (in contrast to the swift moving dactyls* describing the winter sea in 285). *circum-* governs the accusative *annum*. Aeneas' narrative is rarely so explicit in marking the passage of time (8 n.); we are presumably to imagine that one winter or more (as well as a summer, 141) has already been spent on Crete.   **magni gestamen Abantis...figo**: 'the leader of those who survived the Greeks' destruction of Troy dedicates the archetypal Greek ἀσπίς', so J. F. Miller, *CQ* 43 (1993), 447, summing up his persuasive argument for returning to the old view that V. here refers to Abas the son of Lynceus and Hypermestra, acclaimed as the inventor of the shield, and the man who set one up in the temple of Hera in Argos (see also Paschalis 1987: 65); though that Abas belonged to an earlier generation, we may think of a descendant going to Troy with his ancestor's shield. Just as the games look ahead to Book 5, so the dedication is a brief precursor of the trophy Aeneas sets up at 11.5–11 to mark his victory in the previous book over the wicked Etruscan king Mezentius (including a bronze shield among the other, ritually damaged, arms).   **postibus aduersis**: 'on the doorposts opposite', i.e. in full view of anyone approaching, and the standard place for such dedications in the *Aeneid* (2.504, 5.360, 7.183; and at 8.721–2, on the shield, where Augustus fastens up offerings on the temple of Apollo during the triumph after Actium). V. leaves the reader to imagine that the reference is to the temple of Apollo at Actium; but the imprecision may also help evoke the monumental placing at Nicopolis of enormous rams taken from Antony's ships: Suetonius, *Aug.* 18.2 'So that the memory of his victory at Actium might be more celebrated in the future too, he founded the city of Nicopolis near Actium, established games there every four years, and having increased the size of the old temple of Apollo, he adorned with naval spoils the site of the camp he had used and dedicated it to Neptune and Mars'; Cassius Dio 51.1.2–3 also mentions the enlarged temple at Actium, the Games, and an open shrine to Apollo at Nicopolis. On the archaeology of Nicopolis, see W. M. Murray & P. M. Petsas, *Octavian's Campsite Memorial for the Actian War* (Philadelphia, 1989).   **rem carmine signo**: 'I mark the event [*or* the facts] with a verse inscription'. The dedicatory inscription has provoked recent attention as a manifestation of the Roman epigraphic habit (e.g. J. Nelis-Clément & D. Nelis, '*Furor epigraphicus*: Augustus, the poets, and the inscriptions', in P. P. Liddel & P. A. Low (eds), *Inscriptions and their Uses in Greek and Latin Literature* (Oxford, 2013), 317–47, at 325–7, with further references). The poem has quasi-sepulchral epigrams at 5.870–1 and 7.1–4, but more like this are the epitaph for Daphnis at *Ecl.* 5.43–4, and the dedicatory couplets at Tibullus 1.9.83–4 and Propertius 2.14.27–8. The phrasing recalls a verse cited by Herodotus (5.59) from a tripod in Thebes: Ἀμφιτρύων μ' ἀνέθηκεν ἑλὼν [Meineke: ἐὼν codd.] ἀπὸ Τηλεβοάων ('Amphitryon dedicated me, having seized me from the Teleboeae'): see Hutchinson 2013: 338. As a Latin hexameter, it figures Aeneas as the founder of Roman poetry (epigram, and perhaps also epic) as well as the Roman state.   **AENEAS HAEC DE DANAIS VICTORIBVS ARMA**: as often in real inscriptions verbs are to be supplied, e.g. *dat* and *rapta*. A line beginning *Aeneas* and ending *arma* recalls the *Aeneid*'s opening words (*Arma uirumque*), and hints at a potential turning of the tables on the Greeks, a repeated theme of the poem (e.g. 1.283–5, 6.836–40). The phrasing perhaps calls to mind paradoxical language such as Cicero, *Brutus* 254 *uincebamur a uicta Graecia* ('we [Romans] used to be conquered by conquered Greece', discussing rhetoric), a phrase later imitated by Horace (Sillett 2015: 401–2), at *Epistles* 2.1.156 *Graecia capta ferum uictorem cepit* ('captured Greece captured the fierce victor', i.e. Rome was overcome by Greek literary art).

289–93 linquere tum portus iubeo et considere transtris: a hysteron proteron*: they sit in order to row out of port; cf. 5.136 *considunt transtris, intentaque bracchia remis* ('they sit on the cross-benches, and their arms are strained on the oars', before the signal is given to start the boat-race). An accusative is easily understood as the subject of the infinitives: cf. 472.   **protinus aërias Phaeacum abscondimus arces**: 'quickly we make the cloud-capped [*or* lofty] citadels of the Phaeacians disappear below the horizon'; cf. *Ecl.* 9.52 *cantando... condere soles* ('to make the sun set with my singing'). Scherie, the island of the Phaeacians, who finally escort Odysseus back to Ithaca, was regularly identified with Corfu, ancient Corcyra (implicitly at Apollonius 4.982–92, Tibullus 1.3.3). Though V. clearly intends this, another geographical deception is involved, as the highest mountains of Corfu are in the north, close to Buthrotum (Map 3). But he is more interested in marking the swift passing of a location that has delayed the heroes of earlier epics (*Od.* 5.452–13.77; *Arg.* 4.993–1223). **portuque subimus | Chaonio**: i.e. Buthrotum itself. *Chaonius* is an important epithet to introduce the episode, evoking the oracle of Zeus at Dodona, some distance inland, where the priests interpreted the cooing of doves in the oak trees (cf. *Ecl.* 9.13; *Geo.* 1.8, 149; 2.67). Aeneas will not visit Dodona, as he did in the traditions reported by Dionysius (*Rom.* 1.51.1), who has him meeting Helenus there, and Servius (on 256), citing Varro, who attributed the prophecy about eating tables to Jupiter of Dodona: oracular utterance comes from Helenus himself in Buthrotum (374–462). *portu* is dative (cf. 8.125 *subeunt luco*), the normal form for the fourth declension for the Augustan poets, who avoid even *mănūī*, which (unlike *pŏrtūī*, *cŭrrūī*; cf. 541) is possible in dactylic* verse. **celsam**: the city stands 'on a low hill' (*OCD*[4]).

294–355 *Arrival in Buthrotum*
Now that they have passed beyond the territory of hostile Greeks (cf. 270–93 n., and 396–402), it is fitting that the Trojans' first extended stay should be in an allied city, with Helenus, son of Priam, who has now taken Andromache, widow of Hector and Neoptolemus, as his wife, and (astonishingly) become ruler of a Greek kingdom. Buthrotum was a city that mattered in the Augustan age: veterans of Julius and Augustus were settled there. Dionysius 1.51.1 says that the presence of the Trojans at Buthrotum is attested by the fact that the hill on which they encamped was called Troia (cf. 302, 349–51); and Servius (on 349) implies the Roman polymath Varro cited similar evidence. V. varies the traditional story by omitting the visit to Dodona (293 n.) and introducing the memorably sad and poignant figure of Andromache from Euripides' eponymous* tragedy [**H**] and the *Trojan Women*. This is an episode where it is especially valuable to consider the effect of Aeneas' narrative on Dido, another exile, also widowed by the sacrilegious killing of a husband: is it a model when Andromache casts herself as an ever-mournful *uniuira* (488 n.), or encouragement

rather to embrace a new future? After the emotional reunion of this opening section, Aeneas requests prophetic insight from Helenus and receives it, in a long speech (374–462); the departure from these old friends and reminders of Troy is also emotional and drawn out.

294–9 Hic incredibilis rerum fama occupat auris: 'Here a rumour of unbelievable events takes possession of our ears'. *occupat* is a striking metaphor (*OLD* 3), helping to convey the astonishment of the Trojans as they hear this news. Both the rumour and the events are incredible: whereas English tends to put the adjective with the dependent word in such cases, in Latin the genitive can be the noun left unqualified: cf. 131, Conte 2007: 79–80.   **Prīamiden Helenum**: Helenus, a son of Priam (and therefore the brother-in-law of Hector's wife Andromache), is first mentioned as Πριαμίδης Ἕλενος (i.e. V.'s nomenclature in the nominative) in the *Iliad* at 6.76: there too the first syllable is long, though it is short in *Prĭamus*. As well as a warrior (*Il.* 13.576, 758), he is the most prominent seer on the Trojan side; his prophetic powers are vindicated at *Iliad* 7.44–57. He has become Andromache's husband after the death of Neoptolemus, as is prophesied at Euripides, *Andr.* 1243–5 [**H(b)**].   **coniugio...sceptrisque potitum**: lit. 'having taken possession of the marriage and sceptres': *coniugio* is abstract for concrete *coniuge* and *sceptris* is synecdoche* for 'kingdom'.   **Aeacidae Pyrrhi**: Pyrrhus was the great-grandson of Aeacus, son of Achilles and Deidamia, conceived when Achilles was hidden on Scyros before the Trojan War. Called Pyrrhus because of his red hair, he also bore the name Neoptolemus ('New-war'): O'Hara 1996: 133. Aeneas has portrayed him as repulsively violent and sacrilegious in his murder of Priam in Book 2 (526–53). After the fall of Troy, Andromache and Helenus became his captives, the former serving as his concubine and bearing him a son and the latter proving helpful to him as a prophet. When he was killed, Helenus gained a part of his kingdom (330–4).   **Andromachen**: Greek accusative; cf. *Anchisen* (82 n.), *Priamiden* (295), *Hermionen* (328).   **patrio...marito**: 'to a husband of her homeland': Andromache was from Thebe, a city in the southern Troad allied to Troy, which she salutes (in absence) in the first line of Euripides' play [**H(a)**]. At *Iliad* 6.414–28 she describes the capture of the city by Achilles during the war and the killing of her family, and then in 429–30 she movingly expresses her total dependence on Hector, her first Trojan husband.   **cessisse**: 'had passed (to)' (*OLD* 15): as Servius points out, a legal term—as a captive in war Andromache has become a piece of property.   **obstipui**: here of surprise, as opposed to the horror it expresses in 48.   **miroque incensum pectus amore | compellare**: for the infinitive after *amor* compare a line echoed in 299: *Aen.* 2.10 *si tantus amor casus cognoscere nostros* ('if you have such desire to learn our fate'), suggestively addressed to Dido.

300–5 The late placing in this sentence of *Andromache*, its subject, reflects Aeneas' continuing wonder. Who is this woman offering funeral gifts in a grove? It's Andromache! Andromache laments Hector's death already at the end of *Iliad* 22 when, poignantly late, she at last discovers the fact (22.437–515), and more formally at 24.723–45. To Vergil's contemporaries, after 23 BC, it is likely that the depiction recalled also the behaviour of Octavia, sister of Augustus, after the death of her son Marcellus (described at 6.860–86): cf. Seneca, *Dial.* 6.2.4–5:

Through the whole period of her life she put no end to her weeping and groaning, nor did she allow any utterances offering consolation, nor even allow herself to be distracted: intent on one thing and single-mindedly dedicated to it, she was through the rest of her life just as she had been at the funeral, I do not say not daring to rise, but refusing to be comforted, judging it a second bereavement to abandon her tears. She was unwilling to have any image of her beloved son, or to hear any mention of him.

The connexion is enhanced by the story of her weeping and fainting at the Marcellus passage (Servius on *Aen.* 6.861, *Vita Don.* §32).   **cum forte**: 'at a time when, as it happened': inverted *cum* to express a 'useful coincidence' (Horsfall).   **sollemnis…dapes**: 'ritual', 'customary', or 'annual feasts': the last is a common implication in the poem, as at 5.53 *annua uota…sollemnisque…pompas* ('annual sacrifices and ritual processions') and 8.102 *forte die sollemnem illo rex Arcas honorem | Amphitryoniadae magno diuisque ferebat | ante urbem in luco* ('by chance on that day the Arcadian king was bringing the annual offerings to mighty Hercules and the other gods in a grove in front of the city': Aeneas happens to arrive at Rome's future site as Evander is at the Ara Maxima celebrating Hercules' defeat of Cacus).   **tristia dona…libabat**: *libo* can be used both of liquid and solid offerings: at 5.77–9 Aeneas offers wine, milk, sacrificial blood, and flowers at his father's tomb. At *Fasti* 2.533–634, Ovid describes the main Roman festival for the dead, the Parentalia; he commends small gifts—a garlanded tile, fruit, salt, wheat soaked in wine, a scattering of violets

(2.535–40); this culminated in the Caristia on 22 February (631–3 *dis generis date tura...et libate dapes*, 'give incense to the gods of the family...and offer feasts'). There is a hint of necromancy in Vergil's passage: cf. Aeschylus, *Persians* (598–842), where the Queen offers libations at the tomb of Darius, her dead husband, while the Chorus summon up his spirit; and his ghost appears. We might think that deliberately barbarian, but in a famous scene from Aeschylus' *Libation Bearers*, Orestes, Electra, and the Chorus summon up the spirit of Agamemnon (456–509); such scenes are a repeated feature of later epics (e.g. Lucan 6.423–830; Statius, *Theb.* 4.406–645, and R. Parkes (Oxford, 2012), *ad loc.*); Ovid tells at *Fasti* 5.431–44 how during the Lemuria, in May, ghosts were summoned from their tombs to receive beans cast over the worshipper's shoulder. *tristia* is a transferred epithet (hypallage*) referring both to Andromache and the ritual she is performing: Catullus, in the epigram that describes his visit to his brother's tomb, offers *tristes munera ad inferias* (101.8: 'gifts at sad funerals').   **ante urbem in luco**: the law required burials to take place outside Rome and other cities (hence the collections of tombs on the *via Appia* and outside towns such as Pompeii and Ostia). Trees were often planted round tombs, but *lucus* regularly implies a sanctified area, e.g. 8.103 (cited above), 271 *hanc aram luco statuit* ('he [Hercules] set up this altar in the grove').   **falsi Simoëntis**: Aeneas will later discover the name of the river which, in the way of colonists, Andromache and Helenus have named after one of the two rivers of Troy, *Simois* in the nominative (the other river is Xanthus, 350). However, the surprising addition of *falsi* ('pretend') seems to imply a criticism of this and other such attempts to replicate Troy.   **cineri**: Hector had been cremated at the end of the *Iliad*, but the urn containing his ashes has been buried beneath a mound (24.791–9) and Andromache will scarcely have been able to bring them to Epirus. *cinis* is used by synecdoche* for the dead (e.g. 4.552), but again we may find an emptiness in the ritual at the cenotaph.   **manis...uocabat**: cf. 66–8.   **uiridi quem caespite inanem**: the grammar is uncertain here: *quem* is an object of *sacrauerat*, and 'which she had consecrated' makes good sense, but that leaves *uiridi caespite* and *inanem* awkwardly separate, when the reader is expecting a verb to complete the sense ('had built as a cenotaph with green turves'); perhaps best therefore to take as a kind of zeugma*. For the use of turf, cf. the altars built by the Rutulians and Trojans at 12.117–19 (*aras gramineas*). Commemoration of the dead with cenotaphs (lit. 'empty tombs') was customary in the ancient world, but references to the practice in literature tend to emphasize its futility (for example when Aeneas apologizes to the shade of Deiphobus for not burying his body: 6.505–8): *inanis* means 'futile' (*OLD* 13) as well as 'empty'. Panoussi (2009: 146–7) remarks that 'the excess and futility of Andromache's actions permeates the passage...with the adjectives *falsus* (fake) and *inanis* (empty)...poignantly underscoring the ironic contrast between the individual's desire to dwell in the past and the harsh necessity of adjusting to the future'. **geminas...aras**: why 'twin altars'? Servius suggests that they are to Dis and Proserpina; or that one is for Astyanax; but Book 5 strongly implies that both are for the dead hero himself: first Aeneas mentions a plurality of altars by Anchises' burial mound (5.48 *maestasque sacrauimus aras*), then at 5.77–8 he gives two vessels of each offering; cf. *Ecl.* 5.65–6 where two altars and double offerings are promised to the recently deceased and deified Daphnis. **causam lacrimis**: 'the cause of her tears', in apposition to the phrase *geminas...aras* that encloses it: 537 n. The altars have been constructed as the focal point for her grief because she wishes (like Octavia, discussed above) to continue to weep. *causa* is used with the dative also at e.g. 4.290, 11.480 *causa malis tantis* (normalized to the unmetrical *mali tanti* in some MSS), Propertius 3.13.3 *tantis causa...ruinis*. The opening scene of Euripides' play is dominated by Andromache's weeping at the altar of Thetis, e.g. *Andr.* 115–16 'I have come as a suppliant to this statue of the goddess and casting my arms around it I melt away in tears like a trickle dripping from the rocks': this is the end of the only passage of surviving Greek tragedy in elegiac* couplets (103–16). She will cry again at 3.312 and 344, and the tearfulness passes on to Helenus (348) and Aeneas (492).

306–9 me...et Trōĭă circum | arma: we have here an instance of the 'arms and the man' motif (cf. 288, 469). *circum* is adverbial, suggesting 'around her', and *arma* implies the Trojans wearing the recognizable equipment (Aeneas refers to his companions at 347). Contrast the trisyllabic adjective with the disyllabic noun *Trōĭă*. The first *a* in *arma* is long by nature as are the *a* and *e* in *amens* and the first *i* in *uidit*; with the elision of the second *a* in *arma* we have a heavy start to 307 as Andromache struggles to grasp what is happening; and then similarly she struggles to speak in verse 309, which is heavily spondaic* after the first foot. **magnis...monstris**: 'a great marvel': the poetic plural* adds to the sense of wonder. Elsewhere in the book *monstrum* refers to some of the real and horrifying wonders that Aeneas encounters (blood from a plant, 26, 59; the Harpies, 214; Etna, 583; Polyphemus, 658), but here it denotes the shocking coincidence of meeting a friend in distant parts.   **deriguit ..., calor ossa reliquit, | labitur**: Andromache stiffens, turns cold, and falls in a faint: as well as the physiological detail of Aeneas' reaction to Polydorus' blood (29–30) this recalls the reaction Homer gives Andromache when she sees the dead Hector being dragged behind Achilles' chariot at *Iliad* 22.463–7: 'black night covered her eyes and she crashed down and lost consciousness' (466–7). The phrase *calor ossa reliquit* is used again of Euryalus' mother when she hears of her son's death at 9.475; in the next line she drops her shuttle, like Andromache first hearing the cries from the wall at *Iliad* 22.448. Those passages are about death—the shock here is that Aeneas, thought dead, is actually alive: the world has been turned upside down.   **longo uix tandem tempore fatur**: 'at length after a long gap with difficulty she manages to say': the adverbial expressions are pointedly repetitive in force.

310–13 uerane te facies, uerus mihi nuntius adfers: 'do you bring yourself to me as a real image, a real messenger?' The nouns *facies*, *nuntius* are in apposition* to the unexpressed subject (cf. the nominative adjectives in 362 *prospera*; 1.314 *mater... sese tulit obuia*, 2.387–8 *Fortuna... ostendit se dextra*). Andromache, who has been summoning the ghost of Hector, suddenly finds his cousin before her; little wonder that she asks Aeneas if he is real or a spirit. If he is a ghost, he may bring true news of Hector from the underworld. *uerus nuntius* alludes to *Iliad* 22.438, which expresses Andromache's ignorance just after Hector's death: 'no true messenger (ἐτήτυμος ἄγγελος) had come and brought her the news'. The repetition *uera... uerus*, and the brokenness of the following lines, suggest her distress.   **nate dea**: 'son of the goddess' i.e. Venus; *deā* is the ablative of origin usual with such participles (e.g. 608 *quo sanguine cretus*).   **si lux alma recessit**: 'if the life-giving light of day has departed': cf. 600 *hoc caeli spirabile lumen*. After *uiuisne* Andromache wonders whether Aeneas is dead; but the lack of personal pronoun leaves open the possibility that she wonders whether she is dead too (she has just fainted).   **Hector ubi est**: 'Hector—where is he?' If Aeneas is dead, why, she wonders, can she not see Hector, also dead? Her elliptical thought process and her breaking off of her speech in the second foot of the line communicate her intense concentration on her former husband: his name will be the last word of her second speech (343), while her final speech ends with the memory of her dead son Astyanax (489–91).   **impleuit clamore locum**: there is a poignant echo of 2.769 *impleui clamore uias* where Aeneas shouts as he looks for his lost wife Creusa.

313–16 furenti...turbatus: both of them are deeply affected by this surprise meeting—Aeneas himself has seen the ghost of the dead Hector in a vivid dream (2.270–97), we should remember, and both of them have difficulty in speaking (*uix*, 309; *uix*, 313). *furenti* is the more dynamic word, used of Neoptolemus, e.g., at 2.499 and Turnus at 9.691, 11.486, 11.901, but never of Aeneas (though he is described as *furiis accensus* at 12.946): it recalls Homer's description of Andromache as 'like a maenad' when she rushes to the tower to see what has happened to her husband (*Il.* 22.460); and precisely the same form will be used of Dido when she finds she is losing the man she thinks of as her husband (Aeneas) at 4.298.   **uix pauca...subicio et raris...uocibus hisco**: 'with difficulty I interpose [*OLD subicio* 9] a few words and I stammer in broken phrases': again tautology* reinforces the emotion. *hisco* (only here in V.) means 'gape' (*OLD* 1a) and 'open the mouth to speak' (*OLD* 2a): Aeneas gives himself a stage direction for the coming speech (as again in *demissa uoce*, 320).   **uiuo equidem**: *equidem* is an emphatic equivalent of *ego*: 'for my part, I live', 'I DO live'. This sets Aeneas himself in contrast to those who are dead.   **extrema per omnia**: 'through all kinds of extreme situations': the neuter plural adjective *extrema* is used as a noun and then qualified by *omnia*: the emphatic combination also occurs at Sallust, *Cat.* 26.5, Livy 3.15.9 (though of taking the ultimate step of violent revolution).   **ne dubita**: i.e. that I am alive. For the construction, see 394, Penney in Adams & Mayer 1999: 253.   **uera uides** directly answers *uerane te facies* ...? in 310. For the half-line, see Introduction, p. 51: this is a very effective instance, strikingly glossed* by *raris...uocibus* (314); but there is no reason to think V. would have left it so had he given final form to the poem.

317–19 quis te casus...excipit: given that the positive *digna satis fortuna* follows, best taken as 'What misfortune has overtaken you'. The interrogative adjective *quis* instead of *qui* (more common in prose) seems to have been preferred by V. except before a word beginning with *s*: cf. 5.648–9. *te* comes in the second position typical for unemphatic pronouns ('Wackernagel's Law').   **deiectam coniuge**

tanto: 'cast down from [i.e. bereft of] so great a husband'. Hector is a great warrior and an admirable man in the *Iliad*, and his marriage to Andromache represents an ideal relationship (as opposed to that of Paris and Helen and those of the Greek commanders with their concubines).   **quae digna satis fortuna reuisit**: lit. 'what fortune sufficiently worthy visits you again', i.e. 'what fortune that could match what you deserve comes to you now'.   **Hectoris Andromache**: 'Hector's <wife> Andromache'. Most editors attach this to the end of the previous sentence, but Horsfall sees that the contrast with *Pyrrhi* is more pointed if the vocative leads into the rest of 319. Before naming the impious Greek she is known to have married, Aeneas asserts her true identity: whatever fortune has come now, in his mind (as in her own: 488) she will always be the wife of Hector.   **Pyrrhin** = *Pyrrhine*. 'The shortened form is often found in colloquial speech ..., but apart from 6.779 *uiden ut*... V. reserves it for anguished or indignant questions' (Tarrant on 12.503 *tanton*).   **conubia seruas**: 'do you maintain your marriage' to Pyrrhus (*OLD seruo* 5). For the scansion of **cōnūbĭă**, contrast 136.

320–4 dēiēcīt uūlt(um) ēt dēmīssā uōce: the expression is effectively simple: the spondaic* rhythm and the double echo of *deiectam* (317) emphasize Andromache's dejection.   **o felix...Prĭămēĭă uirgo**: this ironic *makarismos** ('fortunate is she who ...') looks back to Aeneas' wish, in his first speech in the poem, as the storm strikes, that he had died at Troy ('three and four times blessed were those who had the fortune to meet death before the eyes of their fathers *Troiae sub moenibus altis*' (1.94–6, a version of Odysseus' words in the storm at *Od.* 5.306–7); cf. also 5.623 *o miserae* (of those who survived Troy). Priam's maiden daughter is defined by what follows as Polyxena, sacrificed on Achilles' tomb as his share in the booty from the sacked city; contrast her sister Cassandra (*Priameia uirgo* 2.403), who is allotted to Agamemnon, and in Aeschylus' tragedy (and other versions) dies alongside her master in his palace. V. again refers to Euripides: (a) *Trojan Women*, in which Andromache argues that her sister-in-law, the dead Polyxena, is better off than she is herself (630–83); (b) *Hecuba*, in which Polyxena is about to be sacrificed on the tomb of Achilles (*hostilem ad tumulum*) at the demand of the latter's ghost. (The play does not take place beneath the walls of Troy but on the Thracian Chersonese: 13–68 n.) In an eloquent speech (342–78) Polyxena tells her mother and Odysseus that she longs to die. She has been a great princess and does not wish to be degraded in slavery; she wants to meet her death as a free woman. As a slave, she says (359–66), 'I may perhaps have a cruel-hearted master who...will force on me the task of making bread in his home, and impose the daily drudgery of sweeping the house and standing by the loom. And a slave bought from I know not where will defile my bed, which was once thought worthy of princes.' **una ante alias**: 'uniquely, more than others': both parts of this give a superlative force to *felix*: cf. 2.426 *Rhipeus, iustissimus unus*, 4.141 *ipse ante alios pulcherrimus omnis* (Aeneas 'himself handsome beyond all the others'), 11.821 *fida ante alias quae sola Camillae* (Acca, 'who alone beyond others was loyal to Camilla'). **sortitus non pertulit ullos**: 'did not endure any drawing(s) of lots': the plural *sortitus* is easily understood of a process that featured many individual actions. Here the reference is to the scene in Euripides, *Trojan Women* (240–77) in which the Greek herald Talthybius announces to the captive Trojan women that each has been allotted to a different Greek. The women specified are Hecuba (allocated to Odysseus), and Cassandra and Andromache, both in fact excluded from the ballot, as chosen by Agamemnon and Neoptolemus respectively. Talthybius also speaks riddling words about Polyxena: 'she has been appointed to serve at the tomb of Achilles' (264); he then advises Hecuba 'count your daughter fortunate: she is lucky' (εὐδαιμόνιζε παῖδα σήν· ἔχει καλῶς, 268). The echo of this in 321, together with the general similarity of sentiment, locates Andromache's speech firmly in the world of Greek—and specifically Euripidean—tragedy (even though stories about the aftermath of the Trojan War were a staple of Roman tragedy). **eri**: the synonym of *dominus* is frequent in comedy but very rare in epic. After the grand *uictoris* 'Andromache's use of the everyday word emphasizes her anger and contempt' (Williams). We may compare what rumour says of Dido's lover at 4.214 *dominum Aenean*.

325–9 nos patria incensa: an echo of Meliboeus' announcement of his exile in the first speech of the *Eclogues*: see Introduction, pp. 6–7. **diuersa per aequora uectae**: V. six times ends a verse with adjective + *per aequora uect-*, alluding to Catullus' visit to his brother's tomb in the Troad, at 101.1 *Multas per gentes et multa per aequora uectus* ('Carried through many peoples and over many seas', itself an epigrammatic version of *Od.* 1.1–4; Elliott (2013: 110) suggests that Catullus mediates existing Latin epic diction): the single line thus combines Andromache's themes of exile and of mourning.

Compare in particular Aeneas' words to the disguised Venus at 1.375–6 *nos Troia antiqua…diuersa per aequora uectos* ('we, carried from ancient Troy…over various seas'): the lots of Aeneas and Andromache here coalesce.   **stirpis Achilleae fastus iuuenemque superbum**: 'the exhibitions of pride of the offspring of Achilles and the arrogant young man': two phrases making much the same point, though the first concentrates on the hated Achilles and the second on the youth of Neoptolemus (whom Andromache will not name till her narrative has him safely dead, at 333).   **seruitio enixae**: 'bringing forth <a child> in slavery': though *enitor* can be intransitive in this sense (*OLD* 3), the three other instances in the *Aeneid* are transitive (391, 7.320, 8.44). The omission of an object draws attention to Andromache's failure to acknowledge the existence of a new son. This is particularly striking because of the importance of the boy in the plot of Euripides' *Andromache*: she announces the hopes connected with the child in the Prologue (24–5: **H(a)**); one of the main themes of the play is the wish of Hermione and her father Menelaus to kill the boy; and Thetis, as *deus ex machina*, reveals that he will be the founder of a dynasty of Molossian kings: though the baby's name is never revealed, this implies that he is called Molossus (as in other sources, e.g. Servius on 297). The word *enixae* that here implies his existence takes the metrical shape called 'molossus' (– – –).   **deīnde** always has trochaic* form in V.: the first two vowels coalesce through synizesis*. **secutus**: with the human and the abstract object there is a mild syllepsis*: 'having pursued' (i.e. as a suitor), *OLD* 2; 'having sought', *OLD* 16.   **Ledaeam Hermionen Lacedaemoniosque hymenaeos**: hendiadys*: 'Hermione, descendant [granddaughter] of Leda, in a Spartan marriage'. Leda gave birth to Helen as a result of her union with Jupiter in the form of a swan. Helen married Menelaus and Hermione was their only child: her marriage to Neoptolemus is being celebrated when Telemachus visits Menelaus in Sparta (*Odyssey* 4.5–7). The mannered form of the line culminates in the unusual four-syllable word, of Greek origin, as at 680.   **me famulo famulamque Heleno transmisit habendam**: 'handed me over to Helenus, for him to possess, a slave to a slave'. Though it is possible to make sense of *que* ('me to a slave and a slave to Helenus'), that obscures the point: the conjunction seems to have been added simply to avoid hiatus* between *famulam* and *Heleno*. For such polyptoton*, used 'to connect two characters', see Wills 1996: 213. Henry helpfully relates this to Euripides, *Andr.* 64 (Andromache to a Maidservant: ὦ φιλτάτη σύνδουλε—

σύνδουλος γὰρ εἶ, 'O dearest fellow-slave—for you are a fellow-slave'). The expression of this line, with its prosaic gerundive, identifies the operation as a business transaction, a passing on of property (cf. 297). The men of Troy were butchered by the Greeks; we are not told why Helenus survives as a slave, but may surmise that his status as a seer has protected him: Servius (on 297) tells a story in which he is useful to Neoptolemus, advising him to return to Phthia overland, thus avoiding the storms that wreck and disperse the Greek fleet.

330-2 V. follows Euripides' *Andromache*, in which Orestes had originally been betrothed to Hermione, but her father Menelaus, on discovering that Troy could only be taken with Neoptolemus' participation, promised her in marriage to the latter if he should sack Troy (966-70); Orestes and Hermione elope, and he arranges the killing of Neoptolemus (who, in the play, is not represented unsympathetically). In Ovid, *Heroides* 8, Hermione, in writing to Orestes, follows the account here and talks as if they had already been married before Neoptolemus seized her.   **ast**: an archaic* word used by Augustan poets mainly as an alternative to *at* where a heavy syllable is needed before a vowel (seventeen times in V., plus *ast de* transmitted at 10.743).   **ereptae... coniugis**: 'of the wife [*or, perhaps,* fiancée] who had been snatched from him': the situation is fundamental to the *Iliad* (Helen, Briseis), and similar language is used in elegy* by Propertius to encapsulate his situation when a rival has won Cynthia (2.8.1 *Eripitur nobis...cara puella*; 2.34.2), and to compare himself to Achilles after the loss of Briseis (2.8.29 *abrepta coniuge*, 36 *erepto amore*).   **scelerum Furiis agitatus Orestes**: 'Orestes, tormented by the madness of [*or* the Furies pursuing] his crimes'. Orestes had killed his mother Clytemestra on Apollo's instructions in requital for her murder of his father Agamemnon. Since all letters in ancient manuscripts were capitals, V.'s text would make no distinction between the abstract idea of madness and the Furies aroused against Orestes by the spirit of his mother, who feature terrifyingly in Attic drama (esp. as the chorus in Aeschylus, *Eumenides*): Lyne 1989: 28-9. At 4.469-73 Dido's dreams are compared to the madness of Pentheus and (according to the manuscripts) *Agamemnonius scaenis agitatus Orestes* (471; it is possible V. wrote not *scaenis* but *Poenis* [= *Furiis*], as the eighteenth-century scholar Markland conjectured). See Introduction, p. 54.   **patrias...obtruncat ad aras**: traditionally (as in Euripides' *Andromache*) Neoptolemus was killed at Apollo's temple at Delphi. *patrias* is chosen to relate Pyrrhus' death to his slaughter of first Polites in front of his father Priam (2.526–32), and then, brutally, Priam himself at the latter's ancestral altar in the palace (2.513–25, 550–3), summed up at 2.663 *natum ante ora patris, patrem obtruncat ad aras*. Within Aeneas' narrative, however, it is harder to see quite how the epithet functions: perhaps 'of his home country', i.e. Greece, in contrast to the murder he committed at Troy. Servius refers to a tradition that Pyrrhus had set up an altar to his father Achilles in the temple; or we might think the killing has been moved to Phthia, or Epirus (so Rebeggiani 2016: 61–5). The expression here also associates him with Pygmalion, Dido's brother, in his slaughter of her husband Sychaeus, whom, as Venus has told Aeneas (1.348–56: **P**), he took *incautum* (cf. 332) *ante aras*. Pyrrhus' end is grimly appropriate. Orestes, a shifty character in Euripides' *Andromache*, is portrayed here as an out-and-out villain. In the play he contrives the murder by spreading rumours among the people of Delphi about Neoptolemus' threat to the shrine.

333–6 regnorum reddita cessit | pars Heleno: *reddita* means 'handed over (appropriately/as called for)'; the dative *Heleno* follows both *reddita*, and *cessit* (cf. 297). V. does not explain how Helenus becomes king, but there is an answer if we ask (one implied by *Andr*. 1243–9: **H(b)**): Andromache is the mother of Neoptolemus' infant heir, and needs a consort to rule the kingdom and pass it on to the line of future kings.   **qui C̲h̲a̲o̲nios c̲o̲g̲n̲o̲mi̲ne c̲ampos | C̲h̲a̲o̲niamque omnem Troi̲a̲no a̲ C̲h̲a̲o̲ne dixit**: 'who called the plains by the name Chaonian and the whole area Chaonia after Trojan Chaon': a very emphatic (and resonant) assertion for a very obscure piece of etymology: we know nothing of a Trojan 'Chaon' and the Chaonians were thought to have existed before the Trojan War. One effect is to bring Dodona to mind (293 n.); for Jenkyns (1998: 439) 'the grinding repetitions suggest an obsessive clinging to names when the substance is gone'.   **Pergamaque Iliacamque iugis hanc addidit arcem**: *Pergama* (neuter plural) was the name for the citadel of Troy, as is indicated by the epexegetic* gloss* *Iliacamque…arcem* (cf. 133). For the expression here, cf. Prop. 4.4.35 *montibus addita Roma* ('Rome built on top of the hills'): the city-founding theme here looks backward to Troy, not forward to Rome: see Morwood, *G&R* 38 (1991), 212–23.

337–43 tibi: the postponement* of *qui* gives this an emphatic position. **qui cursum uenti, quae fata dedere**: an ἀπὸ κοινοῦ* construction:

dedere is understood in the first clause, *cursum* in the second: 'what winds have given you your course, what fates …?' So extraordinary does the meeting seem that Andromache assumes here and in the next line that natural and supernatural causes have brought Aeneas to Buthrotum.   **ignarum**: cf. 7 *incerti quo fata ferant*; moreover Aeneas had no idea that there was a Trojan settlement at Buthrotum.   **nostris deus appulit oris**: *oris* is dative of destination after *appello*, as in the similar phrase at 715 *uestris deus appulit oris*.   **quid puer Ascanius?**: 'what (of) the boy Ascanius?' For the form of question, cf. 7.365, *Geo* 1.111, 3.258, 264–5: it is common enough for the grammar not to need careful attention (and commentators accordingly keep silence); we suppose that *agit* or perhaps *fit* might be implied. Andromache is thinking of her own son Astyanax when she asks about Ascanius. Here, as elsewhere in Books 2 and 3, we may remember that it is not Ascanius whom Dido is cradling in her lap as Aeneas tells his story, but Cupid in his guise.   **superatne et uescitur aura**: 'does he survive and take in the air?' cf. 2.597–8 *superet coniunxne Creusa | Ascaniusque puer?* and 1.546 *si uescitur aura*, where Ilioneus wonders whether Aeneas himself has survived the storm.   **quem tibi iam Troia**: 'whom to you in Troy already…'; for half-lines, see Introduction, p. 51. This instance is the only one in the poem where the sense is incomplete (so already *Vita Don.* §41): perhaps V. could not work out how to complete the sense, but perhaps he saw the aposiopesis* as effective (this is certainly the case for the sentence Neptune begins and breaks off at 1.135): Andromache cannot bring herself to mention the death of Creusa, whether for fear of upsetting Aeneas, or because it reminds her of her own losses at Troy.   **ecqua tamen puero est amissae cura parentis**: 'all the same does the boy have any love for his lost mother?' Though *ecquae* is the standard form of the feminine nominative singular, poets occasionally use *ecqua* as a metrically convenient alternative: Ovid, *Fasti* 4.488; Statius, *Thebaid* 5.129. Andromache was in Troy after Aeneas had fled; it is not hard (if we wonder) to imagine how news of Creusa's fate had reached her. In thinking of the boy and the mother, she is again relating his loss to her own, and she perhaps echoes Hecuba, asking about Polydorus at Euripides, *Hec.* 993 'Has he any memory of his mother here, of me?'.   **ecquid in antiquam uirtutem animosque uirilis | et pater Aeneas et auunculus excitat Hector?**: 'does <the example of> his father Aeneas and his uncle Hector [brother of Creusa] rouse him at all [*ecquid*, adverbial] to old-style courage and manly valour?' The singular verb can be justified by taking the boy's uncle and father as a single example potentially inspiring the boy to become a *man* (**uir**tutem, **uir**ilis): Andromache perhaps remembers Hector's words at *Iliad* 6.479, where (with chilling irony) he hopes people may one day say of their son Astyanax 'he is a much better man than his father'. Servius quotes 9.311 *ante annos animumque gerens curamque uirilem* ('showing a manly spirit and thoughtfulness beyond his years'), which marks how Ascanius has matured; but later in the same book, after his arrow has killed the boastful Italian Remulus Numanus, Apollo congratulates him on his manliness (*macte noua uirtute*, 641), but then tells him to stop fighting, twice addressing him as *puer* (641, 656). Line 343 is repeated at 12.440, at the end of the one speech Aeneas makes to his son in the poem; Andromache addresses him at 486–91, but we never hear anything of the boy's feelings about his mother. The speech that began with praise of death ends with thoughts of Ascanius—but even this is cast in terms that look to the past (*antiquam*, 342; *Hector*, 343), and another member of the future generation, the son who will rule over Buthrotum, is totally elided (327 n.); the account Andromache gives of the city looks persistently back to Troy (334–6).

344–8 fundebat…ciebat: a 'leonine' rhythm, as in 36.   **longosque ciebat | incassum fletus**: 'she was beginning to shed tears in vain at length'. At 6.468 the phrase *lacrimas ciebat* describes Aeneas' reaction to the sight of Dido's ghost.   **sese**: cf. 215. The arrival of Helenus precludes any response to Andromache's questions, and so avoids the repetition of information already known to Aeneas' audience and V.'s readers.   **multum lacrimas uerba inter singula fundit**: some MSS have *lacrimans*, but the noun is needed as the object of *fundit*. The adverbial *multum* is found emphatically placed also at 10.839 *multumque remittit | qui reuocent* (Mezentius 'repeatedly sends men to call back' his son Lausus); here the meaning is 'he pours forth tears much', i.e. copiously. Presumably these are tears of mixed emotion at the sight of fellow Trojans: joy to see them now (347), but pain too at the reminder of what they have all lost.

349–51 paruam Troiam simulataque magnis | Pergama: this is not a 'big' city as the Penates (159–60) and Hector (2.294–5) have commanded Aeneas to aim for: see Fletcher 2014: 125–7, with references to further discussions.   **agnosco**: this is a key word (perhaps emphasized by the echo of *agnoscit*, 347, of Helenus' recognition of his fellow Trojans): Aeneas' reactions are focalized through his own viewpoint. He recognizes the reproduced Troy and notes how small it is. Colonists at all times have used the names of their former homes in their new settlements; but whereas this is journey's end for Helenus and Andromache (493–9), Aeneas must found a city of the future. His response to this theme-park Troy is not entirely negative (351), but it is surely significant that the swirling streams of the Trojan river Xanthus, so eddying and active in Homer (see above all *Iliad* 21 where the river rushes over the plain), are reduced in Aeneas' mind's eye to a dry watercourse (*arentem... riuum*). V. uses *agnosco* to acknowledge his imitation of Homer (cf. Hinds 1998: 8–10).   **Scaeaeque amplector limina portae**: the Scaean gates were the west gates of Troy: the derivation may be from the Greek word σκαιός ('left'). In the *Iliad*, it was by this very gate that Hector and Andromache had their deeply loving exchange in the presence of their son Astyanax (6.392–496). For the embrace of doorways, cf. the women of Troy at 2.490 *amplexaeque tenent postis atque oscula figunt* ('they cling to the doorposts, embracing them and planting kisses'). *limina* is used loosely to mean 'gateway' (*OLD* 2a).

352–5 nec non et: 'additionally too'; the phrase was introduced into poetry by V. in the *Georgics*, perhaps under the influence of Varro's *Res Rusticae*, which four times has *nec non etiam*.   **porticibus... amplis**: at least the colonnades are large in this little city, and Helenus can use them to entertain the new arrivals.   **aulāī** is an archaic* genitive ending found regularly in Ennius and Lucretius. This genitive occurs three times elsewhere in *Aen.* (6.747 *aurai*, 7.464 *aquai*, 9.26 *pictai*), but not otherwise in Augustan poetry. A note of solemnity is struck.   **libabant pocula Bacchi**: 'they make libations from goblets of wine' (*Bacchi* used by metonymy*). Though *libabant* could mean 'were drinking' (as at *Ecl.* 5.26 *nec amnem | libauit quadripes*, 'nor did animal drink river water'), the presence of *paterae* in 355 and the echo of *Geo.* 2.191–2 *hic fertilis... laticis, qualem pateris libamus et auro*, 'this vine is productive of the liquid [i.e. wine] that we offer on golden dishes [hendiadys*]' give a religious feel to the feast. More important still are the echoes of 1.728–40, where Dido has called for a golden *patera* and made a libation to Bacchus and Juno before drinking and passing the bowl on. There is thus an effect of *mise en abyme** here: Aeneas is at a feast of welcome for the Trojan refugees narrating another such feast.

356–462 *The prophecy of Helenus*
In the central section of the central episode of the book Aeneas asks Helenus for clarification of the conflicting prophecies he has heard,

and receives a long prophecy in response (see on 374–462). This consultation takes the place of a trip to the oracle of Zeus at Dodona, mentioned as part of the Aeneas legend by Dionysius Hal., *Rom.* 1.51.1.

356–8 iamque dies alterque dies processit: 'now one day and the next has passed'. As when the Argonauts linger on Lemnos (Apollonius 1.861 ἀμβολίη δ' εἰς ἦμαρ ἀεὶ ἐξ ἤματος ἦεν | ναυτιλίης, 'there was constant postponement of the voyage from day to day') the rapid repetition expresses the rapid passing of days, and hints at the need for Aeneas and his fleet to move on; but it will be verse 505 before they finally depart from the attractions of old friends and a reconstituted Troy. There are explicit markers of delay at 473, 481. *dies alterque dies* is repeated by Valerius Flaccus, at *Arg.* 5.276; similar phrasing occurs earlier in Cicero, e.g. *Verr.* 2.4.66 *dies unus, alter, plures*; *Clu.* 72 *unus et alter dies*.   **aurae | uela uocant**: it is not the weather that is delaying them; cf. 269 *uentus...uocabat*.   **tumidoque inflatur carbasus Austro**: 'the canvas is puffed out by the swelling South Wind'. Though it is the sail that is billowing, not the wind, Latin poets like the expressive usage that applies such epithets to what causes the effect, e.g. Horace, *Odes* 1.5.7 *nigris uentis* ('the darkening winds'); the linguistic process is inverted in 455 *sinus secundos*.   **adgredior**: no conjunction links this to the previous sentence, which gives the circumstances in which Aeneas comes to Helenus: parataxis*. *his dictis* and *talia*, by contrast, look ahead.

359–61 Troiugena: the appeal begins with reference to their shared origin, an obvious *captatio beneuolentiae** and a reflection of Helenus' concern with the past, before moving on to Helenus' capacity for prophecy as a priest of Apollo, astrologer, and augur.   **tripodas laurusque Clari**: 'the tripods and laurels of the Clarian god'. Items particularly associated with the worship of Apollo at Delphi (81, 91) are here transferred to another of the god's oracular centres, Claros, near Colophon (north-west of Ephesus), and thus not far from Troy. V. alludes to both Nicander, *Alexipharmica* 11 τριπόδεσσι...Κλαρίοις, and Lucretius 1.739 (= 5.112) *Pythia quae tripode a Phoebi lauroque profatur* ('what the Pythia utters from the tripod and laurel of Phoebus'). Statius imitates this passage in turn at *Thebaid* 7.707–8 (describing Amphiaraus): *qui tripodas laurusque sequi, qui doctus in omni | nube salutato uolucrem cognoscere Phoebo* ('he who is skilled at following the tripods and the laurels, at hailing Apollo and recognizing a bird in every cloud'). *tripodăs* (Greek third declension) and *laurūs* (fourth declension) are both accusative plurals, perhaps used to suggest the range of Helenus' knowledge. The text we print is a recent conjecture by Silvia Ottaviano (*MD* 62 (2009), 231–7). The text in late antiquity was *tripodas Clarii* (or *Clari*) *laurus*, which lacks the conjunction required by the context. Later manuscripts read *Clarii et*, and Mackail suggested *tripoda* (Greek acc. sing) *ac*; but there is a further problem: the *a* in *Clari* is short (Call. *Hymn* 2.70, Ov. *Met.* 11.399, e.g.) where a long syllable is needed, and the alternative form *Clarii* breaks Vergil's norms for the genitive of second-declension nouns (see 702 n.). Confusion with *clārus* will have been the root of the corruption. **sidera sentis**: 'apprehend the stars'; *sentire* is a very general word for perception and so suits the range of objects it takes here. Attitudes to astrologers in Rome were utterly inconsistent, hence Tacitus' later account of them as something perpetually banned in Rome, and perpetually retained (*et uetabitur semper et retinebitur*, *Hist.* 1.22): though much consulted for personal horoscopes, for example, they were formally expelled from the city by Agrippa in 33 BC, and while Augustus made his horoscope, published in AD 11, a significant part of his self-representation, his edict of the same year forbade private consultations as well as any consultations at all about the date of someone's death (see further F. Santangelo, *Divination, Prediction and the End of the Roman Republic* (Cambridge, 2013), 246–58; and 26, 70 on ornithomancy).   **et uolucrum linguas et praepetis omina pennae**: the line pairs two aspects of augury: listening to the cries of birds and observing their flight; cf. e.g. Ovid, *Fasti* 1.448 *nunc pinna ueras, nunc datis ore notas* ('you [birds] give true information now with a wing, now with your beak'). This recalls the description of Helenus as 'by far the best of the bird-readers' (*Iliad* 6.76). *praepetis* is a formal term from augural language (Gellius 7.6); it means 'flying straight ahead', with the implication 'favourable' (*OLD* 1a). For a similar list of prophetic qualifications, cf. Asilas at *Aen.* 10.175–6 (and Harrison *ad loc.*) *cui pecudum fibrae, caeli cui sidera parent,* | *et linguae uolucrum et praesagi fulminis ignes* ('to whom the entrails of cattle are intelligible, the constellations in heaven, the tongues of the birds and the flashes of the presaging thunderbolt').

362–8 fare age: *age* sometimes attaches an element of impatience to another imperative (e.g. 4.569 *heia age, rumpe moras*, 'hey, come on, break your delay'; 6.629), but this seems rather to belong with instances where it reinforces the request (6.343 *dic age*, 'do tell me' addressed to the ghost of Palinurus; 6.531 *age fare uicissim*, 'please tell me in turn' from Deiphobus to Aeneas; 7.37 *Nunc age... Erato*; 12.832 *uerum age*, Jupiter to Juno). *fare* may be chosen carefully here to reflect the link with *fata* (Introduction, pp. 36–7). **namque omnis cursum mihi prospera dixit | religio**: 'for every divine sign has spoken to me in successful terms of my journey': notably the prophecies of Apollo and the Penates in this book, as well as the directions from the ghosts of Hector and Creusa, e.g. in Book 2 (see 5 n. for further details). *namque* introduces a substantial parenthesis (cf. 1.65–6, 2.604–7, 6.117–18, 6.860–2), in this case extending over five lines; *nam* is used similarly (374). On the application of *prospera* to subject not object, see 310 n., Conte 2007: 107.   **rēligio**: 'a manifestation of divine sanction' (*OLD* 4); cf. 409, and *rēliquiae* (87) for the lengthening of the vowel, standard in poetry.   **cuncti... numine diui** ('all the gods with divine authority') repeats and confirms *omnis religio*, and sets up the contrast with *sola*, 365: Celaeno alone has made a predominantly negative prophecy.   **suaserunt... | Italiam petere**: the infinitive expressing indirect command is a regular construction in Latin verse; V. has it seven times after *suadere*, including 1.357 (**P**; see Tarrant on 12.814). *Italiam petere* recalls Celaeno's phrasing at 253.   **repostas**: syncope* for *repositas*: cf. 6.59–60 *penitusque repostas | Massylum gentis* ('and the utterly distant tribes of the Massyli'), 6.655 *tellure repostos* ('hidden away by the earth', of the dead).   **nouum dictuque nefas... | prodigium**: 'a strange prodigy and one not right to speak of': cf. 256–7, where Celaeno prophesied that hunger would drive the Trojans to eat their tables before they could found a city. Helenus responds to this at 394–5. On the adjectival use of *dictu nefas*, see Wackernagel 715.   **canit**: the verb is common of prophecies (155), and Celaeno spoke in hexameters, like the oracles of Apollo and the Sibyl (*fata canit*, 444).   **tristis denuntiat iras**: 'threatens grim manifestations of anger': see 215 n. for the intimate connexion between the Harpies and *ira*. Beginning from 1.11 and 25, which establish Juno's anger as a theme, the plural of *ira* appears thirty-four times in the *Aeneid*, often as here with the sense 'exhibitions of anger'. *tristis* also picks up on the earlier account of the Harpies (214), as does *obscenam* in the next phrase (241, 262).   **obscenamque famem**: 'and portentous hunger', as threatened at 256–7. The long parenthesis ends on this grim note.   **uito**: for the indicative in a deliberative* question, cf. 88.   **quidue sequens... possim**: the subjunctive shows

Commentary: lines 356–462

that the participle is equivalent to *si sequar*: 'if I were to pursue [= by pursuing] what end could I overcome …?' **tantos…labores**: the speech ends with another echo of a key theme from the proem (1.10 *tot…labores*), also revisited at e.g. 7.117, 12.177 *quam propter tantos potui perferre labores* (the land 'for which I have been able to endure such labours'), 12.435. The word helps figure Aeneas as a hero, undergoing ἄεθλοι as Odysseus does (1.18), and Hercules too (cf. 8.291 *ut duros mille labores…fatis Iunonis iniquae* | *pertulerit*, 'how he endured a thousand tough labours through the fate imposed by unfair Juno'; 10.321).

369–73 hic: 'at this point'. **pacem diuum**: first Helenus seeks divine goodwill, in the traditional Roman way: cf. 251, *OLD pax* 2, and e.g. Oakley on Livy 6.1.12. **uittas…resoluit | sacrati capitis**: 'unties the fillets from his consecrated head'. On 4.518 Servius enunciates the principle *in sacris nihil solet esse religatum* ('in sacred rites it is normal for nothing to be tied'); and in describing direct attempts to channel divine power writers regularly mention (or imply) the absence of belts or knots (4.518; Ovid, *Met.* 1.382), sandals (Ovid, *Fasti* 5.432; Petronius 44.18), and rings (*Fasti* 4.658; Gellius 10.15.6): for the prophet without fillets cf. the Sibyl at 6.48 *non comptae mansere comae* ('her hair was no longer well-arranged'). **ad tua limina, Phoebe**: as at 119 the apostrophe* lends a hymnic quality to the narrative, and perhaps hints at the intimacy with Apollo of another priest, Caesar, who appears *sedens…limine Phoebi* on the shield (8.720). **ipse manu…ducit**: though Horsfall finds here a 'gesture of affectionate reassurance', as he acknowledges, it is hard to find the parallels that confirm the significance of such an act. **multo suspensum numine**: 'anxious at the powerful presence of divinity'. We might expect the prophet about to speak to be the one affected by divine power (cf. the Sibyl at 6.46–51, 77–80), and Servius records the variant *suspensus*, which would refer to Helenus. However, V. uses the participle of those making enquiries (2.114, 6.722), or afflicted by uncertainty (5.827), so *suspensum*, of Aeneas and his anxiety about what he is going to hear, is probably correct.

374–462 Aeneas now delivers Helenus' divinely inspired prophecy (*diuino ore*, 373), aiming to capture its friendly tone (*ore amico*, 463). Three lines of oracular grandiloquence—Aeneas is crossing the deep under higher protection; thus is Jupiter arranging the fated future—

introduce the prophet's wish to make the journey to Italy safer. He begins with a summary of the long voyage ahead, and quickly gets the Trojans to the west coast of Italy: the forecast of the favourable omen of the fecund sow and her thirty young (388–93) outweighs Celaeno's threat about hunger and the eating of tables (394–5). He then returns to more immediate matters: the Trojans should avoid the nearer parts of Italy because of the hostile Greek population (396–402) and should sail round Sicily rather than passing through the narrow channel between Sicily and the mainland and thus encountering the dangers posed by Scylla and Charybdis (410–32). Interspersed with instruction about the journey is important religious advice: the Trojans are to cover their heads during sacrifice, as the Romans will (403–9), and Aeneas is to win over Juno with worship: that, Helenus surprisingly says (see below), will ensure arrival in Italy (433–40). Finally he combines the geographical and the sacred in telling Aeneas to consult the Cumaean Sibyl (441–60).

The prophet says nothing of (a) the Cyclops, (b) the death of Anchises (Aeneas complains about this omission at 712–13), (c) the storm, the arrival in Carthage, and Dido, (d) the return to Sicily and the burning of the ships. Near the start of his speech he says that he will only reveal *pauca…e multis*, explaining that the Fates prevent him from knowing the rest and that Juno forbids him to speak it (379–80); and in his penultimate line, he says that Aeneas has received the advice he is allowed to hear from Helenus (461). These paradoxical comments taken together are appropriately cryptic for an oracular utterance. They invite the reader to consider whether Helenus knows more than he is saying; and they are in line with O'Hara's illuminating comments on the prophecies of Celaeno and Helenus (1990: 25): 'events repeatedly betray Aeneas' expectations, because of what he has been told by gods and prophets'.

Helenus' assertion that Juno forbids him to say more (380) is lent emphasis by the fact that V. alters his source for this line in the *Argonautica* (2.313–16: **M(d)**) where it is Zeus, not his wife, who wishes to put limitations on human prophecy. It links with Helenus' emphatic demand that Aeneas should win the goddess over with suppliant gifts (433–9). The narrative structure of the *Aeneid* means that readers will be aware that any Trojan action to this effect (e.g. at 546–7) will fail (though eventually Roman worship will win Juno round: 1.279–85, 12.838–40). The poem begins with an explanation of her passionate and persistent rage against the Trojans (1.8–49) and her instigation of the terrible storm that drives them to Carthage. Together with Venus, she will engineer a marriage between Dido and Aeneas. She will also instigate the burning of the ships (5.606) and the war in Italy (7.286–640). When she prevents Helenus from saying more, it may be with the intention of keeping Aeneas in ignorance of all of this—and it suits the narrative (see next paragraph). On the other hand, the demand that Aeneas pray to Juno may prove sympathetic to the listening Dido. Carthage is the goddess's most highly favoured city (1.15–18, 441–5) and work on the temple to Juno that Dido is building is essentially finished (446–93).

Though Helenus attributes his omissions to divine constraints, it would make no narratological sense for him to predict all that follows. Aeneas will soon recount the encounter with Polyphemus, and in any case the Trojans escape unscathed. Similarly, he will tell us of the death of Anchises, an event that might be ascribed to Fortune rather than Fate (especially given the inconsistencies over where it happened: 707 n.). The poet himself has already done full justice to the storm, the arrival in Africa, and the meeting with Dido in Book 1: the reader does not need to hear a prophecy of these events, or the return to Sicily, which will be described in Book 5. On the divine level, these are not fated, but the results of Juno's interference—and thus perhaps beyond Helenus' ken. (It would also be distinctly awkward to have Aeneas repeat before Dido that he would meet a woman in Africa who would be a threat to his mission.)

The *Odyssey* provides models for a prophecy which guides a hero on his journey: 11.100–37 and 12.37–141, Odysseus receiving advice from the ghost of Tiresias and Circe respectively. At 11.101–3 Tiresias explicitly warns Odysseus about the wrath of the god Poseidon, who plays the same role as agent of obstruction in the *Odyssey* as Juno does in the *Aeneid*; he advises the hero to sacrifice to the hostile deity, but as a one-off (11.127–34), rather than the habitual act prescribed in V.'s aetiological* poem. Helenus is like Circe in offering advice about the monsters the hero will meet (420–4 n.). The second source of Helenus' speech is Apollonius' *Argonautica*; that poem's most complete account of future events comes from Phineus (2.311–425), already brought to mind by the Harpies episode; later Argus will advise the Argonauts on the return journey (4.257–93), and Hera will seek the aid of Thetis by describing the dangers of Scylla and Charybdis (4.789–832). As we have seen, from Phineus comes the narrator's interest in limiting what is revealed to heroes—and to readers—in advance (2.311–16: **M(d)**);

182   *A Commentary on Vergil,* Aeneid *3*

and his advice about passing through the Clashing Rocks (2.317–40) has obvious resonances in Helenus' warning about Scylla and Charybdis. (For a fuller discussion see Nelis 38–44.)

The speech follows the models of Circe and Phineus in using a primarily didactic* mode rather than the obfuscating or inspired manner of Apollo, Celaeno, or the Sibyl at 6.83–97. Though mysteries are created (386, 439) and maintained (394), Helenus repeatedly explains his advice (the repeated *nam* at 374, 379 might be seen as programmatic*): he tells Aeneas *why* he must avoid *magna Graecia* (396–402), sail round Sicily (410–32), and visit the Sibyl (458–60); he even justifies the covering of the head in sacrifice (406–7). There is much repetition to emphasize key moments of warning or advice (384, 392–3, 396, 408–9, 435–8).

374–6 nate dea (nam …): the parenthesis either explains why Helenus feels able to respond to the request, or introduces the reason for the use of this vocative here (it has more significance than at 311): it is obvious to Helenus that Aeneas continues to be the recipient of divine care, as suits the son of a goddess.   **te maioribus ire per altum | auspiciis manifesta fides**: 'there is clear evidence that you are going over the sea under higher auspices'. *maioribus…auspiciis* (which is quickly glossed* by 375–6) justifies the seriousness with which Aeneas and his father are treating the omens received since the night of Troy's fall (cf. *auguriis…diuum*, 5, as well as the sequence of prophecies heard in this book). *auspicia* (literally, omens gathered by observing birds) and its near synonym *auguria* were fundamental to Rome's religious identity: cf. for example Livy 6.41.4 (speech of Appius Claudius Crassus) *auspiciis hanc urbem conditam esse, auspiciis bello ac pace domi militiaeque omnia geri, quis est qui ignoret?* ('who is there that does not know this city was founded through the taking of auspices, and that all business of war and peace, at home and abroad, is conducted under auspices?'). The longest passage extant from Ennius' *Annales* (72–91 Skutsch) concerns the competitive taking of auspices by Remus and Romulus to decide who should name and rule the new city. These twenty lines are cited in the *de Diuinatione* (1.107) of Cicero, who was himself an augur, though he also presents the classic statement of scepticism about augury in Book 2 of the work. The very name Augustus which Caesar chose for himself evokes augury (Ovid, *Fasti* 1.611); he too served as an augur (*R.G.* 7.3).   **deum rex**: for single monosyllables at the end of a hexameter, see Introduction,

Commentary: lines 356–462 183

p. 49. They frequently occur in traditional phrases, as here and in the repetition at 12.851: V. nods to Ennius, *Ann.* 203 *diuum pater atque hominum rex*: for V.'s use of such phrases to describe the supreme god, see Hutchinson 2013: 334–5. **fata... | sortitur**, lit. 'assigns fates by lot', might be given a less precise sense here, e.g. 'distributes'; but V. nowhere else uses *sortiri* of divine activity, and he has been precise in describing the functions of fate in 1.256–62 (see Introduction, pp. 36–7). At that chronologically later moment Jupiter will not be playing dice with Aeneas' future but setting in motion the inevitable process of history: this, unlike the narrator, Helenus cannot see. **uoluitque uices** reinforces the sense that Helenus' knowledge of the workings of fate is partial: *uices*, like *sortiri*, is not elsewhere used in connexion with the gods, and implies an alternation that only applies on the largest scale to the Trojans' fate—in the fulness of time their successors will defeat the Greeks who have defeated them (1.283–5). What Jupiter rolls at 1.262 are the *fatorum arcana*. In the Introduction (p. 37) we suggest the image of handling a scroll is in play there; here we come closer to the 'wheel of fortune', a concept at odds with the presentation of Jupiter and fate, but certainly available to V., as the phrase *fortunae rota* first appears at Cicero, *in Pisonem* 22 (see R. G. M. Nisbet (Oxford, 1961), *ad loc.* and K. F. Smith (New York, 1913) on Tibullus 1.5.70), and the concept is older. Virgilio expatiates on the topic in Canto 7 of Dante's *Inferno*. **is uertitur ordo**: 'thus the cycle of events proceeds'. *is* is correlated with *sic* (as *ea* with *is* in 393). Though *uertere* can be used of the elemental movements of the heavens (e.g. 2.250), in this context it rather recalls Jupiter's *denial* that he is changed (1.260 *neque me sententia uertit*); *ordo* on the other hand is used by V. of the big movements of history: *Ecl.* 4.5 *magnus ab integro saeclorum nascitur ordo* ('the great cycle of centuries is born anew'; cf. *Aen.* 7.44), 5.707 *quae fatorum posceret ordo* ('what the course of fate demanded'). The employment of three essentially synonymous phrases, the alliteration of *f* in 375, and of consonantal *u* in 376, together with the repetition of other sounds (<u>sortitur</u>...<u>uertitur</u> <u>ordo</u>), build up a feeling of oracular mystery, at least at the start of the speech.

377–80 pauca...e multis: for the selective nature of Helenus' speech, see 374–462 n. **quo tutior hospita lustres | aequora**: 'so that you may more safely pass across the seas that will receive you (*or* foreign seas)'. *hospita*, an adjectival form of the noun *hospes* used in the feminine and the neuter plural, does not necessarily carry the favourable meaning of our 'hospitable' and indeed can mean 'alien' (*OLD* 3). *quo* is the conjunction used to introduce purpose clauses containing a comparative. *lustrare* occurs three times in the speech (385, 429), each time of the Trojans' journeying; though these lack the religious meaning of e.g. 279, a sacred tone may be evoked by the broader themes of the speech.   **Ausonio…portu**: the Penates have told the sleeping Aeneas to go to the Ausonian land in 170–1.   **expediam**: a didactic* form (eleven times in Lucretius, e.g.) introduces a passage in which Helenus tells Aeneas that his current views are ignorantly misguided (381–2); the Sibyl is to provide further instruction (*expediet*, 460).   **prohibent…Parcae…uetat Saturnia Iuno**: the limits on what prophets may know or say is a persistent theme; V. particularly alludes* to Phineus in *Argonautica* 2 (178–86: **M(a)**; 2.311–16 (**M(d)**: see 374–462 n.), along with the hostility to Aeneas of Juno, daughter of Saturn. The epithet (or substantive*) *Saturnia*, which is applied to her fifteen times in the *Aeneid*, is present already in Ennius, *Ann.* 53 Skutsch.

381–3 principio: equivalent to the πρῶτον of Tiresias (*Od.* 11.106) and Circe (*Od.* 12.39), and Phineus' πάμπρωτον at *Arg.* 2.317; but (despite the excitement of first sighting in 523–4) the Italy Aeneas seeks is far off, and the order of Helenus' prophecy is soon disrupted; thus a closer model may be Lycophron 2, where the guard promises to speak 'from the very beginning' (ἀρχῆς ἀπ' ἄκρας), before apologizing for the lengthy and riddling complexity of Cassandra's prophecy.   **quam tu iam rere propinquam | uicinosque, ignare, paras inuadere portus**: 'which you now [i.e. while you are in Buthrotum] think close, and in your ignorance prepare to invade neighbouring ports'. The clause carries on after *que* without a direct link to the relative pronoun. *rere* = *reris* (cf. 440, 7.437); *ignare*, a vocative, is used with adverbial force, as at Ovid, *Met.* 2.100 (the Sun addressing Phaethon) *quid mea colla tenes blandis, ignare, lacertis?* ('why do you ignorantly clasp my neck with persuasive arms?'). *inuadere* can mean 'to enter' (*OLD* 7), but the word predominantly has connotations of aggression; Helenus may be looking forward to the way in which the native inhabitants of Italy will regard the Trojans—or to the invasion of Italy by Pyrrhus, a future king of Epirus, in 280 BC.   **Italiam…| longa procul longīs uĭa dīuĭdĭt ĭnuĭa terrīs**: 'Italy [*appropriately separated from the rest of the clause by the long parenthesis*] a long impassable journey via distant lands separates far off'. *longis…terris* is either instrumental ablative with *diuidit* or descriptive ablative with *uia* (or even the more distant *Italiam*). The line is given an oracular ring by the oxymoron* *uia inuia* (a Grecism: equivalent to Euripides, *Iphigenia in Tauris* 889 ὁδοὺς ἀνόδους: Wills 1996: 455), the repetition of *longus*, and the sequence of long and short *is* (length of vowel is marked here, not quantity of syllable).

384–7 ante looks forward to *quam* in 387, as in 255–6.   **Trinacria...unda**: the 'three-cornered' waters, i.e. those off the coast of Sicily (*Trinacria*); the phrase reproduces πόντου Τρινακρίου from *Argonautica* 4.291. With its three promontories (τρεῖς ἄκραι: Pelorus, Pachynus, Lilybaeum), the island is famously triangular (Call. *Aet*. fr. 1.36, Pliny, *Nat*. 3.86–7), and still symbolized by a three-legged figure on souvenirs. The adjective recurs at 429, 554, the noun at 440, 582. Homer uses the name Θρινάκια (Thrinacia) for the island pastured by the cattle of Helios (*Od*. 11.107, 12.127); the name appears also at Apollonius, *Arg*. 4.965, 994, in a context that identifies it as Sicily, as already in Thucydides (6.2.2).   **lentandus remus**: 'the oar must be bent' (*OLD lento* 1), evoking 'the "give" of an oar in the water due to its slight pliancy' (Williams): cf. Apollonius, *Arg*. 2.591–2 ('the oars bent like curved bows as the heroes strained at them') and C. J. Fordyce (Oxford, 1961) on Cat. 64.183. The effort involved in the journey is brought out, and reinforced by the presence of another spondaic* gerundive (*lustrandum*) in the middle of the next verse.   **salis Ausonii**: V. evokes the travails of the Argonauts in this part of the Mediterranean with his version of Αὐσονίη ἅλς, a phrase that occurs three times in Apollonius (4.590, 660, 846); it refers to the sea west of Italy, usually called the Tyrrhenian.   **lustrandum**, to be taken with all the subjects in 385–6, is used with a mild syllepsis*: the sea is to be 'traversed' (*OLD* 3), the island of Circe 'circled round' (*OLD* 2; cf. 429 *metas lustrare Pachyni*).   **infernique lacus**: when Helenus revisits this part of the journey at 442 *diuinosque lacus et Auerna sonantia siluis*, he changes the epithet and adds the specific mention of Lake Avernus. Avernus was famously an entrance to the underworld, and that would give a possible sense for *inferni* here (so Servius). But the easier way of understanding the phrase is as a direct reference to the waters of the underworld, which Aeneas will cross in Book 6: cf. Propertius 2.28.39–40 *una ratis fati nostros portabit amores...in inferno...lacu* ('A single vessel of fate will carry our love on the infernal lake'; perhaps also 3.18.10) and Tibullus 2.6.39–40 *ab excelsa praeceps delapsa fenestra | uenit ad infernos sanguinolenta lacus* ('having fallen headlong from a high window she came to the infernal lakes covered in blood'). V. uses the phrase *Stygios lacus* at 6.134, in the Sibyl's response to Aeneas' request to visit his father. It seems as if Helenus, having spoken of hell in his initial summary, then adjusts his revelation later, whether from divine constraint or tact.   **Aeaeaeque insula Circae**: Aeneas is to follow the travels of Odysseus and (again) the Argonauts. The Odyssean Circe turns some of his companions to swine before the hero (with divine aid) resists her magic, becomes her lover, and stays with her for a year: 10.133–12.150 (Book 11 narrates the trip to the world of the dead as an interlude); Helenus refers to a character whose eventual hospitality and advice provide a model for his role. At *Argonautica* 4.557–61 and 585–8 first the narrator and then the speaking keel of the Argo, fashioned from Dodonian oak, reveal that the Argonauts cannot return home until they are purified by Circe for the murder of Apsyrtus (Nelis 44); they visit her, successfully, at 4.659–752. Helenus by contrast tells Aeneas to pass by Circe's island (regularly identified as what turned into the promontory Monte Circeo), and this they will do, with Neptune's assistance, at 7.10–24. *Aeaea*, the name of Circe's island, carries with it the Greek cry of woe αἰαῖ ('alas'); the genitive extends the doleful sequence (cf. Propertius 3.12.31 *Aeaeae flentis...puellae*).

388–93 signa tibi dicam: 'I shall tell you signs'. Helenus adds the portent of the sow to that of the tables, but misleads both Aeneas and the reader by discussing the sow first. The verse imitates what Tiresias says to Odysseus before telling him the portent of the oar misidentified as a winnowing fan (the end of his journey to appease Poseidon): *Od*. 11.126 σῆμα δέ τοι ἐρέω μάλ' ἀριφραδές, οὐδέ σε λήσει ('I shall tell you a sign, a very clear one, and you shall not forget it').   **tu condita mente teneto**: reminiscent both of Homeric formulae*, e.g. *Od*. 15.27 σὺ δὲ σύνθεο θυμῷ ('take heed in your heart') and Lucretian didactic*, e.g. 2.582 *conuenit et memori mandatum mente tenere* ('it is good also to hold the instruction in a mindful brain').   **tibi sollicito**: the adjective accurately describes the agitation of Aeneas at the start of Book 8, esp. 18–35; an extraordinarily expressive simile (22–5) compares his thoughts to the darting reflections of sun- or moonlight off water in a bowl.   **secreti**: both 'remote', again (cf. 381–3) stressing the distance the Trojans must travel, and 'hidden', by the trees of 290, 'secluded', in the era before Tiber served an imperial city.   **sus**: for the single monosyllable at the end of the hexameter, see Intro., p. 49;

Commentary: lines 356-462

unlike 12 and 375 this instance is not known to echo Ennius, but cf. Lucretius 5.25 *horrens Arcadius sus*, 'the bristling Arcadian pig'. There it might be tempting to think the reference to Hercules' labour dealing with the 'Arcadian Boar' is undercut by the choice of *sus* rather than *aper* and the considerable emphasis that is thrust on the word by its placement, and here too we might feel there is a conflict between *ingens* and the brief monosyllable *sus*; but V. more closely imitates *Odyssey* 19.439 ἐν λόχμῃ πυκινῇ κατέκειτο μέγας σῦς ('in a thick copse lay a great pig'). It seems that *sus* is not a comic word in itself, and other closing monosyllables are grand (*dis*, 12; *rex*, 375).   **triginta capitum fetus enixa**: 'having delivered a litter [*lit.* offspring: *fetus* is acc. plur.] of thirty young [*lit.* heads]'. For *caput* referring to individual animals in enumeration, see *OLD* 8b. Sows usually had ten or twelve teats according to Pliny (*Nat.* 11.233); and Varro, *Rust.* 2.4.17 writes that piglets in excess of teats are a *portentum*, and then goes on to the story of Aeneas' sow, linking the number thirty to the years of Ascanius' reign at Lavinium before the founding of Alba Longa, as the god Tiber will at 8.47-8 (see below).   **alba solo recubans, albi circum ubera nati**: 'lying white on the ground, white young about her dugs': the repetition emphasizes the etymology of the place name Alba Longa (O'Hara 1996: 143): cf. Prop. 4.1.35 *stetit <u>Alba</u> potens, <u>albae</u> suis omine nata* ('Alba, born from the omen of the white sow, stood as a power'), Varro, *Ling. Lat.* 5.144. *ubera* in combination with the image of the fertile mother recalls Apollo's instruction at 95-6. The legend of the sow survives in subtly different versions: notable besides those already mentioned are Lycophron 1255-8; the historian Fabius Pictor (*c.*200 BC) cited by Diodorus (7.5 = *FRH* 1F3); Dionysius Hal. (*Rom.* 1.56). At *Aeneid* 8.43-5 Tiberinus, the god of the river Tiber, appearing to Aeneas in a dream, repeats Helenus' words in 390-2 (not surprisingly some MSS add 393, with *hic* for *is*). Tiberinus goes on to say (47-8) that after thirty years Ascanius will found Alba Longa (cf. Jupiter at 1.269). V.'s handling of the tradition is well discussed by Harrison, *PLLS* 5 (1985), 135-47.   **is...ea**: pronouns may be attracted into the gender of their predicate without disrupting the stress given by anaphora*: cf. 375-6, 660, 714.

394-5 nec tu mensarum morsus horresce futuros: V. regularly uses a negated imperative in prohibitions: 160, 316. The normal negative in this construction is *ne* and one would expect *neu* (= 'and don't') here; V. may prefer *nec tu* for reasons of euphony: he has it, though not with imperatives, also at 7.733, 12.810 whereas *neu tu* appears only twice in Statius and once in the fragmentary poet Dorcatius. Helenus reassures Aeneas over the anxieties he has expressed about Celaeno's prophecies in 365–7.   **fata uiam inuenient**: the fates will indeed find a way, with the help of Iulus' joke at 7.116 (266 n.): it would spoil the joke to tell it in advance, so divine constraint and narrative benefit combine well here. The reassuring words will be repeated in a more complex context at 10.113, when Jupiter tells the gods not to interfere in the fighting between the Trojans and the Rutuli: it looks there like indifference, but the words Jupiter has spoken at 1.257–66 (see Introduction, pp. 36–7 on *fata*) have already loaded the dice in Aeneas' favour.   **Apollo**: a significant presence in this book through his oracular presence, and involved in the response to the Harpies (264 n.) through his naming at 275 and his implicit presence at Actium (278–88). He is, moreover, the god who speaks through Helenus (359–73, 434).

396–8 has ... terras ... hanc litoris oram: as Servius notes, the deictics* *has* and *hanc* convey a gesture as Helenus points towards Italy. The urgency of the repetition, followed by the delaying relative clause of 397, sets up the powerfully simple denial of these lands in 398. **proxima quae nostri perfunditur aequoris aestu**: 'the closest shore that is washed by the ebb and flow of our sea': *quae* is postponed*, and *proxima* belongs grammatically within the relative clause, as is normal in Latin with superlatives (546).   **effuge**: 'avoid', stressed by enjambment* and by the following pause.   **malis habitantur moenia Grais**: the dative of the agent with *habitari* is mainly found with gerundive or past participle, but we may compare Ovid, *Tristia* 1.1.127–8 *nobis habitabitur orbis | ultimus* ('the end of the world will be inhabited by me'). *malis* defines these Greeks as 'hostile' (*OLD* 5a): Idomeneus and Philoctetes were among the sackers of Troy, and Locri Epizephyrii was to prove an unreliable ally for Rome in the war against Pyrrhus (280–275 BC). For *moenia* ('walls') as a synecdoche* for city, cf. 159.

399–402 Narycii posuerunt moenia Locri: Aeneas is not alone in his quest to find land to found a new city: these Locrians were originally from an unidentified town Narycium opposite the coast of Euboea (*Iliad* 2.535). Returning home from Troy their leader Ajax son of Oileus (called *Narycius heros* by Ovid at *Met.* 14.468) was shipwrecked by Pallas Athena, whose shrine he had desecrated (1.39–41); however, some crews carried on to southern Italy, where they founded Locri

Epizephyrii (= 'Western'). This is the furthest west of the three places listed here (Map 3).   **Sallentinos obsedit milite campos | Lyctius Idomeneūs**: 'Lyctian Idomeneus has fortified the Sallentine plains with his soldiers': the Sallentine plains are in the southern part of Apulia, the heel of Italy, and thus closest to Epirus. *milite* is a collective singular*, frequently used with such nouns (e.g. *eques, pedes, remex*). Idomeneus is *Lyctius* (an epithet V. uses also at *Ecl.* 5.72) because he comes from Crete, and Lyctus is among the Cretan cities named in Homer's catalogue (*Il.* 2.647); cf. Strabo 6.3.5 'they say that the Salentines are colonists from Crete'. Varro (*Ant. rer. hum.* 3.fr.6) has a story in which Idomeneus, after expulsion from Crete (122), joins up with Locrians in Illyria, and together they colonize southern Italy, including *Castrum Mineruae* (531 n.).   **hic illa ducis Meliboei | parua Philoctetae subnixa Petelia muro**: 'here is the famous little Petelia, resting on the wall of the Meliboean leader Philoctetes.' The Greek hero Philoctetes came from Meliboea in Thessaly (*Il.* 2.717). The smell of a festering wound from a snake-bite made the Greeks leave him on the island of Lemnos, till they discovered (from Helenus (!), according to Sophocles, *Philoctetes* 604–13) that his bow and arrows needed to be at Troy for the city to fall. He returned home safely from the war (*Od.* 3.190); but a later account says that he was then expelled from Meliboea to southern Italy, where he founded Petelia (west of the Golfo di Tarento) and Crimisa (Lycophron 911–13, which describes Crimisa as 'a little city', βραχύπτολις). V. is drawing from Cato the Elder who said in the *Origines* (*FRH* 5F64) that Philoctetes built the wall of Petelia. *parua* has been thought to make an etymological point, evoking the old Latin word *petilus* meaning 'thin'. *illa*, with its implication of Petelia's fame, perhaps pays tribute to a town that, unlike other cities of Bruttium, stayed faithful to Rome in the Second Punic War (Livy 23.20.4).

403–9 quin ('further') marks the move to a new, perhaps more important topic as in 1.279 *quin aspera Iuno*, 6.115, 6.824 *quin Decios Drusosque...aspice*, 9.465 (equivalent to the fuller forms *quin et(iam)* found e.g. at 4.309, 6.735, 6.777, 7.177).   **steterint**: 'are moored' (or 'beached': cf. 277); the future perfect marks the first part of the temporal clause as prior to the imperative in the main clause, whereas the fulfilling of vows on arrival (*solues*, 404) occurs at the same time as the veiling of the head: 410–11 follows the same pattern.   **classes**: poetic plural*, 'fleet' or 'ships': cf. 602.   **purpureo...amictu**: though *purpureus* can mean 'bright', the *toga praetexta*, worn by magistrates and priests, had a purple band round the edge: V. gives two aetiologies* in one.   **uelare comas**: *uelare* is passive imperative, with the verb used in a middle* sense, i.e. 'cover yourself' and 'cover your hair'; for the 'retained' accusative, cf. 81, and 545 (where the Trojans obey the instruction). Macrobius (*Sat.* 3.6.17) contrasts uncovered worship at the Ara Maxima (founded in Evander's day for Hercules: 8.102–304) with the usual Roman practice (409), which arose after Aeneas brought the ritual norm of covering the head. V. is also evoking (or perhaps inspiring) the frequent image of Augustus appearing in this manner, familiar to us from the Ara Pacis and the Via Labicana statue (now in the Palazzo Massimo in Rome, and dated later than 12 BC on the assumption that he is depicted as Pontifex Maximus). Highet (1972: 256) notes that 'the prescription to cover the head while sacrificing…has no parallel in Homer or Apollonius'.   **ne qua inter sanctos ignis in honore deorum | hostilis facies occurrat et omina turbet**: 'so that amid the sacred fires while you do the gods honour no hostile shape appear and disrupt the omens'. *quă* is the nominative feminine singular adjectival form of the indefinite pronoun *quis* (as in 433–4, 473; at 453 it is neuter plural). Veiling the head was intended to prevent any ill-omened sight.   **hunc…hunc…| hac**: for such threefold repetition within a sentence, cf. 433–4, 490, 539–40, 608–9, 714–15. Here it brings out the continuity of ritual practice between Aeneas and his followers, between the Trojans and their Roman descendants. The singular future imperative *teneto* (cf. 388) is to be taken ἀπὸ κοινοῦ* with the plural *socii* in the first clause.   **hac casti maneant in rēligione nepotes**: 'let your virtuous descendants continue with this form of religious practice'. *casti* here is equivalent to *pii*, 'showing due respect to the gods', as at Horace, *Carmen Saeculare* 42 *castus Aeneas*.

410–13 ast: cf. 330.   **digressum**: given the disorderly elements in the prophecy (381, 399 nn.), it is unclear whether this refers to departure from the shore where they worship (404, 543–7), or to the initial departure from Buthrotum (cf. 482, 492).   **Siculae…orae**: dative of destination, as at 338.   **angusti rarescent claustra Pelori**: 'the defences [i.e. headlands] of the narrow <strait of> Pelorus begin to separate [*lit.* thin out]': as Aeneas sails east and then perhaps north along the toe of Italy's foot, eventually the separation between the promontories comes to be visible (Maps 3, 4). Pelorus is the promontory

Commentary: lines 356–462   191

forming the north-eastern corner of Sicily; a whirlpool just off the port of Messina was identified as Charybdis (Strabo 6.2.3), and the opposite promontory is the home of Scylla. The tips of these two promontories form a kind of 'gate' (*OLD claustra* 4) enclosing the channel of water, which is 3 km wide. 'The spondaic middle of the line and the conglomeration of consonants slow the movement as Helenus comes to his solemn warning about the Straits of Messina' (Williams). **laeua...laeua**: the repetition is emphatic: the Trojans must not go through the strait but must turn to port (i.e. south) and go round Sicily in a long detour (*longo...circuitu*): *circuitus* is a prosaic word (22 instances in Julius Caesar's commentaries, e.g., and rare in poetry bar Manilius' technical *Astonomica*): Helenus does not seek to glamorize the long-drawn-out journey.   **tibi**: dative of the agent with *petantur*.   **dextrum fuge litus et undas**: the straits, which lie to starboard, are a place of violence, and the home of Scylla and Charybdis, as the following lines tell. There is also a historical reason for Aeneas, the symbolic predecessor of Augustus, to avoid these parts: Messina was the naval base of his opponent Sextus Pompeius in the civil conflicts of the early 30s.

414–19 haec loca...| dissiluisse ferunt: ancient tradition held that Sicily was once joined to Italy: thus the name of Rhegium, the town on the mainland opposite Messina, was derived from ῥηγνύναι ('break asunder'), perhaps hinted at by *dissiluisse. ferunt* is an 'Alexandrian footnote'* evoking this tradition; and later writers mark their accounts in similar ways (Ovid, *Met.* 15.290–2, *dicitur*), Pomponius Mela 2.115 (*ut ferunt*), Justin 4.1.1 (*ferunt*). As in 381–3, the construction of the sentence illustrates the point, through the separation of *haec loca* from its verb.   **ui quondam et uasta conuulsa ruina**: 'once torn by the force of a vast upheaval': *ui* and *uasta ruina* are a hendiadys*.   **tantum aeui longinqua ualet mutare uetustas**: 'so great a change can the long age of time bring about': the separation of Sicily from the mainland as it is described here was not a slow process. The point being made in the parenthesis is that in the course of a long period of time a sudden cataclysm could well happen.   **cum protinus utraque tellus | una foret**: apparently 'when the two countries were one continuous stretch', *protinus* having a local force (*OLD* 2; 10.340 *protinus hasta fugit* 'the spear sped straight on'). One would, however, have expected a pluperfect subjunctive to show that this state was prior to the earthquake; as things stand in most editions (with a comma before *cum* and stronger punctuation after *foret*), we are told of the continuity after the separation, and this awkwardness is exacerbated by the juxtaposition *cum protinus*, which implies that the adverb has its commoner temporal sense ('when immediately'). The difficulty is eased a little with the punctuation adopted here (following Mackail), with a semi-colon before *cum* and a comma after *foret* in the next line: the sense is in any case complete with *ferunt*, and *cum*-clauses regularly begin new sentences. It is also possible that *utraque tellus una foret* should rather be understood as 'one land was becoming a pair'; for *utraque* meaning 'two' cf. 504, and Ovid, *Fasti* 6.287 (Saturn and Ops had three daughters) *utraque nupserunt* ('two married'; Vesta did not); *protinus* would then be temporal ('in an instant').   **medio**: either dative ('to/into the middle'; cf. 410) or ablative of route ('through the middle').   **ui**: 'with force', 'violently': the abrupt monosyllable (alliterative with *uēnit*) is apt for the sudden cataclysm.   **Hesperium Siculo**: here the effect of separation is conveyed by the juxtaposed proper names: what was one land has now become two separate places.   **abscĭdit**: perfect tense; the line thus has five dactyls*, with coincidence of accent* and ictus* in the last three feet.   **aruaque et urbes | limite diductas angusto interluit aestu**: 'and once the fields and the cities were separated by a narrow border it flowed between them with its heaving swell'. A *limes* is a boundary between parcels of land (12.898, *Geo.* 1.126), typically a path that runs between two fields, just as the straits separate the neighbouring Sicily and Italy; *limite* is a conjecture by the great nineteenth-century critic Emil Baehrens, replacing (as at 6.900) the transmitted *litore*, which does nothing to clarify *diductas* (it is not a 'shore' that divides fields and cities). There is an intertext* here with Lucretius' description of the same strait at 1.720–1 [**O**]; he goes on to mention Charybdis and Etna, both of which Vergil will describe at greater length. The lines may be read as a programmatic* introduction to the grandeur of Sicily as expressed in the cosmic nature of Empedocles' thought and Lucretius' verse.

420–3 *Odyssey* 12 thrice features Scylla, a monster with six necks, and the whirlpool Charybdis: first when Circe explains to Odysseus how best to travel between them (12.81–110: **B(a)**), then when the ship does so (12.201–62: **B(b)**), and finally at 12.426–36, when Odysseus is alone and the wreckage he is using as a raft is first swallowed by Charybdis while he clings on to the figtree above, and then disgorged, so he can escape. Thrice too in Aeneas' account: first he is warned to avoid the strait by Helenus, then the Trojans nearly pass through at 3.554–67 and again at 684–6.   **implacata**: 'insatiable', 'unappeasable': a word first extant here and taken over by Ovid at *Met.* 8.845 (of the insatiable appetite of Erysicthon).   **obsidet**: 'occupies', with hostile intention: cf. Ovid, *Met.* 4.490 *aditumque obsedit Erinys* ('a Fury blocked the entrance').   **imo barathri ter gurgite uastos | sorbet in abruptum fluctus rursusque sub auras | erigit alternos**: 'thrice with the deep whirlpool of her abyss she sucks down huge waves into the chasm, and each time she sends them up again to the air'. According to Servius Charybdis was a gluttonous woman, the daughter of Neptune and Earth, who stole the cattle of Hercules (cf. Cacus in Book 8), was struck by Jupiter's thunderbolt and hurled headlong into the sea, where she preserved her former characteristic. Cicero (*Philippics* 2.67) observes that his political enemy Mark Antony outdoes Charybdis (*quae Charybdis tam uorax?* 'what Charybdis is so voracious?'); cf. 632 n. *barathri*, 'abyss' (Greek βάραθρον), is often used of the underworld (e.g. 8.245, Lucr. 3.966): Charybdis is given hellish associations. *uastus*, with its connotations of devastation as well as size, aptly becomes Charybdis' epithet (7.302, Lucr. 1.722 [**O**], Cat. 64.156). The neuter participle *abruptum* is used as a noun, as at 12.687. The phrasing of *sub auras erigit* looks ahead also to the encounter with Etna (576).   **sidera uerberat unda**: as again at 567, V. caps Homer's phrasing: at *Od.* 12.238–9 [**B(b)**] the foam simply falls on the cliff-tops.

424–5 For Homer's Scylla see **B**: at *Od.* 12.86 Scylla has a voice like a new-born hound; her name links etymologically with σκύλλειν ('tear', 'molest'), and σκύλαξ ('young dog'), which may have been the origin of the later version of her appearance (followed here), endowing her with dogs below the waist: the image was used on coins issued by Sextus Pompeius (see Powell 2008: 102; and J. Gerrish, '*Monstruosa species*: Scylla, Spartacus, Sextus Pompeius and Civil War in Sallust's *Histories*', *CJ* 111 (2015), 193–217). The dolphins and 'wolves' of 428, plus the dogs of 432, may also derive from *Odyssey* 12.97, where dolphins and 'dogs' (i.e. dogfish or sharks) are Scylla's normal diet. Lycophron 669 denotes her with the phrase 'mixed-maiden hound Fury' (Ἐρινὺς μιξοπάρθενος κύων); a rationalizing fragment of Sallust's *Histories* (4.27) describes the rock identified as Scylla as *formam hominis capitibus caninis succinctam* ('the shape of a human girt with dog's heads below'), Lucretius 5.892–3 speaks of *rapidis canibus succinctas* *semimarinis* | *corporibus Scyllas* ('Scyllas that are half sea-creatures, girt with snatching dogs below'), which V. had reworked at *Ecl.* 6.75 *succinctam latrantibus inguina monstris* ('girt round her sexual organs with barking monsters'). Ovid's narrative (*Met.* 13.730–14.74: partly in **T**) portrays her as a girl transformed by Circe in jealousy over Glaucus' love of her. Milton bases on Scylla his description of Sin, the monster met by Satan (along with her son Death) as he leaves Hell (*Paradise Lost* 2.650–61). For the sculpture of Scylla found in a cave at Sperlonga, see 588–691 n. V. makes use of many sound effects, e.g. the harsh alliteration of *c* and *s* in 424–5, 430–2; the echo effect of *exsertant(em)* and *trahentem* in 425; the explosive alliteration of *ps* in 426–7.   **caecis... latebris**: for the meaning 'devoid of light', 'dark' (of places), see OLD *caecus* 6. The phrase recalls the Harpies' lair (232).   **exsertantem**: 'thrusting out', equivalent to Homer's ἐξίσχει ('puts...forth', *Od.* 12.94): the only earlier example of the frequentative* *exserto* (which implies 'repeatedly') is in a passage of the lost historian Quadrigarius, cited by Gellius (9.13.12 = *FRH* 24F6), where a Gaul sticks out his tongue (*linguam exsertare*) to mock the Romans: V.'s word perhaps adds a note of grotesquerie.   **nauis in saxa trahentem**: in Homer Scylla grabs individual sailors with her heads; V. makes her a danger to the whole of Aeneas' fleet, thus evoking the disasters suffered by Caesar in this area during the conflict with Sextus Pompeius (Powell 2008: 96–107).

426–8 prima hominis facies et pulchro pectore uirgo | pube tenus, postrema immani corpore pistrix: 'her immediate appearance is that of a human and she is a fair-bosomed maiden down to her pubic region, below she is a sea-monster with a monstrous body'. A model for these lines is Lucretius 5.905 *prima leo, postrema draco, media ipsa Chimaera*, which is itself a close translation of *Iliad* 6.181 πρόσθε λέων, ὄπιθεν δὲ δράκων, μέσση δὲ χίμαιρα ('a lion in front, a serpent behind, Chimaera in the middle'). Hopman (2012: 180, 228) notes how later Roman poets draw on Lucretius' vocabulary to bring out the tension between Scylla's parts. At the start of the *Ars Poetica* Horace supposes his readers would laugh if a painter presented an image cobbled together from various parts, 'so that a woman beautiful above ended up foully in a black fish' (*ut turpiter atrum* | *desinat in piscem mulier formosa superne*, 3–4): did he find V.'s presentation of Scylla comic? Or would he have regarded her as generically appropriate, and so not contravening the demands of unity that he goes on to stress? We may note that the fantastic image is reported by Aeneas from the mouth of the prophet Helenus, and thus doubly distanced from the poet.   **pulchro pectore**: ablative of description, as is the contrasting *immani corpore* immediately below (Hopman 229).   **pube tenus**: *tenus* ('as far as') is accompanied by the ablative in the singular (but genitive in the plural); though functioning as a preposition, it follows its noun. Adams (*BICS* 27 (1980), 51) finds *pube* to be 'the only possible reference to the sexual organs in the *Aeneid*' (but cf. 428). As K. S. Myers (Cambridge, 2009) remarks on Ovid, *Met.* 14.59–67, 'Scylla was allegorized as a symbol of lust, with the dogs below her groin representing her shamelessness and rapacity.'   **delphinum caudas utero commissa luporum**: a monstrously difficult line, literally 'joining the tails of dolphins onto the belly of wolves'; contrast the easily comprehensible Ovid, *Met.* 12.478 *qua uir equo commissus erat* ('where the man had been joined to the horse', of a centaur). *caudas* is an accusative 'retained' with the passive: cf. 81, 405. Given the middle* use of *commissa*, one would expect *utero* to refer to the *uirgo*, and after *pube* it is tempting to give it a sexual sense; but then *luporum* has no function. As *luporum* is an untraditional element and confuses both the grammar and the image, we wonder whether it has replaced an adjective, e.g. *lupino*, which would soften the oddities of the genitive, keep the evocation of quasi-canine creatures around the groin, and allow a play on *lupa* (= prostitute) that would emphasize Scylla's sexual voracity (Hopman 230). Alternatively one might wonder whether the whole verse is an interpolation*: the weighty *pistrīx* would make a fine end to the sentence.

429–32 praestat ... quam: 'it is better that ... than that': *praestat* is followed by accusative-and-infinitive constructions both before and after the *quam*.   **Trinacrii metas lustrare Pachyni**: 'go round the point of Sicilian Pachynus': *meta* means the turning point at either end of a race track (*OLD* 2; at 5.129 of the turning point for the Trojans' ship-race). Here it refers to the turning point represented by the promontory of Cape Pachynus (see Map 4). *Trinacrii* is particularly apt here, where it is applied to one of the points of the 'triangle' (384 n.).   **cessantem**: i.e. 'losing time': i.e. it will obviously take far longer to go round Sicily than to pass through Scylla and Charybdis—if that could be done safely. The sequence of spondees* contributes to the sense of delay.   **longos et circumflectere cursus**: 'and sail round in a long detour'. *circumflectere*, 'to bend (one's course) round a turning point', appears to be a Vergilian coinage.   **semel...uidisse**: 'to have seen just once'. Circe had said that no one, even a god, could take pleaure in seeing Scylla (*Od.* 12.87–8), and Donatus wryly remarks that nobody can see Scylla for a second time.   **S̱cyllam...c̱aeruleis̱ c̱anibus̱**: Scylla's dogs (424–5 n.) are the colour of the sea: *caeruleus* means 'blue' or 'greenish-blue' (*OLD* 2); it is frequently applied to the sea, its occupants, and its divinities (e.g. 12.182, and Cat. 36.11, *ponto*; 5.123 Cloanthus' ship, called *Scylla*; *Geo.* 4.388 *Proteus*; so already Plautus, *Trin.* 834, Ennius, *Ann.* 378 Sk.).   **res̱onantia s̱ax̱a**: the description ends by drawing attention to the sound play that has continued in various forms since S̱cyllam c̱aec̱is̱ in 424; Aeneas will echo Helenus' words in reminiscing at 1.200–1. At the same time V. hints at the rationalizing explanation found already in Sallust: cf. the 'barking waves' (*latrantibus undis*) on the shore at 7.588.

433–40 praeterea strikes a didactic* note (93 instances in Lucretius) in marking a move to a different section, perhaps the most important of the speech.   **si qua...| si qua...si**: the first of a series of repetitions, which help to lend emphasis to the instruction.   **prudentia**: 'foresight' (i.e. *prouidentia*, from which the form derives), rather than general 'wisdom', a concept strangely absent from the diction of the *Aeneid*: this is the only instance of *prudentia*; there are none of *prudens*, *sapiens*, or *sapientia*.   **proque omnibus unum**: picking up *unum illud* from the start of the line (Wills 1996: 74) Helenus says that that one thing outweighs all the rest: *pro* here means 'in preference to' (*OLD* 7); Horsfall cites Cicero, *Dom.* 30 *me unum pro omnibus* ('me alone rather than everybody else').   **repetens iterumque iterumque**: 'repeating again and again': the repetition of *iterum* clearly figures the point being expressed (Wills 116).   **Iunonis...| Iunoni**: the anaphora* imitates the style regularly adopted in hymns (so e.g. Callimachus, *Hymn* 1.6–7: **I(a)**; cf. 119, and the repetition of Ceres' name in a religious context at *Geo.* 1.339–49). Despite the instruction Aeneas does not offer prayer to Juno when he visits her temple at Carthage (1.446–95), and instead finds misguided consolation in the sympathy of foreigners for the Trojans' suffering in the pictures presumably chosen to celebrate the victory of her beloved Greeks. But the Trojans do make offerings to Juno on first arrival in Italy (546–7), and when the fertile sow is discovered (8.81–5). Juno's devastating hostility to the Trojans is made plain at the outset of the poem (1.25–32) and remains implacable until near its conclusion (12.841). Tiberinus will likewise urge Aeneas to propitiate her at 8.60–1. Models here are Tiresias advising Odysseus to sacrifice to Poseidon (*Od.* 11.127–34) and Phineus telling the Argonauts that success in Colchis depends on Aphrodite (*Arg.* 2.423–4).   **supera**: i.e. 'win over', but the military implication is maintained by *uictor*.   **sic denique uictor**: 'in this way at last as victor': the phrasing seems designed to mislead Aeneas—prayer and sacrifices to Juno will not help him reach Italy. What matters is that she will not prevent Trojan arrival and success, and the Romans will be in the habit of worshipping her in the future. *denique* hints at the omission here of what happens in Books 1, 4, 5; *uictor* figures Aeneas as a victor on arrival in Italy, ahead of his war against the Latins, and as representative of the race that will in the long run conquer Carthage (and Greece: cf. 288).   **Trinacria finis Italos mittere relicta**: 'having left Sicily behind you will be sent to Italian lands': *mittēre* is the shortened second-person singular (cf. *rere*, 381) future passive, *finis* a poetic accusative of destination (cf. 254). Helenus' revisiting of Sicily (figured in the repetition of the syllable *re*) hints at the Trojans' return there in Book 5, before they head on to Italy in Book 6.

441–4 huc ubi delatus: cf. 154, 219.   **Cumaeam acceseris urbem**: Aeneas and his men will arrive at Cumae close to the joined Lucrine and Avernian lakes at the start of Book 6.   **diuinosque lacus et Auerna sonantia siluis**: see on 386 *infernique lacus*. Lake Avernus gave access to the underworld: hence the aura of divinity (*diuinos*). *et* is epexegetic*: rather than adding a fresh point, it partially defines *lacus*. V. normally uses the form *Auernus*; but the neuter plural *Auerna* was current too (Lucretius 6.740). *siluis* is instrumental ablative: the wind rustling the trees creates noise round the area of the lake. From the first speech in the *Eclogues* (1.5 *resonare doces . . . siluas*), woods are a resonant landscape in V. (e.g. *Ecl.* 2.13, 5.64, 10.58; *Aen.* 5.149, 6.704, 8.305; echoing those of Lucretius 4.572–89); and the woods near Cumae will play a far more important role in the story than this passing reference might suggest; for it is there that the Trojans seek the wood for Misenus' funeral pyre (6.179–82) and there that Aeneas finds the Golden Bough that will be his passport to the underworld (6.186–211).   **insanam uatem**: the Sibyl of Cumae, Deiphobe by name (6.36). Her frenzied possession by Apollo is forcefully described at 6.46–51, 77–80. This instruction is analogous to Circe's sending Odysseus to consult Tiresias, among the dead (*Od.* 10.490–5).   **fata canit**: 366, 375–6, 559 nn. Helenus sends Aeneas on from one declaration of his fate to another (494).   **foliisque notas et nomina mandat**:

'and entrusts marks and words to leaves'. Servius says that Varro described the Sibyl as writing her prophecies on palm leaves; but V. has just mentioned local woods and says nothing of such exotic imports.

445–7 carmina: the Sibyl will necessarily utter her prophecies in hexameters at 6.83–97; but this is in any case the traditional metre for oracles, including the Greek material collected in the Sibylline books (cf. Tibullus 2.5.16 *abdita quae senis fata canit pedibus*, the Sibyl, 'who sings hidden fates in hexameters'). The word sets up the implicit analogy between her method of composition and Vergil's, as he writes his poem close by. He too produces his work in a disorderly fashion (Introduction, p. 51), speaking it as well as committing it to leaves (of papyrus, presumably); he too disappointed those who wished to hear (or read) his words (*Vita Don.* §11, 31–3; Macrobius, *Sat.* 1.24.11); and in later centuries his work will provide a form of divination, the *sortes Vergilianae*, by which the curious chose a passage at random and then sought meaning in what they read there (J. M. Ziolkowski & M. C. J. Putnam (eds), *The Virgilian Tradition: The First Fifteen Hundred Years* (New Haven, 2008), 829–30).   **uirgo**: the noun is used at 6.47 and thrice when Aeneas addresses the Sibyl in Book 6; this part of her identity will play a large part in Ovid's account, where the trip to the underworld is described in four verses (*Met.* 14.116–19), and the long journey back to the light is occupied by the Sibyl's story of how she tricked Apollo into granting her prophetic powers while denying him sex (14.120–53).   **digerit in numerum**: 'arranges in order', so that the short jottings on each leaf can be set next to each other in the order in which they make sense (Servius).   **illa manent immota locis neque ab ordine cedunt**: given that *illa* refers to physical objects here (and *eadem* likewise in the following antithesis*), it is easiest to take it as standing for *folia*; but the *folia* and the *carmina* (or *fata*, 444) written on them are effectively equated. *manent immota* echoes Jupiter's assertion about the *fata* of the Trojans at 1.257–8 (Introduction, p. 36), and *ordine* makes a link with Helenus' words on fate at 375–6: all is as it should be—until the wind blows and the door opens.

448–52 uerum eadem: both words point to a strong antithesis* (*OLD uerum* 2; *idem* 10a).   **uerso tenuis cum cardine uentus | impulit et teneras turbauit ianua frondes**: 'but, when the hinge <on the door> turns and a breeze has set them in motion and <the movement of> the door has disturbed the light leaves'. Lines 448–51 each have four dactyls*, giving a lightness to the rhythm that is appropriate for the flitting leaves; the enjambed* *impulit* at the start of 449 strikingly communicates the sudden effect of the wind on the leaves. The account of the disorder of the Sibyl's oracles perhaps evokes the loss Rome suffered when the temple of Jupiter Optimus Maximus, in which the Sibylline Books were kept, was destroyed by fire in 83 BC; the senate arranged for a new collection to be put together from a variety of sources. The collection, seen as fundamental to the religious well-being of the Roman state, was moved by Augustus to two chests under the statue of Palatine Apollo (Suetonius, *Aug.* 31.1), apparently while V. was writing the *Aeneid* (6.71–4). **numquam deinde cauo uolitantia prendere saxo | nec reuocare situs aut iungere carmina curat**: 'after that she never concerns herself to take hold of them as they flit around in the rocky cave nor to recall their positions or join up the verses': it is tempting to see this as a depiction of despair from an author who had found his own *carmina* in disorder, whether physical or metaphorical. **inconsulti abeunt**: 'they go away without advice'. The abrupt start, with no expressed subject to the verb, may suggest the failure of the consultation, an effect heightened by elision of the long vowel at the end of *inconsulti* before the short vowel at the start of *abeunt*. *inconsultus* can mean both 'not having taken counsel' (hence 'rash') and, as clearly here, 'not having received advice (at a consultation)' (*OLD* 1c, Servius). **sedemque odere Sibyllae**: the choice of *sedem* anticipates some of the sounds of *odere Sibyllae* and thus increases the sense of disappointed distaste here.

453–7 hic tibi ne qua morae fuerint dispendia tanti...quin adeas uatem: 'Here let no expenditure of <time in> delaying be so valuable to you...as to prevent you from (*quin*) approaching the prophetess': *ne* + perfect subjunctive is regular for a negative command; *tanti* is genitive of value; *quin* follows the idea that concern for the loss of time might *prevent* a properly conducted consultation. **quamuis increpitent socii**: a touch of realism—the sailors may well be impatient over such apparently frivolous delay; cf. 4.418, where Dido thinks Aeneas' men are happy at the thought of leaving Carthage. **ui cursus in altum | uela uocet**: 'the journey forcefully (*ui*) calls the sails onto the deep': the alliteration of *u* suggests the summons of the breezes; but both the adverbial *ui* and *cursus* as the subject are surprising here, and Slater ingeniously suggested in their place *Volturnus*, a southern Italian name for the East Wind (cf. 356). **sinus...secundos**: there is tautology* here: *sinus* means 'sails bellying in the wind'

(*OLD* 7a); *secundus* is used 'of sails spread before a favourable wind' (*OLD* 1b).   **oracula poscas | ipsa canat**: a paratactic* indirect command: 'you should request that she utter prophecies', *oracula* being the object of *canat* (despite the word order): cf. Aeneas to the Sibyl at 6.76 *ipsa canas oro* (after asking her not to entrust her *carmina* to easily disordered leaves).   **uocemque uolens atque ora resoluat** stresses the need for orality, with an echo of Cassandra at Lycophron 3–4: οὐ γὰρ ἥσυχος ... ἔλυσε χρησμῶν ... αἰόλον στόμα ('not calmly did she loose the varying voice of her oracles': noted by Pillinger (forthcoming)).   **uolens**: 'willing(ly)': cf. Nisbet & Rudd on Horace, *Odes* 3.30.15–16: *uolens* 'is found in prayers for a god's goodwill, particularly in granting a request that could be refused'; like much religious diction it appears already in Cato's *de Agri Cultura* (141.2).

458–60 uenturaque bella: a brief reference to what dominates the narrative of the second half of the poem (as well as the Sibyl's words at 6.86 *bella, horrida bella*, and their terrifying context). Ironically Aeneas has just disposed of his *arma* (286–8), but Helenus will generously supply what the Trojans will need (467–71).   **quo quemque modo fugiasque ferasque laborem**: in addition to her warnings about a repeat of the Trojan War, the Sibyl will advise Aeneas to be bold, to seek help from a Greek city (6.95–7), and that he needs to bury a dead comrade and secure the Golden Bough if he is to visit the underworld and return (6.125–55). But the line itself is repeated (with third-person verbs) of Anchises' teaching at 6.892, the culmination of the repeated deferral of prophetic guidance (though even there the narrator passes on no details).   **cursusque dabit uenerata sacerdos**: 'revered, the priestess will supply (*i.e.* tell) the course'. The past participle of the deponent verb *ueneror* is used in a passive sense: cf. Horace, *Satires* 2.2.124 *uenerata Ceres*. *sacerdos* is an emendation for the transmitted *secundos* (drawn from 455, where the meaning is very similar). Horsfall says 'the adj. re-used so soon at v.-end bothers V. not at all'; however, the claim is not based on the evidence (the lists he adduces in his note on 7.554 cite no such repeated adjectives). Moreover, the Sibyl is not the kind of power who can control the winds (as Helenus has just revealed): she helps Aeneas on his various roads with advice.

461–2 quae nostra liceat te uoce moneri: 'the sort of things which it is allowed for you to be warned [i.e. told] by my voice' (taking *liceat* as a generic subjunctive): Helenus encloses* his advice with a return to the topic of 379–80. *moneo*, as often, takes two accusatives, one of the person advised or warned, one of the warning.   **uade age et ingentem factis fer ad aethera Troiam**: 'go then and raise Troy <made> great by your deeds to the skies'. The proleptic* *ingentem* offers a strong contrast with the *parua Troia* in which Helenus lives. *aethera* is Greek accusative singular. The encouragement matches that of the Penates at 158 *tollemus in astra nepotes*, and in echoing 1.259–60 *sublimemque feres ad sidera caeli | magnanimum Aenean* provides another moment of enclosure* to a speech that began with complex allusion* to Jupiter's prophecy (cf. also 7.98–9). The sardonic reader may notice that the Trojans will indeed soon be raised to the heavens—in the hyperbolic* description of their encounter with Charybdis at 564.

463–505 *Departure from Buthrotum*
After his long prophecy Helenus passes on wealth that he has inherited from Neoptolemus (some of it doubtless booty from Troy), and practical help too. At 472–3 departure seems to be imminent but the farewells are drawn out for a further thirty lines, as both Helenus and Andromache reprise elements of their earlier speeches: leaving the past behind proves both emotional and difficult. But the episode ends with Aeneas making promises that look ahead to the future contact and alliances between Epirus/Buthrotum and Rome.

463–71 uates recalls Aeneas' approach to Helenus at the start of the consultation (358).   **ore...amico**: *ore* frequently accompanies verbs of speaking in the poem, both unqualified (e.g. 1.614) and with an epithet, as here and at 373 *canit diuino ex ore*; most similar is *haec...placido...edidit ore* (Latinus 'uttered these words in a welcoming voice', 7.194; cf. 11.251). The prophecy has been friendly; and so are the kindnesses that follow.   **dona**: the giving of gifts upon departure is a repeated feature of the *Odyssey*, notably the presents given to Odysseus by the Phaeacians (13.10–15, 67–9, 217–18): that departure is the prelude to the return home to Ithaca; here the Trojans are heading to a home in Italy (but their future is far more distant and uncertain: 493–7). In two other instances in the *Odyssey* the gifts come after prolonged feasting and some attention to the delay it is causing: at 10.1–18 Odysseus stays for a month with Aeolus, and when the hero asks to depart the god helps him on his way with the favourable West Wind and a bag that contains all the others (cf. 481); at 4.587–619 Menelaus invites Telemachus to stay for eleven or twelve days before heading off with horses, a chariot, and a gold cup, but Telemachus says that his comrades are waiting for him, and Ithaca is not suitable land for horses, so a mixing bowl is offered instead, and eventually given at 15.113–19, along with other gifts, after discussion about the duty of a host not to detain a guest (15.59–91).   **dĕhīnc**: five times scanned thus, as an iambus*, by V., and four times as a monosyllable, with synizesis* (e.g. 1.131).   **auro grauia ac secto elephanto**: 'heavy with gold and cut ivory'; *elephas* is used by metonymy* for 'ivory' (as already in Homer). The hiatus* between *secto* and *elephanto* makes for an elegant allusion* to Homer's πριστοῦ ἐλέφαντος ('sawn ivory', *Od*. 18.196, 19.564), likewise with a hiatus. This helps confirm Schaper's conjecture *ac secto* for *sectoque* (found in all the MSS together with Servius and various grammarians). The scansion *auro grauiā sectoque elephanto* would be anomalous: such lengthening occurs in V. only in the case of the *e* of *que* (91; see also 702 n.). The corruption of the MSS is easily explained: *ac* was omitted between *grauia* and *secto*, and *que* was then added in order to replace the vanished conjunction.   **imperat … ferri**: *impero* with a passive infinitive (rather than *ut* + subjunctive) is not simply a poetic usage: it occurs e.g. in Caesar (*Ciu*. 1.61.6, 3.42.2) and Cicero (*Verr*. 2.2.56, 2.5.88). Verses 465–8 have seventeen spondees* and only seven dactyls*, which helps to evoke the impressiveness, weight, and heavy texture of the gifts; the mannered phrasing likewise evokes the craft of construction in 467–8.   **stipatque carinis**: 'and packs into the vessels', i.e. he gets the cargo packed by others. *carina* ('keel') is commonly used by synecdoche* for the boat as a whole.   **ingens argentum Dodonaeosque lebetas**: either two items in the catalogue, 'a great mass of silver and Dodonaean cauldrons', or one, 'massive pieces of silver, namely cauldrons from Dodona', with an epexegetic* use of *que*: cf. the same phrase *ingens argentum* of tableware at 1.640. Servius mentions bronze basins used as part of the oracular mystery at Dodona (cf. *cortina*, 92); V. presumably pictures similar vessels. For the importance of Dodona in the tradition of Aeneas' visit to Epirus, see 293, 334–5, 356–462 nn.; Dionysius Hal. (1.51.1) reports that the sanctuary still had various dedications inscribed as given by the Trojans, including bronze mixing bowls. For V.'s love of *ingens* see 62 n.; *lebetăs* is Greek accusative plural (from λέβης, a prized object already in Homer, e.g. *Il*. 23.259).   **loricam consertam hamis auroque trilicem**: 'a corselet interwoven with links [*lit*. hooks] and triple-meshed with gold', i.e. a chainmail corselet of gold: a particularly complex form of hendiadys*, as *hamis* and *auro* refer to the shape and material of the parts that make up the mail, but are associated grammatically with different epithets. **conum insignis galeae cristasque comantes**: 'a splendid helmet with flowing plumes set at its apex' (lit. 'the crest and flowing plumes of a splendid helmet'): the expression sets the focus on the apex (*cōnus* = Greek κῶνος) and especially the plumes. V. follows Homer in giving waving crests to heroic helmets, e.g. those of Turnus, *triplici crinitā iubā galeā* ('haired with a triple mane', 7.785) and Aeneas, *terribilem cristis galeam* ('frightening with its plumes', 8.620). **arma Neoptolemi**: these arms have been passed on as gifts, not stripped from a defeated enemy, and so they come without the disastrous connotations of Hector's donning the armour stripped from Patroclus (*Iliad* 17.192–209) or Pallas' arms worn by Turnus (10.495–505, and Harrison *ad loc.*). But the etymology of *Neoptolemus* (296 n.) may be important: these are arms to be worn in the 'new war' to be fought in Italy. Eventually the descendants of the Trojans will turn arms against Greece; cf. Putnam 1995: 59. **sunt et sua dona parenti**: 'my father gets special gifts too'; the application of *sua* to the grammatical subject is common when it refers to the notional subject (here expressed by the dative of advantage *parenti*): cf. 1.461 *sunt hic etiam sua praemia laudi* ('here too there are appropriate rewards for glory'). Though the gifts for the infirm Anchises would not be military equipment, we are left to guess what they might be. The sentence comes with the implication that the preceding lines list gifts for Aeneas, 470–1 gifts for 'the expedition as a whole' (Horsfall). **equos**: Epirus was famous for its horses (*Geo.* 1.59), and so they make a suitable gift from Helenus to his Trojan guests, whose city Homer describes as 'rich in horses' (*Il.* 5.551) and whose champion Hector he often refers to as 'tamer of horses'. Horses will be needed for the *lusus Troiae* display at 5.545–603 (though there is no sign of them when they arrive in Italy: n.b. Latinus' gift of horses at 7.274–85); horses were offered by Menelaus to Telemachus at *Odyssey* 4.590. Thus they are thematically and generically appropriate in a way that another local breed, Molossian dogs (*Geo.* 3.405), would not be. **duces**: probably 'pilots' for crossing the Adriatic, as in Dionysius' account (ἡγεμόνας ... τῆς ναυτιλίας, 'guides for the voyage', 1.51.2). For 'half-lines', see Introduction, p. 51. **remigium supplet**: 'he restores the full complement of oarsmen': Aeneas has left a few men behind on Crete (190). **socios simul instruit armis**: though *arma* can mean 'nautical equipment' (*OLD* 10c), with *socios* as object the phrase may simply mean 'provides with arms'.

472–4 interea: most easily taken as 'subsequently' (cf. 284).   **iubebat**: the omission of an object (e.g. *socios*) after *iubere* is common, especially where a group is being instructed: cf. 9 (Anchises' initial order to sail), 146, 289.   **Anchises**: his leadership here and the grand terms with which Helenus will address him in 475 remind us of his importance in the poem as his death approaches.   **fieret uento mora ne qua ferenti**: 'so that no delay should occur for a following wind' or 'when the wind is favourable': for the sense of *ferens* see *OLD* 1 'carrying in the desired direction, "favourable"' (hence Servius' gloss* *secundo*). The grammar is harder to judge: Vergil has *mora* + dative at 5.749 *haud mora consiliis*, 12.565 *ne qua meis esto dictis mora* ('let there be no delay in carrying out my words'), but in each case the point is that the carrying out of plans might be delayed, whereas the Trojans cannot delay the winds; *uento ferenti* seems therefore to stand for *uobis* (or *nauigationi*), *cum uentus flaret secundus* (which would match Helenus' rhetorical flourish at 480–1 *quid… demoror Austros*, i.e. your using of the winds), but a dative is easily supplied and an ablative absolute would convey the temporal idea more simply. We therefore suggest that *uento ferenti* is an ablative absolute: cf. 5.638 *nec tantis mora prodigiis* ('nor is there delay when the prodigies are so great'). Though the ending *-nti* (as opposed to *-nte*) is not normal in this construction, it is found not only in instances with a strong temporal sense such as Cato, *Agr.* 29 *luna silenti* ('when the moon is dark' [i.e. before the new moon]), Cicero, *de Consolatu* 2.24 *luce serenanti* ('as the day was brightening'), Lucretius 5.664 *orienti lumine*, Catullus 64.376 *orienti luce* (both 'as the sun was rising'), Ovid, *Fasti* 3.459 *uenienti nocte* ('as night comes'), but also elsewhere, e.g. Lucretius 5.887 *fugienti uita* ('as life departs'), Ovid, *Fasti* 5.571 *hinc stanti milite iusto* ('with a just army standing on one side') and perhaps *Her.* 5.155 *fallenti casta marito* ('chaste when her husband was cheating'); V. himself has other ablatives that might best be understood so: 10.292 *crescenti aestu* ('as the water rises'), *Geo.* 2.319 *uere rubenti* ('when spring grows bright'). It may be significant that V. has the participial form in *-nte* only once at line end, at *Geo.* 3.401 *sole cadente*, whereas he freely uses the form in *-nti* there, including ablatives, e.g. 5.820, 6.679, 7.102, 810.   **Phoebi interpres** reminds us that Helenus takes his knowledge of the future from Apollo: cf. 359, 371, 434, 479.

475–81 coniugio, Anchisa, Veneris dignate superbo: 'Anchises, deemed worthy of the proud honour of marriage to Venus'. In some

MSS the name is given in the form *Anchise*, which would match Ἀγχίση at e.g. *Homeric Hymn* 5.108, but grammatical texts (e.g. Quintilian 8.6.42) support *Anchisa*. Some Greek male names of the first declension have vocatives in -α, hence Latin forms such as *Orestă* (Ovid, *Tristia* 1.5.22; Seneca, *Ag.* 933). Here, however, a long syllable is needed, and Quintilian 1.5.61 cites together as archaic* Latin nominatives *Aenea* and *Anchisa* (cf. Naevius, *Poen.* 2 Warmington), and the *ā* matches that in the vocative *Aeneā* (41). For the passive use of the normally deponent verb *dignor*, see *OLD* 1a. Aeneas here quotes Helenus using *coniugium* of the apparently single encounter of Venus and Anchises (as in the Homeric Hymn); in the following book (4.338-9) he will firmly deny that he is married to Dido, even though he is building her city (4.260) and has hung up his arms in her bedroom (4.495-6). **cura deum**: 'darling of the gods', as the partner of Venus, but also in the care taken for his survival, as the rest of the line brings out (cf. 2.687-704). At 1.678 Venus describes Ascanius as *mea maxima cura*, recalled at 10.132 *Veneris iustissima cura*. **bis Pergameis erepte ruinis**: Anchises was saved for the first time when the city was sacked by Hercules (8.290-1) after he had been cheated by the oath-breaking Laomedon (248 n.): at 2.642-3 Anchises says that surviving one sack is enough. **tibi**: ethic* dative reinforcing *ecce* ('I tell you', 'you can see'); the combination is favoured by Cicero, especially in the letters. **Ausoniae tellus**: 'the land of Italy'; the genitive is appositional*, commoner in English than in Latin, which usually says *urbs Roma, terra Hesperia* (2.781), etc. **arripe**: 'seize', 'occupy': the word conveys urgency. **et tamen hanc pelago praeterlābāre necesse est**: 'and yet there is a need for you to sail past the land here.' *praeterlabare* is second person present subjunctive deponent (abbreviated form of *praeterlabaris*), and dependent upon *necesse est*, a regular paratactic* construction (*OLD necesse* 1a). With the four long syllables, compounded by the assonance of the long *a*s, the energy instilled by *arripe* seeps from the verse, as the notion of deferral is introduced. *hanc*, dependent on the preposition in the verb (cf. 688), looks back to *Ausoniae tellus*, but is then more precisely specified by the antithesis* *pars illa* in the next line. In his oracular speech, Helenus has told Aeneas to circumnavigate Sicily and look for a home on the western shores of Italy (381-95), and thus avoid the shores facing Buthrotum (396-402); now in his words to Anchises he pointedly repeats the warning. The feeling of repetition is then increased by the addition of *ait* in 480 (*compellat* has introduced the speech at 474), and by Helenus' comment on

his own prolixity at 480–1. **procul** <*est*>: 'is at a distance': cf. 13, 383. **pandit**: 'reveals': this summarizes the three positive prophecies of the book: Apollo speaks on Delos at 94–8, through the Penates at 154–71, and via Helenus' long speech. The 'heavy alliteration of *p* gives an oracular emphasis to the line' (Williams). **felix nati pietate**: 'blessed in the piety of your son'. Aeneas' hallmark quality of *pietas* is given emphasis by the rare stop after the fifth foot's trochee*.
p. 50 **quid ultra | prouehor**: 'why am I carrying on further?' An ironic foreshadowing of *prouehimur* at 506, where at last the Trojans are making progress again. **quid…fando surgentis demoror Austros**: Servius glosses*, 'i.e. keep you back from making use of the winds': cf. 473. Helenus' words delay the departure of the Trojans, but also the onward movement of the narrative. His last prophetic contribution is to foresee the rising of the South Winds that will help the ships head north-west to Ceraunia (506) and not impede the westward journey across to Italy.

482–5 nec minus: Andromache is as generous, and as sad, as Helenus at the parting (*digressu*, echoed by *digrediens* at 492). **picturatas auri subtemine uestis**: 'garments decorated by a thread of gold'. *picturatas* seems to be a Vergilian coinage. *subtemine* refers to thread which is either woven into the yarn to produce a picture (Ovid, *Met.* 6.56) or used to embroider the cloth (Silius 7.80). It recalls *subtegmina* (as Catullian editors spell it) in the refrain of the song of the Parcae (*currite ducentes subtegmina, currite, fusi*, 'run, spindles, run, pulling the threads', Cat. 64.327 etc., a line V. alludes to at *Ecl.* 4.46–7). The echo draws out other similarities: poem 64 describes a decorated *uestis* (49–266) on which appears Ariadne, repeatedly described as *maesta* (60, 130, 202, 249) at the departure of Theseus. **Phrygiam… chlamydem**: a *chlamys* is a cloak of the Greek type, pinned at the shoulder. The adjective *Phrygiam* (= Trojan) indicates that it was embroidered: cf. Pliny, *Nat.* 8.196 'The Phrygians invented embroidering with a needle and for this reason embroidered cloths are called *Phrygioniae*.' It is appropriate for Andromache, now in Greece, to have embroidered a Greek garment in the style of her homeland. **Ascanio**: Helenus has given presents to Aeneas and Anchises. Andromache, who sees Ascanius as an *alter* Astyanax, gives hers to the boy. (**nec cedit honore**): 'and she does not yield <to Helenus> in honouring <the Trojans>'. The dative *honori* is better attested in the MSS, but attempts to justify it are unpersuasive, and it has presumably arisen because *cedere* is so often followed by a dative.   **textilibusque onerat donis**: 'she loads <Ascanius> with woven gifts'. Verses 483–5 may describe the same gift.

486–91 accipe et haec..., puer: 'accept these gifts too, my boy'; the *et* perhaps adds the woven gifts to the others, or perhaps more loosely marks Andromache's gifts as additional to those already presented by Helenus at 464–71; Horsfall thinks it adds a new category of gift, additional to those already mentioned, but that separates the deictic* *haec* oddly from the narrative context.   **manuum tibi quae monumenta mearum**: 'to be souvenirs for you of my handiwork' (relative with subjunctive expressing purpose). The idea of a gift as a memento is taken from Homer, *Od.* 15.125–7 δῶρόν τοι καὶ ἐγώ, τέκνον φίλε, τοῦτο δίδωμι ('I give this gift to you, dear boy'), where a present for Telemachus' future bride is described as 'a souvenir of Helen's handiwork', μνῆμ' Ἑλένης χειρῶν. We may think of Hector's instruction to Andromache beneath the Scaean gate to go home and see to her weaving (*Iliad* 6.490–2): she weaves when he is already dead at *Il.* 22.440, and still she is obeying him.   **longum...amorem**: Andromache's 'long love' refers to Hector and Astyanax, as well as Ascanius; Servius points out that the phrase refers to the past as well as the future. The echo of Catullus 76.13 *difficile est longum subito deponere amorem* ('it is difficult suddenly to lay aside a long love') re-applies that reflection on sexual love to separation from family; *longus* comes also to mean 'distant' (*OLD* 6).   **Andromachae...| coniugis Hectoreae**: use of the third person adds to the pathos of the scene, and her formal dubbing of herself 'the wife of Hector' while her present husband Helenus stands by indicates that she sees herself as fundamentally *uniuira*: she even echoes Hector's account of her future, when someone will say 'This is the wife of Hector' (*Iliad* 6.460 Ἕκτορος ἥδε γυνή). There is a strong contrast with the listening Dido, who earnestly desires to stay faithful to her murdered husband Sychaeus (4.24–9) but is falling irretrievably in love with Aeneas as he tells his tale (see West, *AJPh* 104 (1983), 257–67; the point is brought out by the echo of 1.749 *infelix Dido longumque bibebat amorem* ('and unhappy Dido drank long draughts of love'). Her love too will involve distant separation.   **dona extrema tuorum**: 'these last gifts of your people', i.e. family or fellow Trojans. The adjective carries a sense of finality: the parting with Helenus and Andromache 'is Aeneas' last link with the tragedy of the past before he finally goes forward into his new world' (Williams).   **mihi sola mei super Astyanactis imago**: 'the only image I have left of my

Astyanax'. The adverb *super* (*OLD* 4a) is used adjectivally in the sense it has in the verb *supersum* ('remain alive, survive', *OLD* 5). After Troy had fallen, Astyanax was thrown to his death from the walls, a fate anticipated at *Iliad* 22.63–4, 24.734–6, and described by Andromache in the prologue to Euripides' play (*Andr.* 9–10: **H(a)**); and by the herald Talthybius at Euripides, *Troades* 1133–5. As Aeneas speaks, Dido has Cupid in her lap, himself an imitation of Ascanius (1.657–722); and at 4.327–30 she will wish she had a child whose features would remind her of Aeneas.   **sic oculos, sic ille manus, sic ora ferebat**: 'his eyes, his gestures, his expressions were just like yours': an ironic reworking of *Od.* 4.149–50, where Menelaus explains how he (like Helen) was able to identify the living Telemachus from his resemblance to Odysseus ('such were his legs, such his hands, and the cast of his eyes, and his head and his hair on top'). The anaphora* of the deictic* *sic* gives a vivid sense of Andromache's gaze passing over Ascanius.   **nunc aequali tecum pubesceret aeuo**: 'he would now be growing up with you, matched in age' (lit. 'of equal age', descriptive ablative); cf. Euripides, *Ion* 354: σοὶ ταὐτὸν ἥβης, εἴπερ ἦν, εἶχ' ἂν μέτρον ('he would be the same age as you if he were alive'). She says nothing to Aeneas: her concentration is on the boy she sees as a double of Astyanax. Having described her son as he was in the past in 490, she now fantasizes about a hypothetical present.

492–4 lacrimis ... obortis: why does Aeneas weep? Is it because of the sorrow of leave-taking or the thought of his uncertain future—or both? The explicit mention of his tears evokes those inherent in Andromache's speech.   **uiuite felices**: a combination of farewell (cf. *ualete*) and *makarismos**: cf. Aeneas' reaction to the city-building Carthaginians at 1.437: *o fortunati quorum iam moenia surgunt*. There too Aeneas generously celebrates those who have founded their city (cf. 498) and have good hopes of prosperity for the future, while all he can see ahead (494) is a succession of labours, threats, and vague promises of long-term success. Though Helenus and Andromache seem to have found little happiness in their recreation of Troy in Epirus, we need not think Aeneas insensitive here: *felix* implies prosperity, good fortune, rather than personal contentment (cf. 321, 480).   **quibus est fortuna peracta | iam sua**: 'as those for whom their fortune is now complete'. For the use of *sua* attached to subject cf. 469; more surprising is its use instead of *uestra*, though that may be eased by the move into the relative clause. *peracta* ('completed', 'brought to an end')

Commentary: lines 463–505   209

implies that this is the end of the story of Helenus and Andromache (cf. *quies*, 495); there is a grim echo when Dido uses *fortuna* and the same verb at 4.653 *uixi et quem dederat cursum Fortuna peregi* ('I have lived and completed the journey Fortuna had given'). **nos alia ex aliis in fata uocamur**: whereas it is *fortuna* that has brought Andromache and Helenus to a settled life in Buthrotum (318), Aeneas and his group of Trojans are controlled by the larger force of Fate (Introduction, pp. 35–8). They see it as something uncertain, driving them from Troy to Thrace, via Delos to Crete, then the Sporades, Actium, and Buthrotum, while ahead lies the labour of bypassing southern Italy and Sicily, in order to reach somewhere quite imprecise on Italy's western shore; but his choice of words make the real point—the destination is fated.

495–9 uobis parta quies: 'you have won rest'. For the ever-toiling Aeneas this is a positive statement, and *quies* is used by V. of pleasant rest (e.g. 1.723, of the pause between courses of the feast, or 2.268 of sleep as a rest from labours); but it is also used of the sleep of death (10.745 = 12.309), which the aged Latinus sees as imminent for him (*nam mihi parta quies*, 7.598).   **nullum maris aequor arandum**: Aeneas reworks the words of Creusa's ghost at 2.780 *longa tibi exsilia et uastum maris aequor arandum* ('you must plough long exile and the vast surface of the sea': a famous zeugma*—seas are 'ploughed' in Latin, but not normally exile). The links between sea and land are then brought out by the use of *arua* (lit. 'ploughland') in 496; but ploughing the sea is futile (Hutchinson in Günther 2015: 272).   **arua neque Ausoniae semper cedentia retro | quaerenda**: Book 3 has given a strong impression of a destination always moving further away, and this has been crystalized by Helenus' prophecy. The feeling continues to be expressed in later books (Barchiesi, *CQ* 44 (1994), 443), notably in the disruptive words of Iris impersonating Beroe at 5.629 *Italiam sequimur fugientem* ('we are pursuing a fleeing Italy') and in Aeneas' address to Apollo at 6.61 *iam tandem Italiae fugientis prendimus oras* ('at last we grasp the shores of fleeing Italy'). When he narrates the story, after the storm has driven them to Carthage, the sense of an ever-receding Italy is especially strong. The enjambment* of *quaerenda* stresses 'the felt distance of the goal' (Perkell).   **effigiem Xanthi Troiamque**: cf. 302, 349–51.   **melioribus, opto, | auspiciis**: 'with better omens for the future, I hope' i.e. than those of Troy.   **quae fuerit minus obuia Grais**: 'and may it have proved to be less in the path of the Greeks': *fuerit* is perfect subjunctive expressing a wish for the future, as the parenthetical *opto* helps the reader to see. Two of the three extant capital MSS (and some other sources) read *fuerint* but the antecedent to *quae* must be *Troiam*, not *auspiciis*: a singular verb is necessary.

500–5 Thybrim uicinaque Thybridis arua: 'the Tiber and the fields bordering on the Tiber': the polyptoton* of the *Thybris* adds emphasis to the river which Aeneas has been told is his goal by Creusa at 2.782. V. prefers the Greek form *Thybris* to the Latin *Tiberis*, which he uses only at 7.715 and *Geo.* 1.499.   **intraro**: syncope* of future perfect *intrauero*.   **cognatas urbes olim populosque propinquos, | Epiro Hesperiam ... unam faciemus utramque | Troiam animis**: 'the cities linked by origin and the related peoples, Hesperia with Epirus ... we shall one day make each one Troy in our hearts': an anacoluthon*, made easier by the parenthesis in 503–4. After the double object referring to the two cities, Buthrotum and Rome (though he will not hear of Rome directly till 4.275), Aeneas puts *Hesperiam* in apposition*, and varies the construction with *Epiro*, as if *coniungemus* were to follow (which can be constructed with plural objects or accusative + dative [= 'join x to y']); but after the parenthesis a more unusual and emphatic expression is used instead. The elision between the names of the two countries stresses their unity; but the Greek meanings of the words ('Mainland', 'Westerland') implies an impossibility to the dream (Jenkyns 1998: 440–1).   **quibus īdem** <s.> **Dardanus auctor | atque īdem** <pl.> **casūs**: 'who have the same origin, Dardanus, and the same fates': the importance of Dardanus (94, 156, 167) has now been understood.   **maneat nostros ea cura nepotes**: as Aeneas could not know, but any reader could, when a future Julian (Augustus), founded the city of Nicopolis (276, 287 nn.) in Epirus, the citizens were to be treated as *cognati* by the Romans. We may compare Cicero, *Verr.* 2.4.72 on the relationship between Segesta (founded by Aeneas, as at 5.746–61) and Rome: 'the people of Segesta think of themselves as joined with Rome not only by continual friendship and alliance, but also by a shared origin'.

506–47 *The voyage to and first landing in Italy*
At last the Trojans depart from the *parua Troia* of Buthrotum, and head towards their future land. The first sight of Italy is a momentous occasion (521–4), and V. builds a sense of expectation in the previous

paragraph (506–20) with a detailed account of their journey, their preparations, and the weather.

506–7 uicina Ceraunia iuxta: *Ceraunia* ('places of thunder') is a mountain range in southern Albania (*montes*, 508); the name is used in Latin to refer to the sheer promontory in which the range ends, marking the southern limit of the Adriatic, and the closest point to the heel of Italy (Map 3). It regularly appears in accounts of journeys east, usually as a danger to be avoided (Caesar, *Bell. Ciu.* 3.6.3; Horace, *Odes* 1.3.20 *infames scopulos Acroceraunia*, 'the notorious cliffs of Acroceraunia', in a poem addressing the ship carrying Vergil to Greece). Here it proves no threat to the Trojans: Jupiter favours their voyage (contrast *Geo.* 1.331–3 *flagranti... alta Ceraunia telo | deicit*, 'he casts down lofty Ceraunia with his blazing weapon'). The distance between Buthrotum and the peninsula is similar to the 72 km crossing to Italy: for narrative economy *uicina* contracts the former; at the same time it evokes the comparative closeness to Italy. For the anastrophe* (postponement of *iuxta*), see 75 n. **unde iter Italiam cursusque breuissimus undis**: 'from where the route <goes> to Italy and the voyage <is> shortest on the waves'. *Italiam* is accusative of motion towards (in prose a preposition would be expected).

508–11 sol ruit interea: the geography of the voyage north-east along the coast has been contracted by the narrative in 506; now the day is cut short too, the pace of time emphasized by *ruit* ('rushes down'). **montes umbrantur opaci**: 'the mountains grew shady and dark': *opaci* is proleptic*. **sternimur**: 'we stretch ourselves out', i.e. lay ourselves down to sleep (the reflexive use of the passive: G&L §218). **optatae gremio telluris**: 'in the embrace of the longed for land', a surprisingly emotional description of a foreign beach visited once after an easy voyage, but perhaps suggesting the pleasure of later Roman visitors who have reached the Greek coast safely. **sortiti remos**: an oddity. Why (even though fortified by the addition of more rowers at Buthrotum: 471) would the Trojans, who have been travelling for years, suddenly allot places on the rowing benches, and do so before sleep after a day's voyage? Contrast Apollonius, *Arg.* 1.395 and Propertius 3.21.12, in each of which the voyage is about to begin. **corpora curamus**: i.e. they eat, drink, and rest, thus dealing with the aches and pains of a day at sea (*fessos artus*). **sopor inrigat**: a nicely chosen verb, which implies not only the spreading of sleep through the body, but also the refreshment it brings, like water irrigating a garden.

512–14 Nox Horis acta: either 'Night proceeding hour by hour' (Servius says *per horas decurrens*, in which case we should not capitalize *Horis*), or 'driven by the Hours', as if the Hours were pulling or guiding the chariot of Night (*bigae*, 5.721) as it passes though the sky, still heading up (*subibat*) to the midpoint of its circuit (*orbem medium*) when Palinurus rises from his bed. The Horae are personified* (like Ὧραι, the Seasons, in Greek) e.g. by Ovid at *Fasti* 1.125; and at *Met.* 2.118–19 they yoke the horses to the chariot of the sun. **necdum ... subibat**: | **haud segnis strato surgit Palinurus**: parataxis*: no conjunction links the sentences; the reader has to supply 'when'. The period of rest is quickly over: the start was signalled by *sternimur* (509), the end by *strato surgit*. Palinurus is presumably keen to start well before dawn, if the weather is good, so that they reach the Italian coast as early in the day as possible. *stratum* (literally 'the strewn thing') is used by synecdoche* for a bed (*OLD* 1b); in this case he has presumably done no more than wrap himself in a blanket (contrast 176). For Palinurus, praised here both by *haud segnis* ('energetic') and by the description of his prompt and alert activity, see Introduction, p. 42: like Anchises he is given due prominence before his death (at the end of Book 5). Nelis (222) notes that the sequence of events begun here imitates Apollonius, *Arg.* 1.1273–83 ('pilot, departure in darkness, daybreak'); but Palinurus has risen even earlier than Tiphys, who is prompted by the morning star, and the Trojans leave no one behind, unlike the Argonauts, who lose Heracles. **omnis**: like *cuncta* (515 and 518) this emphasizes Palinurus' care. **explorat uentos atque auribus aëra** (Greek acc.) **captat**: knowing the direction of the wind will enable Palinurus as helmsman to plan the journey, and before this momentous voyage there is good reason for attention to be given to his investigations. For the procedure, cf. the advice of J. J. & P. Isler in *Sailing for Dummies*: 'Close your eyes and turn your face until you think that the wind is blowing straight at you. Rotate your head back and forth slightly until you sense that the wind is blowing equally hard across each side of your face, and the "sound" of the wind is the same in each ear.' But V. also echoes the heifer at *Geo.* 1.376, which 'has snatched at the breezes with her nostrils' (*captauit naribus auras*), as a sign of imminent rain: Palinurus' ears can find no such portent.

515-17 sidera cuncta notat tacito labentia caelo: having confirmed the direction of the wind, Palinurus observes the stars: this enables him to determine the right course, but perhaps more importantly to check on the weather. V. wrote at length about weather signs in the second half of *Georgics* 1, with occasional reference to the stars, e.g. (as a sign of imminent clear weather) 1.395 *nam neque tum stellis acies obtunsa uidetur* ('for then the sharp appearance of the stars does not appear blunted'). All bodes well as Palinurus gazes: the stars are visible, rotating on their normal courses (*labentia*: *OLD* 2a) in an untroubled sky (*tacito caelo*). **Arcturum pluuiasque Hyadas geminosque Triones** reprises a verse (1.744) from the summary account of the song of the Punic singer Iopas, who just before Aeneas' narrative has delighted the company with his cosmology*. Such lists of stars are found already in Homer, and V. combines names from *Odyssey* 5.272-4 (as he sails, Odysseus looks at the Pleiades, Bootes, the Bear, and Orion), and *Iliad* 18.486-7 (on the shield of Achilles are the Pleiades, the Hyades, Orion, and the Bear), together with Hesiod (*Works & Days* 609-15 includes Arcturus). The three accusatives exemplify the *sidera cuncta*, to which the names are in apposition*. The formulaic* nature of the line fits the ordered sight that encourages Palinurus to sail. The list of constellations here has a similar function to the lists of places passed on other voyages, where land is being skirted rather than open sea crossed.   **Arcturum**: 'the Bear-Warden' is the brightest star in the northern sky, and part of the constellation Bootes; it can prognosticate storms at its setting (Horace, *Odes* 3.1.27) and rising (Pliny, *Nat.* 2.106), as the star himself claims in the prologue of Plautus' *Rudens* (70) *uehemens sum exoriens, cum occido uehementior* ('Rising I am violent, more violent when I set').   **pluuias...Hyadas**: a cluster of stars set in the head of the constellation Taurus. On the evening setting Ovid writes (*Fasti* 5.165-6) *ora micant Tauri septem radiantia flammis, | nauita quas Hyadas Graius ab imbre uocat* ('the face of Taurus flickers shining with seven flames, which the Greek sailor calls Hyades from the rain'; similar is 6.197 on the morning rising); V's epithet *pluuias* likewise indicates derivation from ὕειν ('to rain'). But here the Hyades, like Arcturus and Orion, are simply rotating in a clear sky: sight of them near midnight is not in itself cause for anxiety.   **geminos...Triones**: 'the twin Bears': two constellations adjacent to the pole, also known as *Ursa Major*, the Plough or Big Dipper, and *Ursa Minor*, or Little Dipper (which includes the Pole Star). The obscure name *Triones* is explained by Varro (*L.L.* 7.74; Gellius 2.21.8-10) as meaning 'ploughing oxen'; the form *septem triones* is used to refer to the seven prominent stars of either Bear (e.g. by Cicero, *de Natura Deorum* 2.105–11); Vergil plays with the obscurity of the term in reducing the seven *triones* to two.   **armatumque auro ... Oriona**: Orion is an equatorial constellation, visible in the northern hemisphere in winter. It is seen as having the form of an enormous hunter, wearing a belt and sword (hence *armatum auro*). Aratus (634–46) has him killed by a scorpion when he assails Diana; in Ovid's account of the catasterism* at *Fasti* 5.493–544 he is killed trying to protect the goddess from the scorpion. Again, the morning setting of the constellation (in November) was connected to bad weather (e.g. 7.719 *saeuus ubi Orion hibernis conditur undis*, 'when savage Orion sets in the waves in winter'; 4.52; Horace, *Epodes* 10.10 *tristis Orion cadit*, 'Orion is grim in his setting'); but it is not setting here.   **circumspicit**: either 'surveys' (perhaps implying the scale of the giant) or 'looks around for' (suggesting the need to look in another direction after inspecting the Bears).   **Ŏrīōnă**: a Greek accusative. The name concludes a hexameter with four long syllables already in *Iliad* 18.486 = Hesiod, *Works & Days* 615, at Aratus 636, 754–5, and in Cicero's translation of Aratus (fr. 34.3). Sometimes (e.g. 1.535) V. scans the first O short.

518–20 cuncta ... caelo constare sereno: 'that everything is settled in a calm sky', confirmation of what Palinurus has looked for in 515–17.   **clarum ... signum**: the clear signal to sail matches the clarity of the stars. V. has *clarus* of sound also at 5.139, 7.141; of the brightness of heavenly bodies at 2.696, *Geo.* 1.138.   **castra**: found only here in Book 3, the noun may point to *Castrum Mineruae*, their next landfall (531), where they have been told not to stop (396–402). In Dionysius Hal., *Rom.* 1.51.2, the Trojans cross from 'the harbour of Anchises'; when they reach *Castrum Mineruae* Anchises will play the dominant role.   **temptamus ... uiam**: *uiam temptare* is used of setting out on an unfamiliar route also at 8.113 *ignotas temptare uias*, and *Geo.* 3.8 *temptanda uia est, qua me quoque possim | tollere humo* ('a way must be found by which I too could raise myself from the ground').   **uelorum pandimus alas**: the sails are figured as wings. For the genitive (= 'consisting in sails'), cf. the phrase *remigium alarum* ('oarage consisting in wings'), of Mercury at 1.301 and Daedalus at 6.19.

521–2 After a paragraph that builds a sense of expectation as the Trojans prepare to cross the Adriatic, the first sight of Italy is marked by a bright dawn.   **iamque** marks other significant moments on the journey, in particular the coming of dawn as Aeneas finally abandons Troy at 2.801 (*iamque iugis summae surgebat Lucifer Idae | ducebatque diem*: 'already the morning star was rising from the ridges of highest Ida and bringing on the day'); and in the same phrase **iamque rubescebat** at 7.25, when the Trojans reach the mouth of the Tiber: *iamque rubescebat radiis mare et aethere ab alto | Aurora in roseis fulgebat lutea bigis* ('already the sea was growing red with the sun's rays, and from the heights of heaven saffron-dyed Aurora was shining in her rosy chariot'). The combination of temporal adverb and imperfect verb leads the reader to expect an event that breaks into the process, often introduced (as here) by 'inverted' *cum*. Already in Homer the Greek goddess of dawn is described as 'rosy-fingered Eos'.   **stellis…fugatis**: the image of day or dawn putting the stars to flight is a common one in Latin poetry: cf. 5.42, Hor. *Odes* 3.21.24 *rediens fugat astra Phoebus*; [Sen.] *Octavia* 1–2 *Iam uaga caelo sidera fulgens | Aurora fugat*.   **procul obscuros collis**: what are these hills the Trojans see far off? The heel of Italy, which they are approaching, is rather flat, as *humilem* ('low-lying') immediately reminds us. As happens later in the passage, V. seems to evoke the Rome that lies in the distance of central Italy. Rome's hills are regularly used to refer to the city, e.g. at Horace, *Carmen Saeculare* 7 *dis quibus septem placuere colles* ('to the gods who take pleasure in the seven hills'), Ovid, *Met.* 14.845–6 *Romuleos colles*; and Vergil repeatedly uses the noun when Aeneas visits Pallanteum, on the site of future Rome, in Book 8 (216, 305, 351). *obscuros* is both realistic, implying the hazy impression of hills seen in the distance from the sea, and apt to this evocation of Rome, whose hills are still obscure as Aeneas speaks. Once settled by the Trojans Italy too will emerge from the humble state implied by *humilem*. The present tense of **uidemus**, and the next two verbs, gives vividness to the sight of Italy, and the excited reaction of the Trojans.

523–4 Italiam. Italiam…| Italiam: the enjambment* of the first occurrence of the name conveys the sense of realization: land is seen, and it must be—Italy (so Jenkyns 1998: 442–3). The repetition (a more joyous echo of Celaeno's words at 253–4) then imitates the repeated shouts as first Achates and then the comrades on each ship joyfully salute their future land. The elision of the first *Italiam* before the opening syllable of the second suggest the rapidity with which the cry is taken up. Vergil may be deliberately recalling the sound with which another group of travellers marked the beginning of the end of their long journey: when the Ten Thousand who have marched north from Mesopotamia under the command of Xenophon first catch sight of the sea, troop by troop, repeated shouts ring out of 'θάλαττα, θάλαττα' ('the sea, the sea'): *Anabasis* 4.7.24 (the similarity was noticed already by Thomas Hutchinson, the eighteenth-century commentator on Xenophon, *ad loc.*; note that θ was pronounced as an aspirated *t*). The aural effect here is enhanced by the repeated sounds in *conclāmăt Ăchātes...clāmore.*   **primus** refers to Achates as the first to shout, but also brings this out as a prime moment: cf. in this passage 537, 544; also 3.8 and the application of the epithet to Aeneas himself in the first line of the poem (see Introduction, p. 10). In Book 7 it will be Aeneas himself who sees the wood at the mouth of the Tiber (*atque hic Aeneas...prospicit*, 7.29–30).

525–7 pater Anchises: the phrase occurs eleven times in the poem, five of them in this book, where Aeneas' narrative is leading up to his father's death; but it also marks portentous moments where the old man responds with prayer (2.687, 3.263; cf. also 7.245).   **magnum cratera corona | induit impleuitque mero**: this rephrases actions described at the feast in Dido's palace *crateras magnos statuunt et uina coronant* ('they set up great mixing bowls and crown the wines', 1.724), phrasing repeated, with *laeti* for *magnos*, of the celebration on the banks of the Tiber (7.147): all three passages celebrate arrivals, but despite the friendly welcome arrival in Carthage has a rather different outcome. *cratera* transliterates the Greek form κρατῆρα, a third-declension accusative.   **diuosque uocauit**: both Anchises and Aeneas are represented as invoking the gods for any significant activity: see Introduction, pp. 41–2, and e.g. 2.700, when Anchises acknowledges the shooting star that persuades him to leave Troy. Thus too in Apollonius Jason prays to Apollo for a fair wind when the Argonauts are about to depart (*Arg.* 1.409–24), and pours wine for Earth and the native gods when they arrive in Colchis (*Arg.* 2.1271–4).   **stans celsa in puppi**: the helmsman and normally the ship's captain stood in the raised portion at the stern of an ancient vessel: Anchises is put in the position of honour and control. Significant repetitions of the phrase link Anchises to Aeneas (10.261: see Harrison *ad loc.*) and Augustus at Actium (8.680: **R**): see Introduction, p. 34 (and p. 51 on 'half-lines').

528–9 di maris et terrae tempestatumque potentes: the participle of *possum* has the regular sense 'having power', and is constructed with a

Commentary: lines 506–47   217

genitive to define the sphere in which mastery is exercised. We might expect an address to the gods of the land the Trojans now see for the first time (so, at Ovid, *Fasti* 1.509–11, as they travel up the Tiber, Carmentis, the mother of Evander, hails 'gods of the place we sought, and you land that will provide the heavens with new gods, and rivers and springs, ... '). But Anchises knows that this is only the beginning of the end of the journey, and so concentrates on those with the power to assist its completion. *terrae* acknowledges that difficulties may lie ahead on land, however, and in combination with *maris* echoes the proem, where Aeneas is described as 'harried on land and sea' (*et terris iactatus et alto*, 1.3). To this elemental pair *tempestatum* adds the air.   **uiam uento facilem**: 'a journey <made> easy by [*or* easy thanks to] the wind', *uento* serving as an instrumental or causal ablative.   **secundi**: 'following, favourable', a kind of participle of *sequor*, which with *spirate* figures as winds all the gods addressed. The whole line has a pattern of alliteration (*f- u- u- f- et s- s-*) that is evocative of helpfully blowing winds.

530–2 crebrescunt optatae aurae: the breezes respond to Anchises' prayer (implied by *optatae*) by blowing more strongly, and thus hastening their arrival on the shores of Italy. The elision of *optatae* at 3s may help convey the rapidity with which gust follows gust; there is a similar effect in the repetition of *p* and *t* in 530–1.   **crebrescunt ... patescit**: enclosing the line, the two inchoative* verbs (marked by the presence of *ēsc* at the end of the stem) bring out the sense of excited progress while the ships approach the coast and the port gradually opens out to view, as it gets closer (= *iam propior*, which functions adverbially).   **templumque apparet in arce Mineruae**: According to Dionysius Hal., *Rom*. 1.51.3, 'Landfall ... was at the place called Athenaeum, where Aeneas himself happened to set foot on Italy. The area is a promontory and on it is a harbour in summer, which since then has been called Venus' port.' Servius and the geographer Strabo (6.281) also mention a temple of Athena in the area. Modern Castro, on the coast south of Lecce, is thought to be on the site of the ancient *Castrum Mineruae* (Map 3); excavations in 2007 uncovered the temple of a warrior goddess, plausibly identified as Minerva. It seems appropriate that V. uses the Latin form *Minerua* here, though the goddess's Greek name *Pallas* appears in 544, and each name occurs ten times in the poem. So far in the poem she has been presented as the architect of the Wooden Horse (2.15), the supporter of the Greeks (2.163), the 'savage' protector of the snakes that kill Laocoön (2.226–7), and one of the destroyers of Troy (2.615). The reverence shown here is perhaps a turning point. At 11.477 the women of Latinus' city will take offerings *ad templum summasque ad Palladis arces*, as the Trojan women had done unsuccessfully (*Iliad* 6.269-311; *Aen.* 1.479-82); and on the shield (8.699) she will be set alongside Neptune and Venus as a Roman opponent of the Egyptian Anubis. Minerva was part of the Capitoline triad, alongside Jupiter and Juno, and thus had a home in the temple of Jupiter Optimus Maximus on the Capitol (Varro, *L.L.* 5.158; Livy 6.16.2, 29.9; 7.3.5): *in arce* hints at this; and the sense that we are seeing Rome in the distance will be strengthened in 536.   **uela legunt**: as they come into the mouth of the harbour, they reduce speed by brailing up their sails.

533 portus ab Euroo fluctu curuatus in arcum: the simplest way to understand the phrase with *ab* is to take it as expressing the instrument by which the harbour has been 'curved into a bay'. Such a usage is found in other authors (*OLD ab* 21; e.g. Lucretius 3.820, and Kenney *ad loc.*; Prop. 3.25.5; Ovid, *Met.* 8.514-15), and the phrasing at 570 *portus ab accessu uentorum immotus* supports the notion that *ab* is pleonastic* here (though commentators usually deny that Vergil extended the addition of *ab* from the agent to the instrument). The alternative is in each case to read the preposition as separative, *'away from* the eastern wave, curved into a bay', implying that the bay faces south and is protected from the east (as is the case at Castro). There are similar descriptions of protected harbours also at 1.159-69 (the landfall on the coast near Carthage), *Od.* 9.136-41 (the harbour opposite the land of the Cyclopes), 10.87-94 (the port of the Laestrygonians), 13.96-112 (the harbour of Phorcys on Ithaca, where Odysseus is landed as he returns home, also at dawn [C]: see de Jong *ad loc.*). Behind the calmness of the waters lies in each case a sense of threat. **Euroo fluctu**: *Eurus* is formed from Εὖρος, the Greek name for the East Wind. It occurs nowhere else in classical Latin nor is there an extant Greek equivalent. In an emblematic passage such as this, the choice of an unusual Grecizing word feels important: but is the port offered by Italy protected from the dangers of the Greek world, or has it been formed by Greek influences?

534–6 obiectae ... spumant ... cautes, | ipse latet: the repeated *s*-sounds of 534 contribute to the effective contrast between the foaming rocks cast down in the way of oncoming wind and wave and the port hidden behind (*portus* is shown by *ipse* to resume as subject). Again in 535–6, the ordering of the expression leads us from the twin breakwaters visible to the arriving traveller on to what comes into sight later: the turreted cliffs and the temple further from the shore.   **demittunt**: Vergil has a quasi-reflexive use of the verb (*OLD* 5b) to describe a topographical descent also at *Ecl.* 9.7–8 *qua se subducere colles | incipiunt mollique iugum demittere cliuo* ('where the hills begin to raise themselves up and to let the ridge descend with a gentle slope'). **bracchia**: moles protecting the harbour (*OLD* 6b), here defined further by *gemino muro* as twofold, one on each side. The diction personifies* the landscape (as happens more remarkably in the Cyclops episode).   **turriti scopuli**: Castro has cliffs, and *turriti* can be read as 'tower-like' (*OLD* d; for the picture cf. 1.162–3 *hinc atque hinc uastae rupes geminique minantur | in caelum scopuli*, 'on each side there are desolate crags and twin cliffs threaten up into the sky'), but *muro* has suggested fortifications, and we may think of the more famous towered crags of Rome's hills (cf. *scopuli* at 8.192; *turres* signify the city of Latinus at 7.160, and Rome at Propertius 3.21.15), well back indeed from this shore, along with the temple of Jupiter Optimus Maximus on the Capitol. *campum* in 538 gives a momentary vision of another part of Rome, the Campus Martius.   **refugit**: 'is set back' (*OLD* 3b): another verb with a primarily personal sense used topographically. As Putnam notes (1995: 60), it is also the culmination of a sequence of military words (*arce*, 531; *torquent*, 532; *arcum*, 533; *turriti*, 536): the landscape anticipates the omen (537–40).

537–8 hic returns us to the narrative after the brief ecphrasis* of the port (cf. Introduction, pp. 31–2).   **primum omen**: anything that coincides with initial acts, such as arrival, departure, or a new year, is liable to be read as significant: so Janus at Ovid, *Fasti* 1.178–80:

> 'omina principiis', inquit, 'inesse solent.
> ad primam uocem timidas aduertitis aures,
> et uisam primum consulit augur auem.'

'There are regularly omens in beginnings,' he said. 'You turn fearful ears towards the first word, and the augur seeks information from the bird first seen.'

The interpretation that Anchises gives to the sight is akin to what readers do in finding significance in textual detail; Anchises' reading here is not the only one possible, but the negative aspects are rather less strong than when Aeneas tries to begin the foundation of a city in the place where Polydorus has been killed (n.b. 17 *prima, ingressus*). The enclosure of the appositional* phrase within **quattuor…equos** is a mannerism that becomes a regular feature of Latin poetic style after instances in the *Eclogues* (e.g. 1.57 *raucae, tua cura, palumbes*); Vergil himself uses it sparingly in the *Aeneid* (the catalogue of J. B. Solodow, at *HSCPh* 90 (1986), 129–53, adds only 6.842–3 *geminos, duo fulmina belli, Scipiadas*, but misses at least 3.305, 10.391). The presence of four horses leads on to the image of the chariot at 542.   **tondentis campum late**: grazing implies fertility, and *late* ('far and wide') suggests the horses' freedom, as does the lack of people (cf. the similar circumstances at 221, brought out by *nullo custode*). But the Harpies episode has shown the danger of such assumptions, human inhabitants are implied by the buildings, and it is with the men of Italy that the Trojans will be in conflict.   **candore niuali** 'of snowy whiteness', descriptive ablative with *equos*. White animals were prized: so the horses of Achilles, coveted by Dolon, are described as 'whiter than snow' at *Iliad* 10.437. There is also an evocation of the triumphal chariot, drawn by four white horses according to poetry of the Augustan age (Prop. 4.1.32 *quattuor hinc albos Romulus egit equos*, Tib. 1.7.8, Ovid, *Ars* 1.214, *Fasti* 6.724); see M. Beard, *The Roman Triumph* (Cambridge, MA, 2007), 234–6.

539–43 bellum…pacis: Anchises' speech begins with war and ends with peace. The language of 539–40 strongly emphasizes war, the anaphora* *bellum…bello…bellum* being enhanced by the play between *armantur* and *armenta minantur*. When peace comes, it too is of a singularly warlike kind, symbolized by the possibility of the horses' combining in harmony, but to pull a chariot, itself a symbol of violent competition, war, and the Roman triumph; these lines thus anticipate the climax of Anchises' speech as a ghost, 6.851–3, where again peace is something attained through war and the imposition of order. War and (ambiguously) fertility are predicted on the basis of the horse's head found on the site of Carthage (1.441–5): again Aeneas' experiences match those reported for Dido. Another important intertext* comes at *Georgics* 2.143–8, part of the *laudes Italiae*, Vergil's famous celebration of Italian fertility and security:

>sed grauidae fruges et Bacchi Massicus umor
>impleuere; tenent oleae **armenta**que laeta.

> hinc **bell**ator **equ**us campo sese arduus infert,   145
> hinc *albi*, Clitumne, greges et maxima taurus
> uictima, saepe tuo perfusi flumine sacro,
> Romanos ad templa deum duxere triumphos.

But it [i.e. Italy] has been filled with teeming crops and the Massic liquid of Bacchus [i.e. wine]. It is occupied by olive trees and thriving herds. From here comes the warhorse carrying itself proudly over the plain, from here come the white herd and the bull, noblest of victims, which, often bathed in your sacred waters, Clitumnus, have escorted Roman triumphs to the temples of the gods.

Here V. has more subtly hinted at an etymological link between *armenta* and *bellum* (3.540 serves as a confirmatory gloss* on the earlier passage); here he uses the white cattle pastured on the banks of the Clitumnus to symbolize Italy, and they serve to link agricultural richness with triumph, a topic that is left implied in the *Aeneid* lines.   **hospita** (feminine equivalent of *hospes*) evokes both Italy's unfamiliarity ('foreign') and its desired welcome ('hospitable').   **portas** ('bring') plays on the notion that it is the land that moves when ships sail: 72 n.   **bello**: either ablative ('in war': 2.315, *Geo.* 3.28) or, as Servius thought, dative of purpose ('for war': 4.87).   **armenta**: used of the larger domestic animals. Varro (*L.L.* 5.96) derives it from *arare* ('plough'), but Servius in his commentary on this line links it with *arma*, and similarly writes on *Geo.* 3.49 *haec animalia apta sunt armis, ut scutis boum coria, equi proelio* ('these animals are suited to arms, cowhides for shields, horses for battle').   **idem** ('they too', lit. 'the same') stresses the continuity of subject to emphasize the contrast in the predicate. Given that *idem* makes sense in itself and the delay before we reach *quadrupedes* in the next line, that might be taken as in apposition*, 'four-footed beasts as they are'. The echo of *quattuor* applied to the same animals in 537 brings the implication that they will co-operate as a team in the same way as the four limbs of each horse do.   **olim**: 'on occasion' (*OLD* 4).   **curru** is dative with *succedere* (cf. 292 n.). On such forms, see Gellius 4.16, who cites examples in verse from Lucilius (satire-writer of the second century BC) as well as Vergil, and from Julius Caesar in prose.   **iugo**: probably to be taken as ablative, perhaps instrumental with *ferre* ('by means of') or *concordia* (cf. *Ecl.* 4.47 *concordes stabili fatorum numine Parcae*, 'the Parcae, harmonious thanks to the fixed will of destiny'), rather than dative with *concordia* ('in harmony with the yoke'). *concordia* is transferred from the horses to the bridles that maintain their unity: in Anchises' view good order needs to be imposed.   **spes et**

pacis: 'there is hope of peace too', supplying *est*, as *sunt* in the previous sentence.

543–7 Again Aeneas presents the Trojans as properly pious in response to their circumstances; the effect is increased here by their careful attention to the religious instructions of Helenus (403–9, 434–40). **Palladis armisonae**: the epithet is etymological, for Pallas was said to have her name ἀπὸ τοῦ πάλλειν τὸ δόρυ ('from shaking the spear': Servius, *Aen.* 1.39). The phrase continues the theme of war.   **prima** returns to the theme of primacy (523, 537 nn.).   **accepit**: 'welcomed', as a goddess receiving worshippers (cf. *Geo.* 2.475–7 *me...Musae...accipiant*; Cic. *Sest.* 147 *di immortales...me suis templis aduenientem receperunt*) and the representative of a place offering hospitality to visitors (cf. 79, 210, 708).   **ouantes**: see 189 n.   **capita...uelamur**: like other verbs of dressing (e.g. *redimitus* at 81), *uelare* can be used in the passive with a 'retained' accusative equivalent to that accompanying the active voice ('we cover our heads': see Helenus' instruction at 405; *OLD uelo* 3; G&L §338 n. 2, Woodcock §19).   **ante aras**: Aeneas does not spell out whether they go up to the temple or set up their own altars on the beach (cf. 404). His identification of the temple as Minerva's implies the former.   **Phrygio** helps bring out the opposition between the Trojans and 'Argive' Juno (547), opposition that they now formally begin to undo. The adjective also connects the familiar sight of a Roman priest's covered head and the practice's Trojan origin (cf. 408–9). The passage's use of the present tense (though that is of course conventional in narrative) and of the first-person plural helps link the aetiology* with the continuing practice.   **praeceptisque Heleni dederat quae maxima**: cf. 435–6. It is normal Latin to place the superlative adjective in the relative clause rather than attaching it to the antecedent (G&L §616.3; cf. 27); but the postponement* of the relative pronoun gives *maxima* extra weight.   **Iunoni**: it may not be mere coincidence that Augustus at *Res Gestae* 19.2 lists next to one another temples he built on the Aventine for Minerva and for Juno Regina; both goddesses are part of the Capitoline triad (531 n.) and their equivalents Athena and Hera are leading opponents of Troy in the *Iliad* (which is evoked by *Argiuae* and the epic-sounding compound *armisonae*).

548–69 *The voyage to Sicily*
As the Trojans sail west, the narrative advances swiftly, picking out a few places on Italy's south coast as they pass, and connecting them to

mythological traditions (cf. 692–707). When they approach Sicily, Etna comes to dominate the view, and introduces elements directly from the tales of Odysseus.

548–50 haud mora, continuo: the tautology* emphasizes that Trojans did not even set up camp at Castrum Minervae; they quickly follow Helenus' advice (396–402) to avoid the lands colonized by 'bad Greeks'. As at 207, <est> is notionally to be supplied with *haud mora*, but the phrase is commonly used where another clause follows without a conjunction (parataxis*), and it comes to function like an adverb ('without delay'). *continuo* logically belongs with *obuertimus* ('we immediately reposition'), but Latin regularly places it with an ablative absolute, as here, to stress that the Trojans sail 'as soon as their offerings are completed'. The pleonasm* immediately signals the pace of the paragraph.   **perfectis ordine uotis** marks the completion of the previous scene, *ordine* ('properly') rephrasing *rite* (546): even in their haste they observe due order in their prayers.   **cōrnŭă uēlātār(um) ōbuērtĭmŭs āntēmnārūm**: 'we reposition the horns of the sail-bearing yards'. In its metre this is an extraordinary line: it is a *spondeiazon*; but far more unusual is that it lacks any caesura, with word breaks at the end of the first and the fourth feet, and an elision occluding the gap in the third foot. Norden (423, 446) suggests the rhythm expresses the effort involved in the manoeuvre (comparing the opening spondees* of 562, e.g.). Though we may suspect that the final placing of *antemnarum* goes back to (e.g.) Ennius, the word is not found in the fragments of the *Annales*, nor is the form extant elsewhere in Latin verse. The *cornua* are the horn-like ends of the yards, spars from which the sails hang (an uncommon use of *uelo*: OLD 4b); when the fleet changes direction from south to west, the wind will blow from the other side of the vessel, so the horns are moved from one side of the mast to the other: compare the description of repeated tacking at 5.831–2 *una ardua torquent | cornua detorquentque* ('together they twist the horns above one way, and then back again'), and see L. Casson, *Ships and Seamanship in the Ancient World* (Princeton, 1971), 273–4. **Graiugenum... domos**: the southern parts of Italy, sometimes known as *magna Graecia*, were heavily colonized by Greeks between the eighth and fifth centuries BC (i.e. well after the supposed date of Aeneas). The form *Graiugenum* (genitive plural of *Graiugena*) perhaps evokes the fact that though 'born Greek' these people have migrated (compare Aeneas' use of *Troiugena* at 359 and 8.117).

224 *A Commentary on Vergil, Aeneid 3*

551–3 hinc: 'next'. V. is here (as in 687–707) working within the tradition of the *periplus**, which gives coastal features in order.   **sinus… Tarenti…diua Lacinia…Caulonisque arces…Scylaceum**: The geographer Pomponius Mela describes the coast as a series of bays (*Chor.* 2.68): *Tarentinus* (bounded on the west by the promontory of Lacinium); *Scyllaceus*, the site of *Scyllaceum* (now Squillace) among other towns; and a third, including *Caulonia*, further west: see Map 3. **Herculei (si uera est fama) Tarenti**: Tarentum lies at the north of the enormous Golfo di Taranto. The accounts that associate the city directly with Hercules probably stem from this verse itself (e.g. in Servius). However, it was a colony of Sparta, whose kings claimed descent from the hero; and he was linked to the foundations of the local cities Heraclea (called after Heracles, the Greek form of the name) and Croton (Ovid, *Met.* 15.12–18, Diodorus Sic. 4.23–4). As Horsfall suggests, *si uera est fama* may add a note of caution if the epithet is Vergil's invention.   **attollit se diua Lacinia contra**: Lacinia, a promontory at the extreme south of the bay (hence *contra*), near ancient Croton, is the site of a famous temple of Hera (Juno), hence *diua*.   **nauifragum Scylaceum**: the compound adjective implies that ships were notoriously wrecked on the broad, south-west-facing bay; but Vergil may be more interested in implying a link with Scylla, the ship-wrecking monster (425); her home Scyllaeum was the site of one of Caesar's naval disasters during the war with Sextus Pompey (Dio 48.47.2–5; see further Powell 2008: 103). Though she lies around the corner, on the strait between Italy and Sicily (described by Ovid as *nauifragum fretum* at *Met.* 14.6), the town of Scylaceum produced coins featuring Scylla (Hopman 2012: 192–3). For the rhythm, see p. 49.

554–7 Mount Etna, the largest active volcano in Europe (over 3,300 metres high), dominates the view of those approaching Sicily from the east. The horrors of its activity are postponed till the next paragraph, but its appearance (**cernitur**) is immediately accompanied by threatening noises and turbulent waters. As well as the narrows between Scylla and Charybdis [**B**; Map 3] these recall the encounters of the Argonauts with the Symplegades ('Clashing Rocks': see Apollonius 2.553–4 for the distant roar) and the Planctae ('Wandering Rocks': Ap. 4.924–63; Scylla and Charybdis are seen and heard at 4.922–3). Anchises will attribute the uncanny sounds and violence of the sea to Charybdis in 558, and that judgement is borne out by what follows

(564–7), but in **audimus longe** and **fractas...ad litora uoces** we may catch an echo of other figures from the *Odyssey*: the Sirens (12.39–54, 158–200): see D. Nelis, 'Broken voices on the shore: a note on *Aeneid* 3.556', *REA* 97 (1995), 627–31. These quasi-divine women (cf. 216 n.) lured sailors to their islands with their enchanting song and thus wrecked them on the rocks; however, Odysseus, following Circe's advice, fills his crew's ears with wax and is bound to the mast, so he can listen in safety. Subsequent tradition (the eponymous* vase of the 'Siren Painter', Lycophron 712–16, Hyginus, *Fab.* 125.13, 141) has the Sirens committing suicide in response to this worsting. In a passage that is a doublet of this one (Nelis 208), the Trojan fleet will at 5.864 pass by the *scopulos Sirenum* near Cape Palinurus, and do so safely because, though the sea still resounds on the rocks (866), Odysseus has already dealt with the threat (*difficilis quondam multorumque ossibus albos*, 'difficult once and white with the bones of many men', 865). However, the geographer Strabo mentions theories that place the Sirens on Cape Pelorus near the straits of Messina (1.2.12–13; cf. *SH* 456 (Hedyle), [Seneca], *Hercules Oet.* 189–90, Serv. *Aen.* 5.864), so an evocation of their presence here is apt: the seas crash dangerously on the rocks as we would expect, but the context reverberates with the lamentation (*gemitum, uoces*) of those whose boats they have wrecked (n.b. *fractas*), but perhaps also the woe of the Sirens themselves, who commit suicide on their own rocks (*pulsata saxa*), when their voices are silenced by Odysseus (*fractas uoces*). *uoces* of the sounds of the sea also hints at rationalizing explanations of the Sirens; and the phrasing repeats sounds expressively: *Trinacria cernitur Aetna; gemitum ingentem; pelagi pulsataque saxa*. The frequentative* *pulsata* brings out the repeated pounding of the sea. **aestu miscentur harenae** recalls *furit aestus harenis* ('the sea seethes with sand') in the account of the storm at 1.107, and verses 564–7 echo further details from that passage (notably 103 *ad sidera tollit*, 106–7 on the alternation between the peak of the waves and the trough, 108–10 *tris...tris*). As there and at 3.207–10 escape from the fury of the sea leads through a calm landing towards further danger.

558–60 pater Anchises: as often (e.g. 1.335, 10.62) before direct speech, a verb of speaking is to be understood. Though it is Aeneas to whom instructions have been given by Helenus (410–32 on Scylla and Charybdis), Anchises continues the dominant role he has re-assumed with departure from Buthrotum (cf. 472–9, 525–9, 539–43, 610–11).

His instructions correspond to, but vary, those at *Od.* 12.208–21: Odysseus instructs the crew to row hard and the helmsman to pass close to Scylla (whom he carefully does not mention), a policy that loses six men, while saving the boat as a whole (cf. Circe's words at 12.108–10 [**B(a)**]). The Trojans by contrast circumnavigate Sicily in the hope of reaching Latium with a full complement.　**nimirum haec illa Charybdis**: 'presumably this is the infamous Charybdis': *nimirum* (only here in V., and not common in poetry) marks the speaker as making a reasoned assumption. Though MP, the two antique MSS extant here, read *hic*, that may come from reminiscence of *hic illa* at 401. Most of the medieval MSS have the easier *haec*, which matches the phrasing of 559 ('these are the cliffs, these the rocks'). Servius notes that *illa* has a vituperative tone here; elsewhere the implication of renown is positive.　**hos Helenus scopulos, haec saxa**: again the sounds of the words encapsulate the sounds of the sea on the rocky shore. Horsfall notes that the phrasing is actually closer to *Od.* 12.239–42 [**B(b)**] than to Helenus' prophecy. Unlike the whirlpool Charybdis (a realistic force, even if exaggerated here and in the mythical tradition), the monstrous Scylla is absent from the direct encounter and not named, but mention of the cliffs evokes her (cf. 424–5), as does the interplay of *s* and *c* (cf. 432), and perhaps already *hic illa* in 558.　**canebat**: Helenus 'sang' as a prophet (373; *OLD* 8), but also as the creator of a narrative (*OLD* 3), like Aeneas himself—and Vergil too (cf. 1.1 *Arma uirumque cano*).　**eripite**: in his haste Anchises omits the object, but we easily supply *uos* or *naues*.　**socii**: an epic address for travelling companions (e.g. 1.198); the Greek equivalent ἑταῖροι is used at an analogous moment in Apollonius when the Argonauts are fearfully passing through the Symplegades: *Arg.* 2.588–9 'Euphemus shouted to his companions (ἑταίρους) to put all their strength into their oars' (Nelis 211); cf. e.g. *Odyssey* 1.5, 9.172–7.　**pariter**: 'together' adds due order to the command to row (cf. 5.142 *infindunt pariter sulcos*, 'they cleave furrows together', at the start of the boat race).　**paritérque insúrgite rémis**: the coincidence of íctus* and accent* conveys the regularity of the strokes. V. likes to visualize crews rising vigorously into their stroke on the oar (also 207); at 5.189–90 Mnestheus encourages his crew during the boat-race with the words *nunc, núnc insúrgite rémis, | Hectorei socii.*

561–3 haud minus ac (= *quam*) **iussi faciunt**: despite the urgency of the command, the Trojans respond precisely as ordered (cf. 236; and

Odysseus' crew at *Od.* 12.222). **primus... Palinurus**: as helmsman on the flagship, Palinurus is first to hear Anchises' instructions, and when he turns the ship to port (*laeuas ad undas*; cf. 412–13) the rest of the fleet follows (563). **tridentem... proram**: the three-pronged prow of the Trojan ships (cf. *rostrisque tridentibus* at 5.143, 8.690). *tridentem* is a conjecture by the great seventeenth-century Latinist, Nicolaus Heinsius, for the transmitted *rudentem*; *rudens* normally refers to a 'rope' in a naval context (cf. 267, 682), but would have here to be the present participle of *rudere*, 'roar' or 'bray', and thus inappropriate for the noise of the prow through the water. **laeuam** 'the left', 'the port side' (*partem* is implied): cf. 412.

564–7 Swiftly though they both row and sail away, they are nearly caught by the pull of Charybdis. The description of the effects of Charybdis is closely based on *Odyssey* 12.105–6 (**B(a)**: both authors use anaphora*, 'thrice,... thrice', for the repetitive process of spewing out and sucking in, and V. compounds this with the intrusion of *inter*, 566; *in caelum* treats Homer's ἐπ' ἤματι, 'in a day', as if it meant 'to the light of day') and 12.238–43 (**B(b)**: note the foam and the noise). Vergil's mention of the *Manes* also makes for a more elemental and hyperbolic* vision of the bottom of the sea, while recalling the escape from the Symplegades, which the Argonauts equate to being saved from Hades (Apollonius 2.609–10); *Arg.* 2.568–70 ('the hollow caves at the foot of the jagged rocks roared as the sea surged inside, and above the cliff white foam spurted up from the frothing wave') are imitated in 566–7 (Nelis 47–8). **et idem** (nom. plur.): a regular Latin idiom uses the nominative of *idem* to express 'we also', 'and again': V. anticipates the alternating structure expressed through anaphora* in 566–7. *idem* at the end of the line 'seems to hold them for a moment on the summit of the wave' (Williams *ad loc.*). **tollimur... desedimus**: 'we are raised up... we sank down'. It is unusual to change from the historic* present to the preterite* in verbs as closely linked as this pair are. The pairing perhaps presents the rising as a drawn-out process, the sinking as a sudden action. **ter** s̲copuli c̲lamor(em) inter c̲aua s̲ax̲a: the three *s* and four *c* sounds create a sense of repetitive cacophony, and again hint at Scylla (cf. 559). **spum(am) elis(am) et**: the double elision evokes the squeezing up of the foam. **rorantia uidimus astra**: the hyperbole* rephrases Helenus' account (423), fits the encounter with one phenomenal monster (Charybdis), and prepares us for the hyperbolic sequel (Etna and Polyphemus): the terrestrial will meet the heavens again at 574, and 619–20, and 678; cf. Hardie 1986: 261–2.

568–9 interea fessos: whilst they have been exhausting themselves yet again (78 n.) escaping from Charybdis, almost without noticing (*ignari uiae*) they have come to shore as night falls.   **uentus cum sole reliquit**: a regular phenomenon: as the sun sets, the difference between land and sea temperature disappears, and the sea breeze that has blown during the day stops too: cf. Apollonius, *Arg.* 1.607. As *adlabimur* also shows, their arrival is calm—deceptively so.   **ignari…uiae**: a brief version of *Od.* 9.142–8 [**A(a)**], where Odysseus' ships arrive unsighted on the shore opposite to the Cyclopes' land (cf. 585–7). A broader lack of enlightenment may be implied: Jenkyns (1998: 444) notes the echo of the rustics at *Geo.* 1.41, *ignaros uiae* and thus needing the pity of Caesar and the aid of Vergil. But the narrative function seems more fundamental: *Cyclopum…oris* creates suspense, and *ignari* reminds us that the Trojans do not yet know where they have landed; moreover, Helenus has given no warning about Polyphemus.

570–87 *Etna*
The first Greek colony on Sicily was Naxos (now Giardini Naxos, just south of Taormina, ancient Tauromenium), and Vergil probably thinks of the Trojans as landing there too, below the north-eastern slopes of Mount Etna. The mountain has long been a cause of awe, and an inspiration to a variety of writers, such as Pindar, who describes it in *Pythian* 1, a victory ode written for Hieron, tyrant of Syracuse [**F**], and Lucretius (1.722–5 [**O**], 6.639–702); the fifth-century philosopher Empedocles is said to have thrown himself into the crater; after Vergil come e.g. Seneca's discussion of it as a famous topos* (*Ep.* 79), the 645-line hexameter poem *Aetna* included in the *Appendix Vergiliana*, and the prose dialogue *Etna* in which the Renaissance humanist Pietro Bembo describes his ascent. As Etna underwent major eruptions in 49 and 44 BC Vergil may well be drawing on eye-witness accounts (Scarth, *CW* 93 (1999–2000), 591, 597–8), not least for the darkness that ensues (see P. Y. Forsyth, 'In the wake of Etna, 44 B.C.', *CA* 7 (1988), 49–57). He first describes it realistically, adopting an appropriately grandiloquent register (571–7) and including touches of personification* and hyperbole*; then he touches on one myth that explains the volcanic activity (578–82), while hinting at another. The violence of the volcano is reflected by rumbling and cacophonous language

Commentary: lines 570–87

(572–7, 582), and in considerable clashing between accent* and ictus* (579, 581). The personification of Etna, and the hints at an identification with the Cyclops, fit a theme of the poem which concludes in the comparison of Aeneas to Athos, Eryx, and *pater Appenninus*, the backbone of Italy, at 12.701–3 (J. Morwood, 'Aeneas and Mount Atlas', *JRS* 75 (1985), 51–9).

570–1 portus ab accessu uentorum immotus: for the instrumental use of *ab*, see 533. Like this one, the harbour where Odysseus lands opposite the home of the Cyclopes is good for mooring (εὔορμος, *Od.* 9.136). Vergil describes no further delights, however (contrast the untended goats and vegetation in *Od.* 9.116–41), and with *sed* moves on to set the harbour's excellence against the proximity of the volcano.   **ingens | ipse**: the bay is huge (*ingens* is emphasized by its final position in the line), and *ipse* implies the presence of other huge things, Etna itself (579), the Cyclops too (619, 658), even his eye (636). **horrificis**: the word gives a cue for Aeneas' tone as he relives the horror: cf. *horrendum* (26) in the Polydorus episode.   **tonat Aetna**: cf. 8.418–19 *Cyclopum exesa caminis | antra Aetnaea tonant* ('there is thundering from the caves of Etna, eaten away by the furnaces of the Cyclopes')—a vision of Etna that surfaces in 580.   **ruinis**: for *ruina* in the context of landslips, earthquakes etc., see 414, 8.192, and *OLD* 3b; here it means 'falling material' (i.e. the molten rock thrown out and falling to earth), cf. 1.129 *fluctibus oppressos Troas caelique ruina* ('the Trojans, overwhelmed with waves and what fell from the sky').

572–7 V. imitates Pindar's powerful account of Etna's violent pyrotechnics, *Pyth.* 1.15–28 [**F**] (Thomas 1999: 283–7). The two passages are compared at Gellius 17.10.8–19, quoting an attack on V.'s 'monstrous' excess by a philosopher, Favorinus, who argues that V. has confused night and day in his search for sound-effects, but fails to observe the narrative context or the additional intertextual* complexities. **interdum** looks ahead to *interdum* in 575: sometimes the volcano produces smoke and fire, sometimes molten rock. The first *interdum* continues the sequence of nasals* and dentals* that starts with the onomatopoeic* *tonat Aetna*.   **atram prorumpit ad aethera nubem | turbine fumantem piceo et candente fauilla**: 'shoots out to the sky a dark cloud smoking with a pitchy-black swirl and ash glowing white': the gleam of the ashes heightens the blackness which envelops them. V. reworks in a grander context *Geo.* 2.308–9, where accidental fire in an olive grove *ruit atram | ad caelum picea crassus caligine nubem* ('thick with pitchy darkness rushes a black cloud to the sky'). For V.'s creation of 'darkness visible' (Milton, *Paradise Lost* 1.63), see W. R. Johnson's book of that name, 90–1; cf. also 11.186 *ignibus atris*. The transitive use of *prorumpit* cannot be exactly paralleled; it seems to be based on the passive found at e.g. *hinc prorumpitur in mare uenti | uis* ('the force of the (whirl)wind bursts out from there [the cloud] down to the sea', Lucr. 6.436–7), and may be an easier extension of usage because the *nubes* originates as part of the volcano itself, making the verb quasi-reflexive. Cf. also *rumpere* with the transitive force 'to cause to burst forth' (*OLD* 5), and *erumpere* meaning 'to emit' already at Cicero, *Arat.* 111 (the Dogstar 'emits the fires that bring summer heat', *aestiferos... erumpit... ignes*).   **globos flammarum**: a significant detail amid a persistent rewriting of *Georgics* 1.471–3 (ill-omened signs after Caesar's death): *quotiens Cyclopum efferuere in agros | uidimus undantem ruptis fornacibus Aetnam | flammarumque globos liquefactaque uoluere saxa* ('how often have we seen Etna boiling over onto the fields in waves from its broken furnaces and rolling along balls of flames and molten rocks'). If we look for matching significance in the eruption here, it anticipates an imminent death, again of the great father of a greater son (709–11).   **lambit... uiscera... eructans... cum gemitu**: these hints at personification* are an apt prelude to the stories of the Giant Enceladus trapped beneath the mountain, and of the sky-scraping fiery-eyed Polyphemus too (cf. 619–20 *pulsat sidera*; 622 *uisceribus*; 632 *eructans*; 664 *gemitu*). *eructans* reproduces Pindar's ἐρεύγονται (*Pyth.* 1.21: **F**). Here begins a sequence of corporeal language and description that continues through to 665.   **scopulos auulsaque uiscera montis**: either a hendiadys* ('rocks, the entrails torn out of the mountain') or referring to rocks *and* other features of eruption such as magma.   **cum gemitu glomerat**: after the sound-effects of 571–3, and 574–7 (e.g. *scopulos auulsaque uiscera, erigit eructans liquefactaque saxa*), a further alliteration compounds the first direct reference to sound since *tonat* (571). *cum gemitu* is a humanized version of σὺν πατάγῳ in Pindar's description of the erupting mountain (*Pyth.* 1.24: **F**). *glomerat* ('forms into a ball') is given a directional force by *sub auras* ('up into the air').

578–82 fama est: an 'Alexandrian footnote'*: Aeneas distances himself from the story, while V. draws attention to his use of sources, not least Callimachus (Hollis, *HSCPh* 94 (1992), 273–4). At 4.179 it turns

Commentary: lines 570–87   231

out the personified* *Fama* is sister to Enceladus, on whom she here reports (Hardie 2012: 99–100).   **Enceladi semustum...corpus**: in the myth, the Giants rebelled against Zeus only to be struck by his thunderbolt; their still smoking bodies were buried beneath mountains. The most common version is that Typhoeus (or Typhon) was buried under Etna (Pindar, *Pyth.* 1.16–17 (**F**), *Olymp.* 4.8–9, [Aesch.] *Prometheus Bound* 354–72, Ovid, *Met.* 5.346–8) but, following Callimachus, *Aet.* fr. 1.35–6 βάρος ὅσσον ἔπεστι | τριγλώχιν ὀλοῷ νῆσος ἐπ' Ἐγκελάδῳ ('as heavy as the three-cornered island is on baneful Enceladus'), V. puts Enceladus there, while (through an entertaining misreading of *Iliad* 2.783 εἰν Ἀρίμοις, 'in Arima') Typhoeus is beneath Inarime (an alternative name created for the island of Ischia, near Naples): 9.716 *Inarime Iouis imperiis imposta Typhoeo* ('Inarime placed on Typhoeus by the command of Jupiter'). *sēmustum* = *sēmiustum* (equivalent to the Greek ἡμιδαής used of the body of Phaethon at *Arg.* 4.598: cf. Nelis 50–1).   **urgéri móle hạc**: 'is pressed down by this mass': an appropriately ugly formulation: the spondees* lend weight; the elision before the monosyllable at the caesura adds violence; and the clashes between accent* and íctus* create discord. At Lycophron 688–91 Cassandra foresees Odysseus' visit to Sicily, 'the island which crushed the backs of the giants...boiling with red-hot lava'.   **ruptis...caminis**: 'from its burst furnaces': i.e. the mountain's own furnaces cannot contain the flames within. We get a passing reference to another mythological explanation for volcanic activity. In *Georgics* 4.170–5, *Aeneid* 8.418–43, and Callimachus, *Hymn* 3.46–61 [**K**], the Cyclopes are skilled blacksmiths in Hephaestus/Vulcan's forge in the depths of Mount Etna and the nearby volcanic islands. The primitive, untechnical Cyclopes of both the *Odyssey* and Theocritus' *Idylls* are very different: these are the Cyclopes Aeneas is soon to encounter.   **fessum**: with *latus*: 'when it tires', i.e. gets uncomfortable. V. might have written *fessus*, which would mark the return to Enceladus as subject (cf. Conte 2007: 104).   **mutet latus**: 'changes side', i.e. turns over: cf. Ovid, *Met.* 13.937, Statius, *Theb.* 3.594–5 *aut ubi temptat | Enceladus mutare latus*. Some MSS (including ancient second hands in MP) have *mutat*, but a subjunctive is normal in a subordinate clause in indirect statement (after *fama est*). The picture of the giant shifting position below Etna is drawn from Callimachus, *Hymn* 4.141–3, where it is applied to Briareus [**L(b)**].   **intrémer(e) ómnem**: elision between the fifth and sixth feet normally involves *que* (fourteen times according to Norden 456, including 3.111) or disyllables such as *sine*, *ibi*, *ubi* (perhaps also *neque*, but *nec* is always an easy alternative, often transmitted). More striking elision occurs only here, at 10.508 *haec ead(em) aufert* and 12.26 *hoc anim(o) hauri*, and in both these other cases the monosyllable lessens the conflict between ictus* and accent* in the fifth foot. The effect here is very unusual and unsettling, 'expressive of the upheaval of Sicily by Enceladus' (Wilkinson 1963: 233). **murmure** ('rumbling') helps focus the alliteration of *m*, a frequent device of V.'s to convey storms and earthquakes. **caelum subtexere fumo**: 'weaves a blanket below the sky with smoke'. The metaphor is from weaving a fabric which covers something: cf. Lucr. 5.466 *subtexunt nubila caelum* ('the clouds weave beneath the sky').

583–4 V. gives a more sinister aspect to the darkness under which the Greeks land on the island near the Cyclopes (*Od* 9.142–8: **A(a)**). **noctem illam...| perferimus**: 'throughout that night...we endure'. Both *per-* and the accusative of time emphasize the drawn-out nature of this terrifying ordeal. Hidden in the woods, the Trojans spend the long night in tense wakefulness. **nec quae sonitum det causa uidemus**: for Aeneas as the scientific seeker-out of causes see 32. There is some inconsistency here: the description of Etna has given an explanation for the noise; 574 reports fire and even mentions the stars (absent in 585). Perhaps we are to read those lines as a subsequent rationalization of the *immania monstra* ('dreadful portents'), but we may also perceive a move here to the *monstra* that are still unseen, and that in one case will be unable to see: the Cyclopes (n.b. 658; and cf. *ignari*, 569).

585–7 nam: the sentence explains why they could not see. First six words expressive of light are negated and followed by two implying darkness; then in 587 *lunam* is elided, and overwhelmed by three more words for clouds and night. The impenetrable dark recalls that at Apollonius, *Arg.* 2.1103–5, where Argus and the other sons of Phrixus are shipwrecked, and so sets up the scene in which a helpful traveller (Achaemenides) tells his tale and is rescued, as Argus in *Arg.* 2.1120– 230. **nec lucidus aethra | siderea polus**: 'nor was the sky shining with astral radiance'. *aethra* is a variant of *aethēr*, used in Latin poetry of high register from Ennius on (*Ann.* fr. 416 Skutsch; in V. also at *Aen.* 12.247). Servius distinguishes the two originally Greek words: *aethēr* refers to the sky as the element, while *aethra* communicates its brightness. *polus*, literally the Pole Star, is used by synecdoche* for the sky as a whole (*OLD* 2).   **obscuro sed nubila** <*erant*> **caelo**: 'but there were clouds in an overcast sky' (cf. 572, 582). *caelum*, though easily associated with brightness, was also linked with *celare* ('to conceal'): Varro, *Ling. Lat.* 5.18, Maltby s.v.   **nox intempesta**: 'the dead of night': literally, 'timeless night', i.e. when the utter darkness makes it impossible to register the progression of time. V. is recalling Ennius, *Ann.* fr. 33 Skutsch *cum superum lumen nox intempesta teneret* ('when the dead of night was holding the light of the sky'), itself an imitation of *Od.* 13.269.

588–691 *Achaemenides*
The fundamental intertextual* relationship here is with *Odyssey* 9.106–566, where Odysseus (in Latin *Vlixes*, whence English 'Ulysses') describes with relish (e.g. 413) his encounter with the Cyclops [**A**]. This is the third of Odysseus' narrated adventures, and thus comes shortly after his leaving Troy, but V. places it only three months (645–6) before the arrival of Aeneas, who has been travelling for several years (3.8, 135–9, 284; over six by the time they reach Carthage: 1.755–6). Achaemenides, the 'wretched Greek' (614) left behind by Odysseus, appears to be Vergil's invention. He is important thematically in showing that, despite their disastrous acceptance of Sinon in Book 2 (see below), the Trojans continue to embrace the values implicit in supplication and hospitality. In addition, he gives us a different view of Ulysses from the extraordinarily negative one that we have encountered earlier in the poem.

In his account of the Cyclops episode, focalized through Odysseus' narrative, Homer sets the primitive world of the Cyclopes against the inventive modernity of the Greek hero and his men. These lawless creatures have not developed agriculturally, politically, or socially. They have no technical skills (cf. 580 n.) and do not trade or colonize. As well as having no regard for each other, they care nothing for Zeus or the gods. Thus they feel no obligation to respond (as the Trojans do) to the normal conventions of supplication and hospitality (see esp. 9.105–15, 125–30, 266–8), though Polyphemus does display affection for his favourite ram (9.447–60). Odysseus is the one who shows technical skill in the confrontation (as is made explicit in the similes at 384–6, 391–3: **A**(**d**)), together with inspired planning and verbal dexterity (**A**(**c**): the 'Nobody' trick). This modern man defeats the primitive Cyclops, but (as he tells the story) the last laugh is on him. By insisting on giving his name to Polyphemus while sailing away, he enables the monster to curse him in a speech (528–35) which is the model for Dido's terrifying imprecations against Aeneas (4.612–20). Odysseus ruefully remarks that Zeus did not heed his sacrifice of the Cyclops' ram 'but was planning how all my well-benched ships and trusty companions might be destroyed' (554–5).

Many of these points from Homer are brought out by V. too, as our notes will illustrate. However, he (as usual) adds his own material and gives the narrative a new slant. Odysseus loses men throughout his voyages, a whole fleet indeed, not just those who are graphically described as eaten by Polyphemus, and he will return home alone; Aeneas is hoping to set up a new city based on the remnants of Troy (85–8, e.g.), so for him the loss of people matters (note his distress before leaving behind the old, weak, tired, and female at 5.700–54); it is thus symbolic that he takes on an additional member for his expedition at a point where Odysseus' loss is doubly emphasized (616–17; 623–7). As well as passing the test of humanity posed by Achaemenides, Aeneas broadens his sympathies to include even the (till now) bitterly hated Ulysses; and the final picture of the crowd of one-eyed Cyclopes standing on the beach like a grove is supremely memorable in its grotesquerie.

Within the *Aeneid* the Achaemenides story forms a doublet with the Sinon episode earlier in Aeneas' narration (2.57–198). After ten years of the siege of Troy, Sinon, a brilliantly deceptive Greek, wins the Trojans' sympathy and convinces them that the Greeks really have sailed away and that the wooden horse is a religious offering which will lead to the Trojans conquering Greece if it is taken within the city walls; in fact it leads to the destruction of Troy. The Sinon story is reflected a significant number of times in the present episode: he too begins by admitting that he is a Greek attacker of Troy (2.77–8/3.602–3), sent by a poor father (2.87/3.614–15), for example; Priam himself accepts his plea (2.146–7), as Anchises will that of Achaemenides (3.610–11); for full details see Ramminger, *AJPh* 112 (1991), 56–7. However, this time the Trojans encounter a 'good' Greek and, despite their previous deception, they again respond to the act of supplication with compassion. They have not been dehumanized by the horrors of their defeat; on the contrary, there is a broadening of human sympathy (see 613–15, 687–91 nn.). Their trust is not abused. Indeed, Achaemenides' urgent advice ensures their safety; he is thus like several helpful individuals assisted or rescued by Apollonius' Argonauts (Nelis 52–7), in particular the emaciated Phineus (2.178–497: **M**; see 212 n.).

V. also makes use of the rescue of Theoclymenus by Telemachus from Pylos later in the *Odyssey* (15.256-81: **D**); the passage begins with an account of Theoclymenus' ancestry (223-56), culminating in his name, but it is then he who asks Telemachus who he is and where he comes from (264); and Telemachus replies (267) that he is from Ithaca (like Achaemenides, 613), and that his father is Odysseus (whereas Achaemenides is Ulysses' companion). Theoclymenus is a seer, and later provides prophecies useful to Telemachus and his parents (*Od.* 15.525-43, 17.151-61, 20.350-70); Achaemenides' assistance is more immediate (639-44, 666-7, 690-1). Another influence is Sophocles' tragedy *Philoctetes* (593-4 nn.): the eponymous* Greek hero has been abandoned by his fellow countrymen—because of a disgusting wound resulting from a snake bite—on the volcanic island of Lemnos. Like Achaemenides he barely subsists on what he can catch (*Phil.* 287-9, 710-11), and he pleads with mariners to rescue him (305-11).

In Homer the location of the Cyclopes is unspecified; in Euripides' satyr play *Cyclops* it is Sicily, near Mt Etna (possibly under the influence of a Sicilian comic author called Epicharmus: see *PCG* F 70-2 for the fragments of his *Cyclops*). Thucydides 6.2.1 writes that the Cyclopes and the Laestrygonians are said to have lived in some part of the island (cf. Theocritus 11.7); and the geographer Strabo, a contemporary of V., also connects the Cyclopes with Etna (1.2.9). Euripides gives the Sicilian setting considerable emphasis, referring to it no less than fifteen times (e.g. 114), and it could be that, in using the same location, V. is evoking the satyr play and thus adding weight to the element of grotesquerie that informs his portrayal of the Cyclopes. As has been seen (574-84), he treats the monsters as symbols of the mountain and manifestations of volcanic activity (Scarth, *CW* 93 (1999-2000), 598-601).

In 1957 the fragments of four statue groups were discovered in a coastal cave at Sperlonga 60 miles south of Rome. Among these were a vey fragmentary Scylla group which showed the monster devouring several of Odysseus' companions, and a Polyphemus group in which two of Odysseus' men are about to plunge the pole into the Cyclops' eye while the hero directs them from above. A third companion is running in carrying a wineskin, an allusion* to how Polyphemus was put to sleep. The sculptures, thought to be by the Rhodian creators of the famous Laocoon, date from the late first century BC (see H. A. Weis, 'Odysseus at Sperlonga: Hellenistic hero or Roman heroic foil', in N. T. de Grummond & B. S. Ridgway (eds), *From Pergamon to Sperlonga*

(Berkeley, 2000), 111–65, at 124–5), roughly contemporaneous with V.'s poem. Indeed, Weis argues (119–24) that another of the groups shows Aeneas and Lausus together at the moment of the latter's death in *Aeneid* 10.814–32, and suggests (125–34) that Vergil is the literary model for the cave decoration. She concludes (134) that the organization of the cave programme 'is Vergilian in its context and structure, in its use of Homer as a literary model and foil, and in its use of Odysseus to define the character of Aeneas as a distinctively Roman hero'. A clear response comes at *Metamorphoses* 14.158–441, where Ovid has Achaemenides narrate his story again, this time to a shipmate, Macareus, who in turn tells how he has stayed behind in Italy when Ulysses sails on from Circe's island.

588–90 iamque…cum: cf. 521–2; though the *que* in *iamque* sometimes functions as the conjunction (e.g. 4.157, 6.647, 8.24, 11.766), here, as in *iamiamque*, it perhaps produces a reinforced form of *iam* (cf. 5.225, 6.81, 7.637).   **primo…Ēoo**: perhaps 'with the morning star (appearing) first', the sense the noun certainly has in a fragment of the *Smyrna* by the neoteric* poet Cinna: *te matutinus flentem conspexit Eous, | te flentem paulo uidit post Hesperus idem* (*FLP* 6 = *FRP* 10: 'the Dawn Star of a morning spied you weeping, you weeping a little later also as the Evening Star': both are the planet Venus). However, at Propertius 3.24.7 *roseo…Eoo* ('rosy dawn', reprised at Silius 9.180) and Statius, *Thebaid* 3.40 *gelido…Eoo* ('at the cold time of dawn'), the noun seems not to refer to the star. Likewise in Vergil at *Geo.* 1.288 *sole nouo terras inrorat Eous* we might think it is dawn rather than 'the morning star' that 'bedews the earth with the new sun', and in his commentary on 11.4 *uota deum primo uictor soluebat Eoo* Servius glosses* the phrase with *tempore* ('at the first moment of dawn the victor was paying his vows to the gods'). The first syllable of 'Ἠώς, the Greek for dawn and its goddess, equivalent to Latin *Aurora* (589), is normally heavy, but the form with a short first syllable also exists, and this gets taken over by Latin as an alternative in the adjective *Eous* (V. has the short *e* five times, the long three).   **umentemque Aurora polo dimouerat umbram**: this recalls the dawn of *Od.* 9.151–2 heralding Odysseus' exploration of the Cyclops' land. The line will be repeated at 4.7 (the dawn after Aeneas' narration has concluded). *umentem* is an etymological gloss* on *umbram*, implying that it is so named because shadowed air and ground can be damp (cf. e.g. 4.351 *umentibus umbris*; Servius *ad Aen.* 4.7 *quia nox omnis umida est*; Statius, *Theb.*

2.527-8, Valerius, *Arg.* 5.606, Silius 1.259). As at 586 *polo* is used by synecdoche* for the sky as a whole (cf. *gelidam caelo dimouerat umbram* at 11.210).

590-2 macie confecta suprema | ignoti noua forma uiri miserandaque cultu | procedit: 'there comes, worn out by the final stages of starvation, the strange shape of an unknown man, pitiable in his garb'. In the dawn light the Trojans see an emaciated shape coming out from the trees. The delayed placement of *uiri* implies that it takes a few moments for the Trojans to realize that it is a man: the reader may at first think we are seeing Polyphemus, starving because blinded, and certainly a strange (*OLD nouus* 3) form. However, *noua* (and *ignoti*) also function as a comment on the text: the figure will prove to be a Vergilian novelty. *cultu* refers to his dress and his whole unwashed, unkempt appearance (for the importance and limits of *cultus* in the Augustan age, see e.g. A. S. Hollis (Oxford, 1977) on Ovid, *Ars Amatoria* 1.513-24 and R. K. Gibson (Cambridge, 2003) on 3.101-34). **supplex**: the act of supplication puts pressure on the person supplicated to accede to the request. However, in his important revisionist book *Ancient Supplication* (Oxford, 2006), F. S. Naiden established that by and large the person supplicated had nothing to fear from men or gods if he rejected the appeal. Thus, while the Trojans' generosity of spirit is presented with a challenge here, they could safely have refused to respond. Supplication is a significant and recurring feature of Greek epic and tragedy; V. puts Priam's appeal to Achilles (*Iliad* 24.477-506) on the walls of the Carthaginian temple of Juno (1.487 *tendentem manus*), but ends his own poem with Turnus' failed supplication (12.930-52). **ad litora**: the Trojans have moved from their hiding place in the woods to the shore. The location adds to the parallelism with the Sinon scene; *cum subito* is equivalent to the *ecce* that introduces him (2.57).

593-5 respicimus: 'we look back', i.e. in the direction we had come from; but the verb is used of looking intently (*OLD* 2, 3), and it helps set up the dramatic inspection of the man's entrance on the scene: the sentence that consists only of a verb introduces three lines that have no further verb: the action pauses. **dira inluuies immissaque barba, | consertum tegimen spinis**: 'terrible squalor, and an unkempt beard, clothing held together with thorns'. There is a telegraphic quality here, and perhaps a suggestion of notes for a stage costumier: indeed, the emaciation, filth, and overgrown beard are indebted to a description of Aeetes in a tragedy (probably the *Medus* of Pacuvius) quoted by Cicero at *Tusc. Disp.* 3.26 (P. Schierl, *Die Tragödien des Pacuvius* (Berlin, 2006), fr. 181) *corpus macie extabuit…situm inter oris barba paedore horrida | intonsa infuscat pectus inluuie scabrum* ('his body has wasted away with emaciation; amid the mouldiness of his face his unshaven beard, bristling with filth, darkens his chest which is rough with dirt'). The wildness of the clothing recalls Philoctetes' garb (Sophocles, *Phil.* 226). **at cetera Graius**: 'but as to the rest <he was> Greek'. *cetera* is accusative of respect, an appropriately Greek construction (G&L §338). Servius suggests that they recognized him as Greek because of the way he moved and the sound of his voice, but the arms of 595 would give an immediate clue (cf. 2.386–95, 411–12); so Philoctetes recognizes Neoptolemus as Greek (*Phil.* 223–4 σχῆμα μὲν γὰρ Ἑλλάδος | στολῆς, 'the appearance of your equipment comes from Greece'). **ad Troiam**: this could mean 'to the vicinity of Troy, the Troad' (cf. 1.24), but V. often breaks the rule of the omission of prepositions before the names of cities: for *ad Troiam* so, see 2.342, 9.547. Suetonius tells us that, in the interests of clarity, Augustus 'did not hesitate to use prepositions with the names of cities' (*Aug.* 86.1). **patriis…in armis**: 'in the arms of his country': the man has apparently managed to cling on to some of his distinctively Greek armour through all his travails; but Aeneas may be supplying the fact so he can better dramatize the encounter between Greek arms (594–5) and Trojan (596–7).

596–99 Dardanios habitus: 'Trojan dress': the most identifiable feature of Trojan costume was the Phrygian bonnet, a conical cap with the top leaning forward. **Trōiă uidit | arma**: the Greek from the *Odyssey* now sets eyes on the *Aeneid* (cf. 1.1 *Arma uirumque… Troiae*). For the scansion of the adjective, cf. 306. **procul**: 13 n. **paulum… haesit | continuitque gradum**: the man has emerged from the woods to supplicate the new arrivals; when he perceives that they are Trojans he stops in his tracks horrified. The hysteron proteron* ('he stopped for a little, and checked his steps') focuses attention on his frozen stance. **cum fletu precibusque**: Aeneas cues himself to deliver the Greek's speech with tearful pleading: cf. the emotional language with which he begins his tale (2.3–12 *dolorem, lamentabile, miserrima, lacrimis, horret, luctu*).

599–602 The urgency of the Greek's prayer is reflected in the fact that he bursts into speech only at the fourth-foot caesura, and without a

Commentary: lines 588–691

verb of speaking (but note *precibus*). The start of his appeal is replicated at 6.458–9 *per sidera iuro,* | *per superos* (Aeneas' singularly unsuccessful appeal to the ghost of Dido in the underworld).   **per sidera testor**: 'I entreat you in the name of the stars…': *uos* is easily inferred from context, especially *tollite me, Teucri* in 601.   **hoc caeli spirabile lumen**: 'this light of the heaven which we breathe'. Though we do not literally 'breathe light', and both capital MSS extant here (MP) have *numen* written by the first hand, the second-hand correction *lumen* (also found in the later MSS) is to be preferred. Achaemenides condenses into one two essential supports of life, kept separate at 6.363 *per caeli iucundum lumen et auras* ('by the pleasant light and air of heaven'); and Ovid in his Achaemenides story confirms what stood in his text of Vergil when he follows *quod loquor et spiro* ('the fact that I speak and breathe', *Met.* 14.172) with *lumen uitale* ('the light of life', 175).   **tollite**: 'take me up' (*OLD* 10), specifically 'on board' (as at 6.70; *OLD* 6). The verb can also mean 'do away with', 'kill' (*OLD* 13), a sense Achaemenides will move on to in 605. Compare Philoctetes' plea for Neoptolemus to take him home at Soph. *Phil.* 468–503.   **quascumque…terras**: accusative of motion towards.

602–6 sciŏ: only in *scio* (cf. *Ecl.* 8.43) does V. scan the final syllable of the first-person verb short. This follows spoken usage: see Austin on 2.735.   **me Danais e classibus unum** <*esse*>: 'that I am one man alone from the Greek fleet'. *classibus* may be taken as poetic plural*, which is a particularly easy usage with collective nouns; but we could also read it as 'contingents', and think of the long list of Greek forces described in the catalogue of *Iliad* 2.   **Iliacos fateor petiisse penates**: supply *me* from 602. By *Iliacos…penates* the Greek means the homes of Troy; but in referring to the attack as an assault on gods he increases the rhetorical weight of his admission, and thus shows he understands the *pietas* of the Trojans. The phrase has an added resonance in that the Trojan *penates* are with Aeneas and play a part in the story (12, 148).   **pro quo**: compare Ariadne exploring the reward she is receiving for helping Theseus kill her brother, the Minotaur, at Cat. 64.152 *pro quo dilaceranda feris dabor alitibusque* ('as a return for which I shall be given to the beasts and birds to tear apart').   **spargite me in fluctus uastoque immergite ponto**: this prefigures the action that Dido fantasizes she might have taken against Aeneas: 4.600–1 *non potui abreptum diuellere corpus et undis* | *spargere?* ('could I not have snatched his body, torn it apart and scattered it over the waves?').

V. has in mind the butchering of Medea's brother Apsyrtus in order to delay hostile pursuit (Apollonius, *Arg.* 4.452–81).   **si pereo**: the present is sometimes used to express the future in conditional clauses, especially in less formal speech (Terence, *Andria* 210; Sallust, *Cat.* 20.6, 58.9, both in speeches by Catiline). However, there is a greater oddity about *pereo*—the hiatus* before *hominum*: for discussion see J. Trappes-Lomax, *PCPhS* 50 (2004), 152. He considers the old transposition *manibūs hominum*, but acknowledges that though this gives more typical metre, it removes the appropriate stress from *hominum*: it is not death that Achaemenides is primarily afraid of, but death at the hands of monsters who will devour him. Both oddities could be removed by reading *si moriār* (for the metrical handling, cf. 6.254 *pingue supēr oleum*): this phrase, unlike *si pereo*, recurs in Latin, notably at Ovid, *ex Ponto* 1.2.107 (in a rather similar passage), and *ep. Sapph.* 190. Perhaps V. wanted the play between *pereo* and *periisse*; and he, like Williams, e.g., found the forced pause before *hominum* effective.

607–9 dixerat: 90 n.   **genua amplexus**: this customary mode of supplication may have been a ritualized way of averting the kick that would accompany the rejection of one's plea. W. Burkert (*Structure and History in Greek Mythology and Ritual* (Berkeley, CA, 1979), 52) observes that the ancient appeasement ritual of 'touching the knees—more exactly, the hollow of the knee—of the threatening partner' means 'Sit down, please, and relax'. He shows two illustrations of figures performing this action to plead for their lives, one of them of prisoners in Bangladesh in 1971—moments after the photo was taken they were killed. The salt-caked and naked Odysseus wisely decides not to embrace the knees of Nausicaa at *Od.* 6.141–7; instead he begins his speech Γουνοῦμαί σε ('I supplicate you by your knees', 6.149). *genua* is here trisyllabic and elided (as at 5.468, 10.523, 12.747); contrast 5.432 and 12.905, where it scans as a trochee*, with consonantalized *u*. **genibusque uolutans | haerebat**: the anaphora* tells us that these too are the Trojans' knees; but if Achaemenides is rolling on the ground, he is by their feet (*pedibus*), not their knees. Perhaps we should give point to the polyptoton* by supplying *est* with *amplexus* and translating 'embraced their knees and kept clinging to their knees, rolling about'. In any case the Greek's abject behaviour communicates his desperation. The intransitive use of *uolutare* is unusual; *uolutans* without the reflexive object seems to stand in for the passive present participle (which of course does not exist in Latin): cf. Ovid, *Amores* 3.6.45 *per caua saxa uolutans* (of a river 'rolling over the hollowed out rocks'); and *Geo.* 1.163 *tarda…uoluentia plaustra* (slow-rolling wagons'). Two passages of later authors apparently allude to this passage: Pliny, *Nat. Hist.* 8.56 *leone…suppliciter uolutante* ('a lion rolling on the ground in the manner of a suppliant'); Statius, *Thebaid* 3.138 *canitiem impexam dira tellure uolutans* ('rolling her unkempt grey hair on the dreadful earth': note that he cautiously supplies an object).   **qui sit**: the Homeric τίς πόθεν εἰς ἀνδρῶν; ('who among men are you and where from?'), a question posed by Theoclymenus to Telemachus (**D**; and see 588–691 n.). Note the form *qui*: the evidence of the MS tradition indicates that V. does not use *quis* before a word beginning with *s* though later scribes often normalize to *quis* (the capital MSS are divided at 6.865): presumably he wished to avoid the hissing sound.   **fari…| hortamur**: a strong echo of the Sinon episode: *hortamur fari quo sanguine cretus*, 2.74.   **quo sanguine cretus**: 'of what parentage he was born'. V. took over Lucretius' use (e.g. at 5.6) of the past participle of *cresco* in the same sense as *natus*. He uses the form five times in the *Aeneid*, and it may not be a coincidence that twice (here, and at 2.74, just cited) it invites a reply such as Odysseus repeatedly gives, fabricating a Cretan origin for himself: *Od.* 13.256–87, 14.192–359, 19.165–202.   **deinde**: the usual force of the adverb ('then', 'next') implies that it goes with *fateri*: 'and next to reveal what fortune is troubling him'.

610–12 haud multa moratus: 'after a short delay': *multa* (n. pl. acc.) is very commonly used as an adverb in verse (e.g. 1.465 *multa gemens* 'groaning much'; 4.390 *multa…cunctantem* 'delaying much'). Anchises, the senior Trojan, makes a meaningful but silent gesture to accept the Greek's supplication. *haud multa moratus* shows him thinking over his decision, perhaps in the light of Priam's generosity to Sinon (2.146–51), which turned out to be unjustified; and perhaps with an eye to correcting the less reasonable pause after Odysseus' supplication in the court of Alcinous, for which the king gets upbraided by the senior figure Echeneus (*Od.* 7.153–69).   **dextram…| dat iuueni atque animum praesenti pignore firmat**: the same thing is described twice, first concentrating on the action, and then on the effect. The 'ready pledge of friendship' is the giving of Anchises' right hand (cf. 'the greatest pledge of his right hand', Euripides, *Medea* 21–2); *praesenti* implies promptness and efficaciousness (*OLD* 6, 5). Verses 611–12 imply a more confident and relaxed register for the Greek's second speech.

iuueni shows that at close quarters they have realized that Achaemenides is a young man beneath his filthy exterior.   **tandem**: 'at last' within this brief encounter, but presumably also for the first time in three months, since his companions left (616–18, 645–8).

613–15 cf. *Odyssey* 15.267 [**D**].   **infelicis Vlixi**: 'of unhappy/unlucky Ulysses'. Servius takes *infelix* as meaning 'accursed', believing that Achaemenides is currying favour with the Trojans by speaking pejoratively* of a Greek whom he knows they hate. But surely something more interesting is going on here. Odysseus *was* 'unlucky' (Calypso addresses him as κάμμορε, 'ill-fated one', at *Od.* 5.160 e.g.), and one of his most common epithets is πολύτλας (much-enduring). In addition, as Williams points out, the word *infelix* 'when applied [by V.] to human character always carries a strong association of sympathy' (notably when it is four times applied to Dido in Book 4). Though he has been abandoned by his leader, Achaemenides talks of him with understanding, not animosity. Aeneas, the speaker of the Greek's words, has thus found himself forced to mention an arch-enemy's name with sympathy (cf. 691, and the praise at 628–9). He has previously hissed it out—it is eminently hissable—during in his narrative (e.g. 2.44 *sic notus̱ Vlix̱es̱?* 'is this what we expect from Ulysses?', 90 *pellacis̱ Vlix̱i* 'deceitful Ulysses', 261 and 762 *diru̱s̱ Vlix̱es̱* 'ominous Ulysses', 3.273 *terram … s̱aeui ex̱secramur Vlix̱i* 'we curse the land of savage Ulysses'). Aeneas' father has just shown sympathy towards a Greek and he is beginning to apprehend what he and his enemies have in common rather than what divides them. We may see here an anticipation of the sense of universal sympathy that he misguidedly discovers when viewing the temple of Juno in Carthage (1.459–63). For the genitive *Vlixi* see 273 n.   **nomine** is a significant word in a retelling of the encounter of 'Nobody' with the Cyclops.   **Achaemenides**: a name possibly invented by V. Though there is a similarity to the Persian name *Achaemenes*, the first two syllables are highly appropriate to the Greek's story in echoing ἄχος (distress) and Ἀχαιοί (Achaeans); thus the man left behind by Odysseus ('man of pain') and rescued by Aeneas (from αἰνός, 'terrible') shares an etymology with Achilles (O'Hara 1996: 8–12). See also Carter in *VE* 'Achaemenides'.   **genitore Adamasto | paupere**: 'my father was Adamastus, a poor man' (for ablative absolute without participle to express paternity cf. 10.205–6 *patre Benaco … Mincius*, 11.666 *Eunaeum Clytio … patre*): he is giving a lot of information very swiftly. The phrase could also be causal, poverty forcing Achaemenides to join the expedition to Troy.

Adamastus literally means 'indomitable' in Greek, a good name for a poor Ithacan (cf. *duri Vlixi*, 2.7; *scopulos Ithacae*, 3.272). **mansissetque utinam fortuna**: 'and if only my fortune had remained like that': he refers to his poor lot on Ithaca and his obscurity, and wishes that he had played no part in the *Odyssey* (as he does not, by name) or the *Aeneid* (which conjures him up to rescue him). The account of Achaemenides' identity and origin has not taken long; the account of his *fortuna* will occupy the rest of a substantial speech.

616–18 hic seems to return us to the here and now, but Ach. quickly moves to a story from months before, and the cave of Cyclops. **me** is significantly separated from the verb *deseruere* to which it is the object, as well as the forgetful *socii*. **crudelia limina**: cf. 44 *crudelis terras*, of a land equally inhospitable and blood-soaked. *limen* (again at 626) is used also of the Sibyl's cave (6.45) and Cacus' (8.232). The doorway plays a significant role in Odysseus' story, for the blinded Polyphemus rolls back the vast stone that blocks it, and then sits there trying to catch them as they exit. But as the Cyclops lets his rams out to graze, Odysseus binds his men to their bellies, clings to the largest himself, and they all escape (*Od*. 9.424–66)—all save Achaemenides, it now turns out. There is no obvious space in Odysseus' account to explain his being left behind, so V. has the narrative pass quickly over this part of the story, with some psychological plausibility: Achaemenides does not choose to dwell on the painful moment, nor does he explain how he eventually got out of the cave. **immemores socii**: Donatus suggests that his companions forgot Achaemenides 'in fear [n.b. *trepidi*] of the evident danger, in which each man looked after his own interests rather than anyone else's'; Odysseus gives a rather different account, of course, stressing what care he took to plot 'an escape from death for his companions and himself' (9.420–2); and Achaemenides does not gainsay this directly, blaming the group for his abandonment, and crediting Ulysses for the vengeance (628–9). *immemor* is a significant word in Catullus 64 (58, 123, 135, 248): the echo momentarily aligns Achaemenides with another mythological figure, Ariadne, abandoned on the shore of Naxos by Theseus, but then rescued by a greater figure, Bacchus, and his followers. **uasto Cyclopis in antro**: on *uastus* see Introduction, p. 39, 421 n.

618–20 domus sanie dapibusque cruentis: 'a house of gore and bloody feasts' (ablatives of description). After the grim finality of the enjambed* *deseruere*, and the unusual sense pause after the second trochee*, we are left in the cave. The sentence has no verb: the time of action is over; this is all Achaemenides has to experience now, and the abruptness of the gory details lends them repulsive emphasis. The diction of this and following lines (*sanguine*, 622; *sanie*, 625; *tabo*, 626) seems to owe much to Roman tragedy, especially a fragment of a curse from Ennius' *Thyestes*, fr. 297 Jocelyn: *tabo sanie et sanguine atro* ('with corruption, gore, and black blood').   **opaca, ingens**: like the tree of dreams at the entrance to the underworld (6.283 *ulmus opaca, ingens* 'an elm, shady and huge').   **ipse**: 'himself', i.e. 'the master of the house' (*OLD* 12).   **altaque pulsat | sidera**: Odysseus describes Polyphemus as 'like a wooded peak of lofty mountains' (*Od.* 9.190–2). In Book 3 reference to the stars attributes cosmic scale to Charybdis (423, 564–7) and to Etna (574); similarly for the other Cyclopes at 678–9. This is enhanced in each case by matching evocation of the underworld (421–2, 565, 575–81, 619). These are monsters who can terrorize every part of the universe: heaven and hell, land and sea (cf. Hardie 1986: 297).   **di talem terris auertite pestem!** Horrified in telling of Polyphemus, Achaemenides produces a passionate alliteration of the dentals* *t* and *d*. For the expression, cf. Anchises' prayer after Celaeno's oracular curse at 265 *di, talem auertite casum*, and for the fuller expression with the ablative 1.38 *Italia Teucrorum auertere regem* ('to divert the king of the Trojans from Italy'), 9.77–8 *quis deus, o Musae, tam saeua incendia Teucris | auertit?* ('Which deity, o Muses, turned so savage a burning away from the Trojans?'). At 215 the Harpies have been described as the ultimate *pestis* to emanate from the underworld.

621–2 nec uisu facilis nec dictu adfabilis ulli: editors attach this line to the previous sentence, but the sense is complete after *pulsat sidera* and the reader of an unpunctuated text has no reason to look for a resumption after the exclamation. The double *nec* correlates, as well as negating, the matching adjectives *facilis* and *adfabilis*, which anticipate the unexpressed subject of *uescitur*. The two adjectives match in form, both have their sense complete by *ulli* ('for anyone'), and both are qualified by the ablative of a supine: *uisu facilis* is 'easy to look at' (cf. 1.111 and 9.465 *uisu miserabile*, 'sorrowful to look at'; 10.637 and 12.252 *uisu mirabile*, 'extraordinary to look at'); *dictu adfabilis* means 'approachable to address', a sense that diverges from the normal usage of *dictu* 'to tell of' in combinations such as *mirabile dictu* and *horrendum dictu*: 26 n. The expression is closely based on a line from Accius' tragedy *Philoctetes* (fr. 544 Warmington) cited by Macrobius (*Sat.* 6.1.55) as V.'s source: *quem neque tueri contra nec adfari queas* ('whom you could not look at nor address face to face'); and Statius recalls it at *Siluae* 3.3.72 *terribilem adfatu...uisuque tyrannum* ('a tyrant terrible to address and to see', of Caligula). Approachability in conversation is a humane virtue; cf. Cicero, *Off.* 2.48 'it is hard to say how much friendliness and affability in speech (*adfabilitas*) wins over men's hearts'. The line recalls *Od.* 9.230 οὐδ' ἄρ' ἔμελλ' ἑτάροισι φανεὶς ἐρατεινὸς ἔσεσθαι ('but in fact when he appeared he was going to be no joy to my comrades') in its emphatic litotes*, and in the employment of social commentary ahead of the horrors of cannibalism (cf. also *Od.* 9.356, 370: **A(c)**). *adfabilis* is the first of three plays on Polyphemus' name (644, 653), which could (in Greek) be taken to mean 'destroyer of conversation' (Maltby s.v.).   **uisceribus miserorum et sanguine uescitur atro**: Homer is more brutally specific here: his Cyclops feeds on entrails, flesh, bones, and marrow and leaves nothing over (*Od.* 9.292–3: **A(b)**), whereas *miserorum* expresses sympathy for the victims. On the other hand, the resumption of the letters of *uisceribus* in *uescitur* hints at the way that eating turns the flesh of the victim into the flesh of the consumer: cf. Lucretius' discussion of the Anaxagorean theory of *homoeomeria* 1.837 *uisceribus uiscus gigni* ('flesh comes from flesh').

623–9 uidi egomet...cum: 'I myself saw when...': for Odysseus' version, see **A(b)**. By stressing that the account comes from an eye-witness, Achaemenides brings out the horror, but also stresses the reality of what he saw: cf. Aeneas at 26, and 2.5 *quaeque ipse miserrima uidi* ('and what extremely sad sights I myself saw'), 499, 501; 4.358. *-met* reinforces emphatic pronouns also at 5.650, 6.505 (*egomet*), 4.606, 7.309 (*memet*), 1.207 (*uosmet*).   **resupinus**: 'on his back': this reproduces Homer's ὕπτιος from *Od.* 9.371 but there the Cyclops is lying on his back to sleep. Servius makes the point that killing two men cost V.'s Cyclops so little effort that he could do it lying down.   **frangeret**: another dramatically enjambed* verb (cf. 618).   **sanieque aspersa natarent | limina**: the blood and gore from the killings in the middle of the cave (624) bespattered even the entrance; and the splashes were such it 'swam with blood': for the metaphor cf. *OLD nato* 3, Cicero, *Philippics* 2.105 *natabant pauimenta uino* ('the pavings were swimming in wine'), and *Odyssey* 9.222, where the vessels in the cave flow (or swim) with milk (ναῖον). Lucan combines allusion* to this and the following line in describing the effect of a snake bite at 9.770 *membra natant sanie, surae fluxere* ('the limbs swim with gore, the calves have melted away'). **uidi...cu:n**: the repetition from 623 figures V.'s larger repetition of the Odyssean narrative here. It also implicitly adds a second pair of victims (*Od.* 9.311) to the first (*Od.* 9.289: **A(b)**; a third pair is consumed at 344: **A(c)**). *cum* is again postponed*. **manderet et tepidi tremerent sub dentibus artus**: Horsfall remarks 'Strong alliteration suggestive of effortful mastication.' *tepidi* tells us that the bodies are still warm, a grisly enough detail when V. applies it to the blood or bodies of the slaughtered at 8.196, 9.333, 10.555; but heightened here because the raw human flesh is being consumed. **haud impune quidem**: 'but not with impunity'; *quidem* functions as an adversative here (*OLD* 3c). **nec talia passus**: *non tulit* is similarly used to introduce acts of vengeance, e.g. when Ascanius is about to shoot the boastful Remulus Numanus at 9.622, or when Hercules responds with murderous anger to the fire-breathing of another cave-dwelling monster, Cacus (8.256). **Vlixes...Ithacus**: 'Ulysses...the man of Ithaca': Achaemenides proudly uses the name of his home to denote Ulysses in this moment of heroism (cf. 613), just as Odysseus does when revealing his identity to Polyphemus at *Od.* 9.504–5 Ὀδυσσῆα πτολιπόρθιον...| υἱὸν Λαέρτεω, Ἰθάκῃ ἔνι οἰκί' ἔχοντα ('Odysseus the sacker of cities, son of Laertes, who has his home on Ithaca'). **nec...| oblitus...sui est**: 'nor did [he] forget himself', i.e. (though he forgot Achaemenides) he proved true to his nature: cf. Cicero, *Philippics* 2.10 *ne me hodie...oblitum esse putetis mei* ('and do not think that today I have forgotten myself'). V. brings out a fine irony of *Odyssey* 9: one of Odysseus' most characteristic tricks precisely involves covering up his identity (when he names himself Οὖτις, 'Nobody', 9.364–70; cf. 408: **A(c, d)**); he thus lives up to his epithet πολυμήχανος, 'much-devising'. But at the end of the episode, as we have just seen (9.502–5), he cannot resist revealing his real name.

630–8 nam introduces illustration of the point just made. **simul**: = *simul ac* ('as soon as') as at *Ecl.* 4.26, *Geo.* 4.232. **uinoque sepultus**: in the *Odyssey* Odysseus gets the primarily milk-drinking Cyclops drunk (9.345–74: **A(c, d)**) by feeding him some delicious wine he has been given by a host called Maron (9.196–212). V. conjures up this part of the story with these two words: cf. Ennius, *Annales* 288 Skutsch *nunc hostes uino domiti somnoque sepulti*, also recalled at 2.265 *inuadunt urbem somno uinoque sepultam* and 9.236 *Rutuli somno uinoque* *sepulti* (*soluti* in some MSS), in each case of those about to be slaughtered.   **inflexam**: 'at an angle': cf. *Od.* 9.372 (**A(d)**); the next two lines render 9.373-4.   **per antrum**: 'throughout the cave', Quintilian (8.3.84) finds 'emphasis' in the way the expression implies the size of the Cyclops' extended body—even before we reach the enjambed* *immensus* ('immeasurable'), spilling over into verse 632.   **eructans**: cf. 576: L. Fratantuono (*Madness Unchained: A Reading of Virgil's Aeneid* (Lanham, MD, 2007), 90) observes that the Cyclops 'is the living version of Etna'.   **frusta**: Homer's ψωμοί ('gobbets', 'bits'): cf. Cicero on Mark Antony: *magister equitum... uomens frustis esculentis uinum redolentibus gremium suum et totum tribunal impleuit* ('the master of the cavalry, vomiting, filled his lap and the whole platform with gobbets of food smelling of wine'; *Philippics* 2.63). Is Cicero likening Antony to the Cyclops and has V. picked this up?   **mero**: literally 'unmixed wine', the word is often used (as here) when the alcoholic effect is being stressed; in Odysseus' narrative one cup of Maron's wine was best drunk diluted with twenty measures of water (9.209-10).   **magna precati | numina**: an addition to the story as told by Odysseus (**A(d)**): Achaemenides again assimilates the piety of the Trojans.   **sortitique uices**: 'drawing lots for our parts' in the dangerous blinding of the Cyclops: cf. *Od.* 9.334-5 (and perhaps Euripides, *Cyclops* 483-4). *uices* regularly means 'turns of duty' (*OLD* 2a); here the logic of the context and the Odyssean model imply rather 'roles'.   **circum | fundimur**: 'we pour round': the verb is a middle*, passive in form, and equivalent to a reflexive usage (cf. G&L §218-19). The tmesis* of the verb, emphasized by the line end (as at *Geo.* 4.274-5), imitates *Od.* 9.380-1 ἀμφὶ δ' ἑταῖροι | ἵσταντ' ('my companions took positions around me'), and contributes to the striking sequence of enjambed* verses that stretches from 630 to 636.   **lumen terebramus... | ingens**: 'we bore into his huge eye [*lit.* light]'. Lyne (1989: 115-16) shows how V.'s 'combination of prosaic concrete and expressive abstract' briefly distils what Homer achieves through the simile in which the blinding is likened to the drilling of a ship's timber (*Od.* 9.384-5: **A(d)**). Again enjambment* stresses the adjective *ingens* that is carried over from the previous line.   **quod torua solum sub fronte latebat**: 'which lay, a single eye, hidden beneath his shaggy brow', i.e. his eye was set deep beneath his brow: cf. Cicero, *de Natura Deorum* 2.143 (describing the ingenuity of nature) *latent praeterea utiliter et excelsis undique partibus saepiuntur* ('in addition, <the eyes> are set back to good advantage and shielded on all sides by raised features'). Strangely, though the story in the *Odyssey* depends on the Cyclops having a single eye, this is never mentioned in the poem. In contrast later writers emphasize the fact, as V. does here and in the similes that follow. **Argolici clipei**: when Artemis visits the Cyclopes at Callimachus, *Hymn* 3.53 [**K**] they each have a single eye 'like a shield'. **Phoebēae lampadis**: 'the lamp of Phoebus (the sun god)', i.e. the sun. The similes are appropriate to the Cyclops, whose name means 'circle-eye'. The image of the sun's lamp for the monster's eye (*lumen*) ironically emphasizes that the light of his vision has been extinguished: cf. 658; and Milton's blinded Samson: 'O dark, dark, dark, amid the blaze of noon, | Irrecoverably dark, total eclipse | Without all hope of day!' (*Samson Agonistes* 80–2). **instar** is a neuter noun, probably with the original meaning of 'balance' or 'equivalent weight'; it is commonly used with a genitive to mean 'as big as', 'like'; cf. Ovid's imitation, *Met.* 13.851–2 *instar | ingentis clipei*. **tandem**: as well as bringing out the agonizing slowness with which time can move in such situations, this draws attention to the unusual length of the sentence, and helps convey the connexion between Ulysses' careful planning and the successful outcome. **laeti…ulciscimur**: they take joy in their revenge (see Introduction, pp. 30–1 for the repeated, and contrasting, use of *laeti* of the Trojans). Revenge is a motive for Homer's Odysseus in his dealing with the Cyclops (9.317), as well as with the suitors in the second half of the poem.

639–44 miseri: Achaemenides uses the vocative to evoke the misery that awaits the Trojans unless they flee. **fugite…fugite**: cf. Polydorus' words at 44 *fuge…fuge*. **rumpite**: Servius remarks, *ut festinantes, non 'soluite' sed 'rumpite'* (i.e. since they are in a hurry, they should cut and not untie the mooring ropes). As he recounts his adventures to Dido, Aeneas is unaware that he will cut the cable of his ship in his haste to escape from her (4.580; and cf. Mercury's *rumpe moras* at 569). The 'half-line' is appropriately abrupt (see Introduction, p. 51). **nam qualis quantusque**: the reason the Trojans should flee is that in addition to the blinded Polyphemus, there are a hundred other Cyclopes, equally large, equally uncivilized. Polyphemus is named here for the first time; this distinguishes him from all the others now that they have been brought into the picture. (In Homer the whole group is described at the outset: 9.106–15.) **qualis quantusque… Polyphemus…, | centum alii**: literally 'of what kind and of what size Polyphemus…a hundred others', i.e. a hundred others of the same nature and size as Polyphemus, who... **lanigeras claudit pecudes atque ubera pressat**: the line includes the two products for which sheep are kept (wool and milk/cheese), and two common activities of shepherds, penning (cf. *Od.* 9.220-2) and milking (cf. *Od.* 9. 244, 341). As well as *Odyssey* 9, V. recalls the pastoral Polyphemus of Theocritus, *Idylls* 6 and 11; for a generic reading of the episode see Harrison 2007: 229-31. *laniger* 'wool-bearing' is a common epithet, going back to Ennius (*Satires* 24 Warmington *lanigerum genus*); Vergil has used it at *Geo.* 3.287 *lanigeros agitare greges*, as he turns from cattle and horses to sheep and goats. *claudit* is a word used of penning in animals on a farm, e.g. at *Ecl.* 7.15 *clauderet agnos* ('to pen in the lambs'). *pressare* of milking seems to be a Vergilian development: so *Ecl.* 3.99 *pressabimus ubera palmis* (imitated by Ovid at *Met.* 15.472 *ubera... manibus pressanda*). **uulgo** = *passim* (cf. *Ecl.* 4.25 *Assyrium uulgo nascetur amomum*, 'the balsam of the East will appear far and wide'); it enhances the point of *centum*. **infandi Cyclopes**: the second half of the name Polyphemus is based on the Greek word φημί ('say'): thus O'Hara (*apud* Horsfall) suggests that there is a play on words in calling the Cyclopes 'unspeakable' (*infandi*). The adjective echoes *infandum*, the (ironic) first word of Aeneas' speech (2.3). *Cyclopĕs* is Greek nominative plural. **errant**: the verb is regularly used of pasturing animals (e.g. *Ecl.* 1.9, 2.21 *Siculis errant in montibus agnae*); it implies that the Cyclopes are nomadic.

645-8 tertia iam lunae se cornua lumine complent: 'for the third time now the horns of the moon are filling themselves with light'. This ornate line with its alliteration of *lu-* and *co-* communicates the passing of nearly three months; its elegance throws into relief the horror of the verses that follow. The time-scale does not fit with the *Odyssey*: Odysseus had fled from the land in one of his earliest adventures after the fall of Troy while Aeneas has been travelling for almost seven years. But (despite 5.45-50, 8.268-72) the world of epic poetry does not normally require us to keep an eye on the calendar. Instead V. has his character measuring a realistic period of time by the means available to him, the moon. **cum uitam...traho**: 'while I have been dragging out my life': cf. *OLD traho* 17b, 'to get through (an activity, period of time, usu. by tedious or painful effort)'; Sinon had used the same phrase (2.92). Unlike English (which prefers the perfect) Latin uses the present for actions that extend from the past into current time. The use of inverted *cum* to mean 'in all which time' is relatively unusual (contrast 522, 590, 655), though it is sometimes introduced by *cum interea* (e.g. Cic. *Rosc. Am.* 11; Livy 5.54.5); we find a close parallel with V.'s usage at Prop. 2.20.21–2 *septima iam plenae deducitur orbita lunae | cum de me et de te compita nulla tacent* ('now the cycle of the full moon is being completed for the seventh time while no crossroad has failed to talk of you and me'). **in siluis**: cf. *Ecl.* 10.52 *in siluis inter spelaea ferarum* ('in the woods amidst the caves of wild animals'), where the speaker Gallus is deciding to live a pastoral life (similarly 11.570 in the Camilla story). Here reference to *siluae* marks Achaemenides' move from the world of epic into a life more primitive than that of Vergil's herdsmen: in his diet (649–50) and appearance (593) he is almost more like an animal (or a Cyclops) than a human being. **inter deserta ferarum | lustra domosque**: 'amid the abandoned lairs and homes of wild beasts': abandoned himself, Achaemenides now lives the life of a hunted animal. Donatus makes a distinction between *lustra* ('which beasts make amidst the undergrowth') and *domos* ('which they dig more deeply'); however, the expression could simply be a hendiadys*: 'the dens where wild beasts lived'. **uastos...ab rupe Cyclopas | prospicio**: 'I look out for the huge Cyclopes from a crag'. Achaemenides had presumably spotted the Trojans from such a crag (651–2). Note the scansion of *Cȳclōpăs* (Greek acc. pl.): elsewhere in this episode (569, 617, 644, 675), and throughout Vergil, the first syllable is long: cf. N. Hopkinson, 'Juxtaposed prosodic variants in Greek and Latin poetry', *Glotta* 60 (1982), 162–78. **sonitum pedum uocemque tremesco**: Williams draws attention to the assonance, which suggests the thudding of the Cyclopes' huge feet: cf. Ovid's imitation in Achaemenides' speech at *Met.* 14.214–15 *omnemque tremescens | ad strepitum mortemque timens* ('trembling at every noise and fearing death').

649–50 uictum infelicem: 'a wretched diet' the object of *dant rami*, placed first in the sentence, and thus emphasized. **bacas lapidosaque corna**: 'berries and stony cornels': it is tempting to think the epithet means that 'the fruit is almost all stone' (so Mynors on *Geo.* 2.34, where the phrase *lapidosa corna* originates), but we know of no evidence that *lapis* ('stone') can refer to the 'stones' in fruit; perhaps 'stone-hard' therefore. The cornelian cherry was regarded as food for primitive man (Ovid, *Met.* 1.105) or pigs (*Od.* 10.242). **uulsis pascunt radicibus herbae**: like cornels and acorns (Ovid, *Amores* 3.10.9, *Met.* 1.106, *Fasti* 4.399–400), grass is traditionally the food of primitive man (*Amores* 3.10.10, *Fasti* 2.293, 4.395–8), and Ovid has his Achaemenides driving off hunger 'with acorn and grass mixed with leaves' (*glande... et mixta frondibus herba*, *Met.* 14.216). *uulsis... radicibus* is thus to be taken as ablative absolute ('the roots having been torn'; cf. 27 *ruptis radicibus*) rather than instrumental ('feed with their roots').

651–4 omnia conlustrans: the verb is a rare one, so Vergil may have in mind Cicero, *Tusc.* 5.65 *ego... cum omnia conlustrarem oculis*, where the verb has the same sense ('survey'); the context describes Cicero, also on Sicily, searching woodland thickets near Syracuse for the lost tomb of Archimedes.   **hanc primum ad litora classem | conspexi uenientem**: 'I first saw this fleet coming to the shore': Achaemenides saw the Trojans arriving on the previous day, and waited till dawn, to approach them in the light.   **huic me, quaecumque fuisset, addixi**: 'to this (fleet), whatever it might have proved to be, I handed myself over'. *fuisset* is pluperfect subjunctive, equivalent in the implied indirect discourse to the future perfect of direct speech ('whatever it shall have been'). *addico* is a legal word meaning 'I make (myself) over'.   **satis est** recalls *sat est* (602): both of Achaemenides' speeches end with the declaration of his willingness to suffer any fate rather than falling victim to the monsters. Sinon has also marked the end of one of his speeches with *sat est* and an expression of willingness to be punished (2.102–3).   **nefandam**: 'unspeakable', a metrically useful alternative to *infandus* (644), always placed by V. at line end. As when Ilioneus appeals at 1.543 to the *deos memores fandi atque nefandi* ('the gods who remember right and wrong') the hint at *nefas* is rhetorically apt: this is not the way for Dido to behave there nor the Trojans here.   **uos**: sometimes *uos* and *tu* draw the attention of the addressee (2.712), and sometimes they seem to have an implication like 'please' with imperatives (e.g. 7.267), but here the point seems to be the contrast with the Cyclopes: 'rather (*potius*) may you take away this life (of mine) than they'.   **quocumque... leto**: 'by whatever death <you please>', i.e. any form of death at all.

655–8 uix ea fatus erat... cum: inverted *cum* marks the move from extended narrative to sudden action.   **summo... monte** seems at first an ablative of place 'where', but as the sentence progresses it comes to express 'whence': Homer's Cyclopes dwell on the tops of the mountains (*Od.* 9.113); Polyphemus starts at the top, but heads quickly down to the shore (657, 662). The three and a half verses from *summo* are famously onomatopoeic*: movement is slowed by the five elisions and the fifteen spondees* (only seven dactyls*); there is resonant alliteration of the nasals* *m* and *n*, culminating in the rhyming and assonance of the line-endings <u>mo</u>le <u>mo</u>u<u>entem</u>, <u>petentem</u>, <u>lumen</u> a<u>demptum</u>.   **ipsum**: the Trojans have heard about Polyphemus; now they see him in person.   **uasta...mole**: cf. Cacus, another monstrous embodiment of the forces that militate against civilization, at 8.199 *magna se mole ferebat*.   **<u>pastorem</u> <u>Pol</u>y<u>phem</u>um et litora <u>nota</u> <u>petentem</u>**: 'ponderous alliteration' (Horsfall). The paradox of the man-eating shepherd goes back to Homer, but we should also be reminded of Theocritus, whose sympathetic Polyphemus comes down to the sea to serenade the nymph Galatea (*Idylls* 6, 11): the shores are thus familiar (*nota*) to him, but also to the reader. Polyphemus subsequently features as an erotic/pastoral but also destructive figure in Ovid, *Metamorphoses* 13 (see J. Farrell, *AJPh* 113 (1992), 235–68), and the opera *Acis and Galatea* by Handel and Gay.   **monstr(um) horrend(um), inform(e), ingens**: cf. the description of the horrid Fama at 4.181 *monstrum horrendum, ingens* and (again) the *semihomo* Cacus (*monstrum* at 8.198, *informe cadauer* at 8.264). Thomas (1999: 262–3) notes the revision of *non sum adeo informis* ('I'm not so very ugly', *Ecl.* 2.25), where Corydon imitates the words of the Theocritean Cyclops (6.34–8). This verse is a textbook example of an expressively elided line. Morgan (2010: 206) describes 'the excessive vowel junction' as 'an attempt to capture the monstrosity of the Cyclops by comparably ugly composition: the elision essentially dramatizes the word *informe*, "having no definite or regular shape"' (cf. 330, 'the Cyclops and the civilization represented by metrical form had long been at variance').   **cui** (dative of disadvantage) **lumen ademptum**: this could mean that either his eye or the light of day had been taken from him; Polyphemus' words to his ram at *Od.* 9.452–3 ἄνακτος ὀφθαλμὸν ποθέεις ('you long for your master's eye') might favour the former; *Met.* 14.197 *mihi lucis ademptae* suggests that Ovid read it as the latter. There is a touch of pathos here, above all in the carefully adapted borrowing from Catullus 68B.93 *ei misero fratri iucundum lumen ademptum* ('alas the light [i.e. of life] has been taken from my poor brother').

659–61 trunca manum pinus regit: the capital MSS read the more difficult *manu* ('guides <him> in his hand'); but Quintilian's quotation of these words (8.4.24 'what size of body am I to conceive of for a creature whose "hand a lopped pine guides"') shows the antiquity and aptness of *manum*.   **uestigia firmat**: imitated by Lucan (4.41: slipping soldiers plant their javelins) and Statius, who has the wounded ghost of Laius use a walking-stick (*medica firmat uestigia uirga*, *Thebaid* 2.11).   **lanigerae comitantur oues**: at *Odyssey* 9.469-70 the Greeks rustle the rams that have been the means of their escape; but the ewes were penned separately (439).   **ea sola uoluptas**: 'these (are) his only pleasure': for the attraction of *ea* into the feminine singular by *uoluptas*, see 393. V. glances at Polyphemus' sympathy-winning speech to the ram left behind by the others at *Od.* 9.445-60. Now that the Cyclops represents far less of a danger, the poets evoke pathos for him.   **sola...solamen**: the play was read by Isidore (10.38) as having an etymological point (consolation lightening isolation). To the passages supporting this cited by O'Hara we may add *Geo.* 4.464-5 (Orpheus) *solans...solo in litore*, Seneca, *Tro.* 703-4 *unicum...solamen*, *Phaedra* 267. For the blinded Polyphemus singing is no consolation: contrast Theocritus 11.17, Callimachus, *Epig.* 46.1-4, Harrison 2007: 231. For the 'half-line' 661, see Introduction, p. 51. An attempt was made to complete the verse already in antiquity, with the words *de collo fistula pendet* ('a pipe hangs from his neck'): this adds a musical note to the bucolic presentation of Polyphemus, but the omission of the words in two of the three capital MSS shows that they are not original.

662-5 postquam...uenit: hysteron proteron*: the important feature is mentioned first. Polyphemus has come down to the sea but must wade out until the water is deep before he can bathe his eye.   **luminis effossi**: lit. 'of his dug-out eye'. Though 'digging out' is not quite what has happened, V. has been influenced by the idiomatic phrase *oculos effodere* used by a range of writers with reference to real or imagined punishments and in hyperbolic* threats (Plautus, *Aulularia* 189 *linguam praecidam atque oculos effodiam*, 'I shall cut off her tongue and dig out her eyes', *Capt.* 464; Terence, *Eun.* 740; Laberius, fr. 50(a).3-4 Panayotakis; Catullus 108.5; Caesar, *Bell. Gall.* 7.4.10; Cicero, *Rep.* 3.13; Sallust, *Hist.* 1.*fr.*88).   **fluidum lăuit...cruorem**: 'he washes the flowing blood'. Again, in describing the action, Aeneas creates sympathy.   **inde**: lit. 'from there'. Servius gives the glosses* *aut de fluctibus, aut de spatio oculi*. However, neither is satisfactory, as the blood is not being washed 'from the waves', but 'with them', and the sense 'from the space where the eye was' pointlessly repeats *luminis effossi*. Can *inde* perhaps mean 'therewith'? At present it looks as though the word (repeated in 666) is a space-filler, and perhaps to be set beside the half-lines 640 and 661 as a sign of incompletion. **dentibus infrendens**: a vividly alliterative phrase: 'gnashing' or 'furiously grinding with his teeth'; cf. 8.230 (the hero Hercules trying to get at Cacus), 10.718 (the evil Mezentius).   **gemitu**: 'with a groan', presumably of pain and rage.   **per aequor | iam medium**: 'now through the middle of the sea', i.e. through the high sea: the sequel shows that this is only how it seems (671).   **necdum fluctus latera ardua tinxit**: i.e. the water only came up to the waist of his towering body. After some empathetic verses, we get first a sense of violence (*infrendens*), and now a glance at the threat: he really is a giant.

666–9 nos procul inde: Aeneas returns the narrative to the Trojans, far enough away from Polyphemus to be safe—for the moment. **celerare**: historic* infinitive like *incīdere* in 667, suggesting their frantic speed now they are spurred into action, as does the sequence of dactyls* (five in 666, three more in the first three feet of 667).   **recepto | supplice sic merito**: the Trojans have taken Achaemenides on board, as he deserves, given his suffering and his help: in total contrast to the confidence-trickster Sinon of Book 2, he has alerted them to the terrible danger that now confronts them. Self-interest is in harmony with generosity of spirit.   **taciti** pointedly recalls *Odyssey* 9, where Odysseus first uses his eyebrows (468) to give silent instruction to his men, but when he thinks they are safe he twice taunts Polyphemus, with appalling immediate risk and disastrous eventual results (473–542). (See further on *uocis*, 669.)   **incidere funem**: cf. *Od.* 10.126–7 where Odysseus cuts the ship's cables in order to make a quick getaway from the giant-like Laestrygonians; and Apollonius, *Arg.* 4.208 (the departure from Colchis, and the tyrannous Aeetes). As at 639–40, a prolepsis* of the urgent departure from Carthage (4.575 *incidere funes*).   **uertimus et proni certantibus aequora remis**: 'and leaning forward we turn the sea with striving oars'. *uertimus* is more violent (and perhaps less efficient) than the variant *uerrimus* ('sweep'), found in some later MSS. For the enthusiastic departure cf. the boat-race at 5.140–1 *ferit aethera clamor | nauticus, adductis spumant freta uersa lacertis* ('the sailors' shouting strikes the heavens, the waters foam overturned by applied muscle'), which is followed at 144–7 by a simile comparing chariots beginning a race, with *proni* at 147, graphically presenting the drivers' urgency, as it does the rowers' here. V. recalls *Od.* 9.490 προπεσόντες ἔρεσσον, literally 'falling forward they

Commentary: lines 588–691 255

rowed'. *certantibus* implies the contest between the different crews to get away first (and implies a challenge to the oars at *Od.* 9.472). **sensit**: a dramatically brief clause: Polyphemus—but there is no time for a subject—notices them; and immediately responds (*uestigia torsit*). **ad sonitum uocis**: a puzzle: after they have cast off in silence there is not just noise, but speech; and like Odysseus' taunts (though less disastrously) it gets the attention of Polyphemus. Odysseus' crew understood the danger: 'if he had heard one of us uttering a sound or speaking, he would have hurled a jagged rock and smashed our heads and the timbers of the boat' (9.497–9). Do the Trojans by contrast engage in *nauticus clamor* (128; 5.140–1, cited on 667)? is it the bosun calling time to keep the rowers together? or has some unspecified hero played the Odysseus role and had his folly all but covered over by Aeneas?

670-4 nulla...dextra adfectare potestas: 'no chance to grasp with his right hand'. For *potestas* + inf. cf. 4.565, 7.591, 9.739, 813; for *adfectare* see *OLD affecto* 4. **nec potis**: 'and not able' (repeating *nulla potestas*, before the varied continuation): understand *est* (*potis est* = *potest*). *potis* has markedly archaic* flavour. V, who uses it twice more (9.796, 11.148), has inherited it from second-century drama, Ennius, Cicero's verse, Lucretius, and Catullus; but after V. it occurs in verse only at Persius 4.13, and in a solemn prayer at Silius 12.645. **Ionios fluctus aequare sequendo**: 'to match the waves of the Ionian sea in his pursuit': Polyphemus gets out of his depth: for *aequare* of matching height or depth, cf. *Geo.* 1.113 *cum primum sulcos aequant sata* ('as soon as the blades of corn match the height of the furrows'), *OLD* 10b. *aequare* refers to pace in similar passages elsewhere (6.263 *ducem haud timidis uadentem passibus aequat*, 'he matches the pace of his leader with intrepid step'; 10.248 *uentos aequante sagitta* 'an arrow as fast as the winds'; Silius 15.575 *illum...adnisi aequare sequendo*, 'striving to match him in their pursuit', varying V. in imitating him), and commentators assume that is the sense here; but he is not trying to match the speed of the waves. **clamorem immensum tollit**: Polyphemus has a shout to match his size. It and its reverberation are based on what follows the blinding at *Od.* 9.395 [**A(d)**]; there too the other Cyclopes gather in response, though it is only the 'rock' that resounds with the cry. V. expands the geography in imitation of Artemis' noisy visit to the smithy of the Cyclopes in Callimachus, *Hymn* 3 (**K**: Etna, Sicily, Italy, and Corsica all resound at 56–8). He also gives the shout elemental scale, sea as well as land: cf. *Geo.* 3.223 where the roaring of two fighting bulls causes 'the woods and the full length of heaven' to bellow back (*reboant siluaeque et longus Olympus*). Ovid echoes the shout with an amusingly circular simile at *Met.* 13.876–7: *tantaque uox, quantam Cyclops iratus habere | debuit, illa fuit: clamore perhorruit Aetne* ('that voice was as loud as an angry Cyclops ought to have: Etna shuddered at the shout'). **quo pontus et omnes |…undae**: 'at which all the waves of the sea': hendiadys*. **penitus exterrita <est>**: Italy was 'terrified to its depths', not only on the coast but far inland. This presumably evokes the terror felt by Italy and its people during an eruption of the volcano. **curuis…cauernis**: curved spaces promote echoes, as Servius notes, and the repeated sounds contribute to the point. The blacksmith Cyclopes of 8.418–21 (571 n.) are working in noisy *cauernae*. **immugiit**: V. likes the onomatopoeic* *mūgire* (92), and its compounds *re-* and *immugire*, which appears here for the first time (also at 11.38).

675–81 Compare the gathering of the other Cyclopes in response to the cry at *Od.* 9.399–413 [**A(d)**], only to disperse when Polyphemus falls for Odysseus' trick and blames 'Nobody'. V.'s bizarre variation on the episode is equally inconsequential, but eerily memorable. **excĭtum**: V. uses this form of the past participle here (and 7.623, 7.642, 10.38), but for the feminine singular nominative has the alternative *excĭtă* (4.301, 7.376, 12.445). **complent**: as if the subject were *Cyclopes*, not *genus Cyclopum*. They rushed to the shore as a unit; now Aeneas and his men can see them individually: the effect is similar at 2.63–4 *iuuentus | circumfusa ruit certantque* ('people rush to surround him and compete …'). However, there is a variant *complet*, and it is possible that a scribe has reproduced the phrase *litora complent*, used of the Trojans at 71, and echoed here: the shared language temporarily normalizes the otherwise alien race. **nequiquam**: Aeneas' ships are now too far away for the Cyclopes to be able to reach them. **lumine toruo**: 'with glaring eye', ablative of description, shown by its placing (as well as sense) to belong with *Aetnaeos fratres* rather than *cernimus*. The singular emphasizes that they have only one eye each; the word *lumen* reminds us that they, unlike Polyphemus, can actually see Aeneas and his men escaping (cf. 635, 658). **Aetnaeos fratres**: 'brothers who live on Etna'. **caelo**: either 'to the sky' (cf. 5.451 *it clamor caelo*) or 'in the sky'. **concilium horrendum**: a jocular correction of the Homeric assertion that the Cyclopes have no political

Commentary: lines 588–691　　　　　　　　　257

assemblies (ἀγοραὶ βουληφόροι, *Od.* 9.112).　　**quales cum …**: this is the only developed simile in the book (contrast Book 2, where Aeneas' tale is full of them).　　**uertice celso**: 'with their high tops' (Henry) is to be preferred to 'on a high peak' (Conington): *capita alta* guides the reader, who knows too that the Cyclopes are on the shore; to compare them to trees on a mountain top would be a complicating distraction; and cf. 9.679–82 *quales aëriae…| consurgunt geminae quercus intonsaque caelo | attollunt capita et sublimi uertice nutant* ('just as two airy oaks rise up, and raise their unshaven heads in/to the sky and nod with lofty top').　　**aëriae quercus aut coniferae cyparissi**: a combination of two lines of Catullus 64, which has the phrase *aëria cupressu* at 291, and *quercum aut coniferam…pinum* at 106 (in a simile describing the felling of the Minotaur; *cornigeram* is transmitted, and most editors print *conigeram*, but *-ger* compounds usually indicate 'wearing' rather than 'bearing', and Vergil's text supports the larger change). *cyparissi* is the Greek form for Latin *cupressi*: Ovid, *Met.* 10.106–42 tells the story of how Cyparissus metamorphosed into the tree to mourn for a pet stag that he had accidentally killed. Also Grecizing is the unusual line-ending: see Introduction, pp. 48–9.　　**constitĕrunt**: 'have taken their stand together', i.e. 'stand': cf. Greek ἑστηκέναι; but other gnomic* perfects are used by V. in similes (e.g. 2.380, 11.810–13). The prefix implies that they form a group: V. perhaps has in mind Apollonius, *Argonautica* 1.28–31 'Wild oak trees stand in ordered ranks close together, still tokens of that magic song, growing at Zone on the shore of Thrace: these he [Orpheus] charmed with his lyre and led down from Pieria.' For the metrical form, see Introduction, pp. 47–8.　　**silua alta Iouis lucusue Dianae**: trees in sacred groves would not be felled, and so aptly symbolize great height. Jupiter is regularly associated with oaks (*Geo.* 2.15–16, 3.332) and Diana occasionally with cypress wood (Xenophon, *Anabasis* 5.3.12, Pliny, *Nat.* 16.216), though not directly with groves of cypress (but see Strabo 14.1.20). Our vision of the Cyclopes fades away as they become the woods whence they emerged (cf. 590, 646, 675), and we return to the more comfortable world of Roman deities.

682–3 praecipitis: accusative plural, with *nos* implied: 'acting precipitately, impetuous' (*OLD praeceps* 3): a dramatic start to the line, which continues in dactyls* until the fourth foot, reflecting the Trojans' desperate anxiety to get away (cf. 666–7), even though in reality they are no longer in danger (670–1, 677).　　**quocumque**: literally 'to wherever',

258   *A Commentary on Vergil,* Aeneid *3*

i.e. 'to travel in any direction'.   **rudentis | excutere**: cf. 267 *excussosque iubet laxare rudentis*; and for the infinitive after *ago*, 4–5 n. After rowing initially, they now engage (though hurriedly and without careful planning) in the longer operation of setting the sails; so again at 5.829–30 after 5.778 (777 must be an interpolation* of 3.130, given the intervening conversation where Venus asks Neptune for a fair wind), and implicitly at 4.583/587.   **uentis intendere uela secundis**: 'to spread our sails for following winds'; unfortunately the current wind is from the south, as the next sentence will reveal.

684–6 'The instructions of Helenus warn the opposite, that I should not hold my course between Scylla and Charybdis, a route with a small separation from death on either side.' Note, however, that the order of the Latin takes us to Scylla and Charybdis before we reach the negative command that tells Aeneas not to go that way: it thus partly mimics the pattern of mistake followed by realization. The sentence is very fraught, and the text we print (following Mynors and Horsfall) has two conjectures, Heinsius' *Scyllamque Charybdinque* and Nisbet's *utrimque*, as well as a reading, *teneam* in 686, that is found only in part of the indirect transmission. The further corruptions may have been caused by scribal inattention after confronting the unexpected hypermetric line (684).   **contra**: 'otherwise', 'differently' (*OLD* 10). In 682 they were eager to sail in any direction; Aeneas now sees the problem.   **iussa Heleni**: at 410–32.   **monent…ni**: 'warn (me) not to…': indirect command: *ni* is an old form of *ne*, regularly corrupted in transmission, but also reported for 6.353 (Rufinus 56.7 Halm) and 12.801 (P), as well as at Propertius 2.7.3.   **Scyllamque Charybdinqu(e) | inter**: anastrophe*: for *inter* so cf. 1.218 *spemque metumque inter* and especially *Geo.* 2.344–5 *frigusque caloremqu(e) | inter*, which also exhibits elision of the hypermetric *que* over the break between lines (so too at 1.332–3, 448–9, e.g.). Heinsius' conjecture (for *Scyllam atque Charybdin*) thus restores a distinctively Vergilian styleme*, but one rare enough to confuse scribes and readers.   **utrimque**: Nisbet's conjecture (discussed at *Collected Papers on Latin Literature* (Oxford, 1995), 355) removes the misleading sequence *inter utramque uiam*, and thus helps the reader to link *inter* with what precedes, as well as clarifying that the dangerous route is the single one up the middle of the strait, with Scylla threatening on one side and Charybdis on the other (they cannot each be a *uia* as *utramque uiam* implies).   **uiam** is in apposition* to the route implied by 'between Scylla and Charybdis', and

Commentary: lines 588–691

looks ahead to *cursus*, the object of *teneam*.   **uiam leti discrimine paruo**: an imitation of Hera's words to Thetis about the Argonauts passing between Scylla and Charybdis at Apollonius 4.831–2 ἀλλ' ἔχε νῆα | κεῖσ' ὅθι περ τυτθή γε παραίβασις ἔσσετ' ὀλέθρου ('but guide the ship in the direction where there will be a route, though a narrow one, past destruction'). For the phrase *leti discrimine* cf. 9.143, where Turnus describes the ditches round the Trojan encampment as *leti discrimina parua* ('tiny separations from death'), and 10.511–12 where Aeneas is brought the message 'that his men are a hair's breadth away from death' (*tenui discrimine leti | esse suos*).   **teneam**: though *teneant* is transmitted by the MSS and most of the indirect tradition, it makes no sense in this first-person narrative; and editors rightly choose the first-person singular, preserved only in two MSS of the expanded version of Servius' commentary: Helenus directed his instructions on avoiding Scylla and Charybdis to Aeneas in the singular (*te*, 410; *fuge*, 413). (See also 692–715 n.)   **certum est**: 'I/we decided', a very common impersonal passive (used also at 9.153, *Ecl.* 10.52).   **lintea**, literally 'things made of linen' (cf. 'canvas'), is used as by synecdoche* for *uela* already by Catullus at 64.225, and 4.5 (singular).   **retro**: a fulfilment of the oracular prophecy of Cassandra about Aeneas as παλιμπλανήτης ('backward-wanderer'), at Lycophron 1239.

687–91 ecce...Boreas...| missus adest: As they are now heading south a north wind is just what they need—for once (contrast the storms at 4.442, 12.365)—and suddenly (*ecce*, *OLD* 4) one begins to blow. *missus*, which is emphasized by the enjambment*, implies an unexpressed agent, and helps suggest divine help for the Trojans here: Servius notes Anchises' prayer at 528–9; cf. also 705 *datis...uentis*. **angusta ab sede Pelori**: see 411 n. Though *angusta* refers to the narrow straits between Sicily and Italy, it is here transferred to the promontory Pelorus, described as if it were the seat or abode (*sede*) of a native deity (cf. the eponymous* Eryx in Book 5). Mention of Pelorus, even though the Trojans do not get so far north, allows the description of the circumnavigation of Sicily to begin from one of the three points of the triangular island (Map 4): Pachynus and Lilybaeum follow in 699 and 706; Strabo (6.2) and Pliny (*Nat.* 3.88–90) follow the same sequence.   **uiuo praeteruehor ostia saxo | Pantagiae**: 'I sail past the mouth of the river Pantagia, with its natural rock'. *uiuo saxo* is descriptive ablative with *ostia*, stressing that the harbour is natural, not man-made.   **Megarosque sinus Thapsumque iacentem**: 'and

260   *A Commentary on Vergil, Aeneid 3*

the bay of Megara Hyblaea, and low-lying Thapsus'. All three places named in the line are on the east coast of Sicily, heading south towards Syracuse.   **talia monstrabat...Achaemenides**: 'these and similar things are pointed out by Achaemenides': his provision of information to the Trojans is generalized before he lapses back into anonymity. Like a written *periplus**, listing ports and coastal landmarks, the Greek sailor becomes a source of knowledge that Aeneas will relay as he describes their voyage along the coasts of Sicily (up to 708): contrast *ignari uiae*, 569.   **relegens errata retrorsus | litora**: 'sailing again along the shores he had wandered in the opposite direction'. The passive use of an intransitive verb in *errata* is allowable because the verb can take an internal accusative in the active (*errare litora* = 'to wander past the shores', *OLD* 1b). *relegens* plays with the idea of reading, as well as repetition (which is then stressed by *retrorsus*), and thus offers a final comment on the detailed reworking of the *Odyssey*.   **comes infelicis Vlixi**: the first time Aeneas used this phrase (at 613) he was quoting Achaemenides. Now he uses it in his own narrative voice, charged with emotion in this coda to a factual sentence. His human sympathy has widened sufficiently for him to acknowledge the suffering of a bitter enemy: Putnam (1995: 63) notes the change from 273, where he curses Ithaca, the home of 'savage Ulysses'.

692–715 *The circumnavigation of Sicily and the death of Anchises*
Having corrected their hurried error (sailing north when escaping from the Cyclopes), the Trojan fleet continues its long voyage around Sicily, in a passage that pays homage to a number of Vergil's Hellenistic* predecessors: Theocritus (and other bucolic poets) in 692–6; Apollonius, who followed the *periplus** tradition in listing places passed by the Argonauts (e.g. *Arg.* 1.915–35; 2.1231–50; Nelis 56–9); and Callimachus, who dedicated a passage of *Aetia* 2 (fr. 43) to the foundations of Sicilian cities (see M. Geymonat, 'Callimachus at the end of Aeneas' narration', *HSCPh* 95 (1993), 323–31; Nappa, *CQ* 54 (2004), 640–6): we know he referred to Thapsus, Megara, Syracuse, Camerina, Gela and its river, Selinunte. Sicily also featured heavily in earlier Roman epic, especially Naevius' *Bellum Punicum* and Ennius (Goldschmidt 2013: 111–15). V.'s catalogue is given interest by a sequence of etymological plays (693, 698, 703, 705). It begins and ends with longer accounts of Syracuse and Drepanum, contrasting with the seven places quickly mentioned in 698–706. A pattern of adverbs marks the stages of the voyage (*inde*, 697; *hinc*, 699; *procul*, 701; *inde* 703; *hinc*, 707). Beginning already in

686, 688, and continuing in 698, 705–6, we have a number of first-person singular verbs, where we might expect plurals (as in 668, 677, 697, 700). 'But Aeneas is about to lose Anchises, his co-captain and mentor, and Vergil seems to foreshadow this by the more frequent singulars' (Sanderlin, *CJ* 71 (1975–6), 56). The use of vocatives in 696 and 705 likewise prepares us for the climactic *pater optime* of 710.

692–6 Sicanio praetenta sinu: 'stretched out in front of a Sicilian bay' (the one where Syracuse will sit): *sinu* is dative. The epithet *Sicanio* opens the paragraph with a clear announcement of its topic.   **contra | Plemyrium undosum**: the preposition governs the noun in the following verse (cf. the reverse order at 684–5): 'opposite wave-swept Plemyrium' (Ortygia is at the northern side of the Great Harbour of Syracuse; Plemyrium is the promontory enclosing the southern end: Map 4). As well as leading into a passage where the sea has a metapoetic* function, *undosum* is the first of a succession of etymologically apt epithets in this passage; *Plemyrium* is derived from the Greek πλημυρίς, 'tidal wave'. The interest in etymology is then marked by the start of the following sentence: *nomen dixere priores*.   **Ortygiam. Alpheum...Elidis amnem...Arethusa**: Arethusa is the name of a spring on the small island of Ortygia, part of Syracuse, described by Cicero at *Verr.* 2.4.118 'At the end of this island is a freshwater spring, called Arethusa, of incredible size, very full of fish, which would be entirely covered by the waves if it were not protected from the sea by stone defence-works' (similarly Sen. *Dial.* 6.17.3; the spring is now tainted with salt water). A freshwater source on a small island and so close to the sea was a phenomenon demanding explanation (Seneca, *Natural Questions* 6.8), and already two Greek lyric poets, Ibycus (fr. 323, a reference in scholia* on Theocritus 1.117) and Pindar (*Nemean* 1.1), referred to the story that the fresh water comes from the river Alpheus, the longest river of the Peloponnese, which flows from Arcadia, through Olympia in Elis, and into the Ionian Sea, heading westward towards Sicily (Map 3). The transit is presented as an erotic pursuit of Arethusa already in fragment 3 of the Greek bucolic poet Moschus. For Ovid (*Amores* 3.6.29–30, *Met.* 5.487–508, 572–641) the story will be one of failed rape: an Arcadian water-nymph, Arethusa, tries to escape from the river-god, eventually fleeing under the earth until she surfaces on Ortygia. In *Eclogue* 10.1, 4–5 V. exploited the myth to link Arcadia (the poetic locale of Gallus, the elegiac* love poet celebrated in the poem) with Sicily, origin of his bucolic source, Theocritus:

> Extremum hunc, Arethusa, mihi concede laborem....
> sic tibi, cum fluctus subterlabere Sicanos,
> Doris amara suam non intermisceat undam.

Arethusa, grant me this final labour.... So may Doris [*a sea goddess*] not mix her bitter water with you, when you flow beneath the Sicilian waves.

In the Idyll which V. used as a model for *Eclogue* 10 Theocritus (1.117) employs the spring as a symbol of the Sicilian landscape to which the dying Daphnis says farewell. Springs are regularly sources of poetic inspiration, and Arethusa has this function already in Greek bucolic when the author of the *Epitaphios Bionis* ([Moschus] 3.76–7) describes his predecessor Bion as having drunk from Arethusa just as Homer drank from Hippocrene. The sea on the other hand is regularly associated with *epic* composition especially in contrast to the small fountain or stream (Callimachus, *Hymn* 2.106–12; *Georgics* 2.41–5; Propertius 3.3, 3.9.35–6). The invocation to Arethusa in *Eclogue* 10 thus seeks purity not only for the nymph's water, but also for Vergil's 'final labour' in the field of bucolic poetry.

In the myth that ends the *Georgics* Arethusa features as a sister of Cyrene, the mother of Aristaeus; she it is who first raises her head (4.351–2) from the waters of the river Peneus, by the source of which Aristaeus stands lamenting the loss of his bees (4.317–32); she leads him down into his mother's watery realm, through a cavern flowing with the rivers of the world (4.360–73), to a cave where they pour libations to Ocean (4.380–2) and arrange his visit to Proteus, the 'Old Man of the Sea', in a scene that reworks *Odyssey* 4.351–592. Arethusa's role here can be read as signifying the poetic route of the *Georgics* themselves, which lead the poet from the small-scale pastoral of the *Eclogues* to the epic sea of the *Aeneid*. Once again in 694–6 V. uses the myth with metapoetic* connotations: the sentence recalls *Eclogue* 10 (*Siculis undis* reworking *fluctus Sicanos*, e.g.), but it is dominated by the river Alpheus, not Arethusa, and his waters are confused (*confunditur*) with those of the sea, and not kept separate (*non intermisceat*, *Ecl.* 10.5). The language asserts strongly that we are 'now' (*nunc*, 695) in the world of epic.   **Alpheum**: the normal form in Greek is Ἀλφεός, with a short second syllable (as in Accius, fr. 509 Ribbeck), but to fit the word into dactylic* verse V. takes over the alternative form Ἀλφειός, as used by Moschus (fr. 3.1).   **fama est**: Aeneas repeats a story he has heard (conceivably from their guide Achaemenides, who has been this way before, 690–1); but the phrase is also an 'Alexandrian footnote'* (as at 578), here drawing attention to the metapoetic play the story involves.   **mare**: the placing of this dibrach* in the fifth foot helps give verse 695 a very unusual rhythm; even in the final foot the coincidence of accent* and ictus* in *qui* is lessened by the accent on *nunc* immediately following: the effect may be to suggest the effort of the submarine journey between Elis in 694 and Sicily in 696; there is certainly a contrast with the following two verses, especially 697, where all bar the fourth foot have coincidence of ictus and accent. **ore, Arethusa, tuo**: 'through your mouth, Arethusa' (the ablative expressing the route). Though her part in the narrative is reduced to this half-line, the apostrophe* give a very personal tone, recalling the invocation in *Ecl.* 10.1; reference to her mouth evokes her Muse-like role there, as well as suiting her function as a fountain (cf. 1.245). As an emigrant she may recall Dido, whose life will also be upset by erotic engagement with an epic figure.   **conf<u>und</u>itur <u>und</u>is**: the repetition mimics the sounds of the waves, and reasserts the dominance of the sea is this tale.

697–8 iussi numina magna loci ueneramur: at 435–9 Helenus has instructed Aeneas to worship Juno above all, and the Trojans have piously done so at 546–7; but Juno was not a deity of importance in Syracuse. Servius wonders whether the instruction may alternatively come from Achaemenides or Anchises or an oracle; in Apollonius (1.915–21) the Argonauts follow Orpheus' instructions and put in to Samothrace to become initiates of the local gods (12 n.). Another possibility is that V. is playfully obeying a lost literary instruction, to venerate Alpheus or Arethusa or some other god of Syracuse. The imprecise phrasing of *numina magna loci* seems designed to be evocative, and we may think of Apollo and Artemis, whose shared temple will stand on Ortygia; Artemis was said to have been born there (Pindar, *Nem.* 1.2–4; cf. *Hom. Hymn* 3.16), before Leto moved on to Delos, also called Ortygia (124), where Apollo was born. *uenerari* is an appropriate verb for the pious son of Venus to use (also at 34, 79, 84, 460 in Book 3); here it may evoke Daphnis' refusal to pay reverence to the goddess in Theocritus, *Idyll* 1, brought to mind by the invocation of Arethusa.   **exsupero**: Latin uses verbs of conquering (e.g. *uincere*) to express going beyond a geographical point; when used by Aeneas it also prefigures the Roman conquest of Sicily.   **stagnantis Helori**, 'marshy Helorus': Servius notes that the epithet puns on the Greek for marsh, ἕλος, from which *Helorus* is derived.

699–702 saxa Pachyni | radimus: having avoided passing through the straits at Pelorus they 'scrape past' (*radimus*) the cliffs of the next of Sicily's capes (429, 687 nn.; Map 4).   **fatis numquam concessa moueri**: 'not allowed by the fates to ever be moved', a fittingly oracular assertion. What might appear an announcement that Camerina, like Delos (77), will not suffer earthquakes, refers rather to Apollo's advice μὴ κίνει Καμαρίναν· ἀκίνητος γὰρ ἀμείνων ('do not move Camerina: it will be better unmoved'; alluded to by Callimachus, *Aetia* fr. 64.1–2). This oracle referred not to the city itself, but to a marsh of the same name; when it was drained because of the sickness it caused, it failed to provide protection, and enemy soldiers were able to attack and take the city.   **campique Geloi | immanisque Gelā fluuii cognomine dicta**: the plains of Gela and the town Gela itself will take their name from the river Gelas, perhaps described as 'savage, brutal' (*immanis*, *OLD* 1a) because it was represented on coins as a man-headed bull. The repetition may suggest an etymological point even before the explicit phrasing *cognomine dicta*. The *a* of *Gela* would normally be light, but Latin poets vary in their treatment of the ending in rendering Greek names (e.g. *Phaedrā* at Ovid, *Ars* 1.511, *Rem.* 743; *Phaedră* at *Ars* 1.744), or the syllable may treated as long before the two consonants that begin *fluuii*, though V. normally does this only with *que* (Austin on 4.146; in the case of *que* it happens not only before double consonants: 91). As for *fluuii* itself, V. uses the genitive singular in -*ii* (rather than -*i*) only here in a second-declension noun (9.151 being an interpolation*); for adjectival genitives in -*ii*, see *Ausonii*, 385; *Trinacrii*, 429. This combination of oddities, together with the repetition, make Wagner's deletion of the line persuasive: so M. D. Reeve, *Paideia* 66 (2011), 453–5; though there is a link with Silius 14.218 *uenit ab amne trahens nomen Gela* ('Gela came, which takes its name from a river'), that need not be a copy.

703–6 arduus is another etymological epithet, picking up ἄκρος ('top') in the name of **Acragas**. After two low-lying features (700–2), the account stresses height.   **moenia**: here the underlying anachronism surfaces: the Sicilian cities were not founded until historical times, Acragas in the early sixth century, so its wall can hardly have been visible to Aeneas: his prophetic voice is most explicit here. The point continues in the appositional* phrase **magnanimum quondam generator equorum**: Sicilian victors in chariot races at Olympia used horses from Acragas; *quondam*, which looks as though it points to the

Commentary: lines 692–715   265

past ('once'), in fact refers to the future, 'in time to come' (*OLD* 2). *magnanimum* is the form V. uses for the genitive plural (6.307, *Geo.* 4.476).   **datis linquo uentis**: following winds mean that Selinunte is being left behind, as soon as it enters the text. Again the gods implicitly favour the Trojan journey (cf. 687–8; *Iliad* 7.4–5).   **palmosa Selinus**: the successful race-horses in 704 encourage the reader to think of the palms awarded for Olympic victory (cf. *Geo.* 1.59 *Eliadum palmas... equarum*). V. may have thought or known that palms grew there (so Silius 14.200); but he was also no doubt aware that σέλινον, a form of parsley/celery, symbol of the city on coins, was another plant used to crown victors at athletic games. *Selinūs* is a third-declension feminine, with vocative identical to the nominative.   **uada dura lego saxis Lilybēĭă caecis**: after the monster-infested narrows of Pelorus and the cliffs of Pachynus, at Lilybaeum unseen rocks in the shallows are the danger.

707–11 Aeneas with brief, but marked, emotion (*hic*, 708; *heu*, 709; *hic*, 710; *heu*, 711; *pater optime*, 710) reflects on the death of Anchises. He describes his own past and current state (*tempestatibus actus*; *fessum*); he sums up what his father meant for him ('alleviation for every care and disaster'); and closes with Anchises' survival of a sequence of threats, in particular alluding to his being carried out of a Troy that is sacked and burning. But the death itself is not explained; we are given no clue as to whether illness or accident, sudden stroke or violent act was responsible. The verbs used (both of them stressed by the enjambment*) express it as an active losing by the son (*amitto*, 710) and a desertion by the father (*deseris*, 711): it is as though Aeneas feels both guilty and betrayed.   **Drepani...portus**: It was not a firm tradition that Anchises died at Drepanum: Erskine 2001 finds tombs reported on Mount Ida, at Aeneia in Chalcidice, in Arcadia; Naevius and the Elder Cato in his *Origines* had him reaching Italy (Casali 2007: 119), and so do Strabo (5.3.2), and others mentioned by Dionysius of Halicarnassus (*Rom.* 1.64). Vergil's plot depends on Anchises' absence from the episode in Carthage, so it was sensible to place the death in Sicily. But Drepanum is a striking choice for the death of a father, especially in this etymologically loaded context (Nappa, *CQ* 54 (2004), 645); it gets its name from the sickle (Greek δρέπανον or ζάγκλον) which the god Saturn threw down there after he had emasculated his father Uranus: the story is referred to in Callimachus, *Aetia* fr. 43.69–71 (using both nouns, but talking of Zancle, at the north-eastern corner of the island, of which the same aetion was told), and Apollonius, *Arg.* 4.982–6 (on Corcyra, also called Drepane). Losing his father may seem to free Aeneas to follow his own wishes in Book 4, and perhaps to mark Vergil's escape from the Homeric model (Oliensis 2009: 75–6; Farrell in Perkell 1999: 98–101): but Anchises (and Homer) will keep returning with paternal advice (4.351–3; 5, especially 719–40; 6.679–899). **inlaetabilis ora**: in its final appearance in the book the stem *laet-* is negated; for once it confirms rather than corrects the force of *fessus* (710; cf. 78, 100 nn.). The effect is all the stronger because this is the first occurrence of *inlaetabilis* extant: V. imitates the Homeric ἀτερπέα χῶρον (*Od.* 11.94, 'joyless place', of the home of the dead). Anchises' death would make any shore gloomy for his son; but Goldschmidt (2013: 115) has good reasons to see another prolepsis* here: in 249 BC, during the First Punic War, the Roman fleet was disastrously defeated at Drepanum by Carthage (Polybius 1.49–51). **pelagi tot tempestatibus actus** recalls 1.3 *multum...iactatus et alto* ('much tossed also on the sea') at this transitional moment in the poem (714–15). At the time of Anchises' death, the worst storm lies just ahead for Aeneas, that sent by Juno in Book 1, which threatens to sink the whole fleet, and drives the Trojans to Carthage; but this makes it psychologically plausible for him to associate the death with storms. *actis* is the reading of at least two capital manuscripts (PR) and other sources, but it would mean 'when so many storms had been driven away' (cf. *Geo.* 1.413 *imbribus actis*, 'when the rains have blown away'), a bizarre thing for Aeneas to say when he knows a great storm is imminent. *actus* (preserved only in M, but with a useful parallel at 7.199 *tempestatibus acti*) expresses the sense of injustice felt by the bereaved son. **omnis curae casusque leuamen**: in Book 2, Anchises has been a literal burden to his son (*oneri*, 2.723), if not a heavy one (*nec me labor iste grauabit*, 708: 'nor will the labour of carrying you weigh me down'). Here by contrast we hear that he lightened 'every anxiety and misfortune' for Aeneas. **tantis nequiquam erepte periclis**: Aeneas echoes the phrasing of Helenus at 3.476 *bis Pergameis erepte ruinis*. The expression there singles Anchises out for special praise; here *nequiquam* ('in vain') adds a bitter note. The echo encourages us to take *tantis* as 'so many' as well as 'such great': he survived twice when Troy fell, was not destroyed by the thunderbolt with which Jupiter struck him (2.648–9), and has lived through the plague on Crete and other misadventures suffered by the Trojans on their travels—but he has not reached Rome. Death is a marker of closure at the end of most books of the *Aeneid*: so 2 (Creusa), 4 (Dido), 5 (Palinurus), 6 (Marcellus), 10 (Mezentius), 12 (Turnus).

712–13 nec uates Helenus... non dira Celaeno: again Aeneas complains: a man whose life is determined by the expressions of divine will might hope that his father's death will have been predicted, if not by the kindly prophet, at least by the malevolent Harpy. Having recalled Book 2 in 711, he here reviews the second half of his narrative, and thus gives emphasis to the prophetic element in Book 3 (to Helenus at 374–462, Celaeno at 247–57, we may add Apollo at 94–8; the Penates at 154–71). **cum multa horrenda moneret**: Helenus has mentioned visits to the infernal lakes and Circe's island (386), the need to avoid the wicked Greek inhabitants of south-eastern Italy (396–402), the horrors of Scylla and Charybdis. Even if translated 'when', *cum* clearly has a concessive force here ('though'); hence the subjunctive.

714–15 hic labor extremus: after the closural account of a death and the revisiting of material from Books 2 and 3, Aeneas formally announces the end of his narrative, as the phrase *Extremum...laborem* has signalled the final Eclogue (10.1: see 692–6 n.). **longarum haec meta uiarum**: the tale, like the journey, has been a long one. *meta* is literally 'a turning post' on a race-track, and suits the point where the Trojans have to turn north-east (cf. 429 *metas lustrare Pachyni*), but metaphorically it more often refers to a goal, or finishing line, as at 10.472 *metas...dati peruenit ad aeui* (Jupiter on Turnus' imminent death: 'he has come to the end of the life granted him'). Aeneas has reached the goal of his speech, the end of Trojan wanderings (cf. Apollonius, *Arg.* 4.1775–6 'I have come now to the glorious end [πείρατα] of your labours'); but for the epic as a whole this will prove to be only a turning point, half way to the goal of Latium, at the start of Book 7, and a quarter of the way to the poem's end (cf. Nelis 217–19, 65–6). Moreover, the poem keeps passing through the waters off Drepanum: as the Trojans set sail at the start of Book 1; here; when they return driven by bad weather on their way back from Carthage at 5.12–34; in the boat-race during the games for Anchises (the word *meta* appears at 5.129, 159); and when they set out at 5.774, to reach Italy at last. **hinc me digressum uestris deus appulit oris**: the line summarizes the events that brought Aeneas from Drepanum (*hinc*) to Carthage (*uestris oris*; for the dative, see 338 n.). The line is discussed by Macrobius, *Sat.* 5.2.11 in relation to the narrative design of the

Odyssey: it is equivalent to the brief passage (*Od*. 12.447–8 ἔνθεν...νῆσον ἐς Ὠγυγίην πέλασαν θεοί, 'From here...the gods brought me to the island of Ogygia') in which Odysseus tells how having escaped Scylla and Charybdis he was brought to Calypso's island: ahead of Book 4 *uestris...oris* thus sets Dido and her people in the role of Calypso. Odysseus has already given a proper narrative in Book 7, as he observes at *Od*. 12.451–3 ('I already told the story yesterday...I don't like narrating again things that have been told clearly'); Aeneas can be brief because of the account of the storm given by Ilioneus at 1.527–38, Vergil because of his longer narration at 1.81–173 (cf. also 1.399–400). Aeneas' vague *deus* flatters Dido ('a god brought me here'), but it happens to describe events accurately, whether we see Juno, who caused, or Aeolus, who effected the storm, or Neptune, who quelled it, as responsible for the arrival in Africa. In the conversation with Dido that opens Book 4, her sister Anna will revisit these notions (45–6): *dis equidem auspicibus reor et Iunone secunda | hunc cursum Iliacas uento tenuisse carinas* ('I reckon it was thanks to the protection of the gods and the favour of Juno that the Trojan ships sailed this course'). The verse also maintains the reflexion on the end of the narrative: coming into port is a frequent image for reaching the end of a book or work, as at *Geo*. 4.116–17; Ovid, *Ars* 1.771–2, 3.748, and *Remedia Amoris* 811–12: *hoc opus exegi: fessae date serta carinae; | contigimus portus, quo mihi cursus erat* ('I have finished this work: put garlands on the tired vessel; we have reached the port where our voyage was headed').

716–18 *The end of Aeneas' speech*
The book ends with a brief return to the narrative voice, and a careful echoing of elements from the introduction to the speech at 2.1–2: *Conticuere omnes intentique ora tenebant; | inde toro pater Aeneas sic orsus ab alto* ('Everyone became silent and attentively held their mouths shut; then from the high couch father Aeneas began thus'). Everyone has remained attentive throughout (and presumably silent); now at last the speaker stops talking. On the formal marking of the end of the speech, see 90 n. *Odyssey* 13.1 is similar: 'So he spoke, while they were all rapt in silence.' **pater Aeneas** repeats the phrase from 2.2, but has an added significance here, when Aeneas has just spoken of the death of his father. **intentis omnibus unus**: the juxtaposition of *unus* concentrates the focus on the single speaker in the crowded hall, a scene that Vergil must have known from his own recitations. It may also point to the absence of Anchises. **fata...diuum**

cursusque: Dido asked for *insidias...Danaum casusque tuorum | erroresque tuos* (1.754–5: 'the tricks of the Greeks, the fall of your people, and your wanderings'); what Aeneas has given attributes the fall of Troy to divine will and makes the voyage less arbitrary. **renarrabat**: the verb (used by V. only here) once again hints at the reworking of earlier narratives (690 n.).   **conticuit tandem factoque hic fine quieuit**: 'at last he became silent, and having here made an end he rested [i.e. became quiet]'. Every word of the line contributes to the sense of closure after the long speech; but for the reader who immediately carries on into Book 4 (Harrison, *ANRW* 2.31.1 (1980), 363–5) there is a strong contrast expressed between the calm ending for Aeneas in Book 3 (*quieuit* becomes 'he went to sleep') and Dido's sleepless night that opens Book 4:

> *At regina* graui iamdudum saucia cura
> uulnus alit uenis et caeco carpitur igni.
> multa uiri uirtus animo multusque recursat
> gentis honos; haerent infixi pectore uultus
> uerbaque *nec placidam membris dat cura quietem.*

But the queen long sickening with weighty love nurtures the wound in her veins and is consumed by an unseen fire. The great courage of the hero runs repeatedly through her mind, and the great glory of his race too; his features and his words remain firmly fixed in her heart and *her love grants no calming rest to her limbs.*

The final word thus prefigures the taciturnity of Aeneas in Book 4, and the insomnia of Dido.

Appendix of Major Intertexts

A: Homer, *Odyssey* 9:

Books 9–12 of the Odyssey *contain the hero's account of his travels after the fall of Troy, given at the court of Alcinous, king of the Phaeacians. In Book 9 the main episode (106–566) is his encounter with Polyphemus, one of the Cyclopes, an 'arrogant and lawless people' (107), who 'dwell on the tops of high mountains in hollow caves' (113–14). First the twelve ships reach a nearby island, uninhabited, but full of wild goats (on which they feast).*

(a) *Odyssey* 9.142–51:

> ἔνθα κατεπλέομεν, καί τις θεὸς ἡγεμόνευεν
> νύκτα δι' ὀρφναίην, οὐδὲ προυφαίνετ' ἰδέσθαι·
> ἀὴρ γὰρ περὶ νηυσὶ βαθεῖ' ἦν, οὐδὲ σελήνη
> οὐρανόθεν προύφαινε, κατείχετο δὲ νεφέεσσιν.   145
> ἔνθ' οὔ τις τὴν νῆσον ἐσέδρακεν ὀφθαλμοῖσιν,
> οὐδ' οὖν κύματα μακρὰ κυλινδόμενα προτὶ χέρσον
> εἰσίδομεν, πρὶν νῆας ἐυσσέλμους ἐπικέλσαι.
> κελσάσῃσι δὲ νηυσὶ καθείλομεν ἱστία πάντα,
> ἐκ δὲ καὶ αὐτοὶ βῆμεν ἐπὶ ῥηγμῖνι θαλάσσης·   150
> ἔνθα δ' ἀποβρίξαντες ἐμείναμεν Ἠῶ δῖαν.

There we sailed to land. And some god guided us through the murky night, and it was not possible to see ahead; for the air around the ships was thick, and there was no light from the moon in the sky as it was covered by clouds. No one caught sight of the island and we did not see the long waves rolling to the land until we brought our well-benched ships to shore. We beached the ships, lowered all the sails, and disembarked ourselves by the breakers on the beach. (150) There we went to sleep and awaited bright dawn.

Next day out of curiosity Odysseus crosses over in his own ship to the land of the Cyclopes and finds a cave, and a yard built to protect sheep and goats. This belonged to a monstrous man with no sense of right and wrong: he was not like a bread-eating man but a wooded peak of the lofty mountains which stands out on its own apart from the others (190–2). Odysseus (taking a goatskin of special wine) and twelve of his comrades go into the cave and eat some of the Cyclops' cheese. Polyphemus now appears and blocks the entry to the cave with a huge rock. He quizzes Odysseus and his men about their identity. When Odysseus asks him in the name of Zeus to show the hospitality due to strangers, he refuses, explicitly expressing his disdain for Zeus.

(b) **Odyssey** 9.288–98:

> ἀλλ' ὅ γ' ἀναΐξας ἑτάροις ἐπὶ χεῖρας ἴαλλε,
> σὺν δὲ δύω μάρψας ὥς τε σκύλακας ποτὶ γαίῃ
> κόπτ'· ἐκ δ' ἐγκέφαλος χαμάδις ῥέε, δεῦε δὲ γαῖαν.   290
> τοὺς δὲ διὰ μελεϊστὶ ταμὼν ὡπλίσσατο δόρπον·
> ἤσθιε δ' ὥς τε λέων ὀρεσίτροφος, οὐδ' ἀπέλειπεν,
> ἔγκατά τε σάρκας τε καὶ ὀστέα μυελόεντα.
> ἡμεῖς δὲ κλαίοντες ἀνεσχέθομεν Διὶ χεῖρας,
> σχέτλια ἔργ' ὁρόωντες, ἀμηχανίη δ' ἔχε θυμόν.   295
> αὐτὰρ ἐπεὶ Κύκλωψ μεγάλην ἐμπλήσατο νηδὺν
> ἀνδρόμεα κρέ' ἔδων καὶ ἐπ' ἄκρητον γάλα πίνων,
> κεῖτ' ἔντοσθ' ἄντροιο τανυσσάμενος διὰ μήλων.

But he, leaping up, stretched out his hands towards my companions and, snatching two of them, he dashed them to the ground as if they had been puppies. Their brains flowed out onto the ground and drenched the earth. (290) Tearing them limb from limb he got his meal ready and ate it like a mountain-bred lion. And he left nothing, neither entrails nor flesh nor the bones with their marrow. Weeping, we held up our hands to Zeus as we saw his wicked deeds; but we felt completely helpless. (295) But when the Cyclops had filled his great belly with the human flesh he had eaten and drinking unwatered milk, he lay inside his cave stretching himself out among his flocks.

Odysseus thinks of killing the Cyclops with his sword when he is asleep, but realizes that, if he does that, they will be trapped in the cave because they cannot move the huge rock that blocks its entrance. Instead he cuts off a length of Polyphemus' staff, sharpens, and hides it. Four are selected by lot to help turn the pole in his eye.
At evening the Cyclop returns and milks his ewes.

(c) **Odyssey** 9.343–6, 353–70:

> αὐτὰρ ἐπεὶ δὴ σπεῦσε πονησάμενος τὰ ἃ ἔργα,
> σὺν δ' ὅ γε δὴ αὖτε δύω μάρψας ὡπλίσσατο δόρπον.
> καὶ τότ' ἐγὼ Κύκλωπα προσηύδων ἄγχι παραστάς,   345
> κισσύβιον μετὰ χερσὶν ἔχων μέλανος οἴνοιο·
> ...
> ὣς ἐφάμην, ὁ δ' ἔδεκτο καὶ ἔκπιεν· ἤσατο δ' αἰνῶς
> ἡδὺ ποτὸν πίνων καί μ' ᾔτεε δεύτερον αὖτις·
> 'δός μοι ἔτι πρόφρων, καί μοι τεὸν οὔνομα εἰπὲ   355

Appendix

αὐτίκα νῦν, ἵνα τοι δῶ ξείνιον, ᾧ κε σὺ χαίρῃς·
καὶ γὰρ Κυκλώπεσσι φέρει ζείδωρος ἄρουρα
οἶνον ἐριστάφυλον, καί σφιν Διὸς ὄμβρος ἀέξει·
ἀλλὰ τόδ' ἀμβροσίης καὶ νέκταρός ἐστιν ἀπορρώξ.'
ὣς φάτ', ἀτάρ οἱ αὖτις ἐγὼ πόρον αἴθοπα οἶνον. 360
τρὶς μὲν ἔδωκα φέρων, τρὶς δ' ἔκπιεν ἀφραδίῃσιν.
αὐτὰρ ἐπεὶ Κύκλωπα περὶ φρένας ἤλυθεν οἶνος,
καὶ τότε δή μιν ἔπεσσι προσηύδων μειλιχίοισι·
'Κύκλωψ, εἰρωτᾷς μ' ὄνομα κλυτόν, αὐτὰρ ἐγώ τοι
ἐξερέω· σὺ δέ μοι δὸς ξείνιον, ὥς περ ὑπέστης. 365
Οὖτις ἐμοί γ' ὄνομα· Οὖτιν δέ με κικλήσκουσι
μήτηρ ἠδὲ πατὴρ ἠδ' ἄλλοι πάντες ἑταῖροι.'
ὣς ἐφάμην, ὁ δέ μ' αὐτίκ' ἀμείβετο νηλέϊ θυμῷ·
'Οὖτιν ἐγὼ πύματον ἔδομαι μετὰ οἷς ἑτάροισιν,
τοὺς δ' ἄλλους πρόσθεν· τὸ δέ τοι ξεινήϊον ἔσται.' 370

When he had speedily completed his tasks, he again snatched two of us and got his meal ready. And I stood near the Cyclops and spoke to him, holding in my hands an ivy-wood cup of dark wine [*which he offers to Polyphemus*]. . . . Thus I spoke. He took the cup and drank it and was exceedingly delighted as he drank the sweet drink, and asked for another. 'Kindly give me more, and tell me your name now so that I can give you a gift of hospitality in which you can take pleasure. For the fruitful land does produce wine from grapes for the Cyclopes and rain from Zeus makes them grow for them; but this is a distillation of ambrosia and nectar.' Thus he spoke and I gave him a second drink of bright-shining wine. (360) Three times I brought it to him and gave it to him, and three times he drank in his folly. And when the wine had affected the wits of the Cyclops, then I spoke to him with honeyed words: 'Cyclops, you ask me my famous name. I shall tell you what it is. But you, give me the gift of hospitality as you promised me. Nobody is my name. My mother and father and all my companions call me Nobody.' Thus I spoke. But this was the answer he gave me at once from his pitiless heart: 'I shall eat Nobody last of his companions—the others I shall eat before him. That will be my gift of hospitality.'

(d) *Odyssey* 9.371–414:

ἦ καὶ ἀνακλινθεὶς πέσεν ὕπτιος, αὐτὰρ ἔπειτα
κεῖτ' ἀποδοχμώσας παχὺν αὐχένα, κὰδ δέ μιν ὕπνος
ᾕρει πανδαμάτωρ· φάρυγος δ' ἐξέσσυτο οἶνος
ψωμοί τ' ἀνδρόμεοι· ὁ δ' ἐρεύγετο οἰνοβαρείων.
καὶ τότ' ἐγὼ τὸν μοχλὸν ὑπὸ σποδοῦ ἤλασα πολλῆς, 375
ἧος θερμαίνοιτο· ἔπεσσι δὲ πάντας ἑταίρους
θάρσυνον, μή τίς μοι ὑποδείσας ἀναδύῃ.
ἀλλ' ὅτε δὴ τάχ' ὁ μοχλὸς ἐλάϊνος ἐν πυρὶ μέλλεν

ἅψεσθαι, χλωρός περ ἐών, διεφαίνετο δ' αἰνῶς,
καὶ τότ' ἐγὼν ἆσσον φέρον ἐκ πυρός, ἀμφὶ δ' ἑταῖροι   380
ἵσταντ'· αὐτὰρ θάρσος ἐνέπνευσεν μέγα δαίμων.
οἱ μὲν μοχλὸν ἑλόντες ἐλάϊνον, ὀξὺν ἐπ' ἄκρῳ,
ὀφθαλμῷ ἐνέρεισαν· ἐγὼ δ' ἐφύπερθεν ἐρεισθεὶς
δίνεον, ὡς ὅτε τις τρυπῷ δόρυ νήϊον ἀνὴρ
τρυπάνῳ, οἱ δέ τ' ἔνερθεν ὑποσσείουσιν ἱμάντι   385
ἁψάμενοι ἑκάτερθε, τὸ δὲ τρέχει ἐμμενὲς αἰεί.
ὣς τοῦ ἐν ὀφθαλμῷ πυριήκεα μοχλὸν ἑλόντες
δινέομεν, τὸν δ' αἷμα περίρρεε θερμὸν ἐόντα.
πάντα δέ οἱ βλέφαρ' ἀμφὶ καὶ ὀφρύας εὗσεν ἀϋτμὴ
γλήνης καιομένης, σφαραγεῦντο δέ οἱ πυρὶ ῥίζαι.   390
ὡς δ' ὅτ' ἀνὴρ χαλκεὺς πέλεκυν μέγαν ἠὲ σκέπαρνον
εἰν ὕδατι ψυχρῷ βάπτῃ μεγάλα ἰάχοντα
φαρμάσσων· τὸ γὰρ αὖτε σιδήρου γε κράτος ἐστίν·
ὣς τοῦ σίζ' ὀφθαλμὸς ἐλαϊνέῳ περὶ μοχλῷ.
σμερδαλέον δὲ μέγ' ᾤμωξεν, περὶ δ' ἴαχε πέτρη,   395
ἡμεῖς δὲ δείσαντες ἀπεσσύμεθ'· αὐτὰρ ὁ μοχλὸν
ἐξέρυσ' ὀφθαλμοῖο πεφυρμένον αἵματι πολλῷ.
τὸν μὲν ἔπειτ' ἔρριψεν ἀπὸ ἕο χερσὶν ἀλύων,
αὐτὰρ ὁ Κύκλωπας μεγάλ' ἤπυεν, οἵ ῥά μιν ἀμφὶς
ᾤκεον ἐν σπήεσσι δι' ἄκριας ἠνεμοέσσας.   400
οἱ δὲ βοῆς ἀίοντες ἐφοίτων ἄλλοθεν ἄλλος,
ἱστάμενοι δ' εἴροντο περὶ σπέος ὅττι ἑ κήδοι·
'τίπτε τόσον, Πολύφημ', ἀρημένος ὧδ' ἐβόησας
νύκτα δι' ἀμβροσίην καὶ ἀΰπνους ἄμμε τίθησθα;
ἦ μή τίς σευ μῆλα βροτῶν ἀέκοντος ἐλαύνει;   405
ἦ μή τίς σ' αὐτὸν κτείνει δόλῳ ἠὲ βίηφιν;'
τοὺς δ' αὖτ' ἐξ ἄντρου προσέφη κρατερὸς Πολύφημος·
'ὦ φίλοι, Οὖτίς με κτείνει δόλῳ οὐδὲ βίηφιν.'
οἱ δ' ἀπαμειβόμενοι ἔπεα πτερόεντ' ἀγόρευον·
'εἰ μὲν δὴ μή τίς σε βιάζεται οἶον ἐόντα,   410
νοῦσον γ' οὔ πως ἔστι Διὸς μεγάλου ἀλέασθαι,
ἀλλὰ σύ γ' εὔχεο πατρὶ Ποσειδάωνι ἄνακτι.'
ὣς ἄρ' ἔφαν ἀπιόντες, ἐμὸν δ' ἐγέλασσε φίλον κῆρ,
ὡς ὄνομ' ἐξαπάτησεν ἐμὸν καὶ μῆτις ἀμύμων.

He spoke and falling backwards he fell face upwards. He lay there, his thick neck bent to one side, and sleep that tames everything took hold of him and wine and gobbets of men's flesh gushed from his throat. He belched in his drunken stupor. And then I drove the pole beneath the thick ashes until it became hot. And I spoke encouraging words to all my companions in case any of them should hang back in fear. But when the olive-wood pole was just on the point of catching alight in the fire, green through it was, and was glowing terribly, then I carried it closer from the fire and my companions took positions around me. A god inspired us with great boldness. (381) They took the olive pole, which was sharp at the top, and thrust it into the eye. I pressed against it from above and twisted it, as when a man bores a ship's timber with a drill and his fellows below twirl it around with a strap controlling it from both sides, and it spins continuously. Thus taking the pole with its blazing point, we twisted it and the blood flowed around the hot implement. The breath of the heat singed his eyelids and his eyebrows all round as his pupil burnt and its roots hissed in the fire, (390) as when a blacksmith dips a great axe or adze in cold water and there is a loud hiss as they temper it, for that is what gives the iron its strength. So did his eye sizzle around the olive pole. And he howled out a terrible cry and the rock echoed around. We backed away in fear. But he pulled the pole from his eye, stained red with all the blood. Beside himself with the pain, he flung the pole away from him with his hands. He roared loudly to the Cyclopes who lived around in caves along the windy heights. (400) Hearing him shout, they came from all directions and standing around the cave they asked him what the trouble was. 'Whatever is so very wrong with you that you have shouted like this through the immortal night and are stopping us sleeping? Surely nobody is driving off your flocks against your will or is killing you yourself by trickery or force?' The mighty Polyphemus replied to them from the cave: 'O friends, Nobody is killing me by trickery or force.' They spoke winged words in answer: 'If nobody is using force on you in your solitude, (410) there is no way of avoiding a disease sent by great Zeus. But you should pray to your father, king Poseidon.' Thus they spoke as they went away. And my dear heart laughed at the fact that my name and my excellent intelligence had fooled him.

Odysseus ties his men beneath sheep and himself clings beneath the belly of the largest ram. The blinded Polyphemus removes the stone and lets the animals out—and of course Odysseus and his men too. Polyphemus delivers a poignant speech to the ram asking him why he is this once the last of the flock to leave the cave. When on his ship, Odysseus taunts the Cyclops and tells him his real name. The sound enables Polyphemus to throw rocks at the ship, narrowly missing, and he calls upon his father, the sea god Poseidon, to wreak a fearsome revenge on the now identifiable Odysseus. That affects the poem's plot in general, but for now Odysseus and his men escape.

B: Homer, *Odyssey* 12:

(a) *Odyssey* 12.80–110: *Circe's instructions to Odysseus about Scylla and Charybdis*:

> μέσσῳ δ' ἐν σκοπέλῳ ἔστι σπέος ἠεροειδές,   80
> πρὸς ζόφον εἰς Ἔρεβος τετραμμένον, ᾗ περ ἂν ὑμεῖς
> νῆα παρὰ γλαφυρὴν ἰθύνετε, φαίδιμ' Ὀδυσσεῦ.
> οὐδέ κεν ἐκ νηὸς γλαφυρῆς αἰζήιος ἀνὴρ

τόξῳ ὀϊστεύσας κοῖλον σπέος εἰσαφίκοιτο.
ἔνθα δ' ἐνὶ Σκύλλη ναίει δεινὸν λελακυῖα. 85
τῆς ἦ τοι φωνὴ μὲν ὅση σκύλακος νεογιλῆς
γίγνεται, αὐτὴ δ' αὖτε πέλωρ κακόν· οὐδέ κέ τίς μιν
γηθήσειεν ἰδών, οὐδ' εἰ θεὸς ἀντιάσειεν.
τῆς ἦ τοι πόδες εἰσὶ δυώδεκα πάντες ἄωροι,
ἓξ δέ τέ οἱ δειραὶ περιμήκεες, ἐν δὲ ἑκάστῃ 90
σμερδαλέη κεφαλή, ἐν δὲ τρίστοιχοι ὀδόντες
πυκνοὶ καὶ θαμέες, πλεῖοι μέλανος θανάτοιο.
μέσση μέν τε κατὰ σπείους κοίλοιο δέδυκεν,
ἔξω δ' ἐξίσχει κεφαλὰς δεινοῖο βερέθρου,
αὐτοῦ δ' ἰχθυάᾳ, σκόπελον περιμαιμώωσα, 95
δελφῖνάς τε κύνας τε, καὶ εἴ ποθι μεῖζον ἕλῃσι
κῆτος, ἃ μυρία βόσκει ἀγάστονος Ἀμφιτρίτη.
τῇ δ' οὔ πώ ποτε ναῦται ἀκήριοι εὐχετόωνται
παρφυγέειν σὺν νηΐ· φέρει δέ τε κρατὶ ἑκάστῳ
φῶτ' ἐξαρπάξασα νεὸς κυανοπρῴροιο. 100
τὸν δ' ἕτερον σκόπελον χθαμαλώτερον ὄψει, Ὀδυσσεῦ.
πλησίον ἀλλήλων· καί κεν διοϊστεύσειας.
τῷ δ' ἐν ἐρινεὸς ἔστι μέγας, φύλλοισι τεθηλώς·
τῷ δ' ὑπὸ δῖα Χάρυβδις ἀναρροιβδεῖ μέλαν ὕδωρ.
τρὶς μὲν γάρ τ' ἀνίησιν ἐπ' ἤματι, τρὶς δ' ἀναροιβδεῖ 105
δεινόν· μὴ σύ γε κεῖθι τύχοις, ὅτε ῥοιβδήσειεν·
οὐ γάρ κεν ῥύσαιτό σ' ὑπὲκ κακοῦ οὐδ' ἐνοσίχθων.
ἀλλὰ μάλα Σκύλλης σκοπέλῳ πεπλημένος ὦκα
νῆα παρὲξ ἐλάαν, ἐπεὶ ἦ πολὺ φέρτερόν ἐστιν
ἓξ ἑτάρους ἐν νηῒ ποθήμεναι ἢ ἅμα πάντας. 110

In the middle of the cliff is a dark cave, facing the darkness of the west where Erebos lies. You and your crew are to steer your ship past here, heroic Odysseus. Not even a strong man, shooting an arrow from his hollow ship, would reach the depths of the cave. In there the fiercely yelping Scylla lives; her voice is that of a new-born puppy, but she is a nasty monster. No one could take pleasure in the sight, even a god coming across her. She has twelve legs, all shapeless, and six long necks, and on each (90) a terrifying head, and three rows of strong teeth, set close together, full of dark death. From her middle she is sunk in the hollow cave, but she holds her heads outside the terrible chasm, and fishes there, searching round the rock for dolphins and dog-fish, or any larger creature she might catch, of the countless number that deep-groaning Amphitrite sustains. No sailors may yet boast that they have escaped past her in their ship without woe: with each head she snatches and carries off a man from the dark-prowed vessel. (100) The second cliff you will see is lower, close to the other one: you could shoot an arrow across. On it is a great fig-tree, covered in leaves, and below it the immortal Charybdis sucks down the dark water. Thrice a day she releases it, and thrice sucks it down frighteningly. Don't chance to be there when she is sucking in: not even Poseidon would save you from disaster. But drawing very close to Scylla's cliff, row the boat swiftly past, for it is far better to miss six companions from your ship than all at the same time.

(b) *Odyssey* 12.201-2, 235-47: *Odysseus and his crew approach Scylla and Charybdis*:

> ἀλλ' ὅτε δὴ τὴν νῆσον ἐλείπομεν, αὐτίκ' ἔπειτα   201
> καπνὸν καὶ μέγα κῦμα ἴδον καὶ δοῦπον ἄκουσα....

But when we were leaving the island [of the Sirens], immediately I saw smoke and a great wave, and I heard a noise. [*Odysseus then tells the crew what they must do, and prepares to encounter Scylla.*]

> ἡμεῖς μὲν στεινωπὸν ἀνεπλέομεν γοόωντες·
> ἔνθεν μὲν Σκύλλη, ἑτέρωθι δὲ δῖα Χάρυβδις   235
> δεινὸν ἀνερροίβδησε θαλάσσης ἁλμυρὸν ὕδωρ.
> ἦ τοι ὅτ' ἐξεμέσειε, λέβης ὣς ἐν πυρὶ πολλῷ
> πᾶσ' ἀναμορμύρεσκε κυκωμένη, ὑψόσε δ' ἄχνη
> ἄκροισι σκοπέλοισιν ἐπ' ἀμφοτέροισιν ἔπιπτεν·
> ἀλλ' ὅτ' ἀναβρόξειε θαλάσσης ἁλμυρὸν ὕδωρ,   240
> πᾶσ' ἔντοσθε φάνεσκε κυκωμένη, ἀμφὶ δὲ πέτρη
> δεινὸν ἐβεβρύχει, ὑπένερθε δὲ γαῖα φάνεσκε
> ψάμμῳ κυανέη· τοὺς δὲ χλωρὸν δέος ᾕρει.
> ἡμεῖς μὲν πρὸς τὴν ἴδομεν δείσαντες ὄλεθρον·
> τόφρα δέ μοι Σκύλλη γλαφυρῆς ἐκ νηὸς ἑταίρους   245
> ἐξ ἕλεθ', οἳ χερσίν τε βίηφί τε φέρτατοι ἦσαν.

We sailed up the strait, crying out in woe: on this side Scylla, on the other immortal Charybdis frighteningly sucked down the salt water of the sea. When she vomited it out, like a cauldron on a big fire, she bubbled away in utter turmoil, and high up the foam fell on the tops of both cliffs. (240) But when she swallowed the salt water down again, there utter turmoil was visible within, and the rocks roared terribly round about, and at the bottom the earth appeared dark with sand. Pale fear gripped the crew. We looked at her, fearing destruction; but then Scylla seized six of my men from the hollow ship, men who were strong in limb and might. [*He vividly describes their capture, like fish on a line, and their death.*]

C: Homer, *Odyssey* 13.93-104:

> εὖτ' ἀστὴρ ὑπερέσχε φαάντατος, ὅς τε μάλιστα
> ἔρχεται ἀγγέλλων φάος Ἠοῦς ἠριγενείης,
> τῆμος δὴ νήσῳ προσεπίλνατο ποντοπόρος νηῦς.   95
> Φόρκυνος δέ τίς ἐστι λιμήν, ἁλίοιο γέροντος,

> ἐν δήμῳ Ἰθάκης· δύο δὲ προβλῆτες ἐν αὐτῷ
> ἀκταὶ ἀπορρῶγες, λιμένος ποτιπεπτηυῖαι,
> αἵ τ' ἀνέμων σκεπόωσι δυσαήων μέγα κῦμα
> ἔκτοθεν· ἔντοσθεν δέ τ' ἄνευ δεσμοῖο μένουσι   100
> νῆες ἐΰσσελμοι, ὅτ' ἂν ὅρμου μέτρον ἵκωνται.
> αὐτὰρ ἐπὶ κρατὸς λιμένος τανύφυλλος ἐλαίη,
> ἀγχόθι δ' αὐτῆς ἄντρον ἐπήρατον ἠεροειδές,
> ἱρὸν νυμφάων αἳ νηιάδες καλέονται.

When the brightest star rose up, the one that especially comes heralding the light of early-rising Dawn, then the sea-faring ship approached the island. There is a harbour, belonging to Phorcys, the Old Man of the Sea, in the land of Ithaca. There are two headlands on it, sheer cliffs, falling away towards the harbour, which ward off the great sea produced by unruly winds, on the outer side; but within, well-timbered boats rest without a cable once they come to the goal of a mooring. At the head of the harbour is a long-leaved olive, and near it a cave, lovely, misty, sacred to the Nymphs who are called Naiads. [*Here the Phaeacians put in, and leave the sleeping Odysseus, at last returned to his homeland.*]

D: Homer, *Odyssey* 15.256–70:

> τοῦ μὲν ἄρ' υἱὸς ἐπῆλθε, Θεοκλύμενος δ' ὄνομ' ἦεν,
> ὅς τότε Τηλεμάχου πέλας ἵστατο· τὸν δ' ἐκίχανεν
> σπένδοντ' εὐχόμενόν τε θοῇ παρὰ νηὶ μελαίνῃ,
> καί μιν φωνήσας ἔπεα πτερόεντα προσηύδα·
> 'ὦ φίλ', ἐπεί σε θύοντα κιχάνω τῷδ' ἐνὶ χώρῳ,   260
> λίσσομ' ὑπὲρ θυέων καὶ δαίμονος, αὐτὰρ ἔπειτα
> σῆς τ' αὐτοῦ κεφαλῆς καὶ ἑταίρων, οἵ τοι ἕπονται,
> εἰπέ μοι εἰρομένῳ νημερτέα μηδ' ἐπικεύσῃς·
> τίς πόθεν εἶς ἀνδρῶν; πόθι τοι πόλις ἠδὲ τοκῆες;'
> τὸν δ' αὖ Τηλέμαχος πεπνυμένος ἀντίον ηὔδα·   265
> 'τοιγὰρ ἐγώ τοι, ξεῖνε, μάλ' ἀτρεκέως ἀγορεύσω.
> ἐξ Ἰθάκης γένος εἰμί, πατὴρ δέ μοί ἐστιν Ὀδυσσεύς,
> εἴ ποτ' ἔην· νῦν δ' ἤδη ἀπέφθιτο λυγρῷ ὀλέθρῳ.
> τοὔνεκα νῦν ἑτάρους τε λαβὼν καὶ νῆα μέλαιναν
> ἦλθον πευσόμενος πατρὸς δὴν οἰχομένοιο.'   270

It was his son—Theoclymenus was his name—who then approached and stood near Telemachus; and he found him pouring libations and praying by his swift black ship, and he spoke to him, addressing him with winged words: 'My friend, since I find you sacrificing in this place, (260) I beseech you by your offerings and the god and then by your own life and those of your comrades who follow you, give me a truthful answer to what I ask and do not conceal it. Who are you among men and where have you come from? Where is your city and where are your parents?' And wise Telemachus spoke in answer to him: 'Therefore, stranger, I shall speak to you completely truthfully. My family comes from Ithaca, my father is Odysseus, if he ever existed; but now he has perished in grievous destruction. That is the reason why I have taken my companions and a black ship and have come seeking news of my father who has been gone for a long time.'

E: Pindar, *Hymns*:

Fragments 33c–d: *two separate fragments, quoted by Theophrastus and Strabo, presumably from a hymn to one or all of Apollo, Artemis, and Leto*:

(c) χαῖρ', ὦ θεοδμάτα, λιπαροπλοκάμου
 παίδεσσι Λατοῦς ἱμεροέστατον ἔρνος,
 πόντου θύγατερ, χθονὸς εὐρεί-
 ας ἀκίνητον τέρας, ἅν τε βροτοὶ
 Δᾶλον κικλήισκοισιν, μάκαρες δ' ἐν Ὀλύμπῳ   5
 τηλέφαντον κυανέας χθονὸς ἄστρον.

Hail, o god-built one, sapling most lovely to the children of glossy-locked Leto, daughter of the sea, unquaking wonder of the wide earth, whom mortals call Delos, but the blessed gods on Olympus the far-shining star of the blue earth.

(d) ἦν γὰρ τὸ πάροιθε φορητὰ
 κυμάτεσσιν παντοδαπῶν ἀνέμων
 ῥιπαῖσιν· ἀλλ' ἁ Κοιογενὴς ὁπότ' ὠδί-
 νεσσι θυίοισ' ἀγχιτόκοις ἐπέβα
 νιν, δὴ τότε τέσσαρες ὀρθαὶ   5
 πρέμνων ἀπώρουσαν χθονίων,
 ἄν δ' ἐπικράνοις σχέθον
 πέτραν ἀδαμαντοπέδιλοι
 κίονες, ἔνθα τεκοῖ-
 σ' εὐδαίμον' ἐπόψατο γένναν.   10

For previously it was carried on the waves by the blasts of various winds; but when the daughter of Coeus (Leto) set foot on it, maddened by the pangs of imminent birth, then there rose up straight from foundations in the earth and held up the rock on their capitals four columns on adamantine bases, where she gave birth and saw her blessed offspring.

F: Pindar, *Pyth.* 1.15–28:

ὅς τ' ἐν αἰνᾷ Ταρτάρῳ κεῖται, θεῶν πολέμιος,   15
Τυφὼς ἑκατοντακάρανος· τόν ποτε

Κιλίκιον θρέψεν πολυώνυμον ἄντρον· νῦν γε μὰν
ταί θ' ὑπὲρ Κύμας ἁλιερκέες ὄχθαι
Σικελία τ' αὐτοῦ πιέζει
  στέρνα λαχνάεντα· κίων δ' οὐρανία συνέχει,
νιφόεσσ' Αἴτνα, πάνετες χιόνος ὀξείας τιθήνα· 20
τᾶς ἐρεύγονται μὲν ἀπλάτου πυρὸς ἁγνόταται
ἐκ μυχῶν παγαί· ποταμοὶ δ' ἁμέραισιν
  μὲν προχέοντι ῥόον καπνοῦ
αἴθων'· ἀλλ' ἐν ὄρφναισιν πέτρας
φοίνισσα κυλινδομένα φλὸξ ἐς βαθεῖ-
  αν φέρει πόντου πλάκα σὺν πατάγῳ.
κεῖνο δ' Ἁφαίστοιο κρουνοὺς ἑρπετὸν 25
δεινοτάτους ἀναπέμπει· τέρας μὲν
  θαυμάσιον προσιδέσθαι,
  θαῦμα δὲ καὶ παρεόντων ἀκοῦσαι,
οἷον Αἴτνας ἐν μελαμφύλλοις δέδεται κορυφαῖς
καὶ πέδῳ, στρωμνὰ δὲ χαράσσοισ' ἅπαν νῶ-
  τον ποτικεκλιμένον κεντεῖ.

And he who lies in dreadful Tartarus, the enemy of the gods, hundred-headed Typhos, whom once the far-famed cave of Cilicia nurtured, but now the sea-fronting heights above Cumae and Sicily press down on his shaggy breast and the heaven-high pillar of snowy Etna, year-long nurse of freezing snow, holds him fast; (20) from its depths most holy jets of unapproachable fire shoot forth and in the day rivers pour out a lurid stream of smoke. And in the darkness a crimson rolling flame carries down rocks to the sea's deep expanse with a crash. That monster sends up most fearful jets of Hephaestus' fire, a wondrous portent to look upon and a wonder even to hear of from those who have been present. Such a creature is held fast under the dark-wooded crests of Etna and its plain. And the bed he lies on galls and gouges the whole of his back.

G: Euripides, *Hecuba*:

(a) 1–30: *The ghost of Polydorus speaks the prologue*:

Ἥκω νεκρῶν κευθμῶνα καὶ σκότου πύλας
λιπών, ἵν' Ἅιδης χωρὶς ᾤκισται θεῶν,
Πολύδωρος, Ἑκάβης παῖς γεγὼς τῆς Κισσέως
Πριάμου τε πατρός, ὅς μ', ἐπεὶ Φρυγῶν πόλιν
κίνδυνος ἔσχε δορὶ πεσεῖν Ἑλληνικῷ, 5
δείσας ὑπεξέπεμψε Τρωικῆς χθονὸς
Πολυμήστορος πρὸς δῶμα Θρηκίου ξένου,

Appendix

ὃς τήνδ' ἀρίστην Χερσονησίαν πλάκα
σπείρει, φίλιππον λαὸν εὐθύνων δορί.
πολὺν δὲ σὺν ἐμοὶ χρυσὸν ἐκπέμπει λάθρᾳ   10
πατήρ, ἵν', εἴ ποτ' Ἰλίου τείχη πέσοι,
τοῖς ζῶσιν εἴη παισὶ μὴ σπάνις βίου.
νεώτατος δ' ἦ Πριαμιδῶν, ὃ καί με γῆς
ὑπεξέπεμψεν· οὔτε γὰρ φέρειν ὅπλα
οὔτ' ἔγχος οἷός τ' ἦ νέῳ βραχίονι.   15
ἕως μὲν οὖν γῆς ὄρθ' ἔκειθ' ὁρίσματα
πύργοι τ' ἄθραυστοι Τρωικῆς ἦσαν χθονὸς
Ἕκτωρ τ' ἀδελφὸς οὑμὸς εὐτύχει δορί,
καλῶς παρ' ἀνδρὶ Θρῃκὶ πατρῴῳ ξένῳ
τροφαῖσιν ὥς τις πτόρθος ηὐξόμην, τάλας·   20
ἐπεὶ δὲ Τροία θ' Ἕκτορός τ' ἀπόλλυται
ψυχὴ πατρῴα θ' ἑστία κατεσκάφη,
αὐτὸς δὲ βωμῷ πρὸς θεοδμήτῳ πίτνει
σφαγεὶς Ἀχιλλέως παιδὸς ἐκ μιαιφόνου,
κτείνει με χρυσοῦ τὸν ταλαίπωρον χάριν   25
ξένος πατρῷος καὶ κτανὼν ἐς οἶδμ' ἁλὸς
μεθῆχ', ἵν' αὐτὸς χρυσὸν ἐν δόμοις ἔχῃ.
κεῖμαι δ' ἐπ' ἀκταῖς, ἄλλοτ' ἐν πόντου σάλῳ,
πολλοῖς διαύλοις κυμάτων φορούμενος,
ἄκλαυτος ἄταφος·   30

I have left the gates of darkness where the dead are hidden and Hades dwells apart from the gods, and have come (to this place). I am Polydorus, the son of Hecuba, daughter of Cisseus, and of my father Priam. When it seemed dangerously likely that the Phrygians' city would fall to the might of Greece, in fear he smuggled me out of the Trojan land to the house of Polymestor, his Thracian guest-friend, who cultivates the fertile steppe of the Chersonese and rules a horse-loving people by the spear. My father covertly sent out a vast quantity of gold with me (10) so that, if ever the walls of Ilium should fall, there would be no lack of money for his surviving children to live on. I was the youngest of Priam's children—and that was why he smuggled me from the land. For my boy's arm was not able to carry armour or the spear. As long as the boundaries of our country remained secure, the towers of the Trojan land stood unshattered, and my brother Hector still triumphed with his spear, I was treated splendidly at the house of my father's guest-friend. I flourished like a sapling—to my sorrow. (20) But when Troy was lost with Hector's life and my father's house was utterly destroyed, and Priam himself had fallen at the god-built altar, slaughtered by the blood-polluted hand of Achilles' son, my father's guest-friend killed me, unhappy boy, for the sake of the gold. He killed me and flung me into the surging sea so that he could keep the gold in his own house. And I lie sometimes on the shore, sometimes on the rolling water, carried on the constant ebb and flow of the wave. There is no one to weep over me, no one to bury me.

Appendix

(b) 709–18: *Dialogue between the Chorus of Trojan Women and Hecuba after the discovery of Polydorus' corpse:*

Χορός	τίς γάρ νιν ἔκτειν'; οἶσθ' ὀνειρόφρων φράσαι;	
Ἑκάβη	ἐμὸς ἐμὸς ξένος, Θρήκιος ἱππότας,	710
	ἵν' ὁ γέρων πατὴρ ἔθετό νιν κρύψας.	
Χορός	οἴμοι, τί λέξεις; χρυσὸν ὡς ἔχοι κτανών;	
Ἑκάβη	ἄρρητ' ἀνωνόμαστα, θαυμάτων πέρα,	
	οὐχ ὅσι' οὐδ' ἀνεκτά. ποῦ δίκα ξένων;	715
	ὦ κατάρατ' ἀνδρῶν, ὡς διεμοιράσω	
	χρόα, σιδαρέῳ τεμὼν φασγάνῳ	
	μέλεα τοῦδε παιδὸς οὐδ' ᾤκτισας.	

CHORUS. Who killed him then? Does your dream-wisdom give you the knowledge to tell me that?

HECUBA. It was my own guest-friend, yes, my own, the Thracian horseman, with whom his old father had hidden him.

CHORUS. Alas, what do you mean? So that after the murder he could keep the gold?

HECUBA. I cannot find the words for it. It is a deed without a name, beyond amazement. It is unholy, unendurable. Where is just dealing between guest-friends now? O you most accursed of men, how you have butchered this boy's flesh, hacking his limbs with your iron sword and showing him no pity.

(c) 1132–44: *After Hecuba has blinded Polymestor and killed his children in revenge for his murder of Polydorus, the Thracian king defends himself to Agamemnon:*

λέγοιμ' ἄν. ἦν τις Πριαμιδῶν νεώτατος,
Πολύδωρος, Ἑκάβης παῖς, ὃν ἐκ Τροίας ἐμοὶ
πατὴρ δίδωσι Πρίαμος ἐν δόμοις τρέφειν,
ὕποπτος ὢν δὴ Τρωικῆς ἁλώσεως.   1135
τοῦτον κατέκτειν'· ἀνθ' ὅτου δ' ἔκτεινά νιν,
ἄκουσον, ὡς εὖ καὶ σοφῇ προμηθίᾳ.
ἔδεισα μὴ σοὶ πολέμιος λειφθεὶς ὁ παῖς
Τροίαν ἀθροίσῃ καὶ ξυνοικίσῃ πάλιν,
γνόντες δ' Ἀχαιοὶ ζῶντα Πριαμιδῶν τινα   1140
Φρυγῶν ἐς αἶαν αὖθις ἄρειαν στόλον,
κἄπειτα Θρῄκης πεδία τρίβοιεν τάδε
λεηλατοῦντες, γείτοσιν δ' εἴη κακὸν
Τρώων, ἐν ᾧπερ νῦν, ἄναξ, ἐκάμνομεν.

POLYMESTOR. I shall tell you. There was one of Priam's sons, the youngest, Polydorus, Hecuba's child, whom his father Priam sent from Troy for me to bring up in my house, suspecting, I suppose, that Troy would be taken. I killed him. And now you must hear why I killed him and what excellent judgement and foresight I showed in doing so. I was afraid that if the boy were left alive as your enemy, he would rally Troy and colonize it again, and the Achaeans would realize that one of Priam's sons was still living (1140) and launch a new expedition against the Phrygians' land. Then they would plunder and lay waste the plains of Thrace here, and we, the Trojans' neighbours, would suffer the misery which we endured a short while ago.

H: Euripides, *Andromache*:

[Set in Peleus' kingdom, Phthia]

(a) 1-14, 24-31: *Andromache speaks the prologue*:

Ἀσιάτιδος γῆς σχῆμα, Θηβαία πόλι,	
ὅθεν ποθ' ἕδνων σὺν πολυχρύσῳ χλιδῇ	
Πριάμου τύραννον ἑστίαν ἀφικόμην	
δάμαρ δοθεῖσα παιδοποιὸς Ἕκτορι,	
ζηλωτὸς ἔν γε τῷ πρὶν Ἀνδρομάχη χρόνῳ,	5
νῦν δ', εἴ τις ἄλλη, δυστυχεστάτη γυνή·	6
ἥτις πόσιν μὲν Ἕκτορ' ἐξ Ἀχιλλέως	8
θανόντ' ἐσεῖδον, παῖδά θ' ὃν τίκτω πόσει	
ῥιφθέντα πύργων Ἀστυάνακτ' ἀπ' ὀρθίων,	
ἐπεὶ τὸ Τροίας εἷλον Ἕλληνες πέδον·	10
αὐτὴ δὲ δούλη τῶν ἐλευθερωτάτων	
οἴκων νομισθεῖσ' Ἑλλάδ' εἰσαφικόμην	
τῷ νησιώτῃ Νεοπτολέμῳ δορὸς γέρας	
δοθεῖσα λείας Τρωϊκῆς ἐξαίρετον.	
...	
κἀγὼ δόμοις τοῖσδ' ἄρσεν' ἐντίκτω κόρον,	
πλαθεῖσ' Ἀχιλλέως παιδί, δεσπότῃ δ' ἐμῷ.	25
καὶ πρὶν μὲν ἐν κακοῖσι κειμένην ὅμως	
ἐλπίς μ' ἀεὶ προσῆγε σωθέντος τέκνου	
ἀλκήν τιν' εὑρεῖν κἀπικούρησιν δόμον·	
ἐπεὶ δὲ τὴν Λάκαιναν Ἑρμιόνην γαμεῖ	
τοὐμὸν παρώσας δεσπότης δοῦλον λέχος,	30
κακοῖς πρὸς αὐτῆς σχετλίοις ἐλαύνομαι.	

O Asian land, O city of Thebe, from which I came long ago with a dowry of rich gold to Priam's royal hearth when I was given to Hector to be his wife and bear his child, I Andromache, in days gone by a woman to be envied, but now the most wretched of all of them. I saw my husband Hector killed by Achilles, and Astyanax, the son I bore to my husband, flung from our sheer towers after the Greeks took the land of Troy. (10) I myself, born in a home once counted the freest of all, have arrived in Greece as a slave to the islander Neoptolemus as a choice spear-prize from the spoils of Troy…

And I slept with Achilles' son, my master, and have borne him a male child for this house. And until now, despite my evil lot, I was kept going by the hope that, if my son stayed alive, I would find some help and protection amid my misfortunes. However, after my master married the Spartan girl Hermione and stopped sleeping with me, his slave, (30) I have been harried by her cruel abuse.

Hermione's persecution of Andromache is given full rein by the fact that Neoptolemus is absent at Delphi, where he wishes to appease the god Apollo. It seems as if Andromache's son will be killed when suddenly Hermione panics about how the boy's father will view her behaviour. Orestes now appears and runs off with Hermione, who had once been promised to him in marriage. He sets in motion the murder of her husband. A messenger speech (1085–1165) describes the killing of Neoptolemus at the altar of Apollo by the people of Delphi, as a result of suspicions that Orestes has fomented.

(b) 1239–53: *Thetis, Neoptolemus' grandmother, addressing Peleus, his grandfather:*

ὧν δ' οὕνεκ' ἦλθον σημανῶ, σὺ δ' ἐνδέχου.	
τὸν μὲν θανόντα τόνδ' Ἀχιλλέως γόνον	1240
θάψον πορεύσας Πυθικὴν πρὸς ἐσχάραν,	
Δελφοῖς ὄνειδος, ὡς ἀπαγγέλλῃ τάφος	
φόνον βίαιον τῆς Ὀρεστείας χερός·	
γυναῖκα δ' αἰχμάλωτον, Ἀνδρομάχην λέγω,	
Μολοσσίαν γῆν χρὴ κατοικῆσαι, γέρον,	1245
Ἑλένῳ συναλλαχθεῖσαν εὐναίοις γάμοις,	
καὶ παῖδα τόνδε, τῶν ἀπ' Αἰακοῦ μόνον	
λελειμμένον δή. βασιλέα δ' ἐκ τοῦδε χρὴ	
ἄλλον δι' ἄλλου διαπερᾶν Μολοσσίας	
εὐδαιμονοῦντας· οὐ γὰρ ὧδ' ἀνάστατον	1250
γένος γενέσθαι δεῖ τὸ σὸν κἀμόν, γέρον,	
Τροίας τε· καὶ γὰρ θεοῖσι κἀκείνης μέλει,	
καίπερ πεσούσης Παλλάδος προθυμίᾳ.	

I shall tell you why I am here. Listen carefully to me. Carry this dead son of Achilles to Apollo's hearth (1240) and bury him there, so that his grave may declare that he was violently murdered by Orestes' agency and prove a reproach to the Delphians. As for this captive woman—Andromache I mean—she must dwell in the land of Molossus, old man, united with Helenus in the marriage bed, and this boy, now the sole survivor of Aeacus' line, must go there with her. A succession of Molossian kings descended from him is fated to pass through life in prosperity. (1250) For your race and mine must not be so absolutely erased, old man, nor must that of Troy. Yes, the gods are concerned about that city too, even though it fell by the will of Pallas.

I: Callimachus, *Hymn* 1 [to Zeus]:

(a) 1.1-9:

> Ζηνὸς ἔοι τί κεν ἄλλο παρὰ σπονδῇσιν ἀείδειν
> λώιον ἢ θεὸν αὐτόν, ἀεὶ μέγαν, αἰὲν ἄνακτα,
> Πηλαγόνων ἐλατῆρα, δικασπόλον Οὐρανίδῃσι;
> πῶς καί νιν, Δικταῖον ἀείσομεν ἠὲ Λυκαῖον;
> ἐν δοιῇ μάλα θυμός, ἐπεὶ γένος ἀμφήριστον.   5
> Ζεῦ, σὲ μὲν Ἰδαίοισιν ἐν οὔρεσί φασι γενέσθαι,
> Ζεῦ, σὲ δ' Ἀρκαδίῃ· πότεροι, πάτερ, ἐψεύσαντο;
> 'Κρῆτες ἀεὶ ψεῦσται'. καὶ γὰρ τάφον, ὦ ἄνα, σεῖο
> Κρῆτες ἐτεκτήναντο· σὺ δ' οὐ θάνες, ἐσσὶ γὰρ αἰεί.

At Zeus's libations what else would be better to sing than the god himself, forever great, for evermore master, the router of the mud-born Giants, dispenser of justice to the children of Uranos? How are we actually to sing him, as Dictaean or Lycaean? My heart is greatly in doubt, since his birth is disputed. Zeus, some say that you were born in the Idaean mountains; Zeus, some in Arcadia: which were lying, father? 'Cretans are ever liars.' Right, for the Cretans also constructed a tomb for you, lord; but you did not die: you are everlasting.

(b) 1.46-54:

> Ζεῦ, σὲ δὲ Κυρβάντων ἑτάραι προσεπηχύναντο
> Δικταῖαι Μελίαι, σὲ δ' ἐκοίμισεν Ἀδρήστεια
> λίκνῳ ἐνὶ χρυσέῳ, σὺ δ' ἐθήσαο πίονα μαζὸν
> αἰγὸς Ἀμαλθείης, ἐπὶ δὲ γλυκὺ κηρίον ἔβρως.
> γέντο γὰρ ἐξαπιναῖα Πανακρίδος ἔργα μελίσσης   50
> Ἰδαίοις ἐν ὄρεσσι, τά τε κλείουσι Πάνακρα.
> οὖλα δὲ Κουρῆτές σε περὶ πρύλιν ὠρχήσαντο
> τεύχεα πεπλήγοντες, ἵνα Κρόνος οὔασιν ἠχὴν
> ἀσπίδος εἰσαΐοι καὶ μή σεο κουρίζοντος.

Zeus, the companions of the Corybantes, the Dictaean Meliae, took you in their arms, and Adrasteia placed you to sleep in a golden cradle, and you sucked the rich breast of the goat Amalthea, and you feasted on sweet honeycomb too. For suddenly there appeared in the Idaean mountains, which they call Panacra, the produce of the Panacrian bee. (50) And the Curetes danced the war-dance vigorously around you, beating their armour, so that Cronus might hear the shield with his ears and not your crying/growing up.

J: Callimachus, *Hymn* 2 [to Apollo], 1–7:

Οἷον ὁ τὠπόλλωνος ἐσείσατο δάφνινος ὅρπηξ
οἷα δ' ὅλον τὸ μέλαθρον· ἑκάς, ἑκὰς ὅστις ἀλιτρός.
καὶ δή που τὰ θύρετρα καλῷ ποδὶ Φοῖβος ἀράσσει.
οὐχ ὁράᾳς; ἐπένευσεν ὁ Δήλιος ἡδύ τι φοῖνιξ
ἐξαπίνης, ὁ δὲ κύκνος ἐν ἠέρι καλὸν ἀείδει.   5
αὐτοὶ νῦν κατοχῆες ἀνακλίνασθε πυλάων,
αὐταὶ δὲ κληῖδες· ὁ γὰρ θεὸς οὐκέτι μακρήν.

How the laurel branch of Apollo shakes! How shakes the whole shrine! Away, away, anyone who is wicked. Presumably Phoebus is knocking on the door with his beautiful foot. Do you not see? The Delian palm has nodded sweetly all of a sudden, and the swan sings beautifully in the air. By yourselves now be pushed back, bolts of the gates; by yourselves, bars: the god is no longer far off.

K: Callimachus, *Hymn* 3 [to Artemis], 52–61:

πᾶσι δ' ὑπ' ὀφρὺν
φάεα μουνόγληνα σάκει ἶσα τετραβοείῳ
δεινὸν ὑπογλαύσσοντα, καὶ ὁππότε δοῦπον ἄκουσαν
ἄκμονος ἠχήσαντος ἐπὶ μέγα πουλύ τ' ἄημα   55
φυσάων αὐτῶν τε βαρὺν στόνον· αὖε γὰρ Αἴτνη,
αὖε δὲ Τρινακίη Σικανῶν ἕδος, αὖε δὲ γείτων
Ἰταλίη, μεγάλην δὲ βοὴν ἐπὶ Κύρνος ἀύτει,
εὖθ' οἵγε ῥαιστῆρας ἀειράμενοι ὑπὲρ ὤμων
ἢ χαλκὸν ζείοντα καμινόθεν ἠὲ σίδηρον   60
ἀμβολαδὶς τετύποντες ἐπὶ μέγα μυχθίσσειαν.

[*Artemis' nymphs were terrified by the Cyclopes*]…as all of them had single eyes beneath their brow, as big as a shield made from the hide of four oxen, and when they heard the sound of the anvil echoing at a distance, the great blast of the bellows, and the deep groaning of the workers themselves. Etna resounded; Trinacria resounded, home of the Sicilians; and neighbouring Italy resounded, and Corsica gave out a great cry, when they, having lifted their hammers over their shoulders, struck in turn at the bronze or the iron bubbling from the furnace, and snorted loudly.

L: Callimachus, *Hymn* 4 [to Delos]:

(a) 34–45, 51–4:

> καὶ τὰς μὲν κατὰ βυσσόν, ἵν' ἠπείροιο λάθωνται,
> πρυμνόθεν ἐρρίζωσε· σὲ δ' οὐκ ἔθλιψεν ἀνάγκη, 35
> ἀλλ' ἄφετος πελάγεσσιν ἐπέπλεες, οὔνομα δ' ἦν τοι
> Ἀστερίη τὸ παλαιόν, ἐπεὶ βαθὺν ἥλαο τάφρον
> οὐρανόθεν φεύγουσα Διὸς γάμον ἀστέρι ἴση.
> τόφρα μὲν οὔπω τοι χρυσέη ἐπεμίσγετο Λητώ,
> τόφρα δ' ἔτ' Ἀστερίη σὺ καὶ οὐδέπω ἔκλεο Δῆλος· 40
> πολλάκι σε Τροιζῆνος ἀπὲξ Ἄνθοιο πολίχνης
> ἐρχόμενοι Ἐφύρηνδε Σαρωνικοῦ ἔνδοθι κόλπου
> ναῦται ἐπεσκέψαντο, καὶ ἐξ Ἐφύρης ἀνιόντες
> οἱ μὲν ἔτ' οὐκ ἴδον αὖθι, σὺ δὲ στεινοῖο παρ' ὀξὺν
> ἔδραμες Εὐρίποιο πόρον καναχηδὰ ῥέοντος, 45
> ...
> ἡνίκα δ' Ἀπόλλωνι γενέθλιον οὖδας ὑπέσχες, 51
> τοῦτό τοι ἀντημοιβὸν ἁλίπλοοι οὔνομ' ἔθεντο,
> οὕνεκεν οὐκέτ' ἄδηλος ἐπέπλεες, ἀλλ' ἐνὶ πόντου
> κύμασιν Αἰγαίοιο ποδῶν ἐνεθήκαο ῥίζας.

<Poseidon> rooted the others at the bottom so that they would forget the mainland; no compulsion afflicted you, but you floated on the sea without constraint; and in olden times your name was Asteria since you leapt from heaven into the deep moat like a star as you fled from marriage with Zeus. While golden Leto had no dealings with you, then you were still Asteria and not yet called Delos. (40) Often sailors in the Saronic Gulf going from Anthes' town Troezen to Corinth set eyes on you and as they travelled back from Corinth saw you there no longer: you had run to the fast strait of the narrow Euripus with its noisy currents, ... But when you gave your soil to be the birth-place of Apollo, sea-farers gave you this name in exchange because you no longer floated in obscurity (ἄδηλος) but you set the roots of your feet in the waters of the Aegean Sea.

(b) 141–7:

> ὡς δ', ὁπότ' Αἰτναίου ὄρεος πυρὶ τυφομένοιο
> σείονται μυχὰ πάντα, κατουδαίοιο γίγαντος
> εἰς ἑτέρην Βριαρῆος ἐπωμίδα κινυμένοιο,
> θερμάστραι τε βρέμουσιν ὑφ' Ἡφαίστοιο πυράγρης
> ἔργα θ' ὁμοῦ, δεινὸν δὲ πυρίκμητοί τε λέβητες 145

καὶ τρίποδες πίπτοντες ἐπ᾽ ἀλλήλοις ἰαχεῦσιν·
τῆμος ἔγεντ᾽ ἄραβος σάκεος τόσος εὐκύκλοιο.

And just as when, as Mount Etna smoulders with fire, all its inmost depths are shaken when the giant under the earth Briareus shifts onto his other shoulder and the furnaces roar together with the handiwork beneath the tongs of Hephaestus, and fire-wrought cauldrons and tripods clang terribly as they fall on one another—so great then was the ringing of the well-rounded shield.

(c) 191–5: *Apollo addresses Leto from the womb*:

ἔστι διειδομένη τις ἐν ὕδατι νῆσος ἀραιή,
πλαζομένη πελάγεσσι· πόδες δέ οἱ οὐχ ἑνὶ χώρῃ,
ἀλλὰ παλιρροίῃ ἐπινήχεται ἀνθέρικος ὥς,
ἔνθα νότος, ἔνθ᾽ εὗρος, ὅπῃ φορέῃσι θάλασσα.
τῇ με φέροις· κείνην γὰρ ἐλεύσεαι εἰς ἐθέλουσαν.   195

There is to be seen in the water a slender island wandering over the seas; her feet are not in one place, but she floats on the tide like an asphodel stem where the South Wind, where the East Wind, wherever the sea carries her. Please carry me there: you will come to an island that welcomes you.

(d) 266–73:

'ὦ μεγάλη πολύβωμε πολύπτολι πολλὰ φέρουσα,
πίονες ἤπειροί τε καὶ αἳ περιναίετε νῆσοι,
αὕτη ἐγὼ τοιήδε, δυσήροτος, ἀλλ᾽ ἀπ᾽ ἐμεῖο
Δήλιος Ἀπόλλων κεκλήσεται, οὐδέ τις ἄλλη
γαιάων τοσσόνδε θεῷ πεφιλήσεται ἄλλῳ,   270
οὐ Κερχνὶς κρείοντι Ποσειδάωνι Λεχαίῳ,
οὐ πάγος Ἑρμείῃ Κυλληνίῳ, οὐ Διὶ Κρήτη,
ὡς ἐγὼ Ἀπόλλωνι...'

'O great <earth> with your many altars, your many cities, rich in produce, you fertile lands and you islands that dwell around, I am such as you see, hard to plough, but Apollo shall be called "Delian" after me, and no other one of the lands will be loved so much by any other god, not Cenchreae by Poseidon, lord of Lechaeum, not Cyllene's hill by Hermes, not Crete by Zeus, as I by Apollo...'

M: Apollonius, *Argonautica* 2.178-316:

Phineus and the Harpies

(a) 2.178-93:

Ἔνθα δ' ἐπάκτιον οἶκον Ἀγηνορίδης ἔχε Φινεύς,
ὃς περὶ δὴ πάντων ὀλοώτατα πήματ' ἀνέτλη
εἵνεκα μαντοσύνης τήν οἱ πάρος ἐγγυάλιξεν   180
Λητοΐδης· οὐδ' ὅσσον ὀπίζετο καὶ Διὸς αὐτοῦ
χρείων ἀτρεκέως ἱερὸν νόον ἀνθρώποισιν.
τῷ καί οἱ γῆρας μὲν ἐπὶ δηναιὸν ἴαλλεν,
ἐκ δ' ἕλετ' ὀφθαλμῶν γλυκερὸν φάος· οὐδὲ γάνυσθαι
εἴα ἀπειρεσίοισιν ὀνείασιν ὅσσα οἱ αἰεί   185
θέσφατα πευθόμενοι περιναιέται οἴκαδ' ἄγειρον.
ἀλλὰ διὰ νεφέων ἄφνω πέλας ἀίσσουσαι
Ἅρπυιαι στόματος χειρῶν τ' ἀπὸ γαμφηλῇσιν
συνεχέως ἥρπαζον, ἐλείπετο δ' ἄλλοτε φορβῆς
οὐδ' ὅσον· ἄλλοτε τυτθόν, ἵνα ζώων ἀκάχοιτο.   190
καὶ δ' ἐπὶ μυδαλέην ὀδμὴν χέον· οὐδέ τις ἔτλη
μὴ καὶ λευκανίηνδε φορεύμενος, ἀλλ' ἀποτηλοῦ
ἑστηώς· τοῖόν οἱ ἀπέπνεε λείψανα δαιτός.

There Phineus, Agenor's son, had his home on the shore, a man who endured the most destructive woes above all others because of the prophetic skill which Leto's son had endowed him with in the past. (180) He showed not the least reverence to Zeus himself by unerringly prophesying his holy intentions to men. Therefore Zeus sent upon him a long-continuing old age and took the sweet light from his eyes; and he did not allow him to enjoy all the limitless gifts of food which those who lived round about gathered for him in his house whenever consulting him for oracles; but suddenly swooping near him through the clouds, the Harpies continually snatched the food from his mouth and hands with their beaks; sometimes no food at all was left, at other times a tiny bit so that he could stay alive in distress. (190) They shed a putrid smell on it too; and no-one could endure to stand at a distance, let alone to bring it to their throat, so much did the remnants of his meal stink.

(b) 2.213-29: *Phineus recognizes the Argonauts as they pass; knowing that they will prove his salvation, he asks them for assistance, in particular (234-9) the winged sons of Boreas, Zetes and Calaïs, his brothers-in-law:*

χάριν νύ τοι, ὦ ἄνα Λητοῦς
υἱέ, καὶ ἀργαλέοισιν ἀνάπτομαι ἐν καμάτοισιν.

Appendix

Ἱκεσίου πρὸς Ζηνός, ὅτις ῥίγιστος ἀλιτροῖς 215
ἀνδράσι, Φοίβου τ' ἀμφί, καὶ αὐτῆς εἵνεκεν Ἥρης
λίσσομαι, ᾗ περίαλλα θεῶν μέμβλεσθε κιόντες,
χραίσμετέ μοι, ῥύσασθε δυσάμμορον ἀνέρα λύμης,
μηδέ μ' ἀκηδείῃσιν ἀφορμήθητε λιπόντες
αὔτως. οὐ γὰρ μοῦνον ἐπ' ὀφθαλμοῖσιν Ἐρινὺς 220
λὰξ ἐπέβη, καὶ γῆρας ἀμήρυτον ἐς τέλος ἕλκω·
πρὸς δ' ἔτι πικρότατον κρέμαται κακὸν ἄλλο κακοῖσιν.
Ἅρπυιαι στόματός μοι ἀφαρπάζουσιν ἐδωδὴν
ἔκποθεν ἀφράστοιο καταΐσσουσαι ὀλέθροι,
ἴσχω δ' οὔτινα μῆτιν ἐπίρροθον. ἀλλά κε ῥεῖα 225
αὐτὸς ἐὸν λελάθοιμι νόον δόρποιο μεμηλώς,
ἢ κείνας· ὧδ' αἶψα διηέριαι ποτέονται.
τυτθὸν δ' ἢν ἄρα δήποτ' ἐδητύος ἄμμι λίπωσιν,
πνεῖ τόδε μυδαλέον τε καὶ οὐ τλητὸν μένος ὀδμῆς·

I offer up thanks to you, O lord, son of Leto, even in grievous sufferings. In the name of Zeus, god of supplication, who is most terrible to sinful men, and for Phoebus' sake and for the sake of Hera herself, to whom above all the other gods your travels are a concern, I beseech you, help me, save an ill-fated man from defilement, and do not leave me like this and go off without concern for me. For not only has a Fury stamped on my eyes (220) with her foot, and I drag out to the end a tedious old age, but in addition to these evils yet another most bitter evil hangs over me: the Harpies swoop down as symbols of destruction from some unguessable place and snatch the food from my mouth. And I have no plan to help me against this; but when I think about a meal, I could more easily escape my own thoughts than them, so speedily do they fly through the air. And if ever they leave me a little bit of food, it gives off a putrid and unendurably strong smell.

(c) 2.262–303: *After Phineus has sworn an oath that the gods will not punish them for their aid, Zetes and Calaïs chase off the Harpies*:

Τὼ μὲν ἔπειθ' ὅρκῳ, καὶ ἀλαλκέμεναι μενέαινον.
αἶψα δὲ κουρότεροι πεπονήατο δαῖτα γέροντι,
λοίσθιον Ἁρπυίῃσιν ἑλώριον· ἐγγύθι δ' ἄμφω
στῆσαν, ἵνα ξιφέεσσιν ἐπεσσυμένας ἐλάσειαν. 265
καὶ δὴ τὰ πρώτισθ' ὁ γέρων ἔψαυεν ἐδωδῆς·
αἱ δ' ἄφαρ, ἠΰτ' ἄελλαι ἀδευκέες ἢ στεροπαὶ ὥς,
ἀπρόφατοι νεφέων ἐξάλμεναι ἐσσεύοντο
κλαγγῇ μαιμώωσαι ἐδητύος· οἱ δ' ἐσιδόντες
ἥρωες μεσσηγὺς ἀνίαχον, αἱ δ' ἅμ' ἀϋτῇ 270
πάντα καταβρώξασαι, ὑπὲρ πόντοιο φέροντο
τῆλε παρέξ, ὀδμὴ δὲ δυσάνσχετος αὖθι λέλειπτο.
τάων δ' αὖ κατόπισθε δύω υἷες Βορέαο
φάσγαν' ἐπισχόμενοι ἐπ' ἴσῳ θέον. ἐν γὰρ ἔηκεν

Appendix

Ζεὺς μένος ἀκάματόν σφιν· ἀτὰρ Διὸς οὔ κεν ἐπέσθην 275
νόσφιν, ἐπεὶ ζεφύροιο παραΐσσεσκον ἀέλλας
αἰέν, ὅτ' ἐς Φινῆα καὶ ἐκ Φινῆος ἴοιεν.
ὡς δ' ὅτ' ἐνὶ κνημοῖσι κύνες δεδαημένοι ἄγρης
ἢ αἶγας κεραοὺς ἠὲ πρόκας ἰχνεύοντες
θείωσιν, τυτθὸν δὲ τιταινόμενοι μετόπισθεν 280
ἄκρῃς ἐν γενύεσσι μάτην ἀράβησαν ὀδόντας·
ὣς Ζήτης Κάλαΐς τε μάλα σχεδὸν ἀΐσσοντες
τάων ἀκροτάτῃσιν ἐπέχραον ἤλιθα χερσίν.
καί νύ κε δή σφ' ἀέκητι θεῶν διεδηλήσαντο,
πολλὸν ἑκὰς νήσοισιν ἔπι Πλωτῇσι κιχόντες, 285
εἰ μὴ ἄρ' ὠκέα Ἶρις ἴδεν, κατὰ δ' αἰθέρος ἆλτο
οὐρανόθεν, καὶ τοῖα παραιφαμένη κατέρυκεν·
    Οὐ θέμις, ὦ υἱεῖς Βορέω, ξιφέεσσιν ἐλάσσαι
Ἁρπυίας, μεγάλοιο Διὸς κύνας· ὅρκια δ' αὐτὴ
δώσω ἐγών, ὡς οὔ οἱ ἔτι χρίμψουσιν ἰοῦσαι.' 290
    Ὣς φαμένη, λοιβὴν Στυγὸς ὤμοσεν, ἥ τε θεοῖσιν
ῥιγίστη πάντεσσιν ὀπιδνοτάτη τε τέτυκται,
μὴ μὲν Ἀγηνορίδαο δόμοις ἔτι τάσδε πελάσσαι
εἰσαῦτις Φινῆος, ἐπεὶ καὶ μόρσιμον ἦεν.
οἱ δ' ὅρκῳ εἴξαντες ὑπέστρεφον ἂψ ἐπὶ νῆα 295
σώεσθαι· Στροφάδας δὲ μετακλείουσ' ἄνθρωποι
νήσους τοῖό γ' ἕκητι, πάρος Πλωτὰς καλέοντες.
Ἅρπυιαί τ' Ἶρίς τε διέτμαγεν. αἱ μὲν ἔδυσαν
κευθμῶνα Κρήτης Μινωΐδος· ἡ δ' ἀνόρουσεν
Οὔλυμπόνδε, θοῇσι μεταχρονίη πτερύγεσσιν. 300
    Τόφρα δ' ἀριστῆες, πινόεν περὶ δέρμα γέροντος
πάντῃ φοιβήσαντες, ἐπικριδὸν ἱρεύσαντο
μῆλα, τά τ' ἐξ Ἀμύκοιο λεηλασίης ἐκόμισσαν.

Then, in view of his oath, the two of them were keen to drive [the Harpies] away. Quickly the younger men got ready a feast for the old man, the last one for the Harpies to plunder. [Zetes and Calaïs] stood nearby so that they could strike them with their swords as they swooped. And the very instant the old man touched the food, like sudden storm-winds or flashes of lightning, they sprang forth unexpectedly from the clouds and swooped shrieking in their eagerness for the food. However, as they saw them in mid flight the heroes shouted aloud. But as they shouted, (270) the Harpies swallowed down the lot and flew far away over the sea; and an intolerable stink was left there. But the two sons of Boreas raced after them, holding their swords level with them. For Zeus had endowed them with tireless strength, and without Zeus's support they would have followed only at a distance since the Harpies always outran the blasts of the West Winds whenever they went to Phineus or away from Phineus. And as when dogs with skill in hunting run in the mountains tracking down horned goats or deer, and speeding at full stretch a little behind them (280) they snap their teeth in their jaws to no avail, so did Zetes and Calaïs rush extremely near, grazing them with their fingertips to no purpose. Yet they would actually have rent them to pieces against the will of the gods when they got level with them far away at the Floating Islands, if swift Iris had not seen them and leapt down through the sky from heaven and held them back, persuading them thus: 'It is not permitted, O sons of Boreas, to strike the Harpies, the dogs of great Zeus; but I shall swear an oath that they will no longer come anywhere near him.' (290) Thus she spoke and swore on a libation to the Styx, which is the most terrible and awful oath for all the gods, that the Harpies would no longer draw near to the house of Phineus, the son of Agenor, since this was what was fated. They gave in to the oath and turned around to hasten back to the ship. This is the reason why men give these islands the new name of Strophades [Turning Islands] when before they called them the Floating Islands. The Harpies and Iris separated: they went into a hiding place in Minoan Crete, while she went up high in the air on swift wings to Olympus. In the meantime the heroes cleansed the fouled skin of the old man all round, picked out sheep which they had brought from the plunder of Amycus, and sacrificed them.

(d) 2.311–16: *while they are waiting for Zetes and Calaïs to return, Phineus gives a prophecy of the troubles ahead for the Argonauts* (311–407), *beginning thus*:

> Κλῦτέ νυν· οὐ μὲν πάντα πέλει θέμις ὔμμι δαῆναι
> ἀτρεκές· ὅσσα δ' ὄρωρε θεοῖς φίλον, οὐκ ἐπικεύσω.
> ἀασάμην καὶ πρόσθε Διὸς νόον ἀφραδίῃσιν
> χρείων ἑξείης τε καὶ ἐς τέλος. ὧδε γὰρ αὐτὸς
> βούλεται ἀνθρώποις ἐπιδευέα θέσφατα φαίνειν   315
> μαντοσύνης, ἵνα καί τι θεῶν χατέωσι νόοιο. . . .'

'So hear me. It is not permitted for you to learn everything precisely; but all that is pleasing to the gods, I shall not hide. I was deluded previously in crazily prophesying the intentions of Zeus in order and to the end. For Zeus himself wishes to reveal incomplete oracles to men through prophecy, so that they may lack some knowledge of the gods' intentions. . . .'

N: Apollonius, *Argonautica* 4.1694–1730:

> αὐτίκα δὲ Κρηταῖον ὑπὲρ μέγα λαῖτμα θέοντας
> νὺξ ἐφόβει, τήνπερ τε κατουλάδα κικλήσκουσιν.   1695
> νύκτ' ὀλοὴν οὐκ ἄστρα διίσχανεν, οὐκ ἀμαρυγαὶ
> μήνης, οὐρανόθεν δὲ μέλαν χάος, ἠέ τις ἄλλη
> ὠρώρει σκοτίη μυχάτων ἀνιοῦσα βερέθρων·
> αὐτοὶ δ' εἴτ' Ἀίδῃ εἴθ' ὕδασιν ἐμφορέοντο

Appendix

ἠείδειν οὐδ' ὅσσον, ἐπέτρεψαν δὲ θαλάσσῃ 1700
νόστον, ἀμηχανέοντες, ὅπῃ φέροι. αὐτὰρ Ἰήσων
χεῖρας ἀνασχόμενος μεγάλῃ ὀπὶ Φοῖβον ἀύτει,
ῥύσασθαι καλέων· κατὰ δ' ἔρρεεν ἀσχαλόωντι
δάκρυα· πολλὰ δὲ Πυθοῖ ὑπέσχετο, πολλὰ δ' Ἀμύκλαις,
πολλὰ δ' ἐς Ὀρτυγίην ἀπερείσια δῶρα κομίσσειν. 1705
Λητοΐδη, τύνη δὲ κατ' οὐρανοῦ ἵκεο πέτρας
ῥίμφα Μελαντείους ἀριήκοος, αἵ τ' ἐνὶ πόντῳ
ἧνται· δοιάων δὲ μιῆς ἐφύπερθεν ὀρούσας,
δεξιτερῇ χρύσειον ἀνέσχεθες ὑψόθι τόξον,
μαρμαρέην δ' ἀπέλαμψε βιὸς περὶ πάντοθεν αἴγλην. 1710
τοῖσι δέ τις Σποράδων βαιὴ ἀνὰ τόφρ' ἐφαάνθη
νῆσος ἰδεῖν, ὀλίγης Ἱππουρίδος ἀντία νήσου·
ἔνθ' εὐνὰς ἐβάλοντο καὶ ἔσχεθον· αὐτίκα δ' ἠὼς
φέγγεν ἀνερχομένη, τοὶ δ' ἀγλαὸν Ἀπόλλωνι
ἄλσει ἐνὶ σκιερῷ τέμενος σκιόεντά τε βωμὸν 1715
ποίεον, Αἰγλήτην μὲν ἐυσκόπου εἵνεκεν αἴγλης
Φοῖβον κεκλόμενοι· Ἀνάφην δέ τε λισσάδα νῆσον
ἴσκον, ὃ δὴ Φοῖβός μιν ἀτυζομένοις ἀνέφηνεν.
ῥέζον δ' οἷα κεν ἄνδρες ἐρημαίῃ ἐνὶ ῥέζειν
ἀκτῇ ἐφοπλίσσειαν· ὃ δή σφεας ὁππότε δαλοῖς 1720
ὕδωρ αἰθομένοισιν ἐπιλλείβοντας ἴδοντο
Μηδείης δμωαὶ Φαιηκίδες, οὐκέτ' ἔπειτα
ἰσχέμεν ἐν στήθεσσι γέλῳ σθένον, οἷα θαμειὰς
αἰὲν ἐν Ἀλκινόοιο βοοκτασίας ὁρόωσαι·
τὰς δ' αἰσχροῖς ἥρωες ἐπεστοβέεσκον ἔπεσσιν 1725
χλεύῃ γηθόσυνοι· γλυκερὴ δ' ἀνεδαίετο μέσσῳ
κερτομίη καὶ νεῖκος ἐπεσβόλον. ἐκ δέ νυ κείνης
μολπῆς ἡρώων νήσῳ ἔνι τοῖα γυναῖκες
ἀνδράσι δηριόωνται, ὅτ' Ἀπόλλωνα θυηλαῖς
Αἰγλήτην Ἀνάφης τιμήορον ἱλάσκωνται. 1730

Immediately as they ran over the great Cretan gulf, they were given cause for fear by the night that men call 'enveloping'. Stars did not break through the baleful night, nor the rays of the moon, but black emptiness descended from heaven, or some other darkness arose from the cavernous depths. They themselves did not so much as know whether they sailed on hell or high water. They entrusted to the sea (1700) their route home, at a loss where it might carry them. But Jason lifted up his hands and with a great cry called on Phoebus, summoning him to save them; and tears ran down in his distress. Many gifts he promised for Pytho [Delphi], many for Amyclae, and to take many gifts beyond counting to Ortygia [Delos]. Son of Leto, responding readily, you came swiftly down from heaven to the Melantian rocks, which lie in the sea, and darting up one of these two, you held up your golden bow at the top; and the bow shone a gleaming light all around. (1710) Then there appeared a little island for them to see, one of the Sporades, near the small island of Hippuris; there they cast their anchors and moored. Immediately dawn came up and spread its light. They created a splendid precinct and a shadowed altar in a shady grove, calling upon Phoebus as Aegletes [shining one] because of his far-seen brightness. And they named the barren island Anaphe (Revelation), because Phoebus had revealed it to them when they were terror-stricken. They sacrificed the kind of things that men provide for sacrifice on a desolate coast, (1720) so that, when the Phaeacian maidservants of Medea saw them pouring libations of water on the blazing firebrands, they were then no longer able to restrain the laughter in their breasts inasmuch as they had always seen sacrifices of oxen aplenty in the house of Alcinous. The heroes scoffed at them with obscene words as they took pleasure in their jests; and pleasant abuse and scurrilous raillery were kindled between them. And as a result of that play of the heroes the women on the island compete with the men with similar insults whenever in their sacrifices they propitiate Apollo Aigletes, the tutelary* god of Anaphe. (1730)

O: Lucretius 1.716–25:

In criticizing the pluralist phliosophers who think the universe is formed from as few as four elements, fire, air, water, and earth, he celebrates his poetic model Empedocles, while attacking his teaching:

>quorum Acragantinus cum primis Empedocles est,
>insula quem triquetris terrarum gessit in oris,
>quam fluitans circum magnis anfractibus aequor
>Ionium glaucis aspargit uirus ab undis
>angustoque fretu rapidum mare diuidit undis   720
>Aeoliae terrarum oras a finibus eius.
>hic est uasta Charybdis et hic Aetnaea minantur
>murmura flammarum rursum se colligere iras,
>faucibus eruptos iterum uis ut uomat ignis
>ad caelumque ferat flammai fulgura rursum.   725

Of them Empedocles of Acragas is among the first, he whom the island bore on its three-cornered shores of land, the one that the watery expanse flows around with great windings and scatters the saline corruption of the Ionian sea from its grey-green waves, and the rushing sea with narrow strait divides with its waves the shores of the lands of Aeolia [Italy] from its [Sicily's] territory. Here is desolate Charybdis and here the rumbling of Etna threatens to regather the anger of its fires, so that once more violence sends fires bursting from its jaws and again carries up to heaven the flaming lightning.

Vergil, *Aen.* **1.1–7**: See Introduction, p. 10
Vergil, *Aen.* **1.254–71**: See Introduction, p. 36

P: Vergil, *Aen.* 1.343-64:

Venus in disguise tells the story of how Dido came to lead an expedition of her people to found Carthage:

> huic coniunx Sychaeus erat, ditissimus auri
> Phoenicum, et magno miserae dilectus amore,
> cui pater intactam dederat primisque iugarat   345
> ominibus. sed regna Tyri germanus habebat
> Pygmalion, scelere ante alios immanior omnis.
> quos inter medius uenit furor. ille Sychaeum
> impius ante aras atque auri caecus amore,
> clam ferro incautum superat, securus amorum   350
> germanae; factumque diu celauit et aegram
> multa malus simulans uana spe lusit amantem.
> ipsa sed in somnis inhumati uenit imago
> coniugis ora modis attollens pallida miris;
> crudelis aras traiectaque pectora ferro   355
> nudauit, caecumque domus scelus omne retexit.
> tum celerare fugam patriaque excedere suadet,
> auxiliumque uiae ueteres tellure recludit
> thesauros, ignotum argenti pondus et auri.
> his commota fugam Dido sociosque parabat.   360
> conueniunt quibus aut odium crudele tyranni
> aut metus acer erat; nauis, quae forte paratae,
> corripiunt onerantque auro: portantur auari
> Pygmalionis opes pelago; dux femina facti.

Her husband was Sychaeus, richest in gold of the Phoenicians, and loved by the poor woman with a great passion. Her father had given her to him as a maiden and joined them in taking the omens of first marriage. But her brother Pygmalion ruled over Tyre, more monstrous in wickedness than any other. A madness intervened between them. Pygmalion killed Sychaeus by the altar, lacking any sense of righteous behaviour and blinded by love of gold. He caught him unawares in secret and overcame him, careless of the love (350) of his sister. Long he concealed the deed and evilly making up many stories he deceived the love-sick woman with vain hopes. But in her sleep there came the very image of her unburied husband holding up a face of unnatural pallor. He laid bare the cruel altar and his chest pierced by the sword, and revealed all the unseen wickedness of the house. Then he tells her to hasten her flight and leave her homeland, and as assistance for the journey he uncovers from the earth ancient treasure, an unknown weight of silver and of gold. Stirred by this, Dido prepared her flight and companions: (360) it was a gathering of those who felt hatred for the cruel tyrant or sharp fear. They seized ships that chanced to be ready, and loaded them with the gold: the wealth of avaricious Pygmalion was carried off to sea. The leader of the adventure was a woman.

Q: Vergil, Aeneid 7.107–29:

The Trojans eat their tables:

>Aeneas primique duces et pulcher Iulus
>corpora sub ramis deponunt arboris altae,
>instituuntque dapes et adorea liba per herbam
>subiciunt epulis (sic Iuppiter ipse monebat)   110
>et Cereale solum pomis agrestibus augent.
>consumptis hic forte aliis, ut uertere morsus
>exiguam in Cererem penuria adegit edendi,
>et uiolare manu malisque audacibus orbem
>fatalis crusti patulis nec parcere quadris,   115
>'heus, etiam mensas consumimus?' inquit Iulus,
>nec plura, adludens. ea uox audita laborum
>prima tulit finem, primamque loquentis ab ore
>eripuit pater ac stupefactus numine pressit.
>continuo 'salue fatis mihi debita tellus   120
>uosque' ait 'o fidi Troiae saluete penates:
>hic domus, haec patria est. genitor mihi talia namque
>(nunc repeto) Anchises fatorum arcana reliquit:
>"cum te, nate, fames ignota ad litora uectum
>accisis coget dapibus consumere mensas,   125
>tum sperare domos defessus, ibique memento
>prima locare manu molirique aggere tecta."
>haec erat illa fames, haec nos suprema manebat
>exitiis positura modum....'

Aeneas, the captains, and handsome Iulus settle beneath the branches of a tall tree; they put together a celebratory meal and set spelt wafers on the grass below their feast (thus Jupiter himself ordered) (110) and they pile up the trays made of grain with country fruits. When the rest had been eaten, by chance lack of fodder forced them to turn their jaws to the insubstantial bread, and to attack the fateful circle of crust with bold hand and mouth and not to spare the squares of bread [*or* tables], 'Hey, are we eating the tables too?' says Iulus, and not a word more, joking. The hearing of that utterance brought the first end of their labours, and the father snatched the first word from the mouth of the speaker and silenced him, struck by the presence of divinity. Quickly he says, 'Hail, land promised me by the fates, (120) and hail to you, faithful Penates of Troy: this is our home, this is our fatherland. Now I remember, my father Anchises left behind a fateful secret of this kind: "When you are carried to an unknown shore, your food is reduced, and hunger forces you to consume your tables, then, exhausted as you are, expect to find homes, and remember there to place the foundations of your first buildings and establish them with a rampart." This was that hunger, this was waiting to put a final end to our disasters....'

R: Vergil, *Aeneid* 8.675–81:

The central scene on the prophetic shield Vulcan makes for Aeneas:

> in medio classes aeratas, Actia bella,
> cernere erat, totumque instructo Marte uideres
> feruere Leucaten auroque effulgere fluctus.
> hinc Augustus agens Italos in proelia Caesar
> cum patribus populoque, penatibus et magnis dis,
> stans celsa in puppi, geminas cui tempora flammas   680
> laeta uomunt patriumque aperitur uertice sidus.

In the middle bronze-clad fleets, the war at Actium, were visible, and you might see all the island of Leucas in a ferment with armies at the ready and waves gleaming with gold. On this side Augustus Caesar leading the Italians into battle, together with the senators and people, the Penates and the great gods, standing on the high poop; his joyful temples pour forth twin flames and his father's star is revealed on his crown.

S: Vergil, *Aen.* 12.766–87:

An interruption to the final fight between Aeneas and Turnus:

> forte sacer Fauno foliis oleaster amaris
> hic steterat, nautis olim uenerabile lignum,
> seruati ex undis ubi figere dona solebant
> Laurenti diuo et uotas suspendere uestis;
> sed stirpem Teucri nullo discrimine sacrum   770
> sustulerant, puro ut possent concurrere campo.
> hic hasta Aeneae stabat, huc impetus illam
> detulerat fixam et lenta radice tenebat.
> incubuit uoluitque manu conuellere ferrum
> Dardanides teloque sequi quem prendere cursu   775
> non poterat. tum uero amens formidine Turnus
> 'Faune, precor, miserere' inquit 'tuque optima ferrum
> Terra tene, colui uestros si semper honores,

Appendix

> quos contra Aeneadae bello fecere profanos.
> dixit, opemque dei non cassa in uota uocauit. 780
> namque diu luctans lentoque in stirpe moratus
> uiribus haud ullis ualuit discludere morsus
> roboris Aeneas. dum nititur acer et instat,
> rursus in aurigae faciem mutata Metisci
> procurrit fratrique ensem dea Daunia reddit. 785
> quod Venus audaci nymphae indignata licere
> accessit telumque alta ab radice reuellit.

It happened that there was a bitter-leaved wild olive sacred to Faunus that had stood here, its timber previously revered by sailors, where those rescued from the waves used to nail their offerings to the Laurentine god and to hang the clothes they had vowed; but the Trojans had removed the sacred trunk without any distinction (770) so that they could join battle on an open field. Here the spear of Aeneas stood, here its momentum had carried it and made it stick, holding it in the clinging root. The descendant of Dardanus bent over it and aimed to pull the iron point out by force and to pursue with the weapon the man he could not catch through running. Then Turnus, desperate with fear, said 'Pity me, Faunus, I pray, and you, most excellent Mother Earth, hold the iron, if ever I have attended the honours given to you, which the followers of Aeneas by contrast have profaned in war.' That's what he said and he did not summon the aid of the god for an empty prayer. (780) For Aeneas struggled long and was delayed by the clinging stump and did not manage for all his efforts to open up the grip of the wood. While he is eagerly straining and striving, the Daunian goddess [*Juturna, Turnus' sister*] changed again to the appearance of the charioteer Metiscus, runs up and gives her brother his sword. Venus was angry that the nymph had had the daring and licence to do this; she came up and plucked the weapon out from the deep root.

T: Ovid, *Metamorphoses* 13.623–14.81:

(a) 13.623–39:

> non tamen euersam Troiae cum moenibus esse
> spem quoque fata sinunt: sacra et, sacra altera, patrem
> fert umeris, uenerabile onus, Cythereius heros 625
> (de tantis opibus praedam pius eligit illam
> Ascaniumque suum) profugaque per aequora classe
> fertur ab Antandro sceleretaque limina Thracum
> et Polydoreo manantem sanguine terram
> linquit et utilibus uentis aestuque secundo 630

> intrat Apollineam sociis comitantibus urbem.
> hunc Anius, quo rege homines, antistite Phoebus
> rite colebatur, temploque domoque recepit
> urbemque ostendit delubraque nota duasque
> Latona quondam stirpes pariente retentas. 635
> ture dato flammis uinoque in tura profuso
> caesarumque boum fibris de more crematis
> regia tecta petunt, positique tapetibus altis
> munera cum liquido capiunt Cerealia Baccho.

The Fates did not allow Troy's hopes to be overturned along with its walls: holy objects, and another holy object, his father, a burden deserving of honour, are raised on his shoulders by the heroic son of Venus (out of so much wealth the pious man chooses this booty, along with his son Ascanius), and he is carried across the sea from Antandros in a migrating fleet and leaves behind the wicked threshold of the Thracians and the land oozing with the blood of Polydorus and with the help of winds and a favourable current (630) he enters the city of Apollo, accompanied by comrades. Anius, who duly tended the people as king, Apollo as priest, received him in the temple and his home, and showed him the city, the famous shrines, and the two trunks grasped by Latona as she was giving birth. When incense had been given to the fire, wine poured on to the incense, and the entrails of sacrificed cattle ritually burnt, they head for the palace, and reclined on deep rugs they enjoy the gifts of Ceres with liquid Bacchus [i.e. bread and wine].

Anius then gives an account of the transformation of his daughters (640–74).

(b) 13.675–81:

> talibus atque aliis postquam conuiuia dictis 675
> impleurunt, mensa somnum petiere remota
> cumque die surgunt adeuntque oracula Phoebi,
> qui petere antiquam matrem cognataque iussit
> litora. prosequitur rex et dat munus ituris,
> Anchisae sceptrum, chlamydem pharetramque nepoti, 680
> cratera Aeneae.

After the feast was filled with this and other such conversation and the table was removed, they sought sleep, and rise with the day and make for the oracle of Phoebus, who ordered them to seek their original mother and the shores inhabited by relatives; the king accompanies them as they set off and gives gifts, a sceptre for Anchises, a cloak and a quiver for his grandson, and wine-mixing bowl for Aeneas. [*There follows an ecphrasis* of the bowl including a scene of metamorphosis, and other gifts (671–703).*]

(c) 13.705–34:

>   inde recordati Teucros a sanguine Teucri   705
> ducere principium Creten tenuere locique
> ferre diu nequiere Iouem centumque relictis
> urbibus Ausonios optant contingere portus,
> saeuit hiems iactatque uiros, Strophadumque receptos
> portubus infidis exterruit ales Aello.   710
> et iam Dulichios portus Ithacenque Samonque
> Neritiasque domus, regnum fallacis Vlixis,
> praeter erant uecti: certatam lite deorum
> Ambraciam uersique uident sub imagine saxum
> iudicis, Actiaco quae nunc ab Apolline nota est,   715
> uocalemque sua terram Dodonida quercu
> Chaoniosque sinus, ubi nati rege Molosso
> impia subiectis fugere incendia pennis.
> proxima Phaeacum felicibus obsita pomis
> rura petunt; Epiros ab his regnataque uati   720
> Buthrotos Phrygio simulataque Troia tenetur;
> inde futurorum certi quae cuncta fideli
> Priamides Helenus monitu praedixerat, intrant
> Sicaniam: tribus haec excurrit in aequora linguis,
> e quibus imbriferos est uersa Pachynos ad austros,   725
> mollibus oppositum zephyris Lilybaeon, ad arctos
> aequoris expertes spectat boreanque Peloros.
> huc subeunt Teucri, et remis aestuque secundo
> sub noctem potitur Zanclaea classis harena:
> Scylla latus dextrum, laeuum inrequieta Charybdis   730
> infestat; uorat haec raptas reuomitque carinas,
> illa feris atram canibus succingitur aluum,
> uirginis ora gerens, et, si non omnia uates
> ficta reliquerunt, aliquo quoque tempore uirgo.

Then, remembering the Teucrians [i.e. Trojans] took their origin from the blood of Teucer they made for Crete, but did not bear for long the climate [*lit*. Jupiter] of the place, and abandoning the hundred cities they decide to reach the ports of Italy. There is a wild storm that tosses them, and when they were received in the unreliable harbours of the Strophades they were terrified by the winged Aello [a Harpy] (710). Now they had sailed past the ports of Dulichium, Ithaca, Samos, and the Neritian homes, kingdom of lying Ulysses. They see Ambracia, competed over in a contest of the gods, and the rock beneath the image of the transformed judge, which now takes its fame from Apollo of Actium, and the land of Dodona speaking through its oak tree, and the Chaonian gulf, where the sons of the Molossian king fled impious flames by acquiring wings. Next they seek the countryside of the Phaeacians, planted with fertile apple-trees; after this Epiros is made for, and Buthrotum ruled by the Phrygian prophet [Helenus], and an imitation Troy (721); then assured of the whole future, which Helenus, son of Priam, had foretold in a reliable prophecy, they come to Sicily: this runs out into the sea with three tongues of land, of which Pachynos is turned towards the rain-bearing South Wind, Lilybaeum faces gentle westerlies, Peloros looks to the bears who never enter the sea and the North Wind. Here come the Trojans, and with oars and favourable currents the fleet reaches the sand of Zancle just before night; Scylla infests the starboard side, unresting Charybdis the port; the latter seizes boats, drinks them in, and vomits them up; the former has a black belly surrounded by wild dogs, and bears the face of a maiden; and, if poets have not left behind complete fabrications, at one time she was a maiden. [*Metamorphosis of Scylla, and other tales* (13.735–14.69).]

(d) 14.70–81:

>Scylla loco mansit cumque est data copia primum
>in Circes odium sociis spoliauit Vlixem;
>mox eadem Teucras fuerat mersura carinas,
>ni prius in scopulum, qui nunc quoque saxeus exstat,
>transformata foret. scopulum quoque nauita uitat.
>hunc ubi Troianae remis auidamque Charybdin 75
>euicere rates, cum iam prope litus adessent
>Ausonium, Libycas uento referuntur ad oras.
>excipit Aenean illic animoque domoque
>non bene discidium Phrygii latura mariti
>Sidonis, inque pyra sacri sub imagine facta 80
>incubuit ferro deceptaque decipit omnes.

Scylla stayed there and when first the opportunity was given her, robbed Ulysses of companions to exercise her hatred of Circe, and subsequently she would also have sunk Trojan boats, if she had not first been transformed into a cliff, which now too stands out rocky. The sailor avoids the cliff too. When the Trojan boats had made it past this and greedy Charybdis on their oars, with the shore of Italy already close at hand, they are carried by the wind to the coast of Libya. There Aeneas is received into the heart and home of the Sidonian woman who was not going to take well the departure of her Phrygian husband, and who on the pyre made under the pretence of a sacred rite fell on a sword, and herself deceived deceived all.

Bibliography

Abbreviations

Abbreviations for journals follow standard forms; where these are not easily guessed (e.g. *CPh* = *Classical Philology*), they can be found through internet searches.

CCV = *The Cambridge Companion to Virgil*, ed. C. Martindale (Cambridge, 1997)
EV = *Enciclopedia virgiliana* (6 vols; Roma, 1984–91)
FRH = *The Fragments of the Roman Historians*, ed. T. J. Cornell (3 vols; Oxford, 2013)
FRP = Hollis, A. S., *Fragments of Roman Poetry c.60 BC–AD 20* (Oxford, 2007)
G&L = B. L. Gildersleeve & G. Lodge, *Latin Grammar* (1st edn London, 1867; 3rd edn reprinted London 2005)
LIMC = *Lexicon Iconographicum Mythologiae Classicae* (Zurich/Dusseldorf, 1981–99)
OCD[4] = *Oxford Classical Dictionary*, 4th edn, S. Hornblower, A. Spawforth (Oxford, 2012)
OLD = *Oxford Latin Dictionary*
ThLL = *Thesaurus Linguae Latinae*
TrRF = *Tragicorum Romanorum Fragmenta*, vol. 1, ed. M. Schauer (Göttingen, 2012)
VE = *The Virgil Encyclopedia*, ed. R. F. Thomas, J. M. Ziolkowski (Hoboken, NJ, 2014)

Works cited

Adams, J. N., 'Anatomical terminology in Latin epic', *BICS* 27 (1980), 50–62
Adams, J. N. & Mayer, R. G. (eds), *Aspects of the Language of Latin Poetry* (*PBA* 93; Oxford, 1999)
Adler, E., *Vergil's Empire* (Lanham, 2003)
Akbar Khan, H., 'The Harpies episode in *Aeneid* 3', *Prometheus* 22 (1996), 131–44
Allen, W. S., *Vox Latina* (2nd edn, revised reprint; Cambridge, 1989)
Armstrong, R., 'Crete in the *Aeneid*: recurring trauma and alternative fate', *CQ* 52 (2002), 321–40
Austin, R. G., commentaries on Vergil, *Aeneid*, Book I (Oxford, 1971); Book II (Oxford, 1964); Book VI (Oxford, 1977)
Bailey, C., *Religion in Virgil* (Oxford, 1935)

Barchiesi, A., 'Immovable Delos: *Aeneid* 3.73–98 and the Hymns of Callimachus', *CQ* 44 (1994), 438–43

Butrica, J. L., '*Apollo Actius, Apollo Leucadius*: a false problem in Latin poetry', in M. Joyal (ed.), *In Altum: Seventy-five Years of Classical Studies in Newfoundland* (St John's, 2001), 289–311

Cairns, F., *Virgil's Augustan Epic* (Cambridge, 1989)

Carter, M. A. S., *Aeneid 3: A Critical Reassessment* (Oxford D.Phil. thesis, 2004)

Casali, S., 'Killing the father: Ennius, Naevius and Virgil's Julian imperialism', in W. Fitzgerald & E. Gowers (eds), *Ennius Perennis: The Annals and Beyond*, *PCPhS* Suppl. 31 (2007), 103–28

Clare, R. J., 'Catullus 64 and the *Argonautica* of Apollonius Rhodius: allusion and exemplarity', *PCPhS* 42 (1996), 60–88

Coo, L., 'Polydorus and the *Georgics*: Virgil, *Aeneid* 3.13–68', *MD* 59 (2007), 193–9

Cooley, A. E., *Res Gestae Divi Augusti: Text, Translation, and Commentary* (Cambridge, 2009)

Conte, G. B., *The Poetry of Pathos: Studies in Virgilian Epic* (Oxford, 2007)

Conte, G. B., *P. Vergilius Maro, Aeneis* (Bibliotheca Teubneriana; Berlin, 2009)

Cova, P. V., *Il libro terzo dell'Eneide* (Milan, 1994)

de Jong, I. J. F., *A Narratological Commentary on the Odyssey* (Cambridge, 2001)

Durling, R. M., & Martinez, R. L., *The Divine Comedy of Dante Alighieri*, vol. 1: *Inferno* (New York, 1996)

Dyson, J. T., *King of the Wood: The Sacrificial Victor in Virgil's Aeneid* (Norman, OK, 2001)

Elliott, J., *Ennius and the Architecture of the Annales* (Cambridge, 2013)

Erskine, A., *Troy Between Greece and Rome: Local Tradition and Imperial Power* (Oxford, 2001)

Fantham, E., 'Virgil's Trojan Women', in Günther 2015: 103–34

Feeney, D. C., *The Gods in Epic: Poets and Critics of the Classical Tradition* (Oxford, 1991)

Fletcher, K. F. B., *Finding Italy: Travel, Colonization, and Nation in Vergil's Aeneid* (Ann Arbor, 2014)

Fontenrose, J. E., *The Delphic Oracle: Its Responses and Operations, with a Catalogue of Responses* (Berkeley, 1978)

Fordyce, C. J., *P. Vergili Maronis Aeneidos Libri VII–VIII* (Oxford, 1977)

Fowler, D. P., *Roman Constructions: Readings in Postmodern Latin* (Oxford, 2000)

Goldschmidt, N., *Shaggy Crowns: Ennius' Annales and Virgil's Aeneid* (Oxford, 2013)

Gow, A. S. F., & Page, D. L., *The Greek Anthology: The Garland of Philip* (2 vols; Cambridge, 1968)

Günther, H.-C. (ed.), *Virgilian Studies: A Miscellany Dedicated to the Memory of Mario Geymonat* (Nordhausen, 2015)
Hardie, P. R., *Virgil's Aeneid: Cosmos and Imperium* (Oxford, 1986)
Hardie, P. R., *Rumour and Renown: Representations of Fama in Western Literature* (Cambridge, 2012)
Hardy, C. S, 'Antiqua mater: misreading gender in Aeneid 3.84-91', *CJ* 92 (1996), 1-8
Harrison, E. L., 'The structure of the *Aeneid*: observations on the links between the books', *ANRW* 2.31.1 (1980), 359-93
Harrison, E. L., 'Foundation prodigies in the *Aeneid*', *PLLS* 5 (1985), 131-64
Harrison, S. J., *Vergil, Aeneid 10, with Introduction, Translation, and Commentary* (Oxford, 1991)
Harrison, S. J., *Generic Enrichment in Vergil and Horace* (Oxford, 2007)
Harrison, S. J. (ed.), *Oxford Readings in Vergil's Aeneid* (Oxford, 1990)
Henry, J., *Aeneidea* (5 vols; Leipzig, 1873-92)
Heubeck, A., West, S., & Hainsworth, J. B., *A Commentary on Homer's Odyssey*, vol. 1: *Books 1-8* (Oxford, 1988)
Heyworth, S. J., 'Deceitful Crete: *Aeneid* 3.84ff and the Hymns of Callimachus', *CQ* 43 (1993), 255-7
Heyworth, S. J., *Cynthia: A Companion to the Text of Propertius* (Oxford, 2007; corrected reprint, 2009) [= *Cynthia*]
Hickson, F. V., *Roman Prayer Language: Livy and the Aeneid of Vergil* (Stuttgart, 1993)
Highet, G., *The Speeches in Vergil's Aeneid* (Princeton, 1972)
Hinds, S. E., *Allusion and Intertext: Dynamics of Appropriation in Roman Poetry* (Cambridge, 1998)
Hollis, A. S., 'Hellenistic colouring in Virgil's *Aeneid*', *HSCPh* 94 (1992), 269-85
Hopman, M. G., *Scylla: Myth, Metaphor, Paradox* (Cambridge, 2012)
Hornblower, S., *Lykophron: Alexandra* (Oxford, 2015)
Horsfall, N., 'Aeneas the Colonist', *Vergilius* 35 (1989), 8-27
Horsfall, N., *Virgil, Aeneid 7: A Commentary* (*Mnemosyne* suppl. 198; Leiden, 1995)
Horsfall, N., *A Companion to the Study of Virgil* (Leiden, 2000)
Horsfall, N., *Virgil, Aeneid 3: A Commentary* (*Mnemosyne* suppl. 273; Leiden, 2006)
Housman, A. E., *The Classical Papers of A. E. Housman*, ed. J. Diggle & F. R. D. Goodyear (3 vols; Cambridge, 1972) [= *CP*]
Hübner, W., 'Poesie der Antipoesie. Überlegungen zum dritten Buch der Aeneis', *GB* 21 (1995), 95-120
Hunter, R. L., *The Argonautica of Apollonius: Literary Studies* (Cambridge, 1993)
Hutchinson, G. O., *Greek to Latin: Frameworks and Contexts for Intertextuality* (Oxford, 2013)

Janko, R., *The Iliad: A Commentary*, vol. 4: *Books 13–16* (Cambridge, 1992)
Jenkyns, R. H. A., *Virgil's Experience: Nature and History; Times, Names and Places* (Oxford, 1998)
Jocelyn, H. D., *The Tragedies of Ennius* (Cambridge, 1967)
Keith, A. M., *Engendering Rome: Women in Latin Epic* (Cambridge, 2000)
Kenney, E. J., *Lucretius, de Rerum Natura Book 3* (Cambridge, 1971, 2nd ed. 2014)
Knauer, G. N., *Die Aeneis und Homer* (Göttingen, 1964)
Lloyd, R. B., 'On *Aeneid* 3.270–80', *AJPh* 75 (1954), 288–99
Lowe, D., *Monsters and Monstrosity in Augustan Poetry* (Ann Arbor, 2015)
Lyne, R. O. A. M., *Words and the Poet: Characteristic Techniques of Style in Vergil's Aeneid* (Oxford, 1989)
Maltby, R., *A Lexicon of Ancient Latin Etymologies* (Leeds, 1991)
McGushin, P., 'Virgil and the spirit of endurance', *AJPh* 85 (1964), 225–53
Miller, J. F., *Apollo, Augustus and the Poets* (Cambridge, 2009)
Morgan, L., *Musa pedestris: Metre and Meaning in Roman Verse* (Oxford, 2010)
Morwood, J., 'Aeneas, Augustus, and the theme of the City', *G&R* 38 (1991), 212–23
Mynors, R. A. B., *P. Vergili Maronis Opera* (Oxford, 1969)
Mynors, R. A. B., *Virgil, Georgics: Edited with a Commentary* (Oxford, 1990)
Nappa, C., 'Callimachus' *Aetia* and Aeneas' Sicily', *CQ* 54 (2004), 640–6
Nelis, D., *Vergil's Aeneid and the Argonautica of Apollonius Rhodius* (Leeds, 2001)
Nisbet, R. G. M., & Rudd, N., *A Commentary on Horace, Odes, Book 3* (Oxford, 2004)
Norden, E., *P. Vergilius Maro, Aeneis Buch VI* (7th edn, Stuttgart, 1981)
Oakley, S. P., *A Commentary on Livy Books VI–X* (4 vols; Oxford, 1997–2005)
Ogden, D. (ed.), *A Companion to Greek Religion* (Chichester, 2010)
Ogilvie, R. M., *A Commentary on Livy, Books 1–5* (Oxford, 1965)
O'Hara, J. J., *Death and the Optimistic Prophecy in Vergil's Aeneid* (Princeton, 1990)
O'Hara, J. J., *True Names: Vergil and the Alexandrian Tradition of Etymological Wordplay* (Ann Arbor, 1996)
Oliensis, E., *Freud's Rome: Psychoanalysis and Latin Poetry* (Cambridge, 2009)
Panoussi, V., *Greek Tragedy in Vergil's Aeneid: Ritual, Empire, and Intertext* (Cambridge, 2009)
Parke, H. W., & Wormell, D. E. W., *The Delphic Oracle* (2 vols; Oxford, 1956)
Paschalis, M., 'Virgil's Actium-Nicopolis', in *Nikopolis 1: Proceedings of the First International Symposium on Nicopolis* (Preveza, 1987), 57–69
Perkell, C., *Vergil: Aeneid Book 3* (Newburyport, MA, 2010)
Perkell, C. (ed.), *Reading Vergil's Aeneid: An Interpretive Guide* (Norman, OK, 1999)
Pillinger, E., *Translating Cassandra: The Poetry and Poetics of Prophecy* (Cambridge, forthcoming)

Powell, A., *Virgil the Partisan: A Study in the Re-integration of Classics* (Swansea, 2008)
Putnam, M. C. J., *Virgil's Aeneid: Interpretation and Influence* (Chapel Hill, 1995)
Ramminger, J., 'Imitation and allusion in the Achaemenides scene (Vergil, *Aeneid* 3.588-691)', *AJPh* 112 (1991), 53-71
Rebeggiani, S., 'Orestes, Aeneas, and Augustus', in P. Hardie (ed.), *Augustan Poetry and the Irrational* (Oxford, 2016), 56-73
Rüpke, J. (ed.), *A Companion to Roman Religion* (Chichester, 2011)
Sanderlin, G., 'Aeneas as apprentice—point of view in the Third *Aeneid*', *CJ* 71 (1975-6), 53-6
Scarth, A., 'The volcanic inspiration of some images in the *Aeneid*', *CW* 93 (1999-2000), 591-605
Sillett, A. J., *'A Learned Man and a Patriot': The Reception of Cicero in the Early Imperial Period* (Oxford D.Phil. thesis, 2015)
Skutsch, O., *The Annals of Quintus Ennius* (Oxford, 1985)
Sparrow, J., *Half-lines and Repetitions in Virgil* (Oxford, 1931)
Stahl, H.-P., 'Political stopovers on a mythological travel-route: from battling harpies to the Battle of Actium', in H.-P. Stahl (ed.), *Vergil's Aeneid: Augustan Epic and Political Context* (London, 1998), 37-84
Stephens, S. A., *Callimachus: The Hymns, Edited with Introduction, Translation, and Commentary* (New York, 2015)
Tarrant, R., *Virgil, Aeneid Book 12* (Cambridge, 2012)
Thomas, R., *Reading Virgil and his Texts: Studies in Intertextuality* (Ann Arbor, 1999)
Trappes-Lomax, J., 'Hiatus in Vergil and Horace's *Odes*', *PCPhS* 50 (2004), 141-58
Wackernagel, J., *Lectures on Syntax, with Special Reference to Greek, Latin, and Germanic*, ed. D. Langslow (Oxford, 2009)
Warmington, E. H., *Remains of Old Latin* (4 vols; Cambridge, MA; Loeb Classical Library, rev. reprints 1956-9)
Watson, L. C., *A Commentary on Horace's Epodes* (Oxford, 2003)
West, G. S., 'Andromache and Dido', *AJPh* 104 (1983), 257-67
West, M. L., *Greek Metre* (Oxford, 1982)
West, S., 'Notes on the text of Lycophron', *CQ* 33 (1983), 114-35
Wilkinson, L. P., *Golden Latin Artistry* (Cambridge, 1963)
Williams, G. W., *Technique and Ideas in the Aeneid* (New Haven, 1983)
Williams, R. D., commentaries on Vergil, *Aeneid*, Book III (Oxford, 1962; reprinted Bristol, 1981); Book V (Oxford, 1960; reprinted Bristol, 1981)
Wills, J., *Repetition in Latin Poetry: Figures of Allusion* (Oxford, 1996)
Woodcock, E. C., *A New Latin Syntax* (London, 1959; reprinted Bristol, 1985)

Index

References are to page numbers. Capitals in bold refer to passages in the appendix. Readers are also directed to the glossary, which provides references for the explication or illustration of technical terms.

Abas 159
abruptness, brokenness 33, 100, 166–7, 192, 199, 225, 244, 248
Achaemenides 21–2, 233–60
Achilles 5, 8, 20, 109–10, 112, 115, 117, 124, 129, 162, 168–72, 237, 242
Actian Games 42, 153, 156–60
Actium 3–4, 153, 156–60
  battle of 16, 87, 153, 157–9; **R**
Aeaea 186
Aeneadae (city) 42, 90, 91
Aeneas *passim*
  like Apollo 106
  as consul 101
  dedicates shield 153, 159–60
  as father 43–4, 268
  foreshadows Augustus 159, 191
  founder of Roman poetry 160
  giving a *recitatio* 24, 94, 96, 115, 137, 173, 229, 238, 242, 268
  as leader 42, 110
  married to Dido 205
  as narrator 22, 32–3, 83, 96, 99
  and Odysseus 21–2, 141, 179, 186, 234, 260
  pietas 7, 13 n. 23, 41, 91–2, 97, 100, 106, 132, 146, 206
  as priest and prophet 41–2, 264
  as reader 99
  as sceptical inquirer 95, 232
  Stoic hero 133
Aeneia 90, 91, 265
Aenus 42, 90, 91
Aeschylus 90
  Eumenides 171
  Libation Bearers 23, 164
  Persians 164
aetiology 11, 25–6, 32, 42, 101, 116–17, 153, 181, 190, 222
Agamemnon 91, 99, 124
Alba Longa 187

Alexandria 25
Allecto 16, 141, 145
alliteration 93–5, 101, 104, 112, 118, 136, 141, 183, 192, 194, 196, 199, 206, 217, 218, 225–6, 229–30, 232, 242, 244, 246, 249, 252, 254
Alpheus 117, 261–4
altars 102, 117, 157, 164, 171–2, 222
  twin 165
ambiguity 41, 111–12, 126, 156
anachronism 264–5
Anaphe 138, 139
Anchises 13–15, 83, 86, 90, 103, 108, 116, 124–6, 203–5, 268
  death 261, 265–7
  as father 43, 86, 116, 216, 265–6
  as interpreter 33, 114, 219–22, 224
  as leader 42, 86, 110, 117, 204, 214, 216, 221, 225–6, 241
  lover of Venus crippled by Jupiter 114, 204–5, 266
  mistaken 32, 110, 112, 114–15, 117, 131, 133, 137, 151
  as priest 42, 117–18, 151–2, 216–17
  as senator, *princeps senatus* 101, 131
Andromache 6, 24–5, 33, 39, 43–4, 122, 161–75, 206–9; **H**
  fixated on Troy 25, 164, 168, 172–5
  and Hector 33, 162, 166, 168, 173–5, 207
  in *Iliad* 21, 166, 167, 168, 207
  and Neoptolemus 161–2, 169–70, 172; *see also* Molossus
  uniuira 207
anger 178; (of Aeneas) 18; (Allecto) 141; (Hercules) 246; (Juno) 10, 178, 180–1; (Turnus) 16
Anius 107–9
Antandros 86
Antony, Mark 3, 16, 193, 247

Apollo (Phoebus) 4, 15, 26, 92, 103, 105–14, 117–18, 124, 127, 132–5, 138–9, 148, 151, 155–60, 171, 174, 176, 178–9, 182, 188, 197–9, 204, 263, 264; **J, L**
  at Actium 156, 159, 188; **T(c)**
  at Claros 176
  Genetor 109–10
  at Leucas 155
  on Palatine 84, 108, 199
  sun god (= Helios) 142, 248
  at Thymbra 109
Apollonius, *Argonautica* 5, 25–7, 135, 138, 140, 148, 153, 155, 181, 185–6, 216, 224, 234, 240, 260, 263
Apsyrtus 100, 157, 186, 240
Aratus, *Phaenomena* 7, 142, 214
Arcadia, Arcadians 16, 26, 115, 132, 261, 285
Arcturus 213
Arethusa 261–3
Ariadne 114, 119, 206, 239, 243
Aristaeus 8, 124, 262
Arma uirumque 1, 10, 20, 128, 145, 160, 165, 238
arrivals celebrated 175, 216
Ascanius (= Iulus) 12–13, 16–18, 36, 41, 43–4, 85, 124–5, 147, 152, 173, 187–8, 205–8, 246
  as *alter* Astyanax 173–4, 206–8
Asia 84, 85
assonance 205, 250, 252
astrology 176–7
Astyanax 165, 173, 175, 207–8, 283
Attis 94
augury 176–7, 182
Augustus 3–4, 8–10, 15–16, 19, 87–8, 108, 116, 120, 128–9, 156, 159, 179, 182, 199, 210, 224, 238
  building programme 4, 222
  house on Palatine 108
  Res Gestae 4
  with veiled head 190
Ausonia 131, 184–5, 205, 209
Avernus (lake) 185, 197

Bacchus, *see* Liber
Baudelaire x
beaching ships 104, 122, 156–7, 271
beginnings 83, 104
birds 139–42, 146–7, 150–1

as omens 151, 177, 182, 219
blood 92, 94, 98, 103, 244–6, 253; *see also* chill
Boreads 145–6
brevity 25, 30–1, 88, 125, 200, 247, 255, 265, 268
Brutus 43–4
Buthrotum 42, 153, 161–75, 209–11
  future alliance with Rome 201, 210
  veterans settled there 161

cacophony 227–9
Callimachus 25–6, 92, 103–5, 110–11, 114, 132, 137, 156, 230
Calypso 20, 268
Camerina 264
Carter, Matthew xi
Carthage 11–12, 14, 86, 122, 129, 216, 220, 266–8
Cassandra 28, 133–4, 148–9, 152, 168–9; *see also* Lycophron
Castor and Pollux 88
Castrum Mineruae 189, 214, 217, 223
cattle and goats 138–9, 142
Cato the Elder 26 n. 49, 96, 104, 150, 189, 200, 204, 265
Catullus 29, 119, 138, 169, 206, 243, 259
Celaeno 33, 39, 41–2, 140, 143, 146–50, 152, 178, 180, 182, 188, 215, 267
cenotaphs 164–5
Ceraunia 211
Chaonia 161, 172
Charybdis 21, 27, 39, 155, 180–2, 191–3, 201, 224–8, 244, 258–9, 267–8: **B**
chiasmus* 50–1, 134–6
chill, of fear etc. 94–5, 150, 166
chronology, imprecise x, 84–5, 86, 233, 249; *see also* anachronism
Chryses 106, 124, 152
Cicero 142, 156, 176, 182, 183, 205, 214
  de Oratore 24
Circe 20, 152, 155, 157, 181–2, 186, 192, 194, 196, 197; **B(a)**
cities, building/founding 26, 40, 88–91, 107–8, 115–16, 121–2, 124, 149, 156, 159, 172, 175, 182, 187–9, 208, 210, 220, 224, 234, 260
  made by men not walls 110
Cleopatra, flight from Actium 158–9; *see also* Antony
cleansing 41, 153, 157, 292
closure 266–9

Index

Cnossos 117
colloquial speech 168
colonists 40, 108, 124, 164, 174–5, 189, 223–4, 228
comedy 169, 194
contrast 119–20, 121, 126, 133, 178, 201, 218–19, 220–1, 229, 238, 248, 251, 254, 260, 263, 264
Corcyra (= Corfu) 161, 266
Corybantes 116
Corythus 131–2
Crete 85, 103, 114, 117–25, 129–30, 134, 140, 189
　'hundred-citied' 115
　land of deceit 22 n. 37, 114
　place of labyrinth 125
Creusa 13, 83, 85, 126, 130, 173
Cronos 116
cruelty 98–9
cultus 237
Cumae 197
Cupid 12, 173, 208
Curetes 116, 121
curse 14, 149–50, 154, 234, 242
Cybele 17, 85, 112, 116
　lions 116–17
Cyclades 105, 107, 118–20
Cyclopes 20, 38–9, 94, 180–1, 219, 228–36, 243–57, 260; **A, K**
　political assemblies 256–7
cypress 103, 257

Dante x, 92, 183
Daphnis 5, 129, 160, 165, 262–3
Dardanus 85, 88, 99, 112, 115–16, 130–1, 133, 218
darkness 134–40, 155–6, 194, 228–30, 232–3
dawn, *Aurora*, *Eos* 9 n. 16, 34, 215, 218, 236–7
deification 128–9
delay 20–1, 138, 161, 176, 195, 199–202, 204–6, 241
Delos 30, 103–20, 125, 139, 263, 264; **E, L**
　wandering island 26, 105–6
Delphi 108, 111, 171–2, 176
departure 87, 123, 134, 152, 162, 190, 201–10
　gift-giving on 201–3, 206–7
Diana (= Artemis) 105–6, 129, 214, 248, 255, 257; **K**

didactic 1, 7, 8, 19, 25, 104, 182, 184, 186, 196
Dido 11–12, 14–15, 20–1, 23–4, 27, 37, 38, 83, 89, 99, 100, 108, 114, 149, 159, 173, 180–1, 199, 207–9, 220, 234, 239, 242, 248, 251, 263, 268–9; **P**
　parallels with Andromache 161–2, 207
di magni 39, 87–8, 129, 151
Dione 91
Dionysius of Halicarnassus, *Roman Antiquities* 10 n. 18, 22, 88, 153, 161, 176, 187, 202, 203, 214, 217
Dirae 140–1, 143, 150–1
Dodona 124, 148, 161, 172, 176, 202; *see also* oak
Donatus 2, 20 n. 32, 51, 102, 163, 173, 196, 198, 243, 250
Donusa 119–20
dreams 19, 125–7, 132, 167, 171, 187, 244
　in Homer, Apollonius 125
Drepanum 31, 260, 265–7
Dryope 92
Du-Stil 118
Dulichium 154–5

elemental *or* cosmic scale 39, 135–6, 146, 183, 192, 217, 227, 244, 255–6
embroidery, weaving 206–7
Empedocles 192, 228; **O**
Enceladus 49, 107, 230–2
Ennius, *Annales* 19, 29, 83, 232, 260
Ennius, *Hecuba* 29, 89, 91
epic 1, 8, 10, 19–21, 23–4, 26–7, 33–4, 83, 115, 125, 141, 146, 164, 169, 226, 249, 250, 260–3
epigram 26, 160
Epirus 189, 202, 210
　famous for horses 203
　future links with Rome 26, 41, 43, 201, 210
epithets, compound 34, 48, 106, 222
Erysichthon 92
Etna 86, 138, 192–3, 223, 224, 227–33, 235, 244, 247, 255–6; **F, K, L(b), O**
　historical eruptions 228, 256
　writings on 228

etymology 35, 260, 261; (*Achaemenides*) 242; (*Achilles*) 242; (*Acragas*) 264; (*Actius*) 158; (*Aeaea*) 186; (*Aeneas*) 242; (*Alba Longa*) 187; (*Anaphe*) 138; (*Antandros*) 86; (*arma/armenta*) 221; (*caeruleus*) 136; (*caelum*) 233; (*Caieta*) 15; (*Celaeno*) 140; (*Creta*) 121; (*Cyclades*) 120; (*Cyclops*) 248; (*Delos*) 26, 107; (*Dirae*) 141, 143; (*Drepanum*) 265; (*fata*) 36–7, 178; (*Gela*) 264; (*Gradiuus*) 96; (*Harpyiae*) 143; (*Helorus*) 263; (*Hyades*) 213; (*ingens*) 102; (*Neoptolemus*) 162, 203; (*Odysseus*) 242; (*Pallas*) 222; (*Petelia*) 189; (*Plemyrium*) 261; (*Polyphemus*) 245, 249; (*Pyrrhus*) 162; (*Rhegium*) 191; (*Scylaceum*) 224; (*Scylla*) 193; (*Segesta*) 14; (*Sporades*) 120; (*Strophades*) 139; (*umbra*) 236; (*Zancle*) 265–6

Euripides 23–5
  Andromache 161, 162, 165, 170–2, 208
  Cyclops 235, 247
  Hecuba 84, 89–91, 99–100, 103, 168–9
  Trojan Women 103, 161, 168–9, 208

Evander 132
excrement 141, 146

Fama/*fama* 14, 33, 54, 118, 130, 162, 230–1, 262–3
Fate/*fatum/fata* 35–8, 86–7, 91, 180–1, 183, 188, 197, 209, 269
flight 39, 98
food, eating, feasting 16, 21, 38, 83, 141–3, 146, 149, 152, 163, 175, 201, 216, 243, 245–7, 250; **M**
Fortuna 35–8, 168, 181, 183, 208–9, 243
foundation, *see* cities
funerals, burials 89–90, 97, 103
Furies 23, 140, 148, 150, 171
furor 89

Gallus 5–6, 55–6, 250, 261
games 14, 21, 129, 157–8, 264–5;
  see also Actian Games
Gela 264
Gellius, Aulus 177, 213, 221, 229
genre 1, 7, 23, 26, 194, 203, 249, 261–3
geography, imprecise 119, 155, 156, 161, 209, 211

Getae 96
ghost(s) 12–13, 29, 33, 95, 97–8, 125, 137, 164–7, 174
giant(s) 32, 107, 146, 214, 230, 231, 254; **L(b)**; *see also* Cyclopes; Enceladus; Polyphemus
gods 33, 35–8, 39, 84, 85, 87–8, 92, 117, 127, 132, 143, 151, 183, 216–17, 233, 258, 268–9
golden bough 15, 197, 200
Graecia, magna 42, 182, 223–4
grammar, syntax, accidence:
  ablative absolute expressing paternity 242
  ablative, associative 102
  ablative, instrumental 102, 184, 197, 217, 221
  ablative, local 90, 102, 119, 251
  ablative of attendant circumstances 91
  ablative of cause 121, 217
  ablative of description 90, 98, 121, 184, 195, 208, 220, 243, 256, 259
  ablative of manner 100
  ablative of material 94, 98
  ablative of origin 166
  ablative of place whence 251
  ablative of present participle in -*nti* 204
  ablative of quality 90
  ablative of route 124, 192, 263
  accusative, internal 100–1
  accusative, retained with the passive 134
    part of body 98, 103, 108, 190, 195, 222
  accusative of extent 134
  accusative of motion towards 127, 148–9, 197, 211
  accusative of respect 238
  accusative of time throughout which 137, 232
  agreement with subject not object 166, 178
  asyndeton between adjective and participle 104
  attraction of pronoun to complement 187, 253
  collective nouns, used in plural 102, 239
  collective singular 48, 119, 189
    with plural verb 256
  conditional clause in indirect speech 151

Index

conjunctions, postponement of 50–1, 94
cum, inverted 122–3, 163, 215, 249–51
dative of 4th decl. nouns in -*u* 161, 221
dative of advantage 102, 203
dative of destination 173, 190, 192, 267
dative of disadvantage 94, 252
dative of the agent 90, 188, 191
dative of the thing concerned 94
dative, possessive 94, 135
dative, purposive 102, 221
dative with *causa* 165
future imperative 190
future perfect 189
genitive ending -*ai* (archaic) 175
genitive of second declension nouns in -*ius* 177, 264
genitive of definition 149, 214
genitive of value 199
genitive plural forms 48, 92, 99, 101, 223, 265
gerundive expressing purpose after *mittere* 99, 170–1
gerundive of necessity/obligation 129–30, 145, 185
Greek accusative 108, 118, 119, 120, 162, 177, 201, 202, 212, 214, 216, 250
Greek islands, feminine gender 154
Greek nominative plural 90, 249
Greek vocative 97, 205, 265
hendiadys 98, 128, 131, 133, 143, 170, 175, 191, 202, 230, 250, 256
historic infinitive 123, 127, 254
historic present 48
  followed by present subjunctive 113
imperfect subjunctive ('past potential') 134
imperfect, inceptive 86, 96
indicative in deliberative questions 110
indirect command without *ut* 121, 145, 200
indirect statement introduced by *fama* 118, 230–1, 262
infinitive expressing indirect command 178
infinitive expressing purpose 85, 95
locative 130

ne(c) with imperative 167, 187
participle in conditional sense 127, 178–9
passive, impersonal 259
passive, reflexive usage 211, 247
passive use of deponent verb 124, 200, 205
passive use of intransitive verb 260
poetic plural 48, 96, 109, 125, 136, 165, 189
preposition used with name of city 126, 238
present tense for future in *si* clause 240
purpose clauses containing a comparative 184
relative clause, expressing purpose 207
relative clause, extended 184
sequence of tenses 113
singular for plural 134
subjunctive, generic 200
subjunctive, prospective 150
superlative adjective within relative clause 188, 222
supine, ablative 94, 244
suus referring to notional subject 203, 208
unexpressed 3rd-person plural subject 115, 199
vocative with adverbial force 184
vocatives in -*ā* 97, 205
'Wackernagel's Law' 167
Grecism 105–6, 185, 218, 238; *see also s.v.* grammar *and* metre
greed 89, 98, 100
grotesque 194, 234, 235
Gyaros 106–7

half-lines 51, 167, 173, 248, 253–4
harbour(s) 23, 87, 214, 217–19, 229, 259, 261; **C**
Harpies 27, 138–53, 244
  assault on senses 143–4
  invulnerability 146
  wind deities 149
  see also Celaeno
Harrison, E. L. v, ix
Hector 39–40, 126–7, 161, 164, 166, 168; **G**
  as ghost 12, 44, 84, 125–8, 166–7, 178
  in *Iliad* 20, 34, 164, 168, 174–5, 203, 207
  see also Andromache

Helenus 21, 33–4, 38–42, 44, 118, 122, 140, 158, 161–2, 164–5, 170–209, 222–3, 225–8, 258–9, 263, 266
  misleads Aeneas 32, 186
  most prominent Trojan seer 162, 177
  omissions in prophecy 180, 228, 267
  prolixity 205–6
Hellespont 89
helmets, plumed 203
helmsman 14–15, 42, 137, 152–3, 212, 216, 227
Hercules 16, 40, 146–7, 163, 179, 187, 190, 224, 246, 254
Hermione 170–1
Hesiod 7, 86, 140, 146, 213–14
Hesperia 41, 130, 134, 192, 210
hills 83, 172, 215, 219; *see also* mountains
Homer, *Iliad* 5, 8, 15, 18–21, 105, 106, 112–13, 171, 203
Homer, *Odyssey* 8, 18–22, 27, 135, 142, 153, 181, 185, 186, 201, 218, 225, 236, 238, 242–3, 255, 260
Horae 212
horror 33, 92–5, 97, 140, 143–4, 146, 150, 165–6, 224, 229, 238, 244–5, 249, 252, 267
horses 202–3, 220–1, 264
Horsfall, Nicholas x, xi
hospitality, friendship 38, 89, 100, 102, 108, 176, 186, 201–2, 222, 233, 241, 245, 254
hunger 16, 107, 139, 141–2, 148–9, 152, 178, 235, 237–8, 250–1; **Q**
Hyades 213
Hyginus 105, 148
hymns, hymnic form 26, 107, 118, 179

Iasius 130–1
Ida (mountains, near Troy; and on Crete) 85, 86, 114, 116
Idomeneus 85, 118–19, 189
Ilioneus 130
Ilium, *see* Troy
imitation/allusion, markers of 110–11, 133, 138, 140, 144, 145–6, 153, 175, 252, 260, 269 (cf. 'Alexandrian footnote'*)
impiety 7, 11, 16, 38, 89–90, 100, 172, 233
interpolation* 28 n. 55, 52, 144, 195, 258, 264, 276

Ionian Sea 139–40, 153–4, 255, 261
Iris 140, 150, 209, 292
irony 89, 97, 108, 110, 115, 131, 137, 147, 155, 165, 168, 174, 200, 206, 208, 246, 248, 249
Italy 1–3, 6, 10, 13–18, 41, 43, 88, 122, 130–1, 133–4, 148–9, 180, 184, 188–9, 197, 205, 209–11, 214–17, 220–3, 229
  ever-receding 209
  fertility 220–1
Ithaca 153–5, 202, 235, 243, 246; **C**
Iulus, *see* Ascanius

joke 16, 124–5, 152, 188
Julian star 129
Julius Caesar 3, 5, 8, 128–9, 230
Juno (= Hera) 10–11, 14, 16–18, 26, 35, 38, 42–3, 180–1, 184, 196–7, 222, 263, 268
  at Carthage 11–12, 181, 196, 237, 242
  at Lacinia 224
  Moneta 122
  restricting Helenus' prophecy 180–1, 184
  Saturnia 184
Jupiter (= Zeus) 11, 14, 17–18, 35–8, 87, 92, 112, 114, 116, 128–9, 131–2, 140, 148, 157, 179–80, 183, 188, 211, 231, 233–4, 257, 272; **I**
  Optimus Maximus 199, 218
  as weather god 117, 135, 142
juxtaposition of words 84, 97, 127, 268

labours 129, 146, 179, 208–9, 266
Laertes 154–5
Laomedon, perjury of 85, 147
Latium 85
  fertile 'mother' 112
laurel 108, 110–11, 176
Lavinium 129, 187
leadership 42, 86
learning 35, 86
Lemuria, the 164
Leucas 155–6
Liber, Bacchus (= Dionysus) 90–1, 92, 99, 119, 175, 220–1, 243
lightning, thunder 9, 134, 136, 211, 229–31; **O**
Lilybaeum 185, 259, 265
Locri Epizephyrii 188–9

love 38, 122, 207, 261, 269
Lucretius 8, 19, 29, 95, 186, 192
lusus Troiae 203
Lycophron, *Alexandra* 27–8, 145, 187, 189, 225, 231
Lycurgus 90–1, 99
Lydia 13 n. 24, 41

Macrobius, *Saturnalia* 19, 30, 34–5, 88, 92, 106, 109, 112, 132, 135, 148, 153, 190, 198, 245, 267
Maecenas 7
Marcellus 120
marriage 38, 122, 162, 168, 170
Mars (= Mauors) 4, 90, 96
Medea 27, 92, 157–8
Meliboeus 6–7, 123, 128, 169
memory, forgetfulness v, 33, 42, 88, 114–15, 126, 133, 156, 159, 164, 167, 173, 174–5, 186, 207, 243, 246
Messina, straits of 39, 191, 225, 259
metaphor 93, 98, 110, 138, 157, 162, 211–12, 214, 215, 219, 232, 245, 267
metre, verse form 44–52
  anomalies 45, 47, 105–6, 111, 154, 202, 223, 231–2, 240, 263, 264
  caesurae 47
  correption 47, 139
  counter-enjambment 50, 142
  dactylic rhythm 48, 49, 111, 159, 192, 198–9, 254, 257
  elision (prodelision) 45–6
  elision, expressive 96, 98, 99, 141, 143, 155, 165, 199, 210, 215, 217, 227, 231, 232, 252
  enjambment 50, 84, 113, 139, 143, 188, 199, 209, 215, 244, 245, 247, 259, 265
  -ĕrĕ/-ērunt/-ĕrunt 47–8, 145
  et followed by *caesura* 47
  hexameter 46
  hexameter, end 46, 48–9, 127, 170, 182–3, 186–7, 231–2
  hexameter, start 48, 102
  hiatus 47, 105–6, 139–40, 170, 202, 240
  hypermetric line 49, 258
  Greek rhythm 47, 48–9, 105–6, 139–40, 153, 170, 257
  ictus and accent 49, 52, 98, 138, 192, 226, 229, 231, 232, 263

  internal rhyme 96
  intractable forms 48, 99, 133, 139, 149, 161
  molossus 170
  quantity 44–5; (*potĭtur*) 100
  sense pauses, mid-line 98, 100, 188, 244
  spondaic rhythm 45, 48, 49, 99, 106, 138, 147, 155, 159, 165, 168, 185, 191, 195, 202, 205, 223, 231, 252
  spondeiazon 46, 88, 106, 214, 223
  variant forms 47–8, 236, 256
  Zacynthos, short a before 45, 154
Mezentius 16–17, 159
migration ix, 6–7, 88, 113–15, 129, 131, 133–4, 223, 263
Milton, *Paradise Lost* 194, 230
  Samson Agonistes 248
Minerva, Pallas (= Athena) 21, 88, 188, 217–18, 222
Minos and family 114, 117, 118
misdirection, misinterpretation 11, 12–13, 32, 105, 119, 140, 186, 196, 197, 237, 242, 258
Misenus 15, 145, 197
Molossus 44, 170, 172, 174
monsters 22, 27, 39–40, 118, 138–53, 192–6, 224, 227, 232, 235, 244, 246, 265
moon 126, 204, 249–50
mountain(s) 86, 87, 111, 116, 211, 229, 231; *see also* Etna; Ida
Myconos 106–7

Naevius 28–9, 87, 90, 106, 260
nakedness of athletes 158
Naples 2, 198
Nausicaa 20, 21, 240
Naxos 119, 243
necromancy 164
Neoptolemus (= Pyrrhus) 12, 158, 161–2, 168, 170–2, 201, 203
Neptune (= Poseidon) 11, 14, 85, 105, 112–13, 117–18, 152, 155, 160, 186, 218, 268
Neritos 154
Nicopolis 156, 159–60, 210
Nox/nox 125–6, 136, 212, 233; *see also* darkness
nymphs 108, 125; (freshwater) 261–3, 278; (sea) 39, 85–6, 105, 252, 262; (wood) 92, 96

oak 124, 161, 257, 300
Octavia, grieving for Marcellus 163, 165
Oenotri 130
Olearos 119–20
omens, portents 10, 40–1, 85, 93–6, 101, 114, 118, 142, 146, 149–52, 178, 180, 182, 186–7, 190, 209, 212–13, 219–20, 230, 232
optimism 11, 124, 138
oracles, prophecy 5, 10, 27–8, 32–4, 37, 40–2, 85, 91, 105–17, 124–5, 127–30, 133–4, 140, 148–50, 152, 161–2, 175–201, 206, 226, 235, 259, 263, 264, 267; **M**
  cryptic, riddling 27–8, 85, 112, 130, 131, 149, 180, 182, 184
  in hexameters 178, 198
  partial 41, 140, 183
  style 179, 182, 183, 185, 206
Orestes 171–2
Orion 214
orthography 53–4
Ortygia (= Delos) 119, 124, 127, 263
Ortygia (off Syracuse) 32, 261, 263

Pachynus (cape) 185, 195, 259, 264–5, 267
Palinurus 14–15, 34, 42, 104, 131, 135, 137–8, 153, 212–14, 227
Palinurus (cape) 225
Palladium, the 88
Pallanteum 16, 26, 40, 215
Parcae 35–7, 184
Parentalia, the 163–4
Parian marble 120
Paris 147
Paros 119–20
pastoral 4–8, 142, 249–50, 252–3, 261–2
peace 150, 220–2
Pelorus 185, 190–1, 225, 259, 264–5
Penates 12, 29, 39–41, 87–8, 91, 125–34, 149, 178, 184, 201, 239
  on the Velia 4, 88
performance 23–4
Pergama 109–10, 172
Pergamea/um 42, 121, 134
personification* 14, 15, 102, 118, 124, 140, 146, 212, 219, 228–30, 231
Petelia 189
Phaeacians 160–1
Philoctetes 189
Phineus 27, 139–40, 181–2, 184, 197, 234; **M**

Phoebus, *see* Apollo
pietas/piety 7, 13, 28, 33, 92, 106;
  see also s.v. Aeneas; Trojans
pilots 203
Pindar 19 n. 28, 112, 228, 261; **E, F**
plague 106, 118, 119, 123–4
pollution 41, 102, 126, 146, 153, 157
Polydorus 24, 86, 88–90, 97–103, 150, 166, 220; **G, T(a)**
Polymestor 89, 91, 99–100, 102
Polyphemus 5 n. 10, 21, 40, 50, 94, 133, 181, 227–8, 230, 233–5, 237, 243–56; **A**
  sculpture at Sperlonga 235
Polyxena 168–9
Pomponius Mela 86, 191, 224
portent, *see* omen
postponement, of conjunctions etc. 50–1, 94, 123, 140, 172, 188, 222
  of disyllabic prepositions 106, 211, 258
prayer 96, 109, 135, 146, 150–2, 216–17, 223, 238
  form 117–18, 150, 200
  gesture 132, 151
Priam 44, 84, 99, 100, 162, 172, 234, 237, 241
Probus 85
prophecy, *see* oracle
punctuation (incl. capitals) 53–4, 87, 110, 147, 149, 168, 171, 191–2, 212, 244
Pygmalion 89, 172
Pyrrhus, *see* Neoptolemus
Pyrrhus (king of Epirus) 43, 184, 188
Pythia, the 111

rationalization 193, 196, 225, 232
realism 86, 126, 132, 141, 146, 155, 158, 199, 215, 226, 228, 245, 249
reception of *Aeneid* 3 x, 252
religious rites 26, 90–2, 150, 157–8, 175, 179–80; *see also* sacrifice
repetition 33–4, 39, 95, 98, 124, 134, 135, 136, 166, 172, 174, 182, 185, 188, 191, 196, 200, 205, 215, 220, 227, 246, 256, 263
  avoided 125, 268
  see also anaphora*
Rhoeteum 115
ritual 111

Index

Rome 6, 26, 87, 91, 129–30, 180, 210, 218–19, 266
  conquering Greece 160, 197, 203
  hills 87, 172, 215, 219
Romulus 91, 128–30, 182
Rumour, *see* Fama

sacrifice, offerings 91–2, 117–18, 132, 151–3
  of bulls 92, 118
  covering of priests' heads 42, 180, 182, 222
  for dead 90, 103, 163–4
  deferred 142–3, 151
sailing, rowing 26–7, 30–1, 86, 104, 153, 211, 212, 218, 223, 225–8, 258, 260–1, 264–5
  land seeming to move 105, 221
Sallentines 189
Same 154–5
Samothrace 88, 131, 263
Saturn 130, 184
Scaean Gates 175, 207
Scylaceum 224
Scylla 20–1, 27, 39–40, 141, 155, 180–2, 191–6, 224–7, 258–9, 267–8: **B**
  sculpture at Sperlonga 194, 235
  on Sextus Pompeius' coins 193
Scyllaeum 224
Selinus 265
senate 42, 87, 101, 131
Servius 19, 35, 53; 85–263
sex 195, 198 (denied)
Sextus Pompeius 3, 43, 191, 193–4, 224
Shakespeare, *Macbeth* 149
shield(s) 16, 20, 34, 57, 84, 124, 153, 159, 179, 218, 221, 248; **R**
Sibyl, of Cumae 14–15, 180, 182, 184, 197–200
Sibylline Books 178, 198–9
Sicily 11, 13, 14, 29, 43, 179, 180, 185, 191–2, 197, 222–69
  circumnavigation 31, 40, 205, 226, 259–67
silence 41, 96, 116 (ritual), 173, 225, 241, 254, 255, 268–9
simile 8, 20, 23, 33, 84, 99, 106, 186, 233, 247–8, 254, 256, 257
Simois 164
Sinon 12, 38, 233–34, 237, 241, 249, 251, 254
Sirens 141, 225

Sirius 123–4
smell 141, 143–4, 289–90
smiths xi, 231, 255–6, 275; *see also* Cyclopes
smoke 84–5, 89, 138, 155–6, 229, 232, 277, 280
Sophocles, *Philoctetes* 22, 189, 235, 238–9
Sophocles, *Phineus* 141–2
sortes Vergilianae 198
sow, white 34, 40, 112, 118, 180, 186–7, 196
SPQR 87
stage direction 24, 97, 167, 179, 188, 208, 229, 237, 238, 241
stars 5, 36, 57, 129, 136, 146, 177, 213–14, 232, 239
  put to flight by day 215
  (*or* heaven) touched from land or sea 40, 201, 227–8, 230, 244
storm 20, 27, 28, 31, 134–8, 140, 142, 181, 266, 268
Storm (deity) 117, 118
Strabo 105, 217, 225, 235, 265
Strophades 26, 139–40, 148, 155, 157; **M(c)**
style 30–5, 50–1; *see also* brevity; abruptness; chiasmus; Grecism; repetition; variety
supernatural, uncanny 22, 26, 33, 101, 126, 138–40, 173, 224–5, 256; *see also* Cyclopes; ghosts; Harpies; monsters; omens
supplication 111–12, 151, 165, 233–4, 237–8, 240–1
Sychaeus 89, 100, 125, 172, 207; **P**
Symplegades 27, 182, 224, 226–7
synecdoche* 102, 109, 115, 122, 129, 134, 137, 162, 164, 188, 202, 212, 232, 237, 259
Syracuse 40, 228, 251, 260–3

Tarentum 224
tears, mourning 21, 87, 96–7, 129, 161, 163, 165, 169, 174, 208
Telemachus 170, 201–3, 207–8, 235, 241; **D**
temple(s) 4, 9, 11, 15, 86, 88, 108, 109, 155–6, 159–60, 181, 196, 217–19, 222, 263
Teucer 115, 117, 133
text and transmission 52–4 and nn. 116–24, 171, 179, 199, 210, 239, 254, 256, 258, 266;
  see also interpolation

Theoclymenus 21 n. 35, 235, 241; **D**
Theocritus 5, 231, 249, 252–3, 260–3
Thrace 88–103, 108
  cruelty of kings 99
Thrinacia 142, 185
Thucydides 185, 235
Tiber, Tiberinus, *Thybris* 16–17, 40–1, 112, 125, 187, 196, 210, 215–16
Tiresias 181, 186, 197
toga praetexta 190
tragedy 22–5, 27
  Greek 84, 96, 165, 168–71; *see also* Aeschylus; Euripides; Sophocles
  Roman 29, 169, 238, 244
trees 6, 9, 84, 93, 100, 111, 116, 123 150, 257; **S**
  planted round tombs 102–3, 164
  violation of 85, 91–8
  see also cypress; laurel; oak
Triones (the Bears) 213–14
triumphs 220–1
Troad 83, 115
Trojan women 43, 103
Trojans, as aggressive invaders 7, 142–3, 145, 147–8
  avoiding impious, hostile or Odyssean places 98, 137, 155, 160–1, 180, 182, 188, 191, 193, 205, 223, 267
  continuing woe 24–5
  culpability of 84
  dress 238
  eating their tables 150, 152
  like/unlike Odysseus' men 22, 142, 226–7, 234
  looking to future 10–11, 25, 29, 39–41, 128–9, 131, 165, 175, 201, 208–9
  models for Romans 42–3, 145, 189–90, 222
  piety 22, 90, 150, 152, 222–3, 239, 247, 263
  wandering 106, 137
Troy 9, 84, 87, 109–10, 115–16
  departure from 28, 39, 119
  fall of 11–12, 83–4, 234
  royal family 44, 84, 97
  sacked by Hercules 205
Troy, the 'small Troy' 44, 174–5, 201, 209–10
Turnus 15–18, 20, 34, 39 n. 83, 85, 93, 132, 147, 152, 167, 203, 237, 267; **S**

Ulysses (= Odysseus) 21–2, 28, 83, 114, 142, 153–5, 169, 181, 186, 197, 223, 225–9, 231, 233–6, 240–9, 254–6, 260, 268; **A, B**
  'Nobody' 242, 246, 256
uncanny, *see* supernatural
underworld 15, 39 n. 84, 135, 137–42, 144–6, 148, 185, 193, 197, 227, 244

Valerius Flaccus 141, 150, 176
variety 20 n. 32, 25, 30–2, 34, 101, 107, 210, 255
Varro 35, 88, 146, 161, 175, 187, 189, 198, 213–14, 221, 233
veiled hair, in sacrifice 132, 190
vengeance 89, 243, 246, 248
Venus (= Aphrodite) 11–18, 21, 23, 27, 28, 38, 91, 93, 114, 124, 153, 181, 197, 205, 218, 236, 258, 295
Vergil 131, 198–9, 211, 268
  epitaph 2
  poetic career 1–10
Vulcan (= Hephaestus) 28, 165, 231, 280, 288, 297

war, military diction 2–4, 20, 29, 128, 145, 147, 150, 162, 197, 203, 219–22, 263
water imagery 261–3
wheel of fortune 183
white 112, 118, 119–20, 138, 187, 220–1, 225, 229
Williams, R. D. 52 n. 115
Williams, Gordon x, 41 n. 89
wisdom, absence of 196
word order 50–1, 91, 94, 163, 191, 243, 250
word play (*domus...dominabitur*) 113; (*urbes...uberrima*) 115; (*dirae/Dirae*) 150–1; (*Triones*) 213–14; (*armantur...armenta minantur*) 220; (*Inarime*) 231; (*pereo...periisse*) 240; (*cretus*) 241; (*uisceribus...uescitur*) 245; (*sola...solamen*) 253; (*palmosa Selinus*) 265

Xanthus (river) 42 n. 92, 164, 175, 209

Zacynthos 153–4

Index of passages cited, discussed, or scanned

Italicized numbers refer to lines at least partially scanned.

Accius, fr. 544 Warmington
  (*Philoctetes*) 244–5
Anthologia Palatina 9.559 [= Crinagoras
  32 G.-P.] 120
Apollonius, *Argonautica* 1.28–31: 257
Apollonius, *Argonautica* 1.403–4: 158
Apollonius, *Argonautica* 1.861: 176
Apollonius, *Argonautica* 1.929: 115
Apollonius, *Argonautica* 1.1273–83: 212
Apollonius, *Argonautica* 2.178–93,
  213–29, 262–303, 311–16:
  Appendix **M**; *139–40, 143–4, 146,
  148, 150, 180–2*, 234
Apollonius, *Argonautica* 2.423–4: 197
Apollonius, *Argonautica* 2.516–27: 124
Apollonius, *Argonautica* 2.568–70: 227
Apollonius, *Argonautica* 2.609–10: 227
Apollonius, *Argonautica* 2.1103–5: 232
Apollonius, *Argonautica* 3.311: 130
Apollonius, *Argonautica* 3.846–66: 92
Apollonius, *Argonautica* 4.208: 254
Apollonius, *Argonautica* 4.552–3: 131
Apollonius, *Argonautica* 4.598: 231
Apollonius, *Argonautica* 4.831–2: 259
Apollonius, *Argonautica* 4.982–6: 266
Apollonius, *Argonautica* 4.1694–730:
  Appendix **N**; *135, 137–9, 155, 157–8*
Apollonius, *Argonautica* 4.1775–6: 267
Ausonius, *Cento Nuptialis* 108: x

Callimachus, *Aetia* fr. 1.35–6: 231
Callimachus, *Aetia* fr. 17.8–9: 137
Callimachus, *Aetia* fr. 43: 26, 260, 265
Callimachus, *Aetia* fr. 64.1–2: 264
Callimachus, *Hymn* 1 (*Zeus*) 1–9,
  46–54: Appendix **I**; *103, 114, 116–17,
  121, 131–2*, 196
Callimachus, *Hymn* 2 (*Apollo*)
  1–7: Appendix **J**; *103, 110–11*
Callimachus, *Hymn* 3 (*Artemis*)
  52–61: Appendix **K**; *231*, 248, 255
Callimachus, *Hymn* 4.1: 105
Callimachus, *Hymn* 4 (*Delos*) 34–45,
  51–4, 141–7, 191–5, 266–73:
  Appendix **L**; *103, 105–7*, 231

Catullus 63.7: 94
Catullus 63.52, 76, 91: 116
Catullus 64.7, 13: 138
Catullus 64.106: 257
Catullus 64.152: 239
Catullus 64.291: 257
Catullus 64.327: 29, 206
Catullus 68B.93: 252
Catullus 76.13: 207
Catullus 101.1: 169
Catullus 101.8: 164
Cicero, *Brutus* 254: 160
Cicero, *D.N.D.* 3.67: 100
Cicero, *in Catilinam* 4.6: 101
Cicero, *in Verrem* 2.4.72: 210
Cicero, *in Verrem* 2.4.118: 261
Cicero, *Philippics* 2.10: 246
Cicero, *Philippics* 2.63: 247
Cicero, *Philippics* 2.67: 193
Cicero, *Philippics* 2.105: 245
Cicero, *Prognostica* fr. 6.1: 142
Cicero, *Tusc. Disp.* 5.65: 251
Cinna, *FRP* 10: 236

Ennius, *Annales* 20–2 Skutsch 130
Ennius, *Annales* 33 Skutsch 233
Ennius, *Annales* 137 Skutsch 83
Ennius, *Annales* 190 Skutsch 87
Ennius, *Annales* 203 Skutsch 183
Ennius, *Annales* 288 Skutsch 246
Ennius, *Annales* 417 Skutsch 132
Ennius, trag. fr. 297 Jocelyn 94, 244
Ennius, trag. fr. 351 Jocelyn 91
Euripides, *Andromache* 1–14, 24–31,
  1239–53: Appendix **H**; *161–2, 170,
  172*, 208
Euripides, *Andromache* 64: 170–1
Euripides, *Andromache* 115–16: 165
Euripides, *Cyclops* 483–4: 247
Euripides, *Hecuba* 1–30, 709–18,
  1132–44: Appendix **G**; *89–91,
  99–100*
Euripides, *Hecuba* 342–78: 168–9
Euripides, *Hecuba* 993: 173
Euripides, *Ion* 354: 208

Euripides, *Trojan Women* 240–77: 169
Euripides, *Trojan Women* 630–83: 168

Herodotus 5.59: 160
Homer, *Iliad* 1.1: 20
Homer, *Iliad* 1.59–67: 124
Homer, *Iliad* 1.106: 147
Homer, *Iliad* 2.783: 231
Homer, *Iliad* 4.149: 94
Homer, *Iliad* 6.76: 162
Homer, *Iliad* 6.181: 194
Homer, *Iliad* 6.460: 207
Homer, *Iliad* 6.479: 174
Homer, *Iliad* 11.728: 117
Homer, *Iliad* 18.486–7: 213
Homer, *Iliad* 20.216–18: 115–16
Homer, *Iliad* 20.307–8: 21, 112–13
Homer, *Iliad* 22.438: 166
Homer, *Iliad* 22.466–7: 166
Homer, *Iliad* 24.699–776: 103
Homer, *Odyssey* 1.1: 20
Homer, *Odyssey* 1.427: 95
Homer, *Odyssey* 4.149–50: 208
Homer, *Odyssey* 4.351–592: 262
Homer, *Odyssey* 5.272–4: 213
Homer, *Odyssey* 5.306–7: 168
Homer, *Odyssey* 5.408: 157
Homer, *Odyssey* 7.153–69: 241
Homer, *Odyssey* 9.19–24: 154
Homer, *Odyssey* 9.38–9: 83
Homer, *Odyssey* 9.67–81: 135
Homer, *Odyssey* 9.142–51, 288–98, 343–6, 353–70, 371–414: Appendix **A**; 228, 232–4, 236, 245–9, 255–6
Homer, *Odyssey* 9.230: 245
Homer, *Odyssey* 9.452–3: 252
Homer, *Odyssey* 9.490: 254–5
Homer, *Odyssey* 9.497–9: 255
Homer, *Odyssey* 9.504–5: 246
Homer, *Odyssey* 9.507–16: 133
Homer, *Odyssey* 10.126–7: 254
Homer, *Odyssey* 11.10 (= 12.152): 153
Homer, *Odyssey* 11.94: 266
Homer, *Odyssey* 11.100–37: 181
Homer, *Odyssey* 11.126: 186
Homer, *Odyssey* 11.127–34: 197
Homer, *Odyssey* 12.37–141: 181
Homer, *Odyssey* 12.80–110, 201–2, 235–47: Appendix **B**; 192–3, 224, 226–7
Homer, *Odyssey* 12.260–419: 139
Homer, *Odyssey* 12.447–8: 268

Homer, *Odyssey* 12.451–3: 268
Homer, *Odyssey* 13.1: 268
Homer, *Odyssey* 13.93–104: Appendix **C**; 21 n. 35, 218
Homer, *Odyssey* 13.269: 233
Homer, *Odyssey* 14.301–4: 135
Homer, *Odyssey* 15.125–7: 207
Homer, *Odyssey* 15.256–70: Appendix **D**; 235, 241–2
Homer, *Odyssey* 18.196: 202
Homer, *Odyssey* 19.172: 114
Homer, *Odyssey* 19.439: 187
Homer, *Odyssey* 19.547: 132
Homer, *Odyssey* 19.564: 202
Homeric Hymn 3.88: 105
Horace, *Ars Poetica* 3–4: 194
Horace, *Epistles* 2.1.156: 160
Horace, *Odes* 1.10.14–15: 84
Horace, *Odes* 3.2.25–6: 116

Isidore, *Etymologiae* 10.38: 253
Isidore, *Etymologiae* 10.102: 95

Livy 6.41.4: 182
Lucan 4.41: 253
Lucan 5.154–5: 111
Lucan 9.974–5: 42 n. 92
Lucan 9.770: 245–6
Lucretius 1.92: 111
Lucretius 1.145: 95
Lucretius 1.716–25: Appendix **O**; 192, 228
Lucretius 1.739: 176
Lucretius 1.837: 245
Lucretius 2.114–15: 127
Lucretius 2.601: 116–17
Lucretius 3.290–1: 95
Lucretius 4.387–9: 105
Lucretius 4.589: 29, 197
Lucretius 5.25: 187
Lucretius 5.892–3: 193–4
Lucretius 5.905: 194
Lucretius 6.436–7: 230
Lycophron, *Alexandra* 2: 184
Lycophron, *Alexandra* 3–4: 200
Lycophron, *Alexandra* 669: 193
Lycophron, *Alexandra* 1239: 259
Lycophron, *Alexandra* 1250–2: 149

Macrobius, *Sat.* 3.2.7: 35
Macrobius, *Sat.* 5.1.8: 30

Nicander, *Alexipharmaca* 11: 176

Index of passages cited, discussed, or scanned 321

Ovid, *Amores* 1.15.25-6: 1
Ovid, *Amores* 3.6.45: 241
Ovid, *Epistulae* 15.165-6: 155
Ovid, *Fasti* 1.178-80: 219
Ovid, *Fasti* 1.448: 177
Ovid, *Fasti* 3.181-2: 129
Ovid, *Fasti* 4.259: 112
Ovid, *Fasti* 5.165-6: 213
Ovid, *Fasti* 6.715: 104
Ovid, *Heroides* 8: 171
Ovid, *Metamorphoses* 2.100: 184
Ovid, *Metamorphoses* 2.361-2: 97
Ovid, *Metamorphoses* 7.463: 106
Ovid, *Metamorphoses* 9.336-93: 92
Ovid, *Metamorphoses* 12.478: 195
Ovid, *Metamorphoses* 13.623-14.81: Appendix T; 29-30, 104, 154, 194, 248, 252
Ovid, *Metamorphoses* 13.876-7: 256
Ovid, *Metamorphoses* 14.6: 224
Ovid, *Metamorphoses* 14.158-441: 236
Ovid, *Metamorphoses* 14.172-5: 239
Ovid, *Metamorphoses* 14.197: 252
Ovid, *Metamorphoses* 14.214-15: 250
Ovid, *Metamorphoses* 14.216: 251
Ovid, *Remedia Amoris* 811-12: 268

Pacuvius, fr. 181 Schierl 238
Pindar, *Hymns* fr. 33c-d: Appendix E; 105-7
Pindar, *Pythians* 1.15-28: Appendix F; 228-31
Plautus, *Rudens* 70: 213
Pliny, *Nat. Hist.* 4.65: 120
Pliny, *Nat. Hist.* 8.56: 241
Propertius 2.8.1: 171
Propertius 2.20.21-2: 250
Propertius 2.28.39-40: 185
Propertius 2.34.61: 158
Propertius 2.34.66: 19
Propertius 3.1.31-2: 84
Propertius 3.12.31: 186
Propertius 3.24.7: 236
Propertius 4.1.35: 187

Quintilian 8.3.70: 95
Quintilian 8.3.84: 247
Quintilian 8.4.24: 252-3

Sallust, *Histories* 4.27: 193
Seneca, *Phaedra* 267: 253
Seneca, *Troades* 703-4: 253

Silius, *Punica* 3.1: 83
Silius, *Punica* 14.218: 264
Statius, *Thebaid* 2.11: 253
Statius, *Thebaid* 2.442: 101
Statius, *Thebaid* 3.40: 236
Statius, *Thebaid* 3.138: 241
Statius, *Thebaid* 3.437-9: 107
Statius, *Thebaid* 3.594-5: 231
Statius, *Thebaid* 7.707-8: 176
Supplementum Hellenisticum 982: 157

Tibullus 1.1.78: 135
Tibullus 2.5.16: 198
Tibullus 2.6.39-40: 185-6

Vergil, *Aeneid* 1: 10-12
Vergil, *Aeneid* 1.1: 145; see also Arma uirumque
Vergil, *Aeneid* 1.1-7: 10-11, 98, 128, 133, 217, 266
Vergil, *Aeneid* 1.37: 20 n. 31
Vergil, *Aeneid* 1.94-6: 168
Vergil, *Aeneid* 1.103-10: 225
Vergil, *Aeneid* 1.118: 136
Vergil, *Aeneid* 1.254-71: 36-7, 198, 201
Vergil, *Aeneid* 1.276-7: 91
Vergil, *Aeneid* 1.284-5: 113
Vergil, *Aeneid* 1.286-90: 128-9
Vergil, *Aeneid* 1.293: 150-1
Vergil, *Aeneid* 1.310-12: 144
Vergil, *Aeneid* 1.343-64: Appendix P; 87, 89, 142, 172, 178
Vergil, *Aeneid* 1.375-6: 170
Vergil, *Aeneid* 1.437: 208
Vergil, *Aeneid* 1.527-8: 143
Vergil, *Aeneid* 1.530-3: 130
Vergil, *Aeneid* 1.617: 106
Vergil, *Aeneid* 1.724: 216
Vergil, *Aeneid* 1.744: 213
Vergil, *Aeneid* 1.749: 207
Vergil, *Aeneid* 1.753-5: 83
Vergil, *Aeneid* 1.755-6: 86
Vergil, *Aeneid* 2: 12-13, 83
Vergil, *Aeneid* 2.1-2: 268
Vergil, *Aeneid* 2.3: 249
Vergil, *Aeneid* 2.102-3: 251
Vergil, *Aeneid* 2.265: 246
Vergil, *Aeneid* 2.270-1: 126
Vergil, *Aeneid* 2.293-5: 127-8
Vergil, *Aeneid* 2.327: 113
Vergil, *Aeneid* 2.490: 175
Vergil, *Aeneid* 2.597-8: 173

322 *Index of passages cited, discussed, or scanned*

Vergil, *Aeneid* 2.602–3: 84
Vergil, *Aeneid* 2.624–5: 84
Vergil, *Aeneid* 2.663: 100, 172
Vergil, *Aeneid* 2.769: 167
Vergil, *Aeneid* 2.773–4: 98, 126
Vergil, *Aeneid* 2.780–2: 40–1, 209, 210
Vergil, *Aeneid* 2.801: 215
Vergil, *Aeneid* 2.804: 83, 87
Vergil, *Aeneid* 3: ix-x, 13
Vergil, *Aeneid* 3.1: x, xi, *47*
Vergil, *Aeneid* 3.2: *44*
Vergil, *Aeneid* 3.3: *45*
Vergil, *Aeneid* 3.5–6: *46*
Vergil, *Aeneid* 3.7: *47*
Vergil, *Aeneid* 3.9: 30
Vergil, *Aeneid* 3.11: 30
Vergil, *Aeneid* 3.12: *46*
Vergil, *Aeneid* 3.13–16: 31–2
Vergil, *Aeneid* 3.22–4: 31–2
Vergil, *Aeneid* 3.37: *45*
Vergil, *Aeneid* 3.71: 256
Vergil, *Aeneid* 3.73–8: 31–2
Vergil, *Aeneid* 3.112: *45*
Vergil, *Aeneid* 3.115: 51
Vergil, *Aeneid* 3.124: 50
Vergil, *Aeneid* 3.151: *49*
Vergil, *Aeneid* 3.180: 50
Vergil, *Aeneid* 3.188: 50
Vergil, *Aeneid* 3.210–19: 31–2
Vergil, *Aeneid* 3.211: *47*
Vergil, *Aeneid* 3.248: *48*
Vergil, *Aeneid* 3.270: *45*
Vergil, *Aeneid* 3.277: 51
Vergil, *Aeneid* 3.312: x
Vergil, *Aeneid* 3.325: 6
Vergil, *Aeneid* 3.328: *48*
Vergil, *Aeneid* 3.390: *49*
Vergil, *Aeneid* 3.426–8: 141
Vergil, *Aeneid* 3.464: *48*
Vergil, *Aeneid* 3.476: 266
Vergil, *Aeneid* 3.481–3: 50
Vergil, *Aeneid* 3.514–23: 50
Vergil, *Aeneid* 3.522–3: x
Vergil, *Aeneid* 3.533–7: 31–2
Vergil, *Aeneid* 3.553: *49*
Vergil, *Aeneid* 3.574: *45*
Vergil, *Aeneid* 3.606: *47*
Vergil, *Aeneid* 3.630–40: 50
Vergil, *Aeneid* 3.658: *45*
Vergil, *Aeneid* 3.680: *49*
Vergil, *Aeneid* 3.684: *49*
Vergil, *Aeneid* 3.692–7: 5 n. 10, 31–2

Vergil, *Aeneid* 3.695: *49*
Vergil, *Aeneid* 3.702: 45 n. 95
Vergil, *Aeneid* 4: 14
Vergil, *Aeneid* 4.1–5: 269
Vergil, *Aeneid* 4.45–6: 268
Vergil, *Aeneid* 4.173–97: 118, 230–1, 252
Vergil, *Aeneid* 4.214: 169
Vergil, *Aeneid* 4.260: 122
Vergil, *Aeneid* 4.280: 98
Vergil, *Aeneid* 4.298: 167
Vergil, *Aeneid* 4.412: 100
Vergil, *Aeneid* 4.471: 171
Vergil, *Aeneid* 4.542: 147
Vergil, *Aeneid* 4.569: 248
Vergil, *Aeneid* 4.575: 254
Vergil, *Aeneid* 4.580: 248
Vergil, *Aeneid* 4.600–1: 239
Vergil, *Aeneid* 4.653: 209
Vergil, *Aeneid* 5: 14
Vergil, *Aeneid* 5.8–11: 34, 135
Vergil, *Aeneid* 5.604: 38
Vergil, *Aeneid* 5.623: 168
Vergil, *Aeneid* 5.710: 38
Vergil, *Aeneid* 5.763–4: 104
Vergil, *Aeneid* 5.810–11: 85
Vergil, *Aeneid* 5.850–1: 104
Vergil, *Aeneid* 5.866: 225
Vergil, *Aeneid* 6: 15
Vergil, *Aeneid* 6.66–7: 133
Vergil, *Aeneid* 6.355–7: 138
Vergil, *Aeneid* 6.363: 239
Vergil, *Aeneid* 6.458–9: 239
Vergil, *Aeneid* 6.605–6: 148
Vergil, *Aeneid* 6.781–2: 129
Vergil, *Aeneid* 6.789–90: 128
Vergil, *Aeneid* 6.794–5: 129
Vergil, *Aeneid* 6.892: 200
Vergil, *Aeneid* 7: 15–16
Vergil, *Aeneid* 7.25: 215
Vergil, *Aeneid* 7.29–30: 216
Vergil, *Aeneid* 7.107–29: Appendix **Q**; 16, 40–1, 124, 133, 149–50, 152, 188
Vergil, *Aeneid* 7.147: 216
Vergil, *Aeneid* 7.186: *45*
Vergil, *Aeneid* 7.458–9: 132
Vergil, *Aeneid* 7.468–9: 101–2
Vergil, *Aeneid* 7.604: 147
Vergil, *Aeneid* 7.817: 93
Vergil, *Aeneid* 8: 16
Vergil, *Aeneid* 8.26–7: 125–6
Vergil, *Aeneid* 8.43–8: 187
Vergil, *Aeneid* 8.102: 163

Index of passages cited, discussed, or scanned

Vergil, *Aeneid* 8.256: 246
Vergil, *Aeneid* 8.291: 179
Vergil, *Aeneid* 8.675–81: Appendix **R**; 34, 87, 153, 216
Vergil, *Aeneid* 9: 17
Vergil, *Aeneid* 9.236: 246–7
Vergil, *Aeneid* 9.475: 166
Vergil, *Aeneid* 9.622: 246
Vergil, *Aeneid* 9.716: 231
Vergil, *Aeneid* 10: 17
Vergil, *Aeneid* 10.45–6: 84
Vergil, *Aeneid* 10.104: 148
Vergil, *Aeneid* 10.113: 188
Vergil, *Aeneid* 10.175–6: 177
Vergil, *Aeneid* 10.261: 34, 216
Vergil, *Aeneid* 10.508: 232
Vergil, *Aeneid* 11: 17–18
Vergil, *Aeneid* 11.34–5: 103
Vergil, *Aeneid* 11.831: 34
Vergil, *Aeneid* 12: 18
Vergil, *Aeneid* 12.26: 232
Vergil, *Aeneid* 12.236–7: 6, 148
Vergil, *Aeneid* 12.569: 85
Vergil, *Aeneid* 12.766–87: Appendix **S**; 92
Vergil, *Aeneid* 12.952: 34
Vergil, *Eclogues* 4–8
Vergil, *Eclogues* 1.1–5: 5–6, 10, 123, 128, 169, 197
Vergil, *Eclogues* 1.30: 84–5
Vergil, *Eclogues* 1.70–1: 7
Vergil, *Eclogues* 2.25: 252
Vergil, *Eclogues* 4.47: 221
Vergil, *Eclogues* 4.5: 183
Vergil, *Eclogues* 6.75: 194
Vergil, *Eclogues* 6.85–6: 102
Vergil, *Eclogues* 10.1–5: 261–3, 267
Vergil, *Georgics* 7–10
Vergil, *Georgics* 1.41: 228
Vergil, *Georgics* 1.163: 104, 241
Vergil, *Georgics* 1.221: *106*
Vergil, *Georgics* 1.288: 236
Vergil, *Georgics* 1.376: 212
Vergil, *Georgics* 1.437: *106*
Vergil, *Georgics* 1.471–3: 230
Vergil, *Georgics* 1.501–2: 147
Vergil, *Georgics* 2.143–8: 220–1
Vergil, *Georgics* 2.191–2: 175
Vergil, *Georgics* 2.308–9: 229–30
Vergil, *Georgics* 2.344–5: 258
Vergil, *Georgics* 2.447–8: 93
Vergil, *Georgics* 2.487: 119
Vergil, *Georgics* 2.490: 95
Vergil, *Georgics* 2.531: 158
Vergil, *Georgics* 3.1–48: 9, 18–19
Vergil, *Georgics* 3.24–5: 22 n. 29
Vergil, *Georgics* 3.28–9: 104
Vergil, *Georgics* 3.46–8: 9
Vergil, *Georgics* 3.223: 256
Vergil, *Georgics* 3.268: 150
Vergil, *Georgics* 3.476–7: 119
Vergil, *Georgics* 3.478–81: 123
Vergil, *Georgics* 3.495: 123
Vergil, *Georgics* 4: 19, 262
Vergil, *Georgics* 4.4–6: 8
Vergil, *Georgics* 4.559–66: 9–10

Xenophon, *Anabasis* 4.7.24: 216

Index of Latin words

Italicized numbers refer to discussions of quantity.

ab, instrumental 218, 229
abscondere 160–1
ac (= *quam*) 226
accipere 107
Achilles, -i 109–10
adeo 137
aequare 255
aethra 232
age 131, 177–8
agere + infinitive 85, 258
agnoscere 174–5
alterius 45
amor + infinitive 163
animus + infinitive 101
Anchisā (vocative) 28–9, 204–5
ante…quam 149, 185
aperire 138, 155–6
arma 1, 10–11, 203
arquitenens 34, 106
arx 122
ast 171
attollere 122, 138
auertere 244
auspicia 182
Auster 102, 104
auxilium + genitive 125

bacchari 119
barathrum 193
bella 200
bracchium 219

caecus 136–7, 144, 194
caelicola 48, 92
caerul(e)us 102–3, 136, 138, 196
canere 127, 178, 197, 226
castus 190
causa 95
cedere 134, 162–3, 172
celebrare 158
chlamys 206
circuitus 191
circumflectere 195–6
Clarius 177

clarus 214
classes 102, 239
claudere 249
claustra 190–1
cogere 100–1
cognatus 210
colere 90, 105
commissus 195
conlustrare 251
continuo 223
conubium 48, *122*, 168
cornua 223
cornus 93
cortina 111
cothurnus 23
crebri 120
crudelis 243
cunabula 114
Cyclops 45, *250*
cyparissus 257

da 109
debitus 133
dehinc *202*
deinde *170*, 241
demitto 219
deus 48
dextra 108, 241
di magni 87–8
Dictaeus 131–2
dirus 140
discrimen 259
diuersus 85
diuus 48
dominari 113
dulcis 123
durus 112
dum + past tense 91

ecce 142, 205, 237, 59
ecqua (= *ecquae*) 173
edicere 145
effodere 253
en 127

Index of Latin words

eniti 170
Eous 236
equidem 167
ergo 46, 121, 148, 157
ergo agite 117
errare 106, 113, 249, 260
erus 169
esse omitted 98, 99, 141, 223
et 207
euertere 84
Eurous 218
excipere 139
excitus 256
expedire 184
exsertare 194
extremus 167, 207, 267

falsus 164
fari 36–7, 178
fas 37, 100
fatum/fata 30, 35–8, 86–7, 198
felix 208
fenestrae 126–7
ferens 204
ferre 87
fessus 31, 107
fingere 91
finis 124–5, 269
focus 122
foedare 146
forte 93, 163
fortuna 35–8
fui 87
fugere 39, 98
furens 167

genua 240
Gradiuus 96
gurges 136

hinc 116, 224
horridus 93
hortari 121
hospita 183–4, 221
hospitium 91, 102
humilis 215
humus 93–4

iam = tandem 97
iamque 236
iamque fere 122
idem ('and also') 128, 221, 227

ignarus 228
Ilium, Troia 84
ille 99, 189, 226
immemor 243
immotus 36–7, 107, 111, 198
imperium 129
impero + passive infinitive 202
implacatus 193
in somnis 126
inanis 165
inconsultus 199
inde 253–4
infandus 249, 251
infelix 99, 147, 242, 250, 260
infernus 185–6
inferre 103
ingens 39 n. 86, 102, 201, 202, 229
inlaetabilis 266
inrigare 211–12
inruere 142–3
insequi + infinitive 95
insertus 126–7
instar 248
instaurare 102
intempesta 233
interea 159, 204
inuadere 145, 184
ipse 137, 218–19, 229, 244
ipsius 45
ira 141, 178
is 110
Italia/us 48
iubere without expressed personal object 125, 160, 204

labor 1, 124–5, 129, 179, 267
lacrimabilis 96–7
laetitia/laetus 31, 113, 121, 131, 142, 248, 266
laniger 249
lapidosus 250
legere 120
lentus 95
leuamen 266
libare 163–4, 175
limes 192
limen 175, 243
linquere 119, 123, 129
longus 207
lucus 164
lumen 239, 247–8, 256
lupa 195

Index of Latin words

lustrare 157, 184, 185
Lyctius 189

magnus 39–40, 114, 129, 174
mala 150
malus 188
manu ducere 179
mater 112, 116
Mauors 90
merum 247
-met 245
meta 195, 267
mihi 45
miser 97, 168, 245, 248
mixtus 113
moenia 109, 129, 188
monere 134, 200–1
monstrum 94, 101, 165, 232
monumentum 114
mora 204
multa (adverb) 241
multum (adverb) 174
murmur 232
myrtus 93

-n (= *-ne*) 168
nam 182, 232, 248
namque introducing parenthesis 178
nec/neque 48, 146
nefas (adjectival) 178
neu tu 187–8
ni 258
nimirum 226
nouus 145–6

obscenus 146
obscurus 215
obsidere 193
obtruncare 100
operatus 122
ordo 183
ore 201
Orion 214

palaestra 158
pallidus 142
pandere 151
parcere 97
pariter 226
paruus 40, 174, 189
pater 45, 86, 110 (of a god)
patera 175

patria 87, 122, 148, 152
patrius 148, 158, 162, 171–2, 238
pax (*deorum*) 152, 179
perago 208–9
pestis 244
picturatus 206
pius 106, 152
placidus 151–2
polus 232, 237
populus 101
postquam x, xi, 83–5, 135, 140
potens 216–17
potestas + infinitive 255
potiri 100, 157
potis 255
praeda 143
praepes 177
praesens 132
praesidere 96
praestat (impersonal) 195
praeterea 196
pressare 249
primus 10, 86, 91, 101, 104, 216, 219–20, 222
pro 147, 196
procul 90
pronus 254
proprius 109
prorumpo 230
protinus 191–2
prudentia 196
puer 173–4
purpureus 189–90

quā 190
qui (= *quis*) 241
quid puer? 173
quies 209
quiescere 269
quin 189
quis? (adj., = *qui*) 167
quondam 264–5
quoque 134

referre 101
refugere 219
regnare 90
relegere 260
religio 48, 178
relinquere 119, 123
reliquiae 48, 178
renarro 269

Index of Latin words

repeto 133
repostus 178
resonare 196, 197
respicere 237
rex 107–8
Rhoeteus 115
rudens 227
ruina 229
rumpere 147, 248
rursum/rursus 144

sacer 45, 101, 103
scaena 23
scio 239
secretus 186
secundare 96
secundus 200, 217
Selinus 265
sententia 101
sentire 177
sese 141
signum dare 145
silua(e) 1, 6, 93, 197, 250, 257
simul 246
sollemnis 163
sortiri 183
stare 189
sterni 211–12
suadere + infinitive 178
subtemen 206
super 208
superbus 84
surgere 131
sus 186–7
suspensus 179
suus (= *uester*) 208

tandem 121, 138, 242, 248
temptare 146
tenus 195
terra 111–12

Teucri 99, 112
Teucrus 115
tibi 45
tollere 239
trabs 134
trahere 249
tridens 227
Trinacria/us 185, 195
tristis 140–1, 164
Troius 165, 238
tum 144
tumulus 93
turritus 219

uacare 119
uastus 39 nn. 84–6, 193, 243
uber (noun) 112, 130, 187; (adjective) 115
uela dare + dative 86–7
uelatus 223
uertere 36 n. 78, 183
uerus 166–7
uices 183, 247
uictrix 100
uideri 126
uidi 245
uirilis 173–4
uix + pluperfect 86, 110
Vlixes, -i 110, 155, 233, 242
ultro 127
umbra 1, 6
uncus 141–2
unus 146, 169, 196, 268
uocare 104, 176
uolare 118, 119
uolens 200
uolucer 45
uoluere 37, 114, 183
uolutans 240–1
uos 251
uterque 191–2
uulgo (= *passim*) 249

Printed and bound by CPI Group (UK) Ltd, Croydon, CR0 4YY